The
EROSION
of INERRANCY in
EVANGELICALISM

The
EROSION
of INERRANCY *in*
EVANGELICALISM

Responding to New Challenges to Biblical Authority

G. K. BEALE

CROSSWAY BOOKS
WHEATON, ILLINOIS

Dedication

This book is dedicated to my students—past, present and future—who live in a postmodern world in which conviction about anything is out of vogue. Even within significant sectors of the so-called evangelical church and its institutions, a conviction that all of Scripture is true has been eroding over past decades. This book is written with the hope that it may contribute in some small way to a conviction that the entire Bible is God's truthful word.

The Erosion of Inerrancy in Evangelicalism: Responding to New Challenges to Biblical Authority
Copyright © 2008 by G. K. Beale
Published by Crossway Books
         a publishing ministry of Good News Publishers
         1300 Crescent Street
         Wheaton, Illinois 60187

Cover design: Amy Bristow
First printing 2008

Unless otherwise indicated Scripture quotations marked NASB are from *The New American Standard Bible.*® Copyright © The Lockman Foundation 1960, 1962, 1963, 1968, 1971, 1972, 1973, 1975, 1977, 1995. Used by permission.

All emphases in Scripture quotations have been added by the author.

PDF ISBN: 978-1-4335-0557-7
Mobipocket ISBN: 978-1-4335-0558-4

Library of Congress Cataloging-in-Publication Data
Beale, G. K. (Gregory K.)
    The erosion of inerrancy in evangelicalism : responding to new challenges to biblical authority / G. K. Beale.
      p. cm.
    Includes bibliographical references and index.
    ISBN 978-1-4335-0203-3 (tpb)
    1. Bible—Evidences, authority, etc.—History of doctrines. 2. Evangelicalism. I. Title.
    BS480.B43569 2008
    220.1'32—dc22   2008019146

MG   16 15 14 13 12 11 10 09 08
          9   8   7   6   5   4   3   2   1

Contents

List of Abbreviations

AUSS	Andrews University Seminary Studies
BAGD	Bauer, W., W. F. Arndt, F. W. Gingrich, and F. W. Danker. *Greek-English Lexicon of the New Testament*
BECNT	Baker Exegetical Commentary on the New Testament
BBR	*Bulletin for Biblical Research*
BDB	Brown, F., S. R. Driver, and C. A. Briggs. *A Hebrew and English Lexicon of the Old Testament*. Oxford, 1907
ConBNT	Coniectanea biblica: New Testament Series
EBC	Expositor's Bible Commentary
EvQ	*Evangelical Quarterly*
IBS	*Irish Biblical Studies*
IVPNTC	InterVarsity Press New Testament Commentary
JBL	*Journal of Biblical Literature*
JETS	*Journal of the Evangelical Theological Society*
JR	*Journal of Religion*
JSNT	*Journal for the Study of the New Testament*
JSNTSup	Journal for the Study of the New Testament: Supplement Series
JSOT	*Journal for the Study of the Old Testament*
JSOTSup	Journal for the Study of the Old Testament: Supplement Series
JSPSup	Journal for the Study of the Pseudepigrapha: Supplement Series
NICOT	New International Commentary on the Old Testament
NIGTC	New International Greek Testament Commentary
NIVAC	The NIV Application Commentary

NTS	*New Testament Studies*
SBJT	*The Southern Baptist Journal of Theology*
SNTSMS	Society for New Testament Studies Monograph Series
SNTSSup	Society for New Testament Studies Monograph Series: Supplement
Them	*Themelios*
TJ	*Trinity Journal*
TSAJ	Texte und Studien zum antiken Judentum
TynBul	*Tyndale Bulletin*
VT	*Vetus Testamentum*
WTJ	*Westminster Theological Journal*
WUNT	Wissenschaftliche Untersuchungen zum Neuen Testament
ZAW	*Zeitschrift für die alttestamentliche Wissenschaft*

Acknowledgments

I am grateful to number of scholars across the country who have read and given me feedback on much of this manuscript, especially in some of the previously published articles that have been revised for inclusion in this book. I am particularly indebted to Dr. Gordon Hugenberger, pastor of Park Street Church in Boston, who was very helpful in commenting on parts of chapters 6 and 7.

I also want to thank the following journals for granting me permission to reprint (with minor revisions) the following articles:

"Myth, History, and Inspiration: a Review Article of Peter Enns, *Inspiration and Incarnation. Evangelicals and the Problem of the Old Testament*," *JETS* 49 (2006), 287–312.

"Did Jesus and the Apostles Preach the Right Doctrine from the Wrong Texts? Revisiting the Debate Seventeen Years Later in the Light of Peter Enns' Book, *Inspiration and Incarnation*," *Themelios* 32 (2006), 18–43.

"A Surrejoinder to Peter Enns on the Use of the Old Testament in the New," *Themelios* 32 (2007), 14–25.

"A Surrejoinder to Peter Enns's Response to G. K. Beale's *JETS* Review Article of His Book, *Inspiration and Incarnation*," *The Southern Baptist Journal of Theology*, 11 (2007), 16–36.

Finally, I want to offer appreciation to my students Ben Gladd and Stefanos Mihalios, who helped do research, proofreading, and double-checking for this book. I am above all indebted to my teaching assistants, Mitch Kim and Mike Daling, who read, double-checked, and helped to edit the manuscript. They were tireless in their work and were always willing to help. Thank you, Mitch and Mike; your contribution to this book was invaluable.

Introduction

Imagine a discussion between two biblical scholars. Let us call the first Tom. He comes from an evangelical background and holds to fairly conservative and traditional views of the Bible. He is having a discussion with his friend Pat. Pat comes from a very similar evangelical background, but his views are more progressive. Tom (the traditionalist) and Pat (the progressive) are discussing differing evangelical views about the authority of the Bible.

> PROGRESSIVE PAT: I am sure that you are aware that some significant Christian colleges and seminaries are becoming much more flexible in the way they define the authority of the Bible, and yet others want to continue to hold to a definition that includes inerrancy. What do you think about that?

> TRADITIONALIST TOM: Well, it does concern me that there is an ongoing redefinition of what should be the standard "evangelical" meaning of the authority of Scripture. I think the 1978 Chicago Statement on Biblical Inerrancy is a good statement,[1] which at that time was the general consensus of understanding in evangelicalism.

> PROGRESSIVE PAT: The doctrine of inerrancy, including the formulation of it in the Chicago Statement, is really a part of evangelicalism's fundamentalist past. It is now an outdated statement for twenty-first-century evangelicalism. Shouldn't we begin with a positive statement about Scripture's authority rather than begin with a focus on why it does not have mistakes? What I mean is that the doctrine of inerrancy expresses too much of a negative concern for denying "errors" in the Bible instead of first espousing a more positive robust view that God has inspired the Bible, so that it has divine authority

1. The Statement can be found in appendix 2.

TRADITIONALIST TOM: But if God has truly inspired the whole Bible and he is a God who is flawless, then should we not conclude that his Word will be without error? Thus, part of proclaiming the positive fact that the Bible is divinely inspired is to make clear that this written Word is fully truthful and contains no mistakes. This is especially important since there have been many over past years who have contended that the Bible does contain errors.

PROGRESSIVE PAT: I am not sure that your assumption about God's flawless character must carry over and be applied to the Bible. And, furthermore, what do you mean by *error*? Who is to say that our modern definition of *error* is the right one? Perhaps ancient biblical people had a different view of what constitutes an error. In fact, the attempt to defend the Bible's reliability by denying that it has errors can be done only by assuming that our modern definition of *error* is correct and then reading this modern view into the ancient biblical text.

For example, some Christians wrongly assume that our scientific understanding of the world and modern view of history writing—whereby, for instance, all the historical facts have to be presented in the order that they occurred—is the same view held by the ancient people who wrote the Bible. Whereas modern people would never believe that two statements that clearly contradict one another could still be true, it appears that such a phenomenon can be found in the Bible; for example, some parallel accounts in the synoptic Gospels contain such contradictions either in what Jesus said or what is described as happening. We just cannot assume that our definition of *error* is the same as that of ancient people.

TRADITIONALIST TOM: Why can't we assume that our definition of *error* is the same as the ancient definition? And furthermore, how do you understand that ancient people defined *truth* and *error*, if you think it to be different from our modern view? If you are going to make this claim, don't you need to explain the ancient standard in order to contrast it with the modern one?

PROGRESSIVE PAT: Well, that is difficult to say because the Bible is not a scientific textbook or a philosophical treatise propounding abstract propositional formulations about truth and falsehood. Instead, the Bible is the redemptive-historical story about God who has worked to redeem people from sin and bring them back into relationship with him. The idea of inerrancy has distorted this beautiful storyline by focusing on Scripture primarily as a set of propositional truths rather than as "living oracles" (Acts 7:38), which confront people with God's very being and existence.

There are literary genres expressing relational realities such as exhortation, warning, poetry, and apocalyptic, which have the goal of bringing people into relationship with the living God. Thus, the Bible's ultimate purpose is to confront people with the presence of God and not merely (or even primarily) with descriptions about God or reports about biblical history.

TRADITIONALIST TOM: I agree that the Bible confronts us with God's very presence, which, as you said, is the point of Acts 7:38. And it is certainly true that the Bible is about how God has worked to bring sinful humanity back into relationship with him, but the Bible says that he has done this *in history*, and this account of history contains events reported by biblical writers. Is there not some way that we can discern whether these historical reports are true? And does not Scripture assume the veracity of these reports as being important for how God has conveyed his presence to his people in past biblical history?

PROGRESSIVE PAT: Has not postmodernism taught us, at the least, that we moderns have different presuppositional perspectives from one another? Likewise, ancient biblical writers had their own assumptions or lenses through which they interpreted history. It is possible that they could so interpret a historical event that their interpretation distorted some of the actual details of how that event really occurred. That kind of history writing may not have been unacceptable to them, if, indeed, they were conscious of their presuppositions. But either way, the Spirit was inspiring them to interpret history in this manner. They (and the Spirit) may have been more interested in focusing on God's revelation of himself than upon all the pedantic historical details surrounding that revelation.

TRADITIONALIST TOM: But what kind of criteria can we use to decide between what was really history and what was not? I think we are getting bogged down in some heavy, abstract, and theoretical philosophical issues about the nature of historical knowledge, which I doubt is going to be solved in this brief conversation. Though such issues are very important and need more discussion, let's try to get back to some concrete things about the doctrine of inerrancy that you think can no longer be held in the way that traditional evangelicalism of the twentieth century affirmed.

PROGRESSIVE PAT: All right. I have been studying the book of Isaiah over the past few years, and I have decided on the basis of writing style and subject matter that chapters 40 to 66 were not written by Isaiah the prophet but by an anonymous writer, who lived during Israel's Babylonian exile or soon thereafter.

TRADITIONALIST TOM: While I acknowledge that there are cogent arguments for the position you are taking, there are also, in my opinion, good, reasonable, and more persuasive arguments within the book of Isaiah itself for the traditional view. Your view that Isaiah did not write all of the book attributed to him would mean that either the anonymous writer of chapters 40 to 66 was prophesying of Israel's restoration from Babylonian exile, which would occur only perhaps forty, thirty, or twenty years later, or the writer was recording recent history (the restoration from Babylon) as though it were prophecy.

PROGRESSIVE PAT: Yes, that is correct. It is unlikely that Isaiah the prophet prophesied this restoration two centuries before it happened, since prophets usually prophesy or write what is relevant to the audience living in their own time—a hermeneutical rule about prophecy held by the majority of those in the Old Testament scholarly guild.

TRADITIONALIST TOM: But if the writer of chapters 40 to 66 was living in the middle of the exile, then his prophecies would have been predictions only of imminent events thirty or so years later. Would not this amount to the writer appearing to be more like a weather prognosticator? While there are short-term prophecies found elsewhere in Scripture, there are repeated refrains in Isaiah 40–50 affirming that the prophecies there were announced long ago; God long ago prophesied the restoration from Babylon and that he would fulfill this prophecy (e.g., Isa. 46:10: "Declaring the end from the beginning, and from ancient times things which have not been done, saying, 'My purpose will be established, and I will accomplish all My good pleasure'").

On the other hand, if the writer of Isaiah 40–66 was writing after the exile, then he was making recent history—the restoration from Babylon—appear as though it were prophecy. This latter view, as you know, is that which appears to be held by the majority of scholars. This is especially unacceptable since the theme of Israel's restoration is repeated and underscored so much by Isaiah 40–50, in contrast to Babylon's inept idols that cannot predict anything. If this was not genuine long-range prophecy, then the polemic against the idols as false prophetic witnesses is diluted and not effective.

PROGRESSIVE PAT: Well, we will just have to agree to disagree on this point. But let me add that nowhere in the book of Isaiah is there a claim that the prophet Isaiah wrote the whole book, though there are references that he probably wrote chapters 1 to 39 (Isa. 1:1; 2:1; 13:1; 20:2).

TRADITIONALIST TOM: But could not Isaiah 1:1 imply this? ("The vision of Isaiah the son of Amoz concerning Judah and Jerusalem, which he saw during the reigns of Uzziah, Jotham, Ahaz *and* Hezekiah, kings of

Judah.") This implication is made more explicit since Jesus and other New Testament writers often quote from both Isaiah 1–39 and 40–66 and say in each case that Isaiah wrote the entire book.

PROGRESSIVE PAT: But Jesus was merely referring to a collection of writings known as "Isaiah"; this does not have to mean that Isaiah the prophet himself wrote the entire book.

TRADITIONALIST TOM: But why does Jesus use individualistic, personalized phrases such as "Isaiah prophesied," "Isaiah said," and "what was spoken through the prophet Isaiah"? The most natural way to understand these introductory expressions is that a personal prophet by the name of Isaiah was the individual who was prophesying.

PROGRESSIVE PAT: I understand your point, but these references to Isaiah in the New Testament may be explained in another way. In Jesus' day, it is true that all the Jewish people believed that Isaiah the prophet wrote the whole book of Isaiah, even though we now know today that this is not likely. Naturally, since Jesus was a part of this ancient culture that held beliefs that were built into it over centuries, these beliefs came also to form the human understanding and consciousness of Jesus. Thus, it is natural that Jesus reflected these beliefs, since he was not only divine but also fully incarnate as a human who spoke Aramaic, could read Hebrew, and had a Jewish mindset.

Or, alternatively, Jesus, as the God-man, may have known that Isaiah was not the author of the complete work attributed to him, but he "accommodated" himself to the false Jewish view in order to facilitate his communication of the truths from this book. To have addressed the false Jewish tradition of Isaianic authorship would have shifted the important focus from the point of the main theological message from Isaiah to a pedantic point about historical authorship, so Jesus adapted his message sufficiently to allow this belief to remain unchanged.

TRADITIONALIST TOM: On the other hand, part of Jesus' mission was to explode the false assumptions and beliefs that had been held and had come to be accepted by the Jewish culture. So, why would Jesus go along with this false Jewish tradition and not expose it?

PROGRESSIVE PAT: When Jesus introduced quotations referring to Isaiah, it is unlikely that his intended point was that the historical person Isaiah made the prediction; he was primarily concerned about the meaning of the prediction itself. Thus, when particular prophets are quoted in the New Testament, the focus is mainly on their message more than on the identity of the prophet himself.

Perhaps an illustration could help here. When biblical writers say that "the sun rose," it is unlikely that they were attempting to make a scientific statement about the motion of the sun, even according to the scientific standards of their time, but stating what appeared to be the case phenomenologically to their eyes. Similarly, Jesus' reference to Isaiah is not an attempt to make a historically accurate claim about the authorship of the book of Isaiah but a reflection only of what was commonly held by the populace, whether or not he was ultimately aware that Isaiah did not write the whole book. Just as the point is not that the "sun rose" but the meaning of the overall narrative, so Jesus' point is not that Isaiah wrote this passage but the meaning of the passage that is being quoted.

Traditionalist Tom: Your analogy of the appearance of the sun rising is not close enough in nature to the issue of referring to Isaiah. It is like comparing apples to oranges. That is, it is relatively easy to understand the sun illustration as a mere way of describing the world as it appears to the eye, since even we use that idiom often today. On the other hand, the Isaiah issue is not analogous, since, according to your view, Isaiah the prophet did, indeed, write the majority of the book (chaps. 1–39), but another writer(s) wrote the remainder. Thus, if your position is correct, then sometimes Jesus and the New Testament writers are historically, i.e., scientifically, correct in some of their references to Isaiah (the references to Isaiah 1–39) but not in others (Isaiah 40–66).

In addition, the rising sun reference is an attempt to describe external phenomena as they appear to the human eye, but the mention of Isaiah refers to purported historical reality as it is perceived by the collective mind's eye of tradition, which was believed to be really historically true but was not. In contrast, there is a true sense in which the rising sun expression is true.

Consequently, if it is the case that Jesus merely reflected the false tradition of Judaism, then can we really say that Jesus' and the apostles' affirmation that what "Isaiah the prophet" wrote was "inspired" by God? Is it the untrue and irrelevant husk that contains the true message of the particular passage quoted? And if this is so, then not only do we have a limited view of the inspiration of Scripture but also a view where Christ himself could make errors in his statements even about the Bible itself.

Progressive Pat: Well, I cannot continue this stimulating conversation, since I have to finish an article that I am writing on the authorship of Isaiah. Let's continue this discussion later.

Traditionalist Tom: All right. I also have to finish a lecture that I am writing on how Jesus quoted the book of Isaiah. Pat, I would like to read your article when you have finished. Let's continue our discussion later.

The Aims of This Book

The preceding dialogue is only a small peek into a much broader discussion about the authority of Scripture today among evangelical biblical and theological scholars. There is afoot an attempt to redefine what is an "evangelical view of scriptural authority." In 1949, the Evangelical Theological Society (ETS) was founded, and its doctrinal basis was formulated in the following way: "The Bible alone, and the Bible in its entirety, is the Word of God written and is therefore inerrant in the autographs." In 1978 there was a broad consensus among American evangelical scholars about the inerrancy of Scripture.[2]

This consensus was formulated in the Chicago Statement on Biblical Inerrancy, which most saw as a good elaboration of the one sentence ETS inerrancy statement. If the reader is unacquainted with the Chicago Statement, then it is advisable that it be consulted before much more of this book is read, since the Chicago Statement represented at the time what was considered the benchmark for an evangelical view of the inspiration of Scripture (the Statement is found in appendix 2 at the end of this book).

For several reasons that need not be enumerated here, the Evangelical Theological Society saw a need to give greater clarity to its statement about inerrancy. Consequently, a bylaw was proposed and passed at the 2006 annual meeting by about 80 percent of the voters present. The bylaw ("bylaw 12") essentially referred members to the Chicago Statement on Biblical Inerrancy for advice "regarding the intent and meaning of the reference to biblical inerrancy in the ETS Doctrinal Basis." Some scholars at noteworthy evangelical institutions, however, now believe that with the passing of some thirty years the Chicago Statement is outdated in some very important respects,[3] and some of these institutions

---

2. Nearly three hundred evangelical, scholarly leaders played a role in the formulation of this statement.

3. E.g., see K. Vanhoozer, "Lost in Interpretation? Truth, Scripture, and Hermeneutics," *JETS* 48 (2005): 89–114, who offers critiques of what he considers the traditional view of inerrancy but does not give any substantive criticism of the Chicago Statement; however, note his rather pedantic criticism of the Chicago Statement's Article XI, "It [the Bible] is true and reliable in all matters it addresses": "Strictly speaking, however, 'it' neither affirms nor addresses; authors do" (ibid., 106). But I doubt whether the authors of the Chicago Statement meant to downplay either human or divine authorship here; rather, they were using an accepted stylistic convention for referring to such authorship in the Bible. One can easily recall, for example, Billy Graham's repeated refrain in his evangelical sermons, "The Bible says . . . ," not to speak of Jesus' own repeated reference, "Scripture says . . ."(John 19:37; so also John 7:38, 42; 19:28). Perhaps, ironically, Vanhoozer, who criticizes inerrancy as too literal of an approach and as underemphasizing different genres in Scripture, should realize that he may be misinterpreting the genre of this expression used in the Chicago Statement; i.e., he takes it much more literally than was intended.

do not discourage their faculty from having a critical view of important elements of the document.

With reference to the opening dialogue above about the authorship of Isaiah, let us look at part of Article XVIII of the Chicago Statement:

> WE DENY the legitimacy of any treatment of the text . . . that leads to . . . rejecting its claims to authorship.

Yet, as we will see, a variety of evangelical scholars do not believe that a biblical book's claim of authorship necessarily represents the true past historical reality. But, again, this is just one of a number of points in the Chicago Statement that are currently being rejected.

What has happened in the last thirty years to cause such a desire to revise what had been considered the standard North American evangelical statement on Scripture? I think it is safe to say that, at least, two things have contributed significantly to this reassessment. First, the onset of postmodernism in evangelicalism has caused less confidence in the propositional claims[4] of the Bible, since such claims have to be understood only by fallible human interpreters. This influence has also resulted in an attempt to downplay the propositional nature of Scripture itself and to overemphasize the relational aspect of biblical revelation, i.e., Scripture is not some dry set of impersonal propositions but a living communication from God himself, whom we meet in Scripture. For this reason, Karl Barth's relational view of Scripture has seen a revival of interest, especially among evangelical systematic theologians, though most of these theologians would not like the nomenclature of "systematic" anymore, since it smacks of the study of propositional revelation that needs to be systemized.

A second factor leading to reassessment of the traditional evangelical view of the Bible's inspiration is that over the last twenty-five years there has been an increasing number of conservative students graduating with doctorates in biblical studies and theology from non-evangelical institutions. A significant percentage of these graduates have assimilated to one degree or another non-evangelical perspectives, especially with regard to higher critical views of the authorship, dating, and historical claims of the Bible, which have contributed to their discomfort with the traditional evangelical perspective of the Bible. On the other hand, these same scholars, while significantly qualifying their former view

---

4. By the term *proposition* is meant a statement describing some reality that is either true or false; propositions may be expressed through various literary genres, whether that be straightforward didactic discourse, parables, historical narrative, warnings, prophecy, apocalyptic vision, etc.

of inerrancy, have not left their basic position about the truth of the gospel and the Bible's basic authority. Thus, they continue to want to consider themselves "evangelical" but at the same time reformers of an antiquated evangelicalism, represented, for example, by the Chicago Statement on Inerrancy.

In fact, there is an increasingly popular attitude that the Chicago Statement and the term *inerrancy* carry significant "fundamentalist baggage," with all the negative associations that go with the word *fundamentalism* (e.g., narrow, obscurantist, anti-scholarly, unsophisticated). I have found that this perspective is also shared by some more conservative biblical and theological scholars. This is not the place to discuss the origins of the word *fundamentalism* and the development of the use of the word. Suffice it to say that what appears to be "fundamentalist" is in the eye of the beholder.

J. I. Packer in his *"Fundamentalism" and the Word of God* has given a nice, brief discussion of the origins of fundamentalism and how the word has come to be used. Though that was written in the late 1950s, his basic points still hold. There he distinguishes a fundamentalist view of Scripture from an evangelical view, the latter of which he subsequently identified with the Chicago Statement on Inerrancy since he himself was one of the more well known among its signatories in 1978.

The aims of this book are limited. I want to focus on a specific debate that bears upon the broad issue of biblical authority that has arisen recently in evangelicalism. In particular, this is a debate that I have had with another biblical scholar, who has posed what I consider to be some new challenges to the standard evangelical view of biblical inerrancy. In 2005 Peter Enns published a book titled *Inspiration and Incarnation* (Grand Rapids: Baker). I did not read the book when it first came out, and I had not heard much about it. I suspected that it would espouse views similar to some articles that he had written in previous years, especially on the use of the Old Testament in the New.

One was on the Old Testament and Jewish background of Paul's reference in 1 Corinthians 10:4 to Christ's being the "rock which followed" Israel in her wilderness wanderings.[5] Peter Enns actually sent an offprint of that article to me personally. One of the main points of the article, if not the main focus, was that Paul was referring to a Jewish myth, which he believed to be historical reality, and that he was inspired as a biblical writer in doing so. The conclusion is that God can use myth in this way to reveal his theological truth through his inspired apostles.

---

5. "The 'Moveable Well' in 1 Cor. 10:4: An Extrabiblical Tradition in an Apostolic Text," *Bulletin for Biblical Research* 6 (1996), 23–38.

The second article was about how the New Testament writers interpreted the Old Testament.[6] One of the main conclusions, if not the primary point, was to contend that New Testament writers interpreted the Old Testament in a manner different from the original meaning of the texts they were interpreting, because they were influenced to use the non-contextual interpretative method of the Jewish culture around them.

After reading the first article some years ago, I wanted to respond and I set out to do so. But other writing obligations crowded out the effort. Nevertheless, I intended at some point to try to get a reply out, even if it were years later. When Enns's second article came out, I believed that there were a number of inaccuracies in it which needed response. I decided, however, that I did not want to respond, since I thought there were some significant ambiguities about Enns's own viewpoints and positions, which I believed could be difficult to clarify. When Enns's book *Inspiration and Incarnation* came out, I surmised that it likely had some of the same ambiguities, and, accordingly, I did not feel a compulsion to read the book.

In the fall of 2005, however, I attended an academic meeting where a professing evangelical scholar was giving a review of Peter Enns's book. Consequently, I decided to read the book and take notes on it before this meeting occurred in order that I might better be able to follow the review and interact in the question-and-answer session afterward. After summarizing the book, the reviewer offered some critiques but also concluded with a generally favorable view of the overall approach of the book, saying something to the effect that Enns had sailed between the coasts of fundamentalism and liberalism, achieving a nice balance on the issue of biblical authority in relation to some of the difficult historical and literary features of the Bible.

In the light of this reviewer's generally favorable response to the book and the mostly positive reviews of the book at the time, I decided also to take pen in hand and give my own written response. The response grew and grew, and I ended up publishing two responses. One evaluated the bulk of the book, focusing on issues of history and various kinds of literary features in the Old Testament that Enns set forth as inconsistent with the traditional evangelical view of scriptural inspiration. The second article reviewed the last main and very lengthy chapter in his book about the use of the Old Testament in the New Testament. Enns responded

6. "Apostolic Hermeneutics and an Evangelical Doctrine of Scripture: Moving Beyond the Modern Impasse," *Westminster Theological Journal* 65 (2003): 263–87.

to both the first and the second review, and I wrote counter-responses to each of his replies.

It is these exchanges that will form a significant part of this book. The dialogue of these debates will be set out as they were composed in the journals in which they originally appeared.[7] The purpose is to set forth the debates in these articles as somewhat typical of the kind of debates that are emerging in the beginning of this century within the so-called evangelical scholarly community,[8] though such notions were already beginning to be formulated toward the end of the last century by scholars considering themselves to be still within the evangelical fold.

There are other issues pertinent to this debate that this book will not discuss, and there are other books and articles recently written that challenge a traditional evangelical view of Scripture, but limitations of space do not allow for summary and evaluation of such works.[9] This book is but a brief snapshot of the types of dialogue being conducted within what has usually been considered the most conservative sectors of Christianity. For example, when Ennis published his book, he was in his twelfth year of teaching at Westminster Theological Seminary in Philadelphia, long considered to be a bastion of evangelical orthodoxy.

Since, as we will see, Peter Enns has said that he wants to influence a more popular Christian audience by the ideas of his book, I also have written this book to help interested laypeople, students, and pastors to be able to understand better his arguments and what I believe are the fallacies inherent in them. And, like Enns, I have in mind, secondarily, a scholarly audience, whom I hope also will benefit from the discussion. Ultimately, I have decided to write this book because I believe that the issues discussed in it are very important for Christian faith and confidence in our Bible.

---

7. Though Enns's responses will be summarized as accurately as possible, they will not be reproduced in their original form; nevertheless, readers are highly encouraged to consult these responses in their original journal form.

8. I use the phrase "so-called evangelical" and similar phrases at times, since I am unsure about what constitutes the definition of *evangelical* today. So many people of a variety of theological stripes, especially with respect to their stand on the nature of Scripture, take on the name.

9. Representative examples of such books include John Webster, *Holy Scripture: A Dogmatic Sketch* (Cambridge: Cambridge University Press, 2003); N. T. Wright, *The Last Word: Beyond the Bible* (London: SPCK, 2005); Andrew McGowan, *The Divine Spiration of Scripture: Challenging Evangelical Perspectives* (Apollos [Inter-Varsity], 2007). D. A. Carson has given helpful summaries and reviews of the first two books, and provides references to other recent books of relevance and an extended review of Peter Enns's book, *Inspiration and Incarnation*. See "Three More Books on the Bible: A Critical Review," *Trinity Journal* 27NS (2006): 1–62. For a good review of McGowan's book, see J. R. deWitt, "The Divine Spiration of Scripture—A Review," *Banner of Truth* (June 2008). Along similar lines to Enns's approach, see Kenton L. Sparks, *God's Word in Human Words* (Grand Rapids: Baker, 2008).

After laying out my dialogue with Peter Enns in chapters 1 to 4, I will discuss in the remaining chapters (1) the problem of the traditional understanding of the authorship of Old Testament books, especially that of Isaiah; (2) whether the Old Testament's concept of the cosmos is irreconcilable with a modern scientific view; (3) the problem of the nature of the Christian's certainty and confidence in the authority of the Bible and in the task of interpretation itself; (4) the Chicago Statement of Inerrancy which represent generally my own understanding of what should be considered the evangelical view of the authority of Scripture; and (5) quotations from Karl Barth on the limited nature of the authority of the Bible. The quotations from Barth are included since his perspective on the authority of Scripture is appealed to by some evangelicals as a good model.

CHAPTER ONE

Is a Traditional Evangelical View of Scripture's Authority Compatible with Recent Developments in Old Testament Studies? *Part 1*

Below, with minor revisions, is my initial review, "Myth, History, and Inspiration: A Review Article of *Inspiration and Incarnation* by Peter Enns,"[1] which appeared in *JETS* 49 (2006): 287–312.

Introduction[2]

Peter Enns has written a stimulating and yet controversial book on the doctrine of Scripture. Scholars and students alike should be grateful that Enns has boldly ventured to set before his evangelical peers a view of inspiration and hermeneutics that has not traditionally been held by evangelical scholarship.

After his introduction, in chapter 2 Enns discusses the parallels between ancient Near Eastern myths and accounts in the Old Testament. He says that the Old Testament contains what he defines as "myth" (see his definition later below), but, he affirms, this should not have a negative bearing on the Old Testament's divine inspiration. God accom-

---

1. P. Enns, *Inspiration and Incarnation: Evangelicals and the Problem of the Old Testament* (Grand Rapids: Baker, 2005).
2. I am grateful to several scholarly friends around the country who have graciously read this review article and have offered very helpful comments in the revising stage.

modates himself to communicate his truth through such mythological biblical accounts.

In chapter 3 Enns discusses what he calls "diversity" in the Old Testament. He believes that the kinds of diversity that he attempts to analyze have posed problems in the past for the doctrine of inerrancy. He asserts that this diversity must be acknowledged, even though it poses tensions for the inspiration of Scripture. This diversity is part of God's inspired Word.

In chapter 4 Enns shifts to the topic of how the Old Testament is interpreted by New Testament writers. He contends that Second Temple Judaism was not concerned to interpret the Old Testament according to an author's intention or to interpret it contextually or according to modern standards of "grammatical-historical exegesis." This hermeneutical context of Judaism must be seen as the socially constructed framework of the New Testament writers' approach to interpreting the Old Testament, so that they also were not concerned to interpret the Old Testament contextually. Accordingly, they interpreted the Old Testament by a "christotelic hermeneutic," which means generally that they had a Christ-oriented perspective in understanding the purpose of the Old Testament, including the meaning of specific Old Testament passages. This also means that "the literal (first) reading [of an Old Testament text] will not lead the reader to the christotelic (second) reading."[3]

The final chapter attempts to draw out further implications from the earlier chapters for Enns's understanding of an "incarnational" doctrine of Scripture.

At various points throughout the book, Enns appeals to this incarnational notion, contending that since Christ was fully divine and fully human, then so is Scripture. Accordingly, we need to accept the "diversity" or "messiness" of Scripture, just as we accept all of the aspects of Jesus' humanity. Also at various points in the book is the warning that modern interpreters should not impose their modern views of history and scientific precision on the ancient text of the Bible. Such a foreign imposition results in seeing problems in the Bible that are really not there.

The origin of Enns's book and its strength derive from the author's attempt to wrestle with problems that evangelicals must reflect upon in formulating their view of a doctrine of Scripture.

Enns has attempted to draw out the implications of postmodernism for an evangelical doctrine of Scripture further than most other evangeli-

---

3. Enns, *Inspiration and Incarnation*, 158; page references cited in text pertain to this work.

cal scholars to date. He argues that liberal and evangelical approaches to Scripture both have held the same basic presupposition: that one can discern the difference between truth and error by using modern standards of reasoning and modern scientific analysis. He is proposing a paradigm for understanding scriptural inspiration that goes beyond the "liberal vs. conservative" impasse (pp. 14–15). He wants to "contribute to a growing opinion that what is needed is to move beyond both sides by thinking of better ways to account for some of the data, while at the same time having a vibrant, positive view of Scripture as God's word" (p. 15). This, of course, is a monumental task that Enns has set for himself. Enns says we must go beyond this impasse, and he presents himself as one of the few having the balance or the new synthesis that solves these age-old debates.

The book is designed more for the layperson than the scholar but is apparently written with the latter secondarily in mind. He says his thesis is not novel, but, in reality, the main proposal for which he contends throughout is "novel": he is trying to produce a synthesis of the findings of mainline liberal scholarship and an evangelical view of Scripture. Many who will judge his attempt a failure would probably wish that he had written a book that goes into much more depth, and even those who agree with him would probably wish for the same thing.

There is much to comment on in his short book. At some points, especially in the first three chapters, Enns is ambiguous, and the reader is left to connect the dots to determine his view. What follows here is an attempt not only to summarize and evaluate his explicit views but also to connect the dots in the way I think Enns does in areas where he is not as explicit. Thus, I quote Enns sometimes at length in order to let readers better assess his views and to try to cut through the ambiguity.

This chapter will focus primarily on the first part of Enns's book, which deals with Old Testament issues.

Enns's Incarnational Model for Understanding Biblical Inspiration

In Relation to History and Myth

Perhaps the overarching theme of Enns's book is his conception of divine accommodation in the process of scriptural inspiration. For Enns, Scripture is very human, which means that God meets his people in a very human way in his Word. Enns repeatedly compares this to Christ's incarnation: "As Christ is both God and human, so is the Bible" (p. 17; likewise pp. 18, 67, 111, 167–68). It is out of the incarnational analogy that Enns develops his view that "for God to reveal himself means that he accommodates himself" (p. 109; cf. p. 110). Enns is certainly right to underscore that the divine word in Scripture is also a human word. What this means for Enns is that much more "diversity" in the Bible should be recognized by evangelicals than has been typically the case in the past.

In particular, he is concerned that conservatives have not sufficiently recognized ancient Near Eastern (ANE) parallels with the Bible, particularly the parallels with the Babylonian myth of creation and the Sumerian myth of the cataclysmic flood (pp. 26–27). Enns says that "the doctrinal implications of these discoveries have not yet been fully worked out in evangelical theology" (p. 25). For example, he says that if the Old Testament has so much in common with the ancient world and its customs and practices, "in what sense can we speak of it as revelation?" (p. 31). But, as he acknowledges, these discoveries were made in the nineteenth century, and evangelical scholars have been reflecting on their doctrinal implications ever since the early nineteen hundreds.

It is important to remark at this point that (1) some evangelical scholars have seen the presence of similarities to supposed ANE myth due to *polemical intentions*,[4] as have some non-evangelical scholars, or to direct repudiation of pagan religious beliefs and practices. (2) Others see the presence of similarities as rising from a *reflection of general revelation* by both pagan and biblical writers, and only rightly interpreted by the latter.[5] (3) Still others have attributed purported ANE mythical parallels in the Old Testament to a *common reflection of ancient tradition*, the sources of which precede both the pagan and biblical writers, and the historicity of which has no independent human verification (like the creation in Genesis 1) but is based ultimately on an earlier, ancient, divinely pristine revelation that became garbled in the pagan context and reliably witnessed to by the scriptural writer.[6] (4) Yet another view is that revelation did not always counter ANE concepts but often used them in productive ways, though still revised in significant manner by special revelation. For example, ANE concepts may have helped give shape to the theology of sacred space in the building of Israel's tabernacle

---

4. E.g., see in this respect the article by G. Hasel, "The Polemic Nature of the Genesis Cosmology," *EQ* 46 (1974): 81–102. Cf. A. Heidel, *The Babylonian Genesis* (Chicago: Chicago University Press, 1954), 82–140. Hasel does not believe there is enough evidence to be certain that the Old Testament creation narrative was dependent on the Babylonian one and concludes that some of the significant differences in the former are unparalleled in either the Babylonian or the Assyrian cosmogonies.

5. Enns's discussions of wisdom literature and law in chapter 3 of his book would appear to be consistent with this viewpoint.

6. E.g., see D. I. Block, "Other Religions in Old Testament Theology," in *Biblical Faith and Other Religions*, ed. D. W. Baker (Grand Rapids: Kregel, 2004), 43–78, who, in essence, affirms these first three views, though the majority of the article elaborates on the first perspective. See also Heidel, *Babylonian Genesis*, 139, who cites a scholar representing the third view.

and temple, e.g., the eastward orientation, the placement of important cultic objects, the designation of areas of increasing holiness, the rules for access to the Holy Place and the Most Holy Place, etc.[7]

Of course, another option, in contrast to the preceding four views, is that the biblical writers absorbed mythical worldviews unconsciously, reproduced them in their writings, and believed them to be reliable descriptions of the real world and events occurring in the past real world (creation account, flood narrative, etc.) because they were part of their socially constructed reality.[8] Divine inspiration did not limit such cultural, mythical influence.

Does Enns agree with this latter view, still nevertheless contending that God used myths to convey truth? Does Enns believe that these Old Testament "mythical accounts" do not contain *essential historicity*, so that he uses the word *myth* with its normal meaning? The following analysis of Enns will contend that his view, while sometimes consistent with some of the four above views, does not primarily align itself with any of them. He appears to give an affirmative answer to the preceding two questions, though one must work hard at interpreting Enns to come to these conclusions, since, at crucial points in his discussion, he is unclear. It would have been helpful to readers if Enns had acknowledged the above variety of ways that the Old Testament interacts with ANE myth and where precisely he positioned himself with respect to various Old Testament passages.

According to Enns, the ancient peoples around Israel asked questions about their ultimate being and meaning, "so, stories were made up," especially about the creation (p. 41). The Genesis account of creation "is firmly rooted in the [mythological] worldview of the time" (p. 27); in other words the Genesis passage presupposes and utilizes the mythological creation stories circulating in the ANE (including, presumably, the background of the account about "Adam's" creation?). The main point, according to Enns, is to show that Yahweh is the true God and not the Babylonian gods (p. 27). The same conclusion is reached with respect to the flood account (pp. 27–29).

---

7. E.g., see J. H. Walton, "Ancient Near Eastern Background Studies," in *Dictionary for the Theological Interpretation of Scripture*, ed. K. Vanhoozer (Grand Rapids: Baker, 2005), 42; see the entire article (pp. 40–45), which is helpful. Walton registers agreement also with the preceding three perspectives on ANE parallels, though aligning himself most with this fourth view. See also Block, "Other Religions in Old Testament Theology," 47–48, who also appears partly to align himself with this fourth view.

8. See Walton, "Ancient Near Eastern Background Studies," 43. Walton repudiates such unconscious absorption and use of myth in the Old Testament while affirming that "God's communication used the established literary genres of the ancient world and often conformed to the rules that existed within those genres," 41.

Enns likes the use of the word *myth* to describe these biblical accounts, but how does he define *myth* precisely? Enns says that not all historians of the ancient Near East use the word *myth* simply as "shorthand for 'untrue,' 'made-up,' 'storybook,'" a position with which he appears to align himself (p. 40). Yet, enigmatically, he goes on to define *myth* in the ANE as something apparently very close to this. His formal definition of "myth" is as follows: "Myth is an ancient, premodern, prescientific way of addressing questions of ultimate origins and meaning in the form of stories: Who are we? Where do we come from?" (p. 50; so likewise p. 40).

Note well that there is no reference to history or actual events in this definition. But then Enns proceeds to affirm, despite his earlier apparent qualification about "made-up" stories, that ANE myths were "stories [that] *were made up*" (p. 41, my italics) and were composed by a process of "telling stories" (p. 41), and that "the biblical stories" of the "creation and flood must be understood first and foremost in the ancient contexts." This means, interpreting Enns by Enns, that the biblical stories had "*a firm grounding in ancient myth*" (p. 56, my italics); to reiterate, with specific reference to the Genesis creation account, he says it "is firmly rooted in the [mythological] worldview of the time" (previous page). So, what is Enns's view of myth in relation to real events of the past?

In this respect and in connection with some of Enns's directly preceding statements, he poses a difficult question:

> If the ancient Near Eastern stories are myth (defined in this way as prescientific stories of origins), and since the biblical stories are similar enough to these stories to invite comparison, does this indicate that myth is the proper category for understanding Genesis? (p. 41)

He answers this by asking another question:

> Are the early stories in the Old Testament to be judged on the basis of standards of modern historical inquiry and scientific precision, things that ancient peoples were not at all aware of? (p. 41)

He answers by saying that it is unlikely that God would have allowed his Word to come to the Israelites according to "modern standards of truth and error so universal that we should expect premodern cultures to have understood them." Rather, more probably, God's Word came to them "according to standards *they* understood" (p. 41), which included mythological standards of the time. Recall once more that part of Enns's definition of *myth* includes stories that were made up. He concludes that the latter position is "better suited for solving the problem" of how God accommodated his revelation to his ancient people (p. 41).

Enns acknowledges that beginning with the monarchic age (1000–600 BC) more historical consciousness arises, so that history "is recorded with a degree of accuracy more in keeping with contemporary standards" (p. 43). He immediately adds, however, that a negative answer must be given to the question, "Can we not also conclude that the same can be said for Genesis and other early portions of the Bible?" (p. 43). He continues, "It is questionable logic to reason backward from the historical character of the monarchic account, *for which there is some evidence*, to the primeval and ancestral stories, *for which such evidence is lacking*" (p. 43). He says the same thing even more explicitly on page 44:

> One would expect a more accurate, blow-by-blow account of Israel's history during this monarchic period, when it began to develop a more "historical self-consciousness," as it were. It is precisely the evidence *missing* from the previous periods of Israel's history that raises the problem *of the essential historicity* of that period [my italics].

So, in one respect, we are on somewhat firmer ground when we come to the monarchic period because it is there that we see something more closely resembling what one would expect of good history writing by modern standards: a more or less contemporary, eyewitness account.

Likewise, Enns says a little later:

> The Mesopotamian world from which Abraham came was one whose own stories of origins had been expressed in mythic categories. . . . The reason the opening chapters of Genesis look so much like the literature of ancient Mesopotamia is that the worldview categories of the ancient Near East were ubiquitous and normative at the time. Of course, different [ancient] cultures had different myths, but the point is that they all[9] had them.

> The reason the biblical account is different from its ancient Near Eastern counterparts is not that it is history in the modern sense of the word and therefore divorced from any similarity to ancient Near Eastern myth. What makes Genesis different from its ancient Near Eastern counterparts is that . . . the God they [Abraham and his seed] are bound to . . . is different from the gods around them.

---

9. It is probable here that Enns is including the patriarchs and Israel in this "all."

We might think that such a scenario is unsatisfying because it gives too much ground to pagan myths. (p. 53)

God adopted Abraham as the forefather of a new people, and in doing so he also adopted the mythic categories within which Abraham—and everyone else—thought. But God did not simply leave Abraham in his mythic world. Rather; [sic] God transformed the ancient myths so that Israel's story would come to focus on its God, the real one. (pp. 53–54)

The differences notwithstanding [between Babylonian myths and the Genesis creation and flood accounts], the opening chapters of Genesis participate in a worldview that the earliest Israelites shared with their Mesopotamian neighbors. To put it this way is not to concede ground to liberalism or unbelief, but to understand the simple fact that the stories in Genesis had a context within which they were first understood. And that context was not a modern scientific one but an ancient mythic one.

The biblical account, along with its ancient Near East counterparts, assumes the factual nature of what it reports. They did not think, "We know this is all 'myth' but it will have to do until science is invented to give us better answers." (p. 55)

To argue . . . that such biblical stories as creation and the flood must be understood first and foremost in the ancient contexts, is nothing new. The point I would like to emphasize, however, is that such a firm grounding in ancient myth does not make Genesis less inspired. (p. 56)

It is important to note three things that Enns says in these extended quotations. First, if ancient Old Testament writers did not record history according to modern historical and scientific standards, it means that they did not recount historical events that corresponded with actual past reality but that corresponded to ANE myth; indeed, Enns wants to "emphasize" that "such a firm grounding in ancient myth does not make Genesis less inspired" (p. 56)! Thus, uncritical and unconscious absorption of myth by a biblical author does not make his writing less inspired than other parts of Scripture.

Second, and in connection with the first point, Enns says that "the evidence *missing* from the previous [pre-monarchic] periods of Israel's history . . . raises the problem of the essential historicity of that period," which, in the light of all Enns has said above, most likely means for him that these pre-monarchic accounts are not to be viewed as containing "essential historicity."

Third, the main distinction between the ANE myths and Israel's myths lies *not in the latter recording reliable history* but in the latter proclaiming that Israel's God "is different from the gods around them." It appears fairly clear that the distinction between the ANE mythical accounts of creation and the flood and those of the Genesis accounts is not in the former containing non-history and the latter representing reliable historical events, but the difference is to highlight the biblical God as true in contrast to the false ANE gods. This is the primary way, then, that "God *transformed* the ancient myths," not in presenting a historical account that corresponds to past historical reality, but causing "Israel's story . . . to focus on its God, the real one" (p. 54).

Enns concludes those thoughts by saying, "We might think that such a scenario is unsatisfying because it gives too much ground to pagan myths" (p. 53). Yes, I think that many practicing respected Old Testament and New Testament evangelical scholars (and not only fundamentalists) will think that he indeed has given way too much ground to "pagan myth."

In addition, the fact that Enns affirms that the Pentateuch positively adopts *mythical* notions in the essentially normal sense of the word (i.e., non-historical and fictitious narrative) is also apparent later when he addresses the question of polytheism in ancient Israel. Here again Enns explains what he means:

> It is important here that we not allow our own modern sensitivities to influence how we understand Israel's ancient faith. We may not believe that multiple gods ever existed, but *ancient near Eastern people* did. This is the religious world within which God called Israel to be his people. When God called Israel, he *began* leading them into a full knowledge of who he is, but he started where they were.

> We should not be surprised, therefore, when we see the Old Testament describe God as *greater than* the gods of the surrounding nations. In the Psalms, for example, this is seen in a number of passages. (p. 98)

> I suppose one could argue that the psalmists . . . didn't really intend to be taken literally. . . . For the comparison [between God and other "gods"] to have any real punch, both entities must be *presumed* to be real. For example, we may tell our children something like, "Don't be afraid of the dark. God is greater than the Boogey Man." Of course, adults who say this know that the Boogey Man is not real, but they know that their *children* believe he is real. Even in contemporary Christian expression, we compare God to many things: our problems, our challenges, our enemies,

and so on.[10] And each comparison is made between two real (or perceived to be real) entities. This is what these Psalms are doing as well. (p. 99)

What would have spoken to these Israelites—what would have met them where they were—was not a declaration of monotheism (belief that only one God exists), out of the blue. Their ears would not have been prepared to hear that. What we read in Exodus is perhaps less satisfying for us, but it would have set the ancient world on its head: this god Yahweh . . . meets these powerful Egyptian gods . . . and . . . beats them up. (p. 101)

They [Israel] were taking their first baby steps toward a knowledge of God that later generations came to understand and we perhaps take for granted. At this point in the progress of redemption, however, the gods of the surrounding nations are treated as real. God shows his absolute supremacy over them by declaring not that "they don't exist" but that "they cannot stand up against me." (p. 102)

I have quoted Enns as fully as space allows, since his full views should be clearly seen, and my attempt is to present them as accurately as possible within limited space and despite some of Enns's ambiguity. First, he affirms a developmental view (some would call it "evolutionary"), asserting that early on Israel believed in the reality of many mythical gods but was to worship only the one God, Yahweh, and that it was only later that Israel came to have a monotheistic faith.

Part of the problem with Enns's developmental view is that he sees the same non-monotheistic view expressed in some of the psalms, all of which were written after the patriarchal and early Israelite periods (e.g., Psalm 86 is presented as "a Prayer of David"). Enns says that unless these other "gods" are "*presumed* to be real," then the biblical comparisons of God with the other "gods" lacks "punch."

Therefore, he is espousing that early parts of the Old Testament held to henotheism, belief in one god without asserting that this god is the only god. Is this a necessary deduction from the evidence that he has presented? There are other viable interpretative options for understanding the biblical view of these other gods.

Some scholars see that there are real spiritual realities behind pagan idols but that they are demonic rather than divine realities. For example, the view is testified to early on in the Old Testament that demons were behind idols (see Lev. 17:7;[11] Deut. 32:17). Others would understand that though the Old Testament writers refer to "gods," sometimes using

10. The meaning of this sentence is unclear to me.
11. BDB, 972.

the very word *ᵉlōhîm* in Hebrew, they are not divine realities at all but a lie or deception.[12] Both these alternatives have just as much punch, indeed, probably more punch, than making the assumption that these "gods" are really divine realities.

In fact, early on in Israel's history, there are clear statements against the existence of any gods besides the God of Israel: in the directly following context after the statement in Deuteronomy 4:28 that Israel "will serve gods, the work of men's hands," twice God is said to be the only truly existing God (Deut. 4:39, "the LORD, He is God in heaven above and on the earth below; there is no other"; Deut. 4:35, "He is God; there is no other besides Him").[13] This Deuteronomistic affirmation is developed later in the Old Testament (2 Kings 19:18; Jer. 2:11; 5:7). Hence, when Moses calls God "the God of gods" in Deuteronomy 10:17 he is not assenting to the existence of other deities but affirming "Yahweh's supremacy over all spiritual and heavenly powers."[14] In this light, there is no need to compare God's relationship with early Israelites to parents who allow their children to believe in the boogeyman.

However one evaluates Enns's positive approach to myth, what should be kept separate are the notions of history and scientific precision. Recall that he acknowledges elsewhere in the book that modern views of history are very comparable to the historical consciousness of Israel's scriptural historians beginning around the tenth century BC. Thus, his apparent equation of a modern historiography and modern science in the preceding quotation should be qualified: could there not be "history" as we understand it in the Old Testament, including Genesis, but not an expectation that these same writers would intend to write with scientific precision?

---

12. Indeed, the word *ᵉlōhîm* can also reference earthly idols (e.g., Ex. 34:17; Lev. 19:4; 1 Chron. 16:26; 2 Chron. 13:9; Ps. 96:5; Isa. 37:19; 42:17; Jer. 16:20) or gods that the nations (or apostate Israel) worship (Ex. 34:15–17; Num. 25:2; Deut. 6:14; 7:16), though most references in the latter category probably refer to mere idols or idols that represent gods. The word is used also for angels in the heavenly realm (Pss. 97:7; 138:1; cf. also Job 38:7 ["sons of God"]), and it may be used for malevolent, angelic-like deities dwelling in the heavenly realm (see Job 1:6; 2:1; Gen. 6:2, 4, where "the sons of God" [*bᵉnê-hāᵃᵉlōhîm*], according to many commentators, refer to fallen angels), which are viewed as divine by some humans (cf. perhaps Jer. 7:18; in the New Testament see 1 Cor. 8:5; see also Eph. 3:10 and 6:11–12). Paul captures well the Old Testament view when he alludes to Deut. 4:35 in 1 Cor. 8:4: "There is no God but one," and then adds in vv. 5–6, "For even if there are so-called gods . . . as indeed there are many gods and many lords, yet for us there is one God," and in 10:20 Paul affirms that the so-called gods are demons.

13. Of course, critical scholarship would date Deuteronomy around the sixth century BC so that, according to this view, these statements in Deuteronomy would be seen as arising later in Israel's history.

14. Block, "Other Religions in Old Testament Theology," 57.

I think the answer is that Old Testament writers record history as we would understand it—as events that happened and that correspond to past reality—but they do not attempt to record in some sort of strict chronological fashion or with so-called modern scientific precision (which, of course, are kinds of accepted history writing done even in modern times). To say that ancient people could not narrate history in a way that sufficiently represented actual events of the past because they were not modern historians is a false dichotomy.

I want to repeat and underscore that Enns himself states that beginning with the tenth century BC, history "is recorded with a degree of accuracy more in keeping with contemporary standards" (p. 43). If so, why could not earlier writers have written with the same historical awareness? What is particularly troubling about Enns's view is that he does not include "essential historicity" in his definition of the kind of myth contained in the Old Testament (see the above quotations in this respect) in distinction to ANE myth, which is how he categorizes the creation and flood accounts in Genesis and also possibly the narratives about Abraham, Isaac, and Jacob as well as the event of the Exodus, since they are also pre-monarchic. Recall that all pre-monarchic historical narratives, for Enns, face the problem of "essential historicity" in contrast to monarchic history writing; does he see a historical core to such narratives, and if so, how much or how little?[15]

It would be good if Enns could tell us the grounds upon which one can decide what parts of Old Testament history are true and which are not, since some scholars may think that there are more places than Enns has pointed out where mythical or legendary material is positively affirmed by biblical writers. Even when he says that the history recorded in the monarchic period of Israel's time is more reliable than earlier history recorded in the Pentateuch, how can we be sure of that? There may have been other mythical traditions in circulation that had affinities with significant strands of that monarchic history and which could cast doubt on the veracity of that history.

Thus, it *may be* true that Enns almost never makes the explicit *verbal* statement that the accounts in Genesis and Exodus are not historical, but he often conveys the concept. Nevertheless, the following quotations (that I repeat to make the point), especially when understood in their contexts, are virtually explicit statements that these biblical accounts are not essentially history but myth.

---

15. His discussion suggests strongly that he would not take these accounts in their fullness to be reports corresponding to real events of the past.

The reason the biblical account is different from its ancient Near Eastern counterparts is not that it is history in the modern sense of the word and therefore divorced from any similarity to ancient Near Eastern myth. What makes Genesis different from its ancient Near Eastern counterparts is that . . . the God they [Abraham and his seed] are bound to . . . is different from the gods around them. (p. 53)

The biblical account, along with its ancient Near East counterparts, assumes the factual nature of what it reports. They did not think, "We know this is all 'myth' but it will have to do until science is invented to give us better answers." (p. 55)

The point I would like to emphasize, however, is that such a firm grounding in ancient myth does not make Genesis less inspired. (p. 56)

It is striking that the second quotation even affirms that biblical writers "assumed the factual nature" of their "reports," even though they were really not factual but "myth."

Therefore, the most probable assessment of his view so far is that conceptually, at the least, he affirms that the biblical writers imbibed myths at significant points, recorded them, and, though they were not essentially historical, they naïvely affirmed such myths as reliable descriptions of the real world because they were part of their socially constructed reality. Furthermore, divine inspiration did not restrain such social-cultural osmosis. John Walton's assessment of non-evangelical approaches to the ANE and the Old Testament is generally applicable to Enns's: "The attempt has been made to reduce the Old Testament to converted mythology whose dependency exposes its humanity."[16] There are, however, three important caveats to be made about Enns's approach that differ from the customary non-evangelical approach: (1) He believes the point of the Pentateuchal mythical narratives, like that of the creation and of the flood account, is to highlight for Israelites that their God is to be worshiped in contrast to the other ANE Gods. (2) Enns apparently sees more reliable history being recorded beginning with Israel's monarchic period. (3) He believes the Bible is fully inspired by God.

Brief reference must be made to Enns's writing on the use of the Old Testament in the New Testament to demonstrate further that he believes that the Bible records myths that are "essentially unhistorical." In chapter 4 of his book, he recommends for further reading his article on 1 Corin-

---

16. "Ancient Near Eastern Background Studies," 43.

thians 10:4.[17] There he repeatedly labels as "legend" Paul's reference to the purported Jewish tradition about "the rock which followed" Israel in the wilderness. My analysis of his discussion is elsewhere.[18]

It is interesting to ask why in his book Enns never calls the reference in 1 Corinthians 10:4 a "legend" while doing so explicitly and repeatedly in his article. The fact that he concludes chapter 4 with an unqualified recommendation for his article makes apparent that he has not changed his mind. Thus, Enns presents us with another ambiguity, this time between his book and his recommended article.

So, at the end of the day, one has to read Enns very closely over a number of pages to determine precisely what he means by *myth*. I have adduced some extended quotations, and when we let "Enns interpret Enns" from one part of the book to another, letting his clearer statements interpret the unclear, the likely conclusion is that he uses *myth* still in the essentially normal sense, i.e., stories without an "essential historical" foundation (his very language).

The Question of Recording "Objective" History in Relation to the Incarnational Model

In connection to the preceding section, Enns also says, "One must question the entire assumption that good history writing, whether modern or ancient, is concerned to transmit only bare facts of history. Is there really any such thing as a completely objective and unbiased recording of history, modern or premodern?" (p. 45). There may be some scholars, both evangelical and non-evangelical, who hold the assumption that Enns is arguing against, but the majority of conservative Old Testament and New Testament scholars who publish in their fields today would not hold such an assumption.

This does not mean, on the other hand, that evangelical scholars who agree with Enns's general premise—that all history is not completely objective—agree with his deduction of what this premise means for the reliability of historical events recorded in the Bible. Enns thinks this assumption entails the following: "If the Bible does not tell us what actually happened, how can we trust it about anything? Simply put, the problem before us is the historical character of precisely those Old Testament narratives that seem to report historical events" (p. 45).

---

17. Peter Enns, "The 'Moveable Well' in 1 Cor. 10:4: An Extrabiblical Tradition in an Apostolic Text," *BBR* 6 (1996): 23–38.

18. See my review article of Enns's fourth chapter (on his view of the use of the Old Testament in the New): "Did Jesus and the Apostles Preach the Right Doctrine from the Wrong Texts? Revisiting the Debate Seventeen Years Later in the Light of Peter Enns's Book, *Inspiration and Incarnation*." My review in *Themelios* may be found in chapter 3 of this book.

Though there is a rhetorical tone in the first question of this quotation, the words are Enns's own, and they appear to express his skeptical view of the reliability of events reported in purported historical narratives, as the second sentence further suggests. It is apparent that Enns's overall point in this quotation, understood within the context of his discussion here, is to affirm that "interpreted history" means significant varying degrees of distortion of the record of that history for the purpose of making a theological point. Accordingly, one's trust in such biblical narratives is to be in the theological point being made and not in the actual factuality of the events recorded in these narratives.

But cannot historical writers interpret events without distorting the description of how those events occurred? Leading conservative Old Testament scholars answer in the affirmative, but Enns does not make the reader aware of these views.[19] For example, I know of a Jewish scholar who is convinced that the New Testament account about Jesus' resurrection is historically reliable, but he disagrees with the New Testament's interpretation of the resurrection, i.e., that Jesus is the Messiah for Gentiles *and* Jews. (This Jewish scholar believes Jesus was the Messiah only for Gentiles.)

Enns's Incarnational Model in Relation to Jesus' Incarnation

It is curious that in Enns's attempt to argue for an incarnational analogy for the doctrine of Scripture he never attempts to define what he means by Christ's incarnation (i.e., the relation of his human to his divine nature) and, especially, what aspect of it he thinks helps to clarify how God accommodates himself by revealing his truth through such things as myth.[20] Some evangelical theologians speculate that while the human Jesus was perfect morally, he was still imperfect in such things as mathematical computation or historical recollection. Some say, "Could not Jesus have made a B on his fifth grade math test?" or "Could he not have cut a board wrongly from the instructions of his human father?" On analogy with this conception of Jesus' incarnation, Scripture is God's absolutely

---

19. See, e.g., the first six essays, and bibliography, in *Giving the Sense*, edited by D. M. Howard and M. A. Grisanti (Grand Rapids: Kregel, 2003); in particular, see Howard's convenient listings of such leading scholars contributing in varying degrees to this area as Dever, Rainey, and Hurwitz, and evangelicals such as Long, Provan, Hoffmeier, Hess, Younger, Millard, and Baker ("History as History," ibid., 51). See also G. R. Osborne, "Historical Narrative and Truth in the Bible," *JETS* 48 (2005): 673–88, who makes the point with respect to both Old and New Testament historical narratives. Enns does cite works by Hess and Long (on p. 69), but he does not engage their arguments.

20. Note some of the places where Enns appeals to the incarnational model but without explaining his precise view of the human nature of Jesus as it relates to the human writers of Scripture: pp. 17–18, 109, 111, 167–68.

faithful word about morals and theology (e.g., the way to salvation) but not about minute points of history or scientific facts.

Does Enns hold a view like this? If this is Enns's incarnational model—and we have to make our best speculation, since he does not tell us—then its success depends on, among other things, the problematic presupposition that cognitive information not dealing with issues of morality and salvation (historical facts, scientific facts, etc.) can, indeed, be neatly separated from morality and salvific issues.[21]

But whatever Enns's precise view of Jesus' incarnation is, his very attempt to compare Jesus' incarnation with revelation in God's Word may not work as a good analogy. Some evangelical scholars affirm that New Testament Scripture is the result of the exercise of Christ's prophetic office through prophetic and apostolic writers and that this is the best framework through which to understand the nature of Scripture. An incarnational model may not be the best because, whereas with Christ's incarnation there is one person with two natures, with Scripture there are two persons—God and the human prophet—and one nature, i.e., the one scriptural speech act.[22]

Thus, to try to make the analogy may be like comparing apples to oranges. At the very least, the analogy must be carefully qualified, since it cannot "walk on all fours."[23] Unfortunately Enns not only does not qualify his view of the incarnation, but he never tells us what it is.

Enns and Biblical Diversity

The Apparent Use of the Term "Diversity" in Place of "Error"
Enns sees that "diversity" is part of the warp and woof of Scripture: "Diversity is such a prevalent phenomenon in the Old Testament" (p. 107;

---

21. It might be added that since Jesus said he did not know certain things, such as the precise time of the final destruction of the cosmos (Matt. 24:36), then his cognition was not only limited but faulty. This, however, has not been deemed by the church to reflect a human limitation entailing error: a self-imposed lack of knowledge is different from an erroneous claim. Scripture never qualifies any of Jesus' statements by saying that his ignorance means he could say something false about or not know the truth about the past or the present. In fact, the very context of the above statement in Matthew 24 asserts that everything Jesus did affirm has the enduring quality of unalterable truth: "Heaven and earth will pass away, but My words will not pass away" (Matt. 24:35, following J. I. Packer, *'Fundamentalism' and the Word of God* [Grand Rapids: Eerdmans, 1958], 60–61).

22. I am grateful to my colleague Henri Blocher for suggesting this.

23. Enns (p. 18) himself acknowledges this caveat about the incarnational metaphor, but he never explains what aspect of the analogy does fit. On the other hand, see K. J. Vanhoozer, *Is There a Meaning in This Text?* (Grand Rapids: Zondervan, 1998), 86–87, 303–10, 460–61, who attempts to point out the specific aspects of Christ's incarnation that are helpful analogues to an understanding of the hermeneutical meaning of Scripture; e.g., he says, in arguing for a determinate yet thick meaning of Scripture, "As the Logos indwelt the flesh of Jesus, so meaning indwells the body of the text" (ibid., 310).

likewise p. 108). His definition of *diversity* is not clear: does it refer to various but complementary viewpoints or to irreconcilable perspectives on a given topic? At the least, it would appear to mean that it is difficult to harmonize what different biblical writers say who speak to the same issue. It would appear that he has turned the Reformer's notion of the perspicuity of Scripture on its head and affirmed that there is so much diversity in the Old Testament that our view of inspiration must be reassessed. Furthermore, he says, if we were to use our modern definition of *error*, apparently we would judge that there are errors in the Bible. But Enns says that we cannot use modern definitions of *error* to judge biblical literature and that the best term to use is *diversity*:

> For modern evangelicalism the tendency is to move toward a defensive or apologetic handling of the biblical evidence, to protect the Bible against the modernist charge that diversity is evidence of errors in the Bible and, consequently, that the Bible is not inspired by God. Unfortunately, this legacy accepts the worldview offered by modernity and defends the Bible by a rational standard that the Bible itself challenges rather than acknowledges. (p. 108)

> The messiness of the Old Testament, which is a source of embarrassment for some, is actually a positive. On one level it may not help with a certain brand of apologetics, where we use the so-called perfection of the Bible to prove to nonbelievers that Christianity is true. But this method is as wrongheaded as it is to argue that Christianity is true by downplaying the humanness of Christ. (p. 109)

This is another example of his using his view of Christ's incarnation without defining the view. His implied definition indicates that Christ made mistakes of, for example, a mathematical or historical nature, but that he was reliable in his moral and theological statements, though I may well be wrong about his implication. He does appear implicitly to draw the analogy, which he thinks to be fallacious and the opposite of his comparison, of the "wrongheaded" view of "the so-called perfection of the Bible" with "downplaying the humanness [imperfection?] of Christ" and highlighting his divine perfection.

But is there another logical fallacy in Enns's attempt to affirm that the Old Testament cannot be judged by modern standards of "error" (e.g., pp. 80, 108)? Enns's view appears to be non-falsifiable: if a liberal scholar finds a mistake anywhere in Scripture, Enns would say that the biblical writers operated with a different view of *error* than our modern conception. So, what would count for a biblical writer being in error according to their own ancient standards? Enns never formulates an ancient conception of *error*, and until he does, his position must remain more speculative than the so-called modernist with which he disagrees. It is likely for this reason that Enns does not use the word *inerrancy* to describe his own view. As far as I can tell, he only uses it once (p. 168) as a word others may use to describe their view.

It is important to recall that the doctrine of inerrancy was espoused as an orthodox notion long before the Enlightenment and modernism, from the time of the early fathers up through the Reformers and until the end of the twentieth century.[24] Enns's claim is that new ANE discoveries and certain aspects of postmodern thought now make *inerrancy* an anachronistic idea. The reader will have to determine whether Enns has succeeded in overturning in a groundbreaking manner this long-held notion in order to think of scriptural truth through different lenses.

Epistemology and the Relation of Historical to Mythological Genre

These issues that Enns discusses touch on epistemology. I cannot enter into a full-orbed view of epistemology to which I ascribe and how this relates to logic and the modernist-postmodernist debates. Suffice it to say that the laws of contradiction, or non-contradiction, and identity would seem to be part of the faculties of all human beings as a result of their creation by God in his image. Without these abilities humans would not be able to communicate with one another or perceive correctly—not exhaustively but definitely in part—the created world.

Enns seems to have confused the use of reason, which is an aspect of general revelation, with certain kinds of purported modern history writing and precise kinds of modern scientific knowledge. But these most basic laws of logical thought are quite operable for both modern and premodern people. Indeed, people could not communicate without assuming the truth of these foundational notions of logic. If I say something is red, it means that it is red and not green; or if I say the Chicago White Sox won the World Series in 2005, I mean *they* won it, not the New York Yankees. When people do not presuppose these most basic laws of thinking, then they have difficulty communicating and living in the world. The same is true with ancient communication.

---

24. On which see for the earlier fathers, e.g., J. D. Hannah, "The Doctrine of Scripture in the Early Church," in *Inerrancy and the Church*, ed. J. D. Hannah (Chicago: Moody, 1984), 3–5, and W. R. Spear, "Augustine's Doctrine of Biblical Infallibility," in *Inerrancy and the Church*, 37–65; generally see *Inerrancy and the Church*, ed. J. D. Hannah, passim, and J. D. Woodbridge, *Biblical Authority: A Critique of the Rogers/McKim Proposal* (Grand Rapids: Zondervan, 1982), passim, who also includes a good section on the earlier fathers.

In this respect, and in conjunction with these most foundational notions of human thinking, speech act theory is also helpful to consider. Scholars should be interested in trying to perceive the authorial intention of ancient authors. Just as ancient people performed acts of a physical nature, so they committed acts of speech communication. And, just as we can perceive physical acts, so we can perceive the intentions of speech acts, not exhaustively but partially and sufficiently. Indeed, this is just what Enns is also trying to do.[25]

Speech acts are transcultural. The debate concerns the illocutionary mode of the biblical writers' speech acts.[26] Enns contends that the Pentateuch's speech acts in which early history is narrated are a kind of divine genre, whereby God uses what appears to be a historical genre but which is really to be understood as myth, through which God accommodates himself to the mythical notions of the time and teaches truth, just as he teaches truth through parables. The problem with Enns's view is that what appears to be historical genre—compared with other accepted historical genres later in the Old Testament—he sees to be ultimately mythical. We might even call it a genre of divine accommodation, whereby God knew better but the Israelite writers did not. They thought they were writing true history but God knew that they were not. In this respect, has Enns formulated a new version of *sensus plenior*?[27] In reality, in this respect Enns's view is not new but is close to being a flashback to Gerhard von Rad's view that Old Testament writers wrote what appeared to be historical accounts, which were theologically true on a "salvation-historical" plane but which possessed no essential connection with true, past historical reality.[28]

Should scholars not have the moral and cognitive care to discern both modern and ancient speech acts? If an Old Testament author's speech act intends to communicate something as part of a historical genre (in its illocutionary form), but a modern commentator concludes that it is really myth and justifies this by appeal to divine accommodation to myth unknown to the ancient author, isn't this a twisting of the ancient author's intentional speech act? Enns's view appears to be a novel proposal of an incognito genre of divine accommodation to myth, which

---

25. See further Vanhoozer, *Is There a Meaning in This Text?*

26. For the definition of *illocutionary*, see the section titled "The Problem of Equating the Phrase 'New Interpretations' with the Phrase 'New Meanings'" in appendix 1.

27. In the unlikely case that he is not positing such a *sensus plenior*, then the onus is on him to demonstrate that what appears as a historical genre in such Genesis accounts as the creation and flood is not such a genre but a mythical kind of literature.

28. For a convenient summary of this aspect and problem of von Rad's theology, see W. Eichrodt, *Theology of the Old Testament* 1 (Philadelphia: Westminster Press, 1961), 512–20.

was originally unknown by the ancient author and which was originally encased in a historical genre.

Neither Enns nor his evangelical debate partners can get away from using modern analytical abilities and interpretative methods. By the use of the same analytical skills, Enns and other evangelicals disagree about whether there is myth in the Bible. The question is whether Enns has presented a "reasonable" case for the ancient authors not using the basic reasoning abilities common to human beings when these authors wrote historical narrative. Many will not be convinced, except those already on the road to reaching the conclusion that Enns has reached about myth.

Conclusion on Enns's Use of the Word "Diversity"
Therefore, if Enns were to use what he considers a "modern" definition of "error," would he conclude that what he labels "diversity" is really error? The answer is not hard to determine: most likely, at several points he would conclude this. So, his use of *diversity* some of the time appears to be the semantic equivalent of *error* for those who disagree with him and think that the basic standards of truth and error are still the same for ancient and modern people. It should be remembered, of course, that modern historians have a variety of modes and genres to narrate what we would consider *reliable* history, and that modern people often make statements about reality that are reliable but may not be made with the knowledge of or in the language of scientific precision, since that is not their intention. Thus, Enns insists on the term *diversity*, since he opposes judging ancient writers by the modern standards of truth and error. Does Enns imbibe too much postmodern relativity about truth, or has he been chastened properly so that he has been affected by some of the strengths of postmodernism? Readers will make different judgments about this. For myself, I think he has been too influenced by some of the extremes of postmodern thought.

Some Implications of Enns's Book for Biblical Studies
The intent here is to summarize some of the major themes running throughout Enns's book upon which we have earlier only briefly touched, as well as to look at some of the practical ramifications of Enns's book that he himself discusses.

The Issue of Socially Constructed Cultures, Presuppositions, and Biblical Interpretation
Running throughout Enns's book is the following presupposition: "There is no absolute point of reference to which we have access that will allow

us to interpret the Bible stripped of our own cultural context" (p. 169; cf. p. 161). One paragraph later he says that "our theologies are necessarily limited and provisional" (p. 169). I cannot respond at all fully to this. Nevertheless, while it is true that postmodernism—and earlier, the Dutch Reformed tradition!—rightly has taught us that all things are seen through interpretative lenses, so that no human viewpoint is objective, it is also true that a number of scholars rightly acknowledge that interpreters can understand some things definitely and sufficiently but not exhaustively. Any other epistemological approach takes the insights of postmodernism to a skeptical extreme.[29]

Enns is not clear here, since, in apparent contrast with his preceding statements, he also proposes several interpretations of biblical passages where it is clear that he would say that he understands them sufficiently and definitely but not exhaustively. Thus, he operates at numerous points on the assumption that we do have an "absolute point of reference to which we have access that will allow us to interpret the Bible," despite the fact that we are influenced by our own cultural context.

His discussion on page 169 thus lacks clarity and, therefore, gives the impression that to understand any particular part of the Bible definitely is impossible. It also gives the impression that when we think we have grasped part of biblical revelation in some definite way it is because we have imposed our own cultural presuppositional lenses on the biblical data. In the context of his book, however, I take it that what Enns really means here (p. 169) is that the main presuppositional lenses that evangelicals have imposed on Scripture are standards of modern reason—definitions of truth and error with respect to history and science—especially as this relates to the definition of *myth*.

Enns states, *"The problems many of us feel regarding the Bible may have less to do with the Bible itself and more to do with our own preconceptions"* (p. 15; italics in original). As we have seen, for him, both so-called liberals and evangelicals have the same preconceived notion for determining truth and error, though they have disagreed about whether there is error in the Bible; both have formulated a definition of truth and error on the basis of modern science and modern conceptions of history. Enns says that we must go beyond this impasse, and he portrays himself as one of the contemporary evangelicals able to formulate the new synthesis that deals much better with these long-disputed issues. But, as we have seen elsewhere, Enns sets up two polar opposites and

29. On which see more fully D. A. Carson, *Becoming Conversant with the Emerging Church* (Grand Rapids: Zondervan, 2005), 104–24, where also helpful non-postmodern epistemological models are offered.

does not allow for middle ground concerning possibilities of some significant overlap (not equation) between ancient and modern notions of science and historiography.

As far as I can tell, he has somewhat mirrored the problem found in the work of Jack Rogers and Donald McKim, *The Authority and Interpretation of the Bible: An Historical Approach* (New York: Harper and Row, 1979), who also contended for not interpreting the Bible according to the same modern notions with a quite similar result as Enns—the Bible can have what we moderns would consider error but the ancients would not have so considered it.

For the sake of space, I must refer to the larger discussion of John D. Woodbridge and his critiques of Rogers and McKim along these lines,[30] which is representative of other conservative critiques. Generally, the upshot of Woodbridge's conclusion is that ancient peoples "did have categories at their disposal for assessing" the observable world "that are in some regards commensurable to our own."[31] In addition to the supporting literature cited by Woodbridge, there are more recent publications analyzing ancient mathematics, astronomy, and measurements and showing their technological complexity and degrees of significant overlap with modern equivalents.[32]

It is also quite apparent that Scripture uses the words *true* and *truth* to affirm that ancient people could make descriptive statements that corresponded, not exhaustively but truly to actual reality; likewise Scripture uses words such as *know* to indicate that the ancients could know things sufficiently that corresponded to the reality around them.[33] Concerning

---

30. Woodbridge, *Biblical Authority*, e.g., generally see 19–30, and, in particular, see pp. 28–30 titled "The Dubious Presuppositions Concerning the History of Science," 158–63; generally, see pp. 19–27 for other critiques relevant also to other parts of Enns's own work. Woodbridge discusses such issues as the continuity between ancient and modern mechanics, astronomy, mathematics, measurements of space, and measurements of time. One brief quotation is relevant: "In the period of scholarship from 1880 until quite recently, most scholars were operating with two severe handicaps. One of these was a consistent and drastic underestimation of the scientific achievements of the Babylonians and the ancients in general," p. 162, quoting Shlomo Sternberg in Solomon Gandz, *Studies in Hebrew Astronomy and Mathematics* (KTAV Publishing, 1970), viii–ix. Interestingly, Woodbridge says that we moderns "do not attempt to give the full mathematical designation of the symbol π; we usually proffer our approximation, 3.14, which is very close to one of the Babylonian designations for π, 3 and 1/8" (*Biblical Authority*, 162).

31. Woodbridge, *Biblical Authority*, 163.

32. Most recently see J. M. Steele and A. Imhausen, eds., *Under One Sky: Astronomy and Mathematics in the Ancient Near East* (Münster: Ugarit-Verlag, 2002), as well as bibliography cited at the end of the articles therein.

33. See Carson, *Becoming Conversant*, 188–200; see also A. C. Thiselton, *The Two Horizons: New Testament Hermeneutics and Philosophical Description* (Grand Rapids: Eerdmans, 1980), 411: "In Greek literature and in the Old and New Testaments there are abundant examples of uses of the word 'truth' in which the point at issue is correspondence with the facts of the matter."

historiography, note the following position of a recent work by leading conservative Old Testament scholars: "Modern historians, like their precursors, in fact depend on testimony, interpret the past, and possess just as much faith as their precursors, whether religious or not," and, in addition, "ancient, medieval, and post-Reformation historians as a group were no less concerned than their modern counterparts with differentiating historical truth from falsehood."[34]

In the light of these comments in the preceding two paragraphs, I want only to point out a major gap in Enns's discussion with regard to studies of ancient science and some significant scriptural evidence that shows his discussion to be based on selective evidence, thus skewing the evidence that he has chosen to present. Enns could have acknowledged some of the work that has been done in these areas, even if he disagrees with it. Readers would have been helped by knowing that to posit such an "ancient-modern" polarity on issues like science, logic, and historiography is a reductionism. It results in over-generalized labeling, such as "pre-scientific," or "pre-modern," and "scientific," or "modern" (e.g., pp. 40–41), when, in reality, some significant scholars argue that there is a substantial spectrum of positions between these two polar opposites.[35]

There is a sense, however, in which Enns is clearly correct in his contention that we should not evaluate ancient biblical writings by typical modern scientific conceptions and presuppositions, but it is curious that Enns never mentions it: to assess reports of the miraculous in biblical historical narratives to be non-historical because of a modern bias against the supernatural distorts a correct understanding of these ancient narratives.

In this connection, Enns says that modern preconceptions can distort the Bible (see also pp. 14–15), since the ancient biblical culture had different preconceptions about the reality of the world. There has, however, also been scholarly discussion about how different presuppositional paradigms share some commensurable features; otherwise "members of one paradigm could never understand the culture of individuals living

---

34. I. Provan, V. P. Long, and T. Longman III, *A Biblical History of Israel* (Louisville: Westminster, 2003), 50.

35. Enns also employs such contrasting labels as "liberal and evangelical [or conservative]" (e.g., pp. 21, 41, 47, 107–8) throughout his book, even though he himself admits at the beginning that while "such labels may serve some purpose . . . they more often serve to entrench rather than enlighten" (p. 14). My main difficulty with the way Enns uses these labels is that he associates "conservative" or "evangelical" scholars' views with popular "fundamentalist" views, which is not accurate; there is certainly, at least, a spectrum of theologically viable approaches among such scholars, which is consistent with a traditional perspective on inerrancy (as, e.g., represented by the Chicago Statement on Inerrancy).

in another."[36] Thus, there is some kind of bridge between worldview perspectives, whether between that of ancient cultures and that of modern or between different perspectives of modern people themselves who disagree.

Enns needed to reflect awareness of this discussion, even if he evaluates it negatively. Of course, Enns himself also has his preconceptions, which he surely would admit, and these are preconceptions formulated by his socially constructed reasoning abilities. Why could not his preconceptions be the ones that are distorting Scripture? How do we test the validity of preconceptions or presuppositions? The best way is by means of what some call a "critical realism."[37] As we just noted, people holding different paradigms of interpretation can still communicate with one another and understand and evaluate each other's paradigms. The presuppositional lens that makes the most sense of the most data is the more probable lens. Of course, neither Enns nor I have the space to submit our lenses to the test of "critical realism." All we can do is to say that our respective lenses are approaches that have made the most sense of the biblical data that we have looked at, and then we can footnote our published works and let others see how well our lenses work.

Enns and the Ethics of Hermeneutics

Lastly, Enns understands that the proposals of his book will arouse disagreement, and he pleads for a hermeneutic of humility, love, and patience. He wants to be heard fully before readers react negatively. He says:

> It has been my experience that sometimes our first impulse is to react to new ideas and vilify the person holding them, not considering that person's Christian character. We jump to conclusions and assume the worst rather than hearing—*really* hearing—each other out. What would be a breath of fresh air, not to mention a testimony to those around us, is to see an atmosphere, a culture, among conservative, traditional, orthodox Christians that models basic principles of the gospel:
>
> *Humility* on the part of scholars to be sensitive to how others will hear them and on the part of those whose preconceptions are being challenged.

---

36. Woodbridge, *Biblical Authority*, 28, 161, who cites and summarizes the significance of the work of Thomas Kuhn, *The Structure of Scientific Revolutions* (Chicago: University of Chicago Press, 1962).

37. E.g., see N. T. Wright, *The New Testament and the People of God* (Minneapolis: Fortress, 1992), 3–144, and G. K. Beale, "Questions of Authorial Intent, Epistemology, and Presuppositions and Their Bearing on the Study of the Old Testament in the New: a Rejoinder to Steve Moyise," *Irish Biblical Studies* 21 (1999): 1–26 (now included in revised form as an excursus to this book).

Love that assumes the best of brothers and sisters in Christ, not that looks for any difference of opinion as an excuse to go on the attack.

Patience to know that no person or tradition is beyond correction, and therefore no one should jump to conclusions about another's motives.

How we carry on this very important conversation is a direct result of *why*. Ultimately, it is not about us, but about God. (p. 172)

These last four points are well put, and all scholars should keep them in mind. But some readers, in retrospect, will recall places where Enns himself needed to keep in mind these excellent guidelines. The reason I point these things out here is not to unduly criticize Enns but because Enns has made it clear in the directly preceding extended quotation that it is those evangelicals against whom he is writing whom he believes have been guilty of violating these very good standards. Even in the above quotation he portrays "conservative, traditional, orthodox Christians" as those whose "first impulse" is "to react to new ideas and vilify the person holding them not considering that person's Christian character"; they "jump to conclusions and assume the worst" of those who propose such new ideas. Such people "wish to keep [God] small by controlling what can or cannot come into the conversation" (p. 172).

Is Enns conscious of his outstanding guidelines when he paints "conservative, traditional, orthodox Christians" with such a sweeping brush? Perhaps, unfortunately, Enns has experienced these things from some conservatives, but this does not justify such a generalization without extensive footnote support. Furthermore, this kind of emotive language will not encourage further conversation with those whom he disagrees. It is ironic that these comments come in the immediate context of his exhortation to pursue love, patience, and humility.

With specific regard to his exhortation to humility, note the following comments that he makes earlier in the book: "Should Paul's comment [about 1 Cor. 10:4] be understood as another example of this tradition [about the Jewish legend of a traveling well-shaped rock that followed Israel throughout the wilderness wanderings]?[38] I think that is beyond a reasonable doubt" (p. 151). There are well-known commentators,[39] even

---

38. The bracketed wording in this quotation is my insertion. See Enns, "The 'Moveable Well' in 1 Cor. 10:4: An Extrabiblical Tradition in an Apostolic Text," for his use of "legend" in connection to 1 Cor. 10:4, upon which I comment in my review article in *Themelios*, "Did Jesus and the Apostles Preach the Right Doctrine from the Wrong Texts? Revisiting the Debate Seventeen Years Later in the Light of Peter Enns's Book, *Inspiration and Incarnation*": 32–37, now found in chapter 2 of this book.

39. E.g., see E. E. Ellis, *Paul's Use of the Old Testament* (1957; repr., Grand Rapids: Baker, 1981), 66–70.

some who do not believe in inerrancy, who disagree with Enns's statement here, so it would have been more helpful to express his conclusion
in more diplomatic terms in order to allow for more dialogue.

Similarly he comments on the interpretation by some evangelicals
that Jesus' cleansing of the temple at the beginning of his ministry in
John 2 is a distinct event from the cleansing narrated toward the end of
his ministry in the Synoptics. In response to this interpretation of two
cleansings, Enns says, "It is a distortion of the highest order to argue that
Jesus must have cleansed the temple twice," which he thinks is based
on the "unwarranted assumption" that "good historiography . . . must
maintain chronological order" (p. 65).

Consider the prominent scholars who hold the position of two cleansings: among others note A. Plummer, B. F. Westcott, R. V. G. Tasker, R. G.
Gruenler, Leon Morris,[40] D. A. Carson,[41] and more recently A. Köstenberger,[42] as well as Craig Blomberg, who leans toward two cleansings but
believes that neither position has adduced enough evidence definitively
to settle the issue.[43] These are not scholars who have a historiographical
predisposition against topical arrangement of gospel material, nor would
practicing conservative evangelical scholars consider the arguments for
their view "a distortion of the highest order." Unfortunately, this is an
unduly confident statement by Enns, as well as one that distorts this
issue in gospel studies.[44]

Perhaps one could pass over these kinds of comments, but Enns continues to make them. He says, "Therefore, if what claims to be a Christian
understanding of the Old Testament simply remains in the preeschatologi-
cal moment—simply reads the Old Testament 'on its own terms'—such
is not a Christian understanding in the apostolic sense" (p. 159). But
there are very good Christian Old Testament scholars who would beg
to differ but would not, I suspect, say that Enns's hermeneutical approach is "not a Christian understanding." While I myself believe that
the progressive, eschatological, revelatory stage of the New Testament
is decisive for understanding the Old, I believe the Old interprets the

40. Leon Morris, *The Gospel According to John* (rev. ed.; Grand Rapids: Eerdmans, 1995), 166–68,
where also reference to Plummer, Westcott, Tasker, and Gruenler may be conveniently found.
41. D. A. Carson, *Matthew*, EBC (Grand Rapids: Zondervan, 1995): 441.
42. Andreas Köstenberger, *John*, BECNT (Grand Rapids: Baker, 2004): 111.
43. Craig Blomberg, *The Historical Reliability of John's Gospel* (Downers Grove, IL: InterVarsity,
2001), 87–91. See also R. A. Whitacre, *John*, IVPNTC (Downers Grove, IL: InterVarsity, 1999), 82,
who views both options as equally possible, and H. Ridderbos, *The Gospel of John* (Grand Rapids:
Eerdmans, 1997), 115, who is ambiguous about his view on the issue.
44. Enns makes the same kind of statement when he says, "For any interpreter, modern or ancient,
to appeal to Deuteronomy 33:2–4 to support a notion of angels mediating the law *is an indication
of what they wish to find there, not what is there*" (p. 149, my italics).

New, and that a Christianly-conceived messianic understanding can be discovered by reading the Old Testament itself. I am not concerned to defend my statement but merely to say that we should be careful of saying that opposing interpretations are "not a Christian understanding." This would seem to be the very thing Enns is contending against—a so-called fundamentalist, black-and-white view of things.

In another place Enns says, "[To] mount arguments showing that apostolic hermeneutics is actually grounded in the grammatical-historical meaning of the Old Testament" and ". . . [to] talk about the Second Temple context is just nonsense that can be safely avoided" is "untenable because the Second Temple evidence cannot be ignored—or better, it can be ignored only by means of a willful choice to disregard the plain evidence we have" (pp. 159–60).

First, perhaps Enns has laypeople in mind or some idiosyncratic evangelical scholar, but I know of no evangelical scholar in disagreement with Enns who would say that "all this talk about the Second Temple context is just nonsense" or that it should be "ignored." Is this setting up a straw man for the lay reader and then knocking it down? This reveals a pattern at points throughout the book, where Enns erects the position of his opponents in such extreme form that no reputable conservative scholar in disagreement with his general views could identify him- or herself. Has Enns expressed himself consistently here according to his own ideal hermeneutical standards that he lists above (e.g., to "jump to conclusions" about the motives or views of others)?

Similarly, he says with respect to ANE discoveries that "conservatives have tended to employ a strategy of selective engagement, embracing evidence that seems to support their assumptions" (p. 47). He writes:

> Many evangelical scholars do excellent historical work but do not always squarely address the doctrinal implications of their own findings. More than once, I have observed evangelical scholars pursue a line of argumentation about Genesis or some other topic, come close to drawing out the logical implications for how we understand the Bible, but then retreat to traditional, safe categories. Likewise, and perhaps more commonly, problematic evidence is simply ignored or dismissed in an effort to protect the Bible (or better, one's beliefs about how the Bible should be). Even worse, simplistic and irresponsible arguments are sometimes mounted that serve no purpose other than to affirm established positions. (pp. 47–48)

If Enns is going to make this accusation, which represents traditional evangelicalism, is it not incumbent on him, at least, to footnote the representative examples of the "many evangelical scholars" and their works that he has in mind? Without proper documentation, this not only appears misrepresentative but could also mislead the reader. In addition to citing such scholars, Enns needs to explain how they selectively use their evidence and how they do not face up to the evidence that they themselves discover. Without such fleshing out, Enns's statements become platitudes without any basis for the reader.

Furthermore, there have been a number of good Old Testament and ANE evangelical scholars who should not be described in this manner. Among others, I think of Donald Wiseman, Alan Millard, Kenneth Kitchen, Meredith Kline, Daniel Block, John Walton, Lawson Younger, and Richard Hess. These scholars in one way or another have shown how important ANE parallels are for understanding the Old Testament, as well as how the Old Testament differs from such parallels, and several of these scholars have shown the viability of the historical accounts in Genesis and elsewhere in contrast to the non-historical nature of their mythological correspondences. Many, including non-evangelicals, would acknowledge that these and conservative scholars before them have attempted to relate their faith commitments to "what we have learned about the Bible over the past 150 years," contrary to the claims of Enns (in this regard, cf. Enns's wording on p. 48 in relation to the preceding context; similar to the claim that he makes on p. 171).

Likewise, Enns says:

> There is a significant strand of contemporary Christian thinking on the Old Testament that feels that these sorts of things [diversity in Scripture] just shouldn't happen. And, if they do, they just *appear* to be a problem. You just need to read a bit more closely or do a little more research, and if you're patient enough, you'll get the right answer eventually. For others, however (including myself), such an approach comes close to intellectual dishonesty. To accept the diversity of the Old Testament is not to "cave in to liberalism," nor is it to seek after novelty. It is, rather, to read the Old Testament quite honestly and seriously. (p. 107)

No one should doubt that Enns is sincere in attempting to interpret the Bible honestly, but for him, on the other hand, to imply, as he appears to do, that those who disagree with him—not a few people but those who are "a significant strand of contemporary Christian thinking"—practice "an approach [that] comes close to intellectual dishonesty" is, again, not an expression of the excellent hermeneutical ideals that he elaborates above. Such a hermeneutical ideal is an unwillingness to "jump to conclusions" about the motives or views of others (p. 172).

Why cannot he grant that other scholars who differ with him also seek "to read the Old Testament quite honestly and seriously"? The clear implication is that conservative scholars are not serious and honest. And, if he sees such egregiously bad methods practiced and bad motives held by such scholars, he should quote them and point out the evidence for his conclusions. Again, he has painted a wide swath of evangelical scholarship with this reductionistic brush, though I do not doubt that some evangelicals, laypeople, and perhaps a few scholars with whom he has had contact have been guilty of the accusation that he makes.

Nevertheless, Enns's ethical hermeneutical guidelines are an excellent reminder of how to dialogue with those with whom we disagree. May all biblical scholars attempt to model these standards, which none of us will perfectly model until we see Jesus face-to-face in glory or at the eschaton.

Conclusion

I have quoted Enns often and at length in order to attempt, as much as possible within the confines of this essay, to present his statements in context and to reveal his authorial intention. Many of his assumptions are so wide-ranging and debatable—the primary evidence of the Old Testament, Judaism, and the New Testament so selective,[45] as well as the secondary sources he cites[46]—that it is hard to do justice in evaluating his book in a brief manner. Nevertheless, I have tried to review the book as accurately as I could, which has resulted in a longer than usual review and some inevitable repetition at points.

My critique of Enns may be broadly summarized by the following eight points:

> 1) He affirms that some of the narratives in Genesis, e.g., of creation and the flood, are shot through with myth, much of which the biblical narrator did not know lacked correspondence to actual past reality.

45. In this respect, see my earlier-cited article in *Themelios* on Enns's view of the use of the Old Testament in the New Testament in relation to Judaism: "Did Jesus and the Apostles Preach the Right Doctrine from the Wrong Texts? Revisiting the Debate Seventeen Years Later in the Light of Peter Enns's Book, *Inspiration and Incarnation,*" 26–31, now in revised form in chapter 3 below.
46. Enns does cite bibliography for further reading at the end of most of the chapters (with very brief abstracts), but he does not engage them evaluatively in the body of his chapters. This often leaves uninformed readers with the impression that Enns's perspective and evidence for his arguments is the primary or only viable perspective or evidence. The only way they would learn otherwise is by doing some research and reading in secondary literature.

2) Enns appears to assume that since biblical writers, especially, for example, the Genesis narrator, were not objective in narrating history, then their presuppositions distorted significantly the events that they reported. He too often appears to assume that the socially constructed realities of these ancient biblical writers, e.g., their purported mythical mindsets, prevented them from being able to describe past events in a way that had significant correspondence with how a person in the modern world would observe and report events.

3) Enns never spells out in any detail the model of Jesus' incarnation with which he is drawing analogies for his view of Scripture.

4) Enns affirms that one cannot use modern definitions of *truth* and *error* in order to perceive whether Scripture contains truth or error. However, this is non-falsifiable, since Enns never says what would count as an error according to ancient standards. This is also reductionistic, since there were some rational and even scientific categories at the disposal of ancient peoples for evaluating the observable world that are in some important ways commensurable to our own.

5) Enns does not follow at significant points his own excellent proposal of guidelines for evaluating the views of others with whom one disagrees.

6) Enns's book is marked by ambiguities at important junctures of his discussion.

7) Enns does not attempt to present to *and* discuss for the reader significant alternative viewpoints beside his own, which is needed in a book dealing with such crucial issues.

8) Enns appears to caricature the views of past evangelical scholarship by not distinguishing the views of so-called fundamentalists from that of good conservative scholarly work.

Peter Enns might believe that my assessment of his book and its implications are inaccurate, but it would be difficult for him to contend that the evaluation and implications could not be construed as plausibly following from the statements he has made. In other words, he might contend that the conclusions and implications that I have drawn are not conclusions and implications he would draw, but I think many, if not most, readers would likely read him the way that I have. In some cases, perhaps, I have pointed out what is perchance the result of faulty writing or ambiguity rather than faulty theology or hermeneutics. Nevertheless, such things must still be pointed out, since the issues are so significant.

The nature of Enns's book demands not only mere description of the author's views but also, at times, interpretation because of the ambiguities and tensions among his statements. Anyone who wants to attempt to review Enns's book thoroughly and to do justice to it will have to engage in interpretation of these kinds of statements. I have tried my best to do this and to cut through the ambiguities where they occur. Readers will have to decide for themselves whether or not I have succeeded at those points where I have been forced to interpret.

Indeed, why write a lengthy review of a book that is designed primarily to address a more popular audience and only secondarily a scholarly readership?[47] The reason is that the issues are so important for Christian faith, and popular readers may not have the requisite tools and background to evaluate the thorny issues that Enns's book discusses. But I have also written this review for a scholarly evangelical audience, since the book appears to be secondarily intended for them,[48] and there have been different evaluations of Enns's book by such an audience.[49]

Perhaps it is fitting that a *Neutestamentler* should review the chapters on the Old Testament in Enns's book, since he himself has written a chapter on the New Testament, which, for the most part, I have not included in this review. As Christian biblical scholars, despite our specialties, we need as much as possible to be whole-Bible scholars as well. Cross-fertilization between the Testaments is healthy, and I hope that it can continue.

Enns's book has been harder than any other that I have ever reviewed, but I thank Peter Enns for making me think in more depth about the issues that he raises in this book.

---

47. Note where Enns indicates his purpose in addressing a more popular audience (e.g., pp. 13, 15, 168), though these statements do not exclude a scholarly audience.

48. E.g., the publishers distributed complimentary copies to biblical scholars at the November 2005 Institute for Biblical Research Meeting.

49. I have read reviews that differ in their evaluation of the book: e.g., see the reviews of M. Eschle-bach in *JETS* 48 (2005): 811–12; T. Longman, "Divine and Human Qualities of the Old Testament," *Modern Reformation* 14 (2005), 33–34; Susan Wise Bauer, "Messy Revelation," *Books and Culture* (May/June 2006): 8–9; M. Daniel Carroll R. (Rodas), *Denver Journal. An Online Review of Current Biblical and Theological Studies* 8 (2005), which are generally positive; but see critical reviews by D. A. Carson, "Three More Books on the Bible: a Critical Review," *TJ* 27NS (2006): 18–45, J. D. Currid, "Review: *Inspiration and Incarnation: Evangelicals and the Problem of the Old Testament*," *Banner of Truth* 521 (2007): 22–27; P. Helm, http://www.reformation21.org/Life/Shelf_Life/Shelf_Life/ 181?vobId=2938&pm=434; and B. C. Ferry in *New Horizons* (October 2005), 23–24.

CHAPTER TWO

Is a Traditional Evangelical View of Scripture's Authority Compatible with Recent Developments in Old Testament Studies? *Part 2*

Peter Enns responded to my initial review of his book (chapter 1 of the present volume) in "Response to G. K. Beale's Review Article of *Inspiration and Incarnation*" (*JETS* 49 [2006]: 313–26). My reply to his response comprises, with small revisions, the majority of this chapter. My reply originally appeared as "A Surrejoinder to Peter Enns's Response to G. K. Beale's *JETS* Review Article of His Book, *Inspiration and Incarnation*," in *SBJT* 11 (2007): 16–36.

Preceding my counter-reply (in this chapter) is an interpretative summary of Enns's response to my initial review. This summary has been written by my research assistant Mitch Kim.[1] My goal in including the interpretation of a third party is to achieve the greatest possible objectivity.

Mitch Kim's Summary of Peter Enns's Response to Greg Beale's Initial Review of *Inspiration and Incarnation*

In "Response to G. K. Beale's Review Article of *Inspiration and Incarnation*,"[2] Peter Enns registers "many and thoroughgoing" disagreements

---

1. The reader should feel free to consult Peter Enns's full, original response that is being summarized here.
2. *JETS* 49 (2006): 313–26. Henceforth, references to Enns's response will be noted parenthetically in text by page number from this article.

with Beale's review (p. 313). He begins by addressing some "preliminary but vital issues" and then moves on to discuss a few areas of deeper, more substantive disagreement. The preliminary issues revolve around the focus of the book as apologetic, popular, and evangelical. The areas of more substantial disagreement center on the relationship between myth and history, inerrancy, and the incarnational analogy. Enns concludes with a final observation about the varied reception of his work.

Preliminary Issues: Reasserting the Apologetic, Popular, and Evangelical Focus

Enns's work is apologetic—"to help the faithful deal with threats to their faith." However, Enns sees Beale's critique of his book to be "alternatively . . . a failed academic treatise, an ambiguous systematic theology, or a dangerous introduction to Scripture" (p. 315). This genre confusion, according to Enns, accounts for Beale's unwarranted conclusions. As apologetics, Enns attempts to deal with purported "important discoveries" touted by the media or college professors that "demonstrate" the Bible is not the Word of God. His rhetorical strategy seeks to undermine such arguments by unflinchingly presenting the data of the arguments without special pleading or cover-up and then presenting a model that would account sufficiently for this data in an orthodox conception of inspiration. Yet according to Enns this unflinching presentation of the data is portrayed wrongly by Beale as evidence of Enns's own skepticism (p. 318).

Enns's work is also popular, which accounts for "the absence of footnotes, annotated bibliographies at the end of each chapter, and a glossary of terms at the end" (p. 314). According to Enns, while Beale charges that this is "dismissive of the work of other evangelical scholars," the lack of detailed citations and interaction with alternative proposals is simply an expression of Enns's intent to reassure lay readers that, regardless of diverse viewpoints, the Bible is still the Word of God.

Further, although Enns points out that his annotated bibliographies at the end of each chapter reveal his indebtedness to other evangelical scholars, he simultaneously "believe[s] that evangelical biblical scholars need to work harder at presenting the grand picture of what God has done in and through the Bible for the benefit of the thinking lay reader" (p. 316).

Also, Enns's desire is to address evangelicals with a high view of the divine authority of Scripture, which explains why he wants to draw special attention to the "necessary corrective focus on the human element in Scripture" (p. 316). Evangelicals typically do not need a fuller explanation of Scripture's divine element, yet they may be troubled by how the human element of Scripture, as revealed increasingly by modern discoveries, can coexist with their own commitment to its divine origin.

Areas of More Substantial Disagreement: Theology, Methodology, and Epistemology

Myth and History

Here Enns affirms "the basic historical referential nature of the opening chapters of Genesis" (p. 317). Enns explains that his concern is not that conservatives have not sufficiently recognized ANE parallels with the Bible, as, he says, Beale has contended, but that the implications of this recognition for the history, authority, and inspiration of Scripture have not been fully developed. According to Enns, Beale accuses him of an evolutionary model of Israelite religion, moving from a polytheistic to a monotheistic context. Enns responds, however, that he is "working from a progressive-revelational model where God is leading Israel to a fuller knowledge of who he is" (p. 318).

At its core, Enns argues, Beale's assertions of Genesis as "essentially historical" seem to "*begin* the discussion rather than *end* it" (p. 319). The phrase "essential history" does not explain how and in what way Genesis is essentially historical. Does it merely mean that God does something in space/time history? Or does it mean that Genesis 1 describes creation in fully literalistic terms? The question that troubles lay readers is how one can begin to make judgments regarding the extent of the historicity of the events, given the antiquity and foreignness of the Genesis account (p. 320). Enns, therefore, seeks to approach this question by affirming that "the proper starting point is to affirm the roots of the biblical creation account in its ANE setting," not unnecessarily distancing it from its mythical environment.

Inerrancy

Enns's central concern is that:

> Inerrancy . . . must be understood in ways that are respectful and conversant with the parameters set by Scripture's own witness understood in its varying historical contexts. Otherwise, we run the risk of basing our doctrine of inerrancy on a foundation outside of Scripture, and then expecting Scripture to behave in ways that we presume it should . . . rather than trying to define such categories as best we can from within Scripture (p. 321).

While, Enns says, Beale likely would agree with this statement in principle, it seems that his argument regarding diversity rests on "some outside standard by which to define inerrancy," perhaps the law of non-contradiction (p. 321). However, the way in which Scripture is inerrant must be understood not by the universality of rational thought but in connection with the process in which God has inspired Scripture itself.

Enns tackles one example of this diversity—the differences between the accounts in Exodus and Deuteronomy. Enns explains that the choice is not, as Beale contends, between complementary viewpoints and ir-reconcilable perspectives, but it begins by recognizing, on the level of wording, "irreconcilable" differences between the accounts. Such "irreconcilable" differences force the reader to work out this tension, which eventually permits him or her to see a "complementarity on a higher level" without explaining away the tension. This process is more than simply working out an "apparent" tension but rather includes the "proper recognition of the surface 'irreconcilable perspectives' of the texts in question" (322).

Enns's concern is that the doctrine of inerrancy does not marginalize contrary data into preconceived notions of how Scripture *ought* to behave. His avoidance of the term *inerrancy* is that it can "too quickly . . . stifle discussion rather than promote it." The question, then, says Enns, is not "*whether* the Bible is inerrant (which is what Beale seems to think is at stake), but *how* the Bible is inerrant" (p. 323).

The Incarnational Analogy

The ambiguity of this analogy, which, according to Beale, invalidates the analogy, relates to the details of the text. For example, some argue that the Bible cannot be influenced by ANE mythical creation stories since this would constitute historical errors, yet Enns responds that "such culturally laden expressions are what one would expect" (p. 323). Further, Enns grounds this analogy theologically in the work of Herman Bavinck, who states that just as Christ became flesh, "so also the word, the revelation of God, entered the world of creatureliness, the life and history of human-ity" (p. 324). The incarnational analogy of Scripture, then, demands that evangelicals accept the challenge of probing more deeply the creatureliness of the inspired biblical books, in light of our ever-increasing understanding of its historical-cultural context.

Final Observation

Enns contends, "The space and energy—even emotion—Beale and others have devoted to reviewing the book involves more than impressions of my alleged incompetence in scholarship, or writing style, or questionable commitment to evangelical theology. It may tell us something about the reviewers themselves" (p. 326). Enns acknowledges that his book has re-ceived varying, even polarizing, responses. Some have responded positively on a deep level, as it expresses problems with which people were already struggling. Yet others have responded in a decidedly negative fashion, because of where they perceive such thinking might lead us. "Diverse reactions to the book may tell us at least as much about the current state of evangelical thinking as it does about the book itself" (p. 326). So the question is how these important questions will be addressed by the evan-gelical community without a climate of fear, suspicion, and posturing.

Greg Beale's Counter-Reply[3]

My first response to the critique of Enns presented above is to encourage readers to go back and read my full review of his book in chapter 1. I think most readers will see, based on his critique, that Enns has not advanced the argument much beyond what I said in chapter 1, nor has he responded to some of the specific evidence that I adduced.

I have in mind, for example, the evidence that he holds various significant narratives in Genesis to be myth according to its classic definition, and that he acknowledges that the biblical writers mistakenly thought such myths corresponded to real past reality. He never directly addresses this specific issue.

I will respond to what I consider to be some of Enns's major critiques of my review of his book. What follows refers both to the preceding summary of Enns's "Response" in *JETS* and to his original fuller reply there.

The Question of Whether Enns's Book Is Intended for a Popular or Scholarly Audience

Enns contends that I misread the genre of his book and that I reviewed it as scholarly instead of as a popular book. He says that, as a result, though I cite his statements at length, "citations, no matter how lengthy, will not contribute to bringing clarity to an author's intention" and might cause "obscurity" of it, if such citations are "founded on a faulty reading strategy" (p. 313). He says I reviewed the book as if it were "an academic treatise" or "a systematic theology" or "an introduction to Scripture," whereas "its [real] aim is to reach a lay evangelical audience for which the human element of Scripture . . . presents an obstacle to confessing that the Bible is God's word" (pp. 313–14).

He says that his "primary audience" is "evangelical and non-academic" and that the "book's purpose is specifically apologetic" in that it is "intended to help the faithful deal with threats to their faith" (p. 314). This "aim" is not only "announced explicitly, but its popular focus is implied throughout the book, as indicated by the absence of footnotes, annotated bibliographies at the end of each chapter, and a glossary of terms at the end" (p. 314). He continues by saying:

> The fact that my aim is evangelical, non-academic, and apologetic accounts for the rhetorical strategy I adopt throughout the book, which is to lay out

---

3. The remainder of this chapter is a revision of G. K. Beale, "A Surrejoinder to Peter Enns's Response to G. K. Beale's *JETS* Review Article of His Book, *Inspiration and Incarnation*," *SBJT* 11 (2007): 16–36.

a few examples of things that are universally accepted as demonstrations of the human situatedness of Scripture—the very thing that is causing readers problems—and to present these examples unapologetically, in as stark and uncompromising a manner as that of hostile commentators, be it in a book, on cable TV, or in a classroom. As part of this apologetic, it is crucial that the non-scholarly reader understand that nothing in principle has been withheld; no data has been covered over as too damaging or problematic for consideration; no special pleading has been employed against the data themselves, because these data have positive value in helping us understand how Scripture—by God's design—bears perfect witness to the wisdom and glory of God.

To present the matter this way is to attempt to pull the rug out from under the perceived strength of the opposing argument, that for the Bible to be God's word it cannot possibly look the way it does. (p. 314)

Enns asserts that not to review the book according to its popular aims is to criticize him for not writing a book that he never intended to write, an error he feels that I committed: "Beale seems to read the book alternatively as a failed academic treatise, an ambiguous systematic theology, or a dangerous introduction to Scripture. None of these descriptions are valid, but they form Beale's starting point, which leads him to draw unwarranted conclusions" (p. 315). Yet he acknowledges that I "flag various topics for high-level discussion," and in doing so I have "correctly discerned . . . that in addition to the primary purpose, there is a secondary purpose [of the book] as well: to foster further theological discussion among evangelical scholars regarding the implications of the human element of Scripture for how we think about our Bibles, and for how we are equipping our students to do the same" (p. 315).

A number of responses to Enns's reply need to be made here, since Enns is attempting to use this objection to deflect my criticisms of his book. I am going to elaborate a bit on this issue, since we are dealing with the important subject of how Christian scholars should communicate important and very debated interpretative and theological issues to a more popular readership, especially in the church.

First, I clearly noted in my original response the exact dual purpose of the book that Enns has laid out, and which he acknowledges (above) that I perceived correctly. I say:

Indeed, why write a lengthy review article of a book that is designed primarily to address a more popular audience and only secondarily a scholarly readership?[4] The reason is that the issues are so important for Christian faith, and popular readers may not have the requisite tools and background to evaluate the thorny issues that Enns's book discusses. But I have also written this review for a scholarly evangelical audience, since the book appears to be secondarily intended for them,[5] and, I suspect, there will be different evaluations of Enns's book by such an audience.[6]

In point of fact, I reviewed Enns's book with these primary and secondary audiences in mind; at the beginning of my review in chapter 1, I said, "The book is designed more for the lay person than the scholar but is apparently written with the latter secondarily in mind." And, how could citing quotations from Enns at length in order to understand what he says in context be a misreading of the popular genre, as he contends? Are popular readers to be kept from the contextual meaning of his statements? This critique by Enns would seem to be an attempt to say that no one should give serious scrutiny to the cogency and validity of his arguments. So I am mystified by his response here.

So, why does Enns think that I misjudged the popular genre of his book? Enns thinks that his book is at such a popular level that he need not discuss alternative views of major explosive issues addressed in the book, nor should such issues be footnoted, even in a brief representative manner.

But one must ask whether it is appropriate to address such important interpretative and theological issues and give only one side. To give alternative viewpoints does not necessitate heavy footnoting but only a brief representation of sources supporting various sides, and these could be put in the form of endnotes after the chapters or at the conclusion of the book—something one typically finds in more serious *popular* kinds of books. Here, for example, I think of John Piper's and J. I. Packer's books, as well as those by Don Carson. Additionally, it is surprising that Enns did not do this since he considers that part of his popular audience is "graduate students" and "college students," though he states this negatively: the popular audience "is not restricted to" such students (p. 314).

Since Enns acknowledges, however, that the book's primary readership, a popular audience, includes undergraduate and graduate students

---

4. Note where Enns indicates his purpose in addressing a more popular audience (e.g., pp. 13, 15, 168), though these statements do not exclude a scholarly audience.

5. Recall that the publishers distributed complimentary copies of Enns's book to biblical scholars at the November 2005 Institute for Biblical Research Meeting.

6. G. K. Beale, "Myth, History, and Inspiration: A Review Article of *Inspiration and Incarnation* by Peter Enns" *JETS* 49 (2006): 312.

and its formally intended secondary readership is scholars, does this not make entirely appropriate, even necessary, that the best of representative positions be presented and lightly footnoted? I have taught on both the undergraduate and graduate level, and when I order textbooks that address major interpretative and theological issues, I consider it normal for such books to have brief though representative footnoting of alternate sides of debated topics.

Even if footnotes were judged to be inappropriate, is it not incumbent in such crucial discussions, at least, to lay out the main sides of the debate and the primary evidence supporting each side, and then to argue for the view the author prefers? But, by his own admission, Enns has not even done this: his popular "rhetorical strategy adopted throughout the book . . . is to lay out a few examples of things that are universally accepted as demonstrations of the human situatedness of Scripture" and "present these examples unapologetically, in as stark and uncompromising a manner as that of hostile commentators" (p. 314).

Any reading of Enns's book will reveal that a number of the issues he discusses are of crucial theological significance and vigorously debated by scholars of varying theological perspectives—indeed, to say the least, these are matters about which there is no "universally accepted" position, especially if one is comparing traditional non-evangelical, neo-evangelical, and traditional evangelical positions. However, if one has in view that the only viable positions to survey are non-evangelical positions, then one might be able to say there is "universal acceptance" within this restricted community on such issues. But he has chosen to present only one side on these issues, and, strikingly, it is the side that has been traditionally held by non-evangelical scholars.

Specifically, let us review some of these major issues. I summarized the primary points of my critique in my initial review in the preceding chapter, the first four of which elaborate on specific interpretative and theological issues of great import:

- Enns affirms that some of the narratives in Genesis (e.g., creation and the flood) are shot through with myth because in many instances the biblical narrator did not know the narrative lacked correspondence to actual past reality.
- Enns appears to assume that since biblical writers, especially, for example, the Genesis narrator, were not objective in narrating history, then their presuppositions distorted significantly the events that they reported. He appears too often to assume that the socially constructed realities of these ancient biblical writers (e.g., their

purported mythical mindsets) prevented them from being able to describe past events in a way that had significant correspondence with how a person in the modern world would observe and report events.

- Enns never spells out in any detail the model of Jesus' incarnation with which he is drawing analogies for his view of Scripture.

- Enns affirms that one cannot use modern definitions of *truth* and *error* in order to perceive whether or not Scripture contains truth or error. First, this is non-falsifiable, since Enns never says what would count as an error according to ancient standards. Second, this is reductionistic, since there were some rational and even scientific categories at the disposal of ancient peoples for evaluating the observable world that are in some important ways commensurable to our own.

It is surprising to me that Enns would say that there "are universally accepted" positions on these issues, since he considers only non-evangelical views to be the "accepted" ones and does not seriously consider the most viable alternative viewpoints set forth by evangelical scholarship. Furthermore, note that only one of my eight major criticisms (summarized at the end of chapter 1) concerns Enns's complaint about "footnoting," and actually this point demands only that Enns present the various major competing views on these debated issues, even if footnotes are excluded. Now, he does typically present only in passing and very briefly another viewpoint, different from the non-evangelical one, but it is usually a fundamentalist view that does not represent the mainstream evangelical position on the matters that he addresses.

I do not see how any of these eight criticisms are inconsistent with normal expectations of a popular book, which would include serious laypeople, undergraduate students, and graduate students. The first four points involve substantive issues that need well-balanced discussion. Instead, Enns appears to have approached his discussion rhetorically, attempting to persuade by presenting only one side of a biblical or theological issue.

There is, however, one area in which Enns affirms that he has been as thorough as he could be within the parameters of the aims of his book:

> As part of this apologetic [in the book], it is crucial that the non-scholarly reader understand that nothing in principle has been withheld; no data has been covered over as too damaging or problematic for consideration; no

special pleading has been employed against the data themselves, because these data have positive value in helping us understand how Scripture . . . bears perfect witness to the wisdom and glory of God. (p. 314)

Should not Enns have been just as careful in presenting the best of traditional evangelical positions on the controverted issues as he has been in laying out the non-evangelical critical viewpoint? He likely would respond by saying that the difficulties he adduces should be recognized by all evangelical scholars. And—this is the very nub of the problem—many, if not most, evangelical scholars, I dare say, do not see the difficulties to be as problematic as does Enns (though he will sometimes say that not to recognize the problems the way he does is to be guilty of "special pleading" and refusing to recognize the reality of the biblical data).

I want to repeat from chapter 1 that the reason that alternative views should be carefully explained in such a popular book is that the issues are so important for Christian faith, and popular readers may not have the requisite tools and background to evaluate the thorny issues that Enns's book discusses. As scholars, I believe that we should be as careful when writing for non-scholars as for scholars and distill difficult scholarly issues and debates in a way understandable to laypeople, which includes, of course, a level of communication not employing scholarly jargon or Greek or Hebrew or other technical language. But the concepts should be there for them, including concepts representing the best of both sides of an argument. Accordingly, the vast majority of my review in chapter 1, as can be seen from the four-point summary critique (pp. 64–65), dealt with substantive issues that Enns was discussing and was not primarily a critique of the fact that he did not include footnotes.

Consequently, Enns and I disagree about whether he should have engaged with the best of representative positions on various significant interpretive and theological matters. I believe he made an infelicitous choice in adopting the rhetorical strategy that he did, since it can and likely will mislead the typical lay reader, despite the fact that he repeatedly says that he wants to help lay readers better understand how ANE parallels relate to the Bible. In particular, recall that he says that the purpose of his book "is specifically apologetic, that is, intended to help the faithful deal with threats to their faith" (p. 314). Ironically, the likelihood is that most of what Enns discusses lay readers will confront for the first time. (I do find that graduate students sometimes have these problems and questions.)

Furthermore, most of the problems that he poses are not that hard to solve, though he gives the impression that they are difficult to square with a traditional view of inerrancy. Indeed, this is partly why I felt a burden to write the review that I did. Instead of helping people in the church gain confidence in their Bibles, Enns's book will likely shake that confidence—I think unnecessarily so.

The Question of Enns's View of Biblical Inspiration

Enns says that I call into question (by insinuation) his "basic conviction" that "the Bible is from God—that every bit of it, no matter how challenging or troublesome, is precisely what God wanted us to have and perfectly formed to do what God has designed it to do" (p. 317). Enns has misread me. A careful reading of my initial review in chapter 1 reveals that I do not call into question Enns's own *conviction* that *all* of "the Bible is from God,"[7] but I do question the viability of his attempt to hold to plenary inspiration while at the same time affirming that biblical writers unconsciously imbibed mythical stories and mistakenly thought that they corresponded to past historical reality. I do not think I have misunderstood him on this matter. He holds to a fully inspired Scripture, though this inspired Scripture contains "myths" (unbeknownst to the biblical writers themselves) at various significant points in describing redemptive-historical events. Consequently, while I believe that Enns holds to a fully inspired Bible, I do not think his view of the nature of inspiration is persuasive.

According to Enns, biblical writers were consciously intending to be understood as writing a historical genre, *but, in fact, we now know such events are myth*. Enns says that though such accounts do not convey historical truth, they still have important theological truth to tell us: that we are to worship the God of the Bible and not pagan gods. Enns even differs here from Robert Gundry, who contended that some narratives by Gospel writers, which traditionally had been taken to be history, in fact are not, since they were intentionally and consciously employing a midrashic method that added significant non-historical but interpretative features.

But Enns is saying much more than this: the biblical writers thought they were recording history but they were wrong; they were unaware that they were recording myth. This is a conclusion that does not appear to pay due hermeneutical respect to the conscious historical genre signals by biblical writers, however interpretative they may be.

Thus, one problem with his view of inspiration is that he ends up with a completely inspired Bible in which the biblical authors narrate what

7. See also my original *JETS* review, "Myth, History, and Inspiration," 287, 293, and 297.

they thought was history; but now we know they were wrong. This is tantamount to saying that the biblical writers made mistakes, but these mistakes were divinely inspired. His affirmation of inspiration, thus, dies the death of a thousand qualifications.

The Question of Enns's View of Myth and History

Enns has several responses to my discussion of his section on myth and history. First, he affirms that a "potentially misleading impression" could result from my "claim that his concern is that 'conservatives have not sufficiently recognized ANE parallels with the Bible,' when in fact the entire chapter is based on the opposite assumption that these things have been duly recognized by evangelicals" (p. 318). Instead, Enns says his concern is "to bring to the forefront the implications of these parallels for how evangelicals can think of Genesis as historical, authoritative, and inspired" (p. 318).

But Enns does not present the full picture of what either of us has said. Here is what I say in chapter 1:

> In particular, [Enns] is concerned that conservatives have not sufficiently recognized ANE parallels with the Bible, particularly the parallels with the Babylonian myth of creation and the Sumerian myth of the cataclysmic flood (pp. 26–27). Enns says that "the doctrinal implications of these discoveries have not yet been fully worked out in evangelical theology" (p. 25). For example, he says that if the Old Testament has so much in common with the ancient world and its customs and practices, "in what sense can we speak of it as revelation?" (p. 31). But, as he acknowledges, these discoveries were made in the nineteenth century, and evangelical scholars have been reflecting on their doctrinal implications ever since the early nineteen hundreds (p. 289).[8]

It is true that Enns is most concerned with the implications of ANE parallels for the doctrine of Scripture (Genesis in this case) as inspired and historical, and he does not feel that evangelicals have reflected on this sufficiently. My comment above focuses on this very point.

But Enns also believes specifically that evangelicals *have not sufficiently recognized the ANE parallels* because of their commitments to a traditional view of scriptural inspiration. This is part of what I have in mind in the first sentence of my comment above. In his book Enns says, "It is also ill advised to make such a sharp distinction between [ANE and OT parallels] that the clear similarities are brushed aside [which, from the context of this chapter, he thinks conservatives have

---

8. See p. 28 above.

too often done]."[9] Again he says: "The conservative reaction . . . tends to minimize the ancient Near Eastern setting of the Old Testament, at least where that setting poses challenges to traditional belief,"[10] and again, "conservative Christian scholars, particularly early on, have tended to employ a strategy of selective engagement of the evidence: highlighting extrabiblical evidence that conforms to or supports traditional views of the Bible, while either ignoring, downplaying, or arguing against evidence to the contrary."[11]

Thus, my statement that Enns believes "that conservatives have not sufficiently recognized ANE parallels with the Bible" is part of what Enns is saying. I was not saying that Enns believes that evangelical scholars have been ignorant about the existence of these parallels but that they have not "sufficiently recognized" their bearing on scriptural inspiration.

Second, as we saw earlier, he says in his book that there are biblical texts that presuppose the real existence of other gods, arguing that God led Israel slowly but surely from partial knowledge, i.e., from revealing to them that other real gods in addition to himself did actually exist, to fuller monotheistic knowledge of himself. I refer to this as a developmental view and say that "some would call it 'evolutionary.'" Enns considers my use of "evolutionary" as a pejoratively "visceral" expression of his view, but it is unclear why he says this.[12]

---

9. Enns, *Inspiration and Incarnation,* 27.
10. Ibid., 32.
11. Ibid., 39.
12. Enns chaffs at my labeling of his position as "evolutionary" and says I should have been "more circumspect than to use such a visceral term," since evolutionary models are naturalistic and exclude divine "direction and involvement" (p. 318). He says he is "working from a progressive-revelational model." Perhaps, he thinks the word is visceral since it may evoke associations with the notion of, for example, biological evolution and its applications to the history of intellectual and social thought. But is it not well known that there are two dominant "evolutionary" models: an atheistic one and a theistic one, the latter in which God is involved and directing the evolutionary process? There are significant Christian scholars (some of whom even hold to inerrancy) who hold to the latter view. In fact, it is well known among church historians that the great Princeton New Testament exegete, theologian, and scholar still greatly revered by both Westminster seminaries, B. B. Warfield, accommodated some qualified aspects of theistic evolution within his Calvinistic approach to Scripture. E.g., see B. B. Warfield's articles "Creation, Evolution, and Mediate Creation" and "The Manner and Time of Man's Origin," in *B. B. Warfield, Evolution, Science, and Scripture: Selected Writings,* ed. M. A. Noll and D. N. Livingston (Grand Rapids: Baker, 2000), a collection of writings by Warfield that Enns even cites in his "Response" (pp. 313–14, n. 3; p. 318, n. 9). In this light, it is difficult to see how Enns could think that I meant the naturalistic, atheistic model of evolution, since he clearly espouses belief in God. I don't think that I needed to qualify the word, since Enns expresses such belief in God, and, thus, I do not think that reference to theistic evolution is "visceral" (especially since I do not refer to it as my own opinion but that others "would call it 'evolutionary'").

Third, Enns is concerned about my use of the phrase "essential historicity" in my discussion of his analysis of the "myth-history issue" in Genesis, for which he says I have "lack of appreciation" of the complexities of this topic (p. 318). Enns says that I "err in thinking that such an affirmation is crucial to addressing the very difficult but real myth-history problem in Genesis," and that "the phrase amounts to little more than a slogan that obscures the issue when further explanation is not given to how, in what way, and to what extent Genesis is essentially historical" (p. 319).

But I have chosen to use this phrase to summarize the problem because it is the phrase that Enns himself used to contrast the problem of the records of "the previous periods of Israel's history," to the historical record of the "monarchic period, when it began to develop a more 'historical consciousness.'"[13] Similarly, he says, "It is precisely the evidence *missing* from the previous periods of Israel's history [e.g., the Pentateuch] that raises the problem of the *essential historicity* of that period" (italics mine).[14] Enns appears to assume a typical definition of *essential history*; otherwise his statement about monarchic and pre-monarchic history would not make good sense. I take the same fairly normal definition of the phrase—that writers record events that correspond with real past events. Of course, as I mentioned earlier, though historians certainly interpret history, such interpretations do not necessarily distort the historical actions and events being recorded, as I would hold in the case of biblical writers.

It also bears repeating that Enns does not include "essential historicity" in his definition of *myth*,[15] which he sees present in Genesis, and that he does not see the pre-monarchic biblical accounts to contain "essential historicity."[16]

Enns asserts in his *JETS* "Response" that he "would have liked to have been clearer" about his "affirmation of the basic historical referential nature of the opening chapters of Genesis" (p. 317). But he really says no more to clarify this very brief statement, which is also ambiguous.

One reason this lack of elaboration is problematic is that Enns has used the analogy of an artist painting a portrait or a painting to describe how the event of the exodus might be understood. After acknowledging that some have compared the exodus to a portrait, he qualifies the comparison by saying, "In Exodus the whole question is, 'are we deal-

---

13. Enns, *Inspiration and Incarnation*, 44.
14. Ibid.
15. See this in my original *JETS* review article, "Myth, History, and Inspiration," 290, 296.
16. Ibid., 293.

ing with a life-like portrait such as that of Norman Rockwell or are we closer to the impressionism of a Monet or even the abstract art of a Picasso or Jackson Pollock?'"[17] I suggest going online to look at some of the abstract art of Picasso and, especially, Pollock to visualize the kind of comparison that Enns appears implicitly to be posing as a possibility for understanding the event of the exodus.

Accordingly, Exodus appears to be a work of literary art that in significant ways indirectly imitates other ANE mythical works to depict something that is historical, but it may be difficult to discern how much of the actual historical kernel of the event is present in the narrative "painting." According to Enns's abstract art analogy, the event of the exodus may be hardly discernible at all. At best, this may merely be another of the several ambiguities that I discussed in my review in chapter 1.

Though Enns contends that he is among those "evangelicals [who] would generally affirm" that "Genesis 'appears to be a historical genre' and therefore is 'true history' and records 'real' events of the past" (p. 319), he immediately backtracks and asks, "What type of historical genre does Genesis appear to be, and how does the ANE evidence affect how we formulate such a definition? What constitutes 'true' history or 'real' events?" (p. 319). The sharp edge of the problem for him is that "Genesis shares the cosmology of its ancient analogs, even while it contests their theology," and this "cannot help but affect how we think about the 'essential historical' nature of Genesis" (p. 319). He sees the polemical contrast between the pertinent Genesis narratives and their ANE analogues to be only in the area of "theology," i.e., the God of Genesis is the only God that deserves worship. Enns would not say at this point that the polemic is that the God of Genesis is the only real God, since, as we have seen, he affirms that God's revelation at this point did not deny the existence of other real gods.

But why does the polemic not also involve a contrast with history, in the sense that the God of the patriarchs really does work in history as opposed to the unreal ANE gods? I would say that the biblical account gives the record that corresponds with what God actually did in space-time history in contrast to the ANE accounts of false gods who really did not act in history.

Thus, though Enns claims to hold to some kind of general affirmation of the historicity of Genesis 1–11, the way he specifically fleshes this out is quite different from other evangelical Old Testament scholars. He gives so many qualifications that it is unclear what he really affirms. In

17. Peter Enns, "Exodus and the Problem of Historiography," paper delivered at the 56th Annual Meeting of the Evangelical Theological Society in San Antonio, Texas, November 2004.

chapter 1 I went to great lengths to cite Enns's very words—indeed paragraphs—to show that he affirms that the Pentateuch positively adopts mythical notions in the essentially normal sense of the word (i.e., nonhistorical and fictitious narrative).[18]

Of course, Enns must see some actual history in Genesis, perhaps the core of the patriarchal narratives, though he never spells out for the reader what narratives he sees to correspond to actual past events and to what degree he sees them as not "historical." In fact, the problem for him is significant, since he says that all pre-monarchic historical narratives face the problem of "essential historicity" in contrast to monarchic history writing.[19] In this respect, recall that he says, "It is questionable logic to reason backward from the historical character of the monarchic account, *for which there is some evidence*, to the primeval and ancestral stories, *for which such evidence is lacking*."[20]

Enns gives a fairly clear answer to his question about what kind of genre Genesis is. He says it is a "mythic" genre, explaining *myth* as "an ancient, premodern, pre-scientific way of addressing questions of ultimate origins and meaning in the form of stories: Who are we? Where do we come from?" (p. 50 of Enns's book). Note, again, that Enns's definition does not include a reference to recording history that corresponds to an actual past state of affairs. I labored to show in my review in chapter 1 that Enns's definition of *myth* is normal in that for him it refers to "stories [that] were made up" especially about "origins."[21] Thus, he says that "myth is the proper category [genre] for understanding Genesis."[22]

Enns says that V. P. Long's discussion in his *Art of Biblical History* gives an excellent beginning point about genre considerations, especially in relation to his own concern about "what role ANE literature should play in 'calibrating' our genre discussions" about Genesis ("Response," p. 320). But Long is much more cautious than Enns; one of his main points is that while genre categories derived from study of ancient extra-biblical and cultural contexts can be helpful, "it is important to bear in mind that genre categories that have been developed through study of literatures outside the Bible may not be fully applicable to the biblical texts."[23]

18. This is found also in my original *JETS* review, "Myth, History, and Inspiration," 293, 289–97.
19. Enns, *Inspiration and Incarnation*, 43–44.
20. Ibid., 43 (emphasis in original).
21. Ibid., 41.
22. Ibid., though the wording is part of a question in his book ("does this [Genesis's similarity to ANE myth] indicate that myth is the proper category for understanding Genesis?"), in context, he answers the question positively.
23. V. P. Long, *The Art of Biblical History* (Grand Rapids: Zondervan, 1994), 40.

Again, Long says, especially with respect to ANE mythological parallels, "The temptation must be avoided either to insist that only those biblical genres are possible that find analogies outside the Bible . . . or to assume that whatever genres are attested outside the Bible may without qualification find a place in the Bible."[24] And once more, "the Ancient Near East, then, offers little that can compare to the larger discourse units of the Old Testament, or of the whole Old Testament."[25] At points in the same chapter, Long says that smaller discourse units in the Bible also contain unique genres that have no parallel in the ancient literary world[26] or they contain mixed or blended genres.[27] Furthermore, extrabiblical genre categories are merely "descriptive" and must never become "prescriptive" for the Bible,[28] and some "might be deemed unacceptable."[29] In contrast, even in his response, Enns lacks nuance in his understanding of how ANE mythic genre relates to Genesis. Part of the upshot of Long's chapter is about how difficult it is to define genre both theoretically and specifically.

It is striking that Enns affirms that "the biblical account, along with its ancient Near Eastern counterparts, assumes the factual nature of what it reports. They did not think, 'We know this is all "myth" but it will have to do until science is invented to give us better answers'" (*Inspiration and Incarnation,* p. 55). Thus, the biblical writers absorbed mythical worldviews unconsciously, reproduced them in their writings, and believed them to be reliable descriptions of the real world and events occurring in the past real world (creation account, flood narrative, etc.) because they were part of their socially constructed mythical reality.[30]

Enns presents the problem of Genesis 1 as a classic case of the problem about which he is concerned:

> What, for example, is "essentially historical" about Genesis 1? Is it the bare affirmation that God did "something" in space/time history? Or, at the other end of the spectrum, is it the affirmation that Genesis 1 describes creation in literalistic terms (literal 24-hour days, canopy of water, etc.)?

24. Ibid., 45–46.
25. Ibid., 48.
26. Ibid., 44–45.
27. Ibid., 57.
28. Ibid., 43.
29. Ibid., 46.
30. See J. H. Walton, "Ancient Near Eastern Background Studies," *Dictionary for the Theological Interpretation of Scripture,* ed. K. Vanhoozer (Grand Rapids: Baker, 2005), who repudiates such unconscious absorption and use of myth in the Old Testament while still affirming that "God's communication used the established literary genres of the ancient world and often conformed to the rules that existed within those genres" (p. 41).

If the former, are the specific form and content of Genesis 1 just decorative flourishes (which leaves one wondering why God put them there in the first place)? If the latter, are we to say that Genesis 1 can be safely understood at arm's length from the ancient world in which the texts were intended—by God—to speak? What precisely about Genesis 1 needs to be affirmed as "accurate, true, real" (to use Beale's terms), and how does one even begin to make these judgments, given the antiquity and foreignness of Genesis vis-à-vis modern historical standards? These are the kind of things that can and do trouble lay readers. (pp. 319–20)

In reply, there are several possible well-known interpretations of Genesis 1 that can be quite consistent with a notion of "essential historicity": (1) a literal creation by God during a literal six days composed of 24-hours each; (2) a literal creation by God over a long period of time, understanding the days to be figurative for a long period; (3) a creation that is to be seen as a literal description of a chaotic, non-functional cosmos followed by a description of God "setting up the functions that will establish an ordered, operational cosmos,"[31] which is conceived of as a temple for himself and his people in which to dwell.[32]

There are, of course, subcategories of these basic views, some of which hold to theistic evolution and some of which do not. Thus, both the two views that Enns cites, as well as the third view, would be within the range of correspondence to "essential historicity." Varying interpretations of the creation and flood narratives do not necessitate a different view of the narratives' "essential historicity." A view inconsistent with "essential historicity" is one that holds to the depiction of God's creative activity as merely a reflection of other ANE mythical creation narratives and that claims the only point being made by the Genesis writer is that the God of Genesis is the God to be worshiped instead of the various other ANE gods who purportedly participated in the creation of the cosmos.

I must stop here and refer readers back to my initial review reproduced in chapter 1. Enns has not addressed the specific evidence that I laid out there—he, indeed, affirms that significant narratives in the Pentateuch are shot through with myth. I concluded in the review that he understands myth "in the essentially normal sense, that is stories without an 'essential historical' foundation."[33] Since, in his response to my initial

31. J. H. Walton, *Genesis*, NIVAC (Grand Rapids: Zondervan, 2001), 84, though see the entire section on 65–159.
32. Ibid., 147–52; though, while this is a literal depiction, the time scope may be difficult to pin down. Also, the cosmos is defined as the literal macrocosmic temple, of which small ANE and Israel's architectural temples were microcosmic models.
33. See Beale, "Review Article," 297.

review, he has not distanced himself from the evidence that I laid out for his view in this respect or disagreed with my conclusions about his view, then I must assume that I was correct in my conclusion about his view of the mythical nature of accounts in Genesis.

Therefore, how is Enns's view different from that of Gerhard von Rad's perspective, that Old Testament writers wrote what appeared to be historical accounts, which were theologically true on a salvation-historical plane, but which possessed no essential connection with true, past historical reality?[34] I mentioned this in my initial review, but Enns never addresses it in his response.

Consequently, when Enns challenges me and others about our simplistic view of essential history, what he wants us to agree with is that Genesis is shot through with a mythic genre, though the writer, and those who passed on the early traditions that the writer received, thought they were passing on accounts that corresponded with true past historical events. I am unconvinced by Enns's challenge.

Issues of Science and Myth in Relation to Enns's Use of the Term "Diversity"

Enns is also troubled by my discussion of inerrancy as it is related to his view of myth and theological diversity. First, in responding to Enns's dichotomy between the pre-scientific and the scientific worlds, I pointed out in my review that there are significant overlaps between modern mathematics and astronomy. Enns responds that he fails to see how such overlaps help with understanding "the relationship between Genesis 1 and *Enuma Elish*, or any other ANE analog" (p. 320). But the very reason that I made the point is that Enns repeatedly in his book made the unqualified distinction between the purported pre-scientific and scientific ages:

> Ancient peoples were not concerned to describe the universe in scientific terms . . . scientific investigation was not at the disposal of ancient Near Eastern peoples. (p. 40)

> Are the early stories in the Old Testament to be judged on the basis of standards of modern historical inquiry and scientific precision, things that ancient peoples were not at all aware of? (p. 41)

> [The historical context of Genesis] was not a modern scientific one but an ancient mythic one. (p. 55)

---

34. Again, for a convenient summary of this aspect and problem of von Rad's theology, see W. Eichrodt, *Theology of the Old Testament*, vol. 1 (Philadelphia: Westminster Press, 1961), 512–20.

My point about the existence of ancient mathematics and astronomy that overlaps with modern notions of these areas is relevant, at least, because it qualifies Enns's sweeping generalizations and reductionisms about an absolute gap between the two worlds. Furthermore, these overlaps are specifically significant for the present discussion, since Enns himself relates "modern historical inquiry and scientific precision." He elaborates on this by referring to "modern standards of truth and error." Without any further qualification, I assume that he includes scientific precision in describing the cosmos and such things as scientific precision in measurements, calculations, etc., which may sometimes form part of historical narrative reports. Indeed, that he does have in mind descriptions of the cosmos is apparent from his above reference to ancients not "describing the universe" in scientific terms, and from the context where he includes reference to ancient perceptions of how the sun and the moon travel and the ancient view of the cosmos (p. 54).

Certainly, to some significant degree the overlap with astronomy is relevant here. Furthermore, also relevant is that ancient and modern peoples share strikingly similar phenomenological portrayals of the cosmos. Our common reference to the sun rising or setting is one that was also common in the ancient world of the Old Testament (e.g., see Gen. 15:12, 17; 19:23; 28:11; 32:31).[35]

Lastly, while it is true that there are unusual portrayals of the cosmos in the ANE and Old Testament according to modern standards, which some might be tempted to call premodern, the reason is likely theological. For example, it is clear in the ANE and Old Testament that temples were designed to be symbolic representations of the cosmos. Why? There is evidence in both the ANE and in the Old Testament that the cosmos was conceived of as a huge temple. Earthly temples were little models of God's entire creation as a macrocosmic temple in which he was present in a much grander way than in the small architectural sanctuaries.[36] Since the temples were symbolic of God's heavenly dwelling, it is unlikely that the Israelites actually believed the cosmos was literally structured like a giant temple merely on a bigger scale than Israel's earthly temple, though there is not space here to elaborate on how this is so.[37]

I also do not have room here to explain the possible relationships between ANE and Israelite temples, but suffice it to say that it is unlikely

35. In this respect, see briefly D. A. Carson, "Three More Books on the Bible: A Critical Review," *TJ* 27NS (2006): 34–35, as well as chap. 7 below.

36. On which see G. K. Beale, *The Temple and the Church's Mission* (Leicester: Inter-Varsity, 2004), 29–80, and chaps. 6–7 of this book.

37. On which see ibid., 29–80 and chaps. 6–7 herein.

that Israel merely unconsciously modeled their temple on the temples of the foreign false, mythical gods around them.[38] One must be cautious in setting up other symbolic cosmic perspectives purportedly shared by the ANE and Israel and calling them premodern.[39] In the case of Israel, what some may call premodern or pre-scientific cosmology is, in reality, a theological and symbolic conception of the whole cosmos pointed to symbolically by Israel's small temple, which served as a kind of miniature cosmos. I have dedicated chapters 6 and 7 to the specific issue of how Israel's theological view of the cosmos relates to Israel's temple and how both of these are related to a modern understanding of the cosmos.[40]

In connection again to inerrancy, Enns is uncomfortable with my effort to show that there are certain universal categories of rational thought by which truth is discerned.[41] Enns responds, "Even though there are certainly categories of thought that are universally and time-lessly part of the human condition, the Bible, precisely because it is a product of God's self-revelation in *history*, has, by God's design, a local, timely dimension to it" (p. 321). But Enns never tells us what human categories of thought are universally and timelessly applicable, so the concession is a platitude without content. Essentially, I am saying that ancient peoples had categories of thought "at their disposal for assess-ing" the observable world that are in some regards commensurable to our own.[42] Furthermore, if the categories of thought that I offer above are not applicable, then how can we make any sense of Scripture? It would merely become so much gibberish.

Despite the fact that Enns says that I am defining the nature of Scrip-ture by an outside criterion, it is quite evident that Scripture reflects and presupposes this notion, since Scripture itself often uses the word *true* or *truth* to affirm that ancient people could make descriptive statements that corresponded, not exhaustively but truly, to actual reality; likewise Scrip-ture uses words such as *know* to indicate that the ancients could know things sufficiently that corresponded to the reality around them.[43]

In fact, to turn the tables on Enns, it appears to be Enns who is allow-ing extrabiblical sources to define the nature of scriptural inspiration.

---

38. For my explanation of the relationship, see *Temple and Church's Mission*, 29–167.
39. As, e.g., that depicted in A. P. Dickin's chart in Enns, *Inspiration and Incarnation*, 54.
40. On which see pp. 161–218.
41. Note my discussion of this in chap. 2 and in my *JETS* "Review Article," 301.
42. Quoting in part J. D. Woodbridge, *Biblical Authority: A Critique of the Rogers/McKim Proposal* (Grand Rapids: Zondervan, 1982), 163.
43. See D. A. Carson, *Becoming Conversant with the Emerging Church* (Grand Rapids: Zondervan, 2005), 188–200; see also A. C. Thiselton, *The Two Horizons: New Testament Hermeneutics and Philosophical Description* (Grand Rapids: Eerdmans, 1980), 411.

He affirms that the genre of Genesis is best defined as "myth." And why does he define the genre of Genesis in this way? Because he believes there is such a close conceptual similarity between the opening chapters of Genesis and Mesopotamian myth.[44]

So do we let the mythical genre of the ANE stories determine the genre of Genesis or do we let Genesis itself determine its own genre and then go outside to the ANE environment to see how it is related?[45] In the initial part of my review in chapter 1,[46] I contended that on its own, Genesis portrays itself as a historical genre. Of course, there is interpretation interspersed, as is true with any ancient or modern history writing. As one attempts to see the relationship between this genre in Genesis and other ANE writings, there are at least five ways that one can perceive of such a relationship, the last of which, unconsciously imbibed myth, favored by Enns, is the least probable.

Among the most viable suggestions are that Genesis alludes to ANE religious myth in order to conduct polemic against it, or it reflects, along with the ANE myths, general revelatory truth or a common ancient tradition, both of which are only rightly interpreted by the divine Scripture. Each of these perspectives could be applicable to understanding the example of cosmic temple symbolism discussed above. While one may disagree with this assessment, it is not forced harmonization nor special pleading but a reasonable evaluation of the evidence.

Interestingly, Enns makes the same mistake in starting points in his chapter on the use of the Old Testament in the New, where he affirms that one first must understand Second Temple Jewish hermeneutics, and then one can understand New Testament hermeneutics only through the lens of early Judaism. Enns's approach must be turned on its head or radically altered: start first with examining the interpretative approach of Jesus and the apostles, and then study Judaism to see the relationship between the two or, at least, study the various sectors of Judaism and the New Testament, and then compare and contrast them.[47] Enns appears typically to interpret special revelation by general revelation, e.g., extrabiblical tradition, rather than vice versa. In other words, with

---

44. *Inspiraton and Incarnation*, 55; so also p. 41: "The biblical stories are similar enough to invite comparison with the category of ANE myth."

45. Interestingly, in contrast to Enns's approach, C. Van Til's presuppositionalist perspective, the most well-known apologist of the Westminster Seminary tradition, of which Enns identifies himself, starts first with Scripture and judges all things by Scripture.

46. See also my original *JETS* "Review Article," 289–90.

47. For my fuller argument in this respect, see my "Did Jesus and the Apostles Preach the Right Doctrine from the Wrong Texts? Revisiting the Debate," and my "A Surrejoinder to Peter Enns on the Use of the Old Testament in the New," *Them* 32 (2007), 14–25, which are now respectively reproduced here in chaps. 3–4.

regard to Old Testament issues he wants to "calibrate our genre discussions" by letting the ANE literature play a more dominant role than the biblical literature.[48]

Enns says, "Some of our differences can be attributed to my Reformed, specifically presuppositional, theological and epistemological starting point."[49] I doubt that this is helpful, since I cut my teeth early in my graduate studies on the presuppositional viewpoints of such Reformed theologians as John Calvin, Abraham Kuyper, and Cornelius Van Til and on the biblical-theological approach of Geerhardus Vos, perspectives which I still hold.[50]

In relation also to the issue of inerrancy, Enns says I affirm that recognition of diversity in Scripture is close to denial of inerrancy.[51] He says that I "seem to suggest that the choice is between 'complementary viewpoints' and 'irreconcilable perspectives,'" though he says it is "more complex" than this.[52] Actually what I say is that his definition of *diversity* in the book is not clear: does it refer to various but complementary viewpoints or to irreconcilable perspectives on a given topic? His only answer is that it is a "more complex matter than this."

In reality, much of what Enns discusses is not difficult to relate or harmonize, if I may use such a worn word, which Don Carson has well discussed in his review of Enns.[53] After reading Carson and Enns again, I think readers will discern a penchant in Enns to make diverse molehills into irreconcilable hermeneutical mountains. Like Carson, I just don't see the problem in a number of diverse examples that Enns gives. Part of Enns's concern is excellent: let us not jump immediately to trying to harmonize before we have *fully* explored on the exegetical level each particular text of concern, seeing its role within its own literary and historical context. He is afraid that people with "inerrancy on their brain" will too quickly start trying to harmonize. His caution in this respect is outstanding.

On the other hand, he does not appear to see a role for rigorous analysis of how the two "diverse" texts may relate. This is really part of

---

48. Note Enns, "Response to Beale," 320, n. 14, where he uses this language to pose the question of how to determine genre, a question that he answers in his book and in his "Response" that I lay out above.

49. Enns, "Response to Beale," 315, n. 6.

50. It may be true that our differences are due to presuppositional perspectives, but, if so, it may be because Enns and I interpret the presuppositional approaches of old Princeton and old Westminster differently. I am sure, however, that we could not get to the bottom of this particular disagreement without some in-depth face-to-face discussion and debate.

51. Enns, "Response to Beale," 323.

52. Ibid., 322.

53. Carson, "A Critical Review," 37–40.

the work of biblical theology, not merely a knee-jerk reaction by those preoccupied to solve scriptural problems. Enns himself says that a biblical-theological approach should be used in the face of the diversity, not so much to solve it but to recognize that such diversity, e.g., in the case of the law codes, "is not ultimate, but are steps along the way leading up to Christ . . . helping us to see that the Law is not meant to be an ultimate unchanging statement of God's will but penultimate, awaiting the coming of Christ who . . . fulfills the law" (p. 322).

This particular example with respect to the law I find very interesting, though in order to make a persuasive case Enns would have to flesh it out more. Nevertheless, he has offered here an ultimate redemptive-historical rationale that actually does have great potential to resolve the problem of diversity, which Enns most of the time denies can be done. Indeed, I think it would be difficult to use this particular christocentric (or christotelic, as Enns prefers) rationale to understand other kinds of diversity that Enns sees throughout the Bible; it is unclear how such diversity—diversity in historical parallel accounts, apparent mistakes in numbers, place names, etc.—relates to Christ's eschatological coming, a critique also offered in Don Carson's review.

But it is clear that Enns does see that, at least, some of what he discusses involves such radical diversity that it cannot be resolved according to modern standards of rationality, and we must leave such diversity to stand as it is. Now, in part, I agree that when diversity appears irresolvable on the literary or biblical-theological level, then we let it stand, and we do not foist some precarious harmonization onto the text. What we philosophically label such irresolvable diversity will differ with the presuppositions of the individual interpreter: some will call it *error*, some *difficulty*, and some, like Enns, just *diversity*, since it appears that the term *error* is for him an anachronistic modern word that is inapplicable to ancient thought. This was my assessment of Enns's view of diversity in the chapter 1 review, and that assessment has not changed despite his further response.

Enns does not like my application of *postmodern* to his view, since he thinks it is "a loaded, emotive" term (p. 317). I do not mean it in any emotive sense. What I mean is that modern standards of rational thought are inapplicable to judging ancient expressions of thinking, a typical trait of even those who would refer to themselves as evangelical "soft" postmodernists and do not see it as a negative term.

The Question of Enns's Incarnational Analogy
Enns's last major concern is with my evaluation of his incarnational analogy. In my review I questioned the validity of the way Enns uses

this analogy in understanding Scripture as both a divine and a human word, since he was ambiguous about what parts of the analogy apply and which do not. He admits that, if he were writing the book again, he would be clearer about how the incarnational analogy applies to Scripture:

> As there is no sin in the God-man Jesus, so too there is no error in Scripture. The human situatedness and diverse nature of Scripture, then, are not to be understood as errors corresponding to some putative sin on Christ's part, but rather as the condescension of God corresponding to Christ's humanity. (p. 323)

Enns admits that the analogy is large enough to drive a hermeneutical truck through, since he can see how some would use it to disallow myth in Scripture, yet he believes that he can use it to see "that such culturally laden expressions" of myth "are what one would expect" (p. 323). Enns appeals to some wonderful quotations by Bavinck, Green, Warfield, and Gaffin on the incarnational analogy with Scripture (with which I agree), but the question remains as to how to flesh out further what they say.

It is in the attempt to flesh out that the disagreements arise. He tries to give concrete details of his view: "'Does Genesis 1, bearing strong similarities to ANE myth, correspond to Jesus "sinning" or to the fact that he had olive skin, wore leather sandals, and spoke Aramaic?' I am of the latter opinion" (p. 323). But this kind of alternative incarnational example does not get to the heart of the matter of Enns's proposals. Enns wants to see that myth can be naturally though unconsciously woven into God's revelation in its human situatedness. So the better incarnational question should be formulated in this manner, which I repeat from chapter 1:

> Some evangelical theologians speculate that while the human Jesus was perfect morally, he was still imperfect in such things as mathematical computation or historical recollection (e.g., some say, could not Jesus have made a "B" on his fifth grade math test? Or could he not have cut a board wrongly from the instructions of his human father?). On analogy with this conception of Jesus' incarnation, scripture is God's absolutely faithful word about morals and theology (e.g., the way to salvation) but not about minute points of history or scientific facts.[54]

To get more at the heart of the issue for Enns's proposals, it would seem that his above question should be reformulated as follows: "Does

54. Also see my *JETS* "Review Article," 299.

Genesis 1, bearing strong similarities to ANE myth, correspond to Jesus unconsciously in his human nature accommodating himself to the mythical or non-historical traditions of Jewish culture,[55] which would not be moral sin, or does the Genesis 1-ANE relationship correspond more to the fact that Jesus had olive skin, wore leather sandals, and spoke Aramaic?" (p. 324).

Now, I wonder, which option Enns would choose with this new alternative? I posed the same question in the review in chapter 1, but Enns has chosen not to address it, even though it is the most pertinent aspect of the incarnational paradigm that would seem to have most relevance for supporting his argument about myth. Of course, it would mean holding to a lower Christology than that to which the church has dominantly held throughout her existence. If Enns holds to an unconscious accommodation to myth by Old Testament writers and by Paul (e.g., see chaps. 3 and 4 for his view of 1 Cor. 10:4), then it would appear that he likely holds the same view about Jesus.

This is made even clearer, as we will observe in chapter 3, as Enns explicitly affirms that Jesus' use of the Old Testament in the New was a thoroughgoing accommodation to Judaism's uncontrolled and non-contextual use of the Old Testament. Thus, Jesus was not concerned with the original meaning of Old Testament authors, and he read in meanings that had nothing to do with such original meaning.[56] We will also see in chapters 4 and 5 that Enns implicitly believes that Jesus purportedly uses a Jewish interpretative method that involves the unconscious absorption of myth, though Enns discusses this aspect of Jewish exegesis explicitly only in relation to Paul (as in the case, e.g., of 1 Cor. 10:4).

Thus, my objection is not that the incarnational analogy cannot be validly used, but that, if it is used, it must be carefully defined, which Enns still does not do in his response.

Enns concludes his response to this topic by saying that "the precise nature of this analogy . . . cannot and need not be worked out with the kind of precision [Beale] seems to demand before the analogy can be used to benefit lay readers who confess by faith the mystery of the incarnation . . ." (p. 324). But this is an insufficient response, since the way he has defined the incarnational analogy is very general and, by his own admission, is susceptible of widely varying applications, so that, as it stands, it is not a very helpful model for trying to resolve the

55. Which some moderate evangelicals would say, e.g., was that Adam was a real figure in history or that there really was a flood in Noah's day or that the prophet Isaiah wrote the entire book of Isaiah or that Moses was the author of the Pentateuch, etc.
56. Enns, *Inspiraton and Incarnation*, 114–15, 132.

kinds of problems that Enns has set up throughout his book. To appeal to "the mystery of the incarnation" at this point would appear to be special pleading.

Conclusion

Enns concludes his response by reflecting upon why there is so much controversy over his "little book, written in a popular style for a popular audience" (p. 326). He answers that the controversy tells as much about "the reviewers themselves" and "the current state of evangelical thinking as it does the book itself" (p. 326). While this is a very generally correct statement, it is virtually a truism.

Part of the fuel that fired my motivation to write the review was to give laypeople and students another perspective on the issues that Enns addresses, especially since I believe there are people who will be disturbed and have their faith *unncecessarily* unsettled by a writer long associated with Westminster Seminary, a traditionally orthodox school. Contrary to Enns's view, I have written partly because I don't want laypeople to have the impression that Enns has laid out all the relevant evidence on both sides of the debate and then to think that Enns's conclusions, based on such selective evidence, are viable for evangelical faith.

As Don Carson has noted, while Enns says that he wishes Christians troubled by contemporary scholarship's objections to the Bible's authority would come to terms with what the Bible really says and to see that an evangelical faith in the Bible is viable, almost every sentence in Enns's book is in fact an attempt to acknowledge the viability of these objections and to undermine what he takes to be conservative (mis)conceptions of what the Bible is.[57]

The last sentences of Enns's response are a plea not to perpetuate a "climate of fear, suspicion and posturing" that produces "a climate [that] does not honor Christ" (p. 326). I completely agree, as long as this does not mean that vigorous critique of one another's views is disallowed.

---

57. E.g., see Carson, "Three More Books on the Bible," 29.

CHAPTER THREE

Is a Traditional Evangelical View of Scripture's Authority Compatible with Recent Developments in the Study of the Old Testament in the New? *Part 1*

This chapter is a slightly revised version of my review of the portion of Peter Enns's book that concerns how the New Testament writers interpret the Old Testament. This review appeared originally as "Did Jesus and the Apostles Preach the Right Doctrine from the Wrong Texts? Revisiting the Debate Seventeen Years Later in the Light of Peter Enns's Book, *Inspiration and Incarnation*" (*Them* 32 [2006], 18–43).

Seventeen years ago, I wrote an article in *Themelios* titled "Did Jesus and His Followers Preach the Right Doctrine from the Wrong Texts?"[1] which was partly in response to Richard Longenecker's work on the use of the Old Testament in the New. Much related work has happened since then in this field, especially among evangelical scholars. The appearance of the recent book by former Westminster Seminary professor Peter Enns, *Inspiration and Incarnation*,[2] represents a similar position to that of Longenecker, yet in significant ways goes beyond it. For this reason,

1. G. K. Beale, "Did Jesus and His Followers Preach the Right Doctrine from the Wrong Texts? An Examination of the Presuppositions of the Apostles' Exegetical Method," *Them* 14 (1989): 89–96.
2. Peter Enns, *Inspiration and Incarnation: Evangelicals and the Problem of the Old Testament* (Grand Rapids: Baker, 2005).

I have thought it fitting to readdress the issue of my 1989 *Themelios* article in the light of Enns's recent work.

While the majority of Enns's book concerns a discussion and evaluation of evangelicals' views of the Old Testament, his lengthy fourth chapter (over 50 pages) is about the use of the Old Testament in the New Testament, based partly on an earlier article.[3] Here Enns has written a stimulating and thought-provoking chapter, one that will cause Christians to think long and hard about their own views on this important issue.

One of Enns's main points is his emphasis on interpreting the Old Testament according to a "christotelic" hermeneutic, an approach of the apostles that he believes the contemporary church should follow. I like this term *christotelic* better than *christocentric*, since it refers more explicitly to approaching Old Testament texts without attempting to read Christ into every passage—something which some wrongly construe to be a christocentric reading. The goal of the whole Old Testament is to point to the eschatological coming of Christ, and, therefore, I think Enns has made a very helpful improvement on a Christian approach to the Old Testament. I also think that his stress on reading the Old Testament from the eschatological perspective of the New Testament age is crucial and absolutely correct. Though I am in general agreement with his approach, the way Enns often defines a christotelic reading is not, in my view, as felicitous nor are several other significant points that he makes about how the New Testament uses the Old Testament.

Five Issues of Concern about Enns's View of the New Testament's Use of the Old Testament

1) Odd Uses

Enns contends that there are "odd uses" of the Old Testament in the New Testament in terms of modern readers' perceptions. Enns also says that such uses occur "often" in the New Testament: "Time and time again the New Testament authors do some odd things, by our standards, with the Old Testament."[4]

Other New Testament scholars have found that these so-called odd uses adduced by Enns can viably be understood also as "grammatical-historical" exegesis. But why does Enns not acknowledge these other plausible interpretations, especially since they are given not by funda-

---

3. Peter Enns, "Apostolic Hermeneutics and an Evangelical Doctrine of Scripture: Moving Beyond the Modern Impasse," *WTJ* 65 (2003): 263–87.

4. Peter Enns, *Incarnation and Inspiration*, 114; so also 115–16, 152. Henceforth, in this chapter references to Enns's book will be noted parenthetically in text. Enns appears to acknowledge that exceptionally there is some "grammatical-historical" exegesis by the apostles (e.g., p. 158).

mentalists but by active New Testament scholars who are publishing in the field, some of whom also do not affirm inerrancy? This is misleading because he does not give the reader—whether layperson or scholar—an opportunity to judge his interpretation of these purported "odd uses" in the light of other competing interpretations.

In addition, Enns proposes that New Testament writers use either a "grammatical-historical" exegetical method *or* a "christotelic" approach (e.g., pp. 158–60), the latter of which Enns says is usually not related contextually to the original intention of the Old Testament author (pp. 156–60). In this respect, he says that "final coherence" of meaning in Christ is often not consistent with the original meaning of the Old Testament human author (p. 160).[5] He writes:

> To read the Old Testament "christotelically" is to read it *already knowing* that Christ is somehow the *end* to which the Old Testament story is heading. . . . It is the Old Testament as a whole, particularly in its grand themes, that finds its *telos*, its completion, in Christ. . . . What constitutes a Christian reading of the Old Testament is that it proceeds to the second reading, the eschatological, christotelic reading—and this is precisely what the apostles model for us. (p. 154)

One who disagrees with Enns's thesis can agree with his definition of a christotelic reading just quoted but not necessarily with his contention that such a reading means that "New Testament authors were not engaging the Old Testament in an effort to remain consistent with the original context and intention of the Old Testament author" (p. 115).

But are there other interpretative methods to keep in mind besides those mentioned by Enns that can show significant degrees of consistency with Old Testament contexts? Other good scholars would say that there are other viable interpretative approaches along the spectrum between these two opposite poles of grammatical-historical exegesis and non-contextual exegesis. For example, the New Testament authors may be using a *biblical-theological approach* that could be described as a canonical contextual approach. This approach is not a technical *grammatical-historical* one but takes in wider biblical contexts than merely the one being quoted, yet is not inconsistent with the quoted context.[6]

Were not the apostolic writers theologians, and can we not allow that they interpreted the Old Testament not always according to a

---

5. On p. 153 he says explicitly "that apostolic hermeneutics violates what is considered to be a fundamental interpretive principle: don't take things out of context."

6. For examples of this, see G. K. Beale, *The Temple and the Church's Mission* (Leicester: Inter-Varsity, 2004), passim.

grammatical-historical exegetical method but theologically, in ways that creatively developed Old Testament texts yet did not contravene the meaning of the original Old Testament author? Or, could New Testament writers be permitted the liberty to use a "typological approach," whereby historical events come to be seen as foreshadowings of events in New Testament times? Some think this is not a viable approach while others do. The latter see that underlying the approach was a philosophy of history whereby God designed earlier events to point to later events, e.g., the death of the Passover lamb was an event foreshadowing and fulfilled in Christ's death (John 19:36). The later use grows out of the earlier narrated event and, thus, is organically or contextually related to it and its meaning; while being a progressive revelatory development of the Old Testament text, it is not inconsistent with the original context.

When one considers all of these different approaches, what the New Testament writers do with the Old Testament does not seem so "odd."[7] In fact, in his discussion of the use of Hosea 11:1 in Matthew 2:15, after Enns says that this does not reflect grammatical-historical exegesis, he proposes what I would call a quite viable biblical-theological approach. This approach, which Enns says is employed by Matthew in his use of Hosea 11:1, is not inconsistent with the original intention of the Hosea verse and is understandable to both ancient and modern readers. Accordingly, Enns viably proposes:

> Matthew's use of Hosea reflects broader theological convictions. Although neither I nor anyone else can step into Matthew's head and outline precisely how he understood Hosea, the following suggestion is quite reasonable. It may be that Matthew had in mind not simply this one verse in Hosea 11, but the larger context of that chapter. There were no verse numbers in Matthew's day. Quoting one verse may have been a way of saying "that part of Hosea that begins with 'out of Egypt I called my son.'"

> If this is true (and although this is not merely a private opinion, it is conjectural nonetheless), we may be able to trace some of Matthew's broader theological underpinnings. The son in Hosea and the son in Matthew are a study in contrasts. Israel came out of Egypt, was disobedient, deserved punishment, yet was forgiven by God (Hos. 11:8–11). Christ came out of Egypt, led a life of perfect obedience, deserved no punishment, but was

---

7. E.g., see E. E. Ellis, *Paul's Use of the Old Testament* (Grand Rapids: Baker, 1991), 52–53 (on the purported allegory of Galatians 4), 66–70; 131 (on the "following rock" of 1 Cor. 10:4); and 70–73 (on Abraham's seed in Galatians); and S. J. Hafemann, "The Glory and Veil of Moses in 2 Cor. 3:7–14," in *The Right Doctrine from the Wrong Texts?* ed. G. K. Beale (Grand Rapids: Baker, 1994), 295–309 (on the use of Exodus 32–34); etc.

crucified—the guiltless for the guilty. By presenting Jesus this way, Matthew was able to mount an argument for his readers that Jesus fulfilled the ideal that Israel was supposed to have reached but never did. Jesus is the true Israel.

Again, this is just one way of putting together Matthew's theological logic, and it is certainly up for debate. What is certain, however, is that Matthew's use of Hosea most definitely had an internal logic that was meaningful to his readers. Our obligation is to try to understand Matthew as he would have been understood by his original audience, not as we would like to understand him. (p. 134)

I would rather say that this "internal logic" suggested by Enns is also quite understandable to modern readers as a viable biblical-theological reading, consistent with the original contextual understanding of Hosea 11. Thus, I like this proposal by Enns. It shows that, whether Enns realizes it or not, in reality he is showing another interpretative approach besides grammatical-historical or non-contextual christotelic that New Testament writers could employ and that is not inconsistent with the original Old Testament context. One wonders what Enns's conclusions might be if he had tried more to explore other kinds of approaches like this one before making final overall conclusions about how the New Testament uses the Old.

Enns's list of "strange" uses are not that many; indeed, he lists only eight (pp. 114–42): Exodus 3:6 in Luke 20:27-40; Hosea 11:1 in Matthew 2:15; Isaiah 49:8 in 2 Corinthians 6:2; Abraham's seed in Galatians 3:16, 29; Isaiah 59:20 in Romans 11:26–27; Psalm 95:9–10 in Hebrews 3:7–11. Yet he claims that these unusual uses are "such a very common dimension of the New Testament" (p. 116). He needs to list many more texts in order to support this claim, and he needs to give representative surveys of the various interpretations of each passage in order to show their varying interpretations and whether some of them contest the oddity.[8]

---

8. For a listing of other purported "odd" uses and some counter responses, see Beale, "Did Jesus and the Apostles Preach the Right Doctrine from the Wrong Texts?" in *Right Doctrine from Wrong Texts*, 388–389. The same kind of responses could be given to the list adduced by Enns; e.g., see, among others, Enns's own above analysis of Hos. 11:1 in Matt. 2:15; on "seed" in Gal. 3:16, 29, see E.E. Ellis, *Paul's Use of the Old Testament*, 66–73, and, more recently, C. John Collins, "Galatians 3:16: What Kind of Exegete was Paul?" *TynBul* 54 (2003): 75–86; on Isa. 49:8 in 2 Cor. 6:2, see G. K. Beale, "The Old Testament Background of Reconciliation in 2 Corinthians 5–7 and Its Bearing on the Literary Problem of 2 Cor. 6:14–7:1," *NTS* 35 (1989): 550–81.

The reader is left to trust Enns's word for it. In contrast to Enns's assessment, there is significant past scholarship[9] and a recent large-scale, detailed work that argue that the dominant approach of New Testament writers was to develop Old Testament texts in various ways that emerge out of and are not inconsistent with the original intention of Old Testament writers.[10]

2) Options for Handling Problematic Uses of the Old Testament

Enns identifies four views of dealing with these problems (p. 115), the last of which he espouses and which some will find difficult to accept. He says:

> There are three popular options in evangelical scholarship for addressing the odd manner in which the New Testament authors use the Old Testament:
>
> 1) To argue, wherever possible, that the New Testament authors, despite appearances, were actually respecting the context of the Old Testament text they are citing. Although it may not be obvious to us, there must be some *legitimate* trigger in the Old Testament text, since no inspired writer would handle the Old Testament so irresponsibly. Careful examination will reveal that the New Testament's use of the Old Testament text is actually based in and is consistent with that Old Testament author's intention.
>
> 2) To concede that the New Testament author is not using the Old Testament text in a manner in which it was intended, but then to say that the New Testament author himself does not intend to "interpret" the text, only "apply" it. Since the New Testament does not intend to present us with hermeneutical models for how it handles the Old Testament, it poses no difficulty for us today.
>
> 3) To concede, on a variation of option 2, that the New Testament authors were not following the intention of the Old Testament authors, but to explain it as a function of apostolic authority. In other words, since they

---

9. In addition to works indicated throughout this essay, see also, among a number of others, e.g., R. T. France, *Jesus and the Old Testament* (Grand Rapids: Baker, 1984); S. J. Hafemann, *Paul, Moses and the History of Israel*, WUNT 81 (Tübingen: Mohr [Paul Siebeck], 1995); R. Watts, *Isaiah's New Exodus in Mark* (Grand Rapids: Baker, 2000); D. W. Pao, *Acts and the Isaianic New Exodus* WUNT 2.130 (Tübingen: Mohr Siebeck, 2000); J. Fekkes, *Isaiah and Prophetic Traditions in the Book of Revelation*, JSNTSup 93 (Sheffield: JSOT Press, 1994); G. K. Beale, *John's Use of the Old Testament in Revelation*, JSNTSup 166 (Sheffield: JSOT Press, 1999); and D. Mathewson, *A New Heaven and New Earth*, JSNTSup 238 (Sheffield Academic Press, 2003).

10. G. K. Beale and D. A. Carson, eds., *A Commentary on the New Testament Use of the Old Testament*, (Grand Rapids: Baker, 2007), 1,280 pp. (Of course, Enns would not be expected to be aware of the contents of this source, since this commentary was published after he wrote his book.)

were inspired, they could do as they pleased. We are not inspired, so we cannot follow their lead. (p. 115)

Enns responds to these three views in the following manner:

> In my opinion, all three of these views—although motivated by noble concerns to protect the Bible from abuse—will not stand up to close examination. As we go through the examples in this chapter, we will comment on these views here and there, but I will state my conclusions up front:
>
> (1) The New Testament authors were not engaging the Old Testament in an effort to remain consistent with the original context and intention of the Old Testament author.
>
> (2) They were indeed commenting on what the text *meant*.[11]
>
> (3) The hermeneutical attitude they embodied should be embraced and followed by the church today.
>
> To put it succinctly, the New Testament authors were explaining what the Old Testament means *in light of Christ's coming*. (pp. 115–16)

I believe, contrary to Enns, that view 1 can be held without embarrassment and can stand up to close examination, particularly when one remembers that there are other viable forms of relating the Old Testament to the New Testament than mere grammatical-historical exegesis. In fact, I would contend that it is the view that likely makes most sense of the data, without strained interpretations.

Again, to demonstrate the probability of his view, Enns would have to adduce many, many more examples of so-called non-contextual exegesis than he has. What is especially striking is Enns's claim that "the odd uses of the Old Testament by New Testament authors are such a very common dimension of the New Testament that it quickly becomes special pleading to argue otherwise" (p. 116). But must not "special pleading" remain in Enns's lap, since he does not attempt to adduce all the many examples of odd uses that he claims exist? Remember that he only adduces eight examples. He could have listed others, even if he did not have the space to discuss them. One can agree with Enns that the New Testament writers were interpreting the Old Testament "in light of

---

11. Note significantly here that Enns distinguishes "what the text meant" from "the original context and intention of the Old Testament author" that he mentions in his preceding point 1.

Christ's coming" (pp. 115–16), but this does not have to mean that they were contradicting the original meaning of the Old Testament.

3) Second Temple Judaism

Enns claims that the interpretative world of Second Temple Judaism is the primary context within which to understand the New Testament's use of the Old Testament (e.g., pp. 116–17). The problem with this is that the Jewish interpretative world is not uniform. There are some wild and crazy uses of the Old Testament, but there is also some good and sophisticated exegesis. Enns makes no acknowledgment of the two kinds of exegesis (biblical-theological and typological) that I refer to in the New Testament (above), which also is present in early Judaism. He assumes that the warp and woof of Jewish hermeneutics is not grammatical-historical or concerned with an Old Testament author's original intention or with Old Testament context (pp. 130–31). But he offers only a few examples that he believes support his view, again without entertaining other possible interpretative perspectives on these texts (pp. 121–31). His view, therefore, becomes a presupposition with little adduced evidence supporting it. Again, he could have listed more examples, even if he did not have the room to elaborate on them.

It is significant that Enns does acknowledge elsewhere some diversity in early Judaism:

> What has become clear from these [pseudepigraphical] texts is that Judaism in the centuries following the exile was a diverse phenomenon: there are *Judaisms* but no "Second Temple Judaism." This is important for both Christians and Jews to keep in mind. The line from biblical Israelite religion does not run straight to either of its two heirs, Judaism or Christianity. Rather, the Second Temple evidence in general shows a number of varied and competing trajectories, all of which claim biblical precedent.[12]

But then, in the same article, Enns goes on to deduce just what he does in his book and *WTJ* article: that Second Temple Judaism, while diverse in other respects, reflected a common hermeneutical approach that influenced the way New Testament writers interpreted the Old Testament:

> The ways in which both rabbinic Judaism and the NT authors interact with their Scripture did not arise in a vacuum. Rather, both demonstrate hermeneutical methods and conclusions demonstrable in many, many Second Temple texts. . . . In fact, similar hermeneutical trajectories were

---

12. P. Enns, "Pseudepigrapha," in *Dictionary of the Theological Interpretation of the Bible*, ed. K. Vanhoozer (Grand Rapids: Baker, 2005), 652.

already set within the Hebrew Scriptures (the Chronicler's interpretation of Israel's history; Daniel's interpretation of Jeremiah's seventy years as seventy "sevens" of years). How the rabbis and the apostles handled their Scripture must be understood within the context of earlier interpretative activity. . . . The Pseudepigrapha, therefore, contribute to the church's own understanding of its Bible, insofar as they outline general interpretative trajectories adopted by NT authors.[13]

In the context of the article, and especially the wider context of Enns's book and *WTJ* article, the main "interpretative trajectories" influencing New Testament writers were the non-contextual Jewish exegesis of the Old Testament and a dependence on Jewish interpretations of Old Testament history that had dubious historical claims. (With respect to the latter, Enns cites Acts 7:53; 1 Cor. 10:4; Gal. 3:19; and Heb. 2:2). Thus, while recognizing in a number of respects that Second Temple Judaism was composed of many "Judaisms," with regard to hermeneutics, Enns believes that there was a generally uniform non-contextual approach to Old Testament interpretation, which was the dominant influence on the New Testament approach.[14]

Enns needed to acknowledge that early Judaism was characterized by diverse exegetical methods or approaches. Jewish communities were likely not identical in their interpretative approach to the Old Testament (DSS, Philo, pre-AD 70 Pharisaic Palestinian Judaism, and some Jewish apocalyptic communities). Thus, it is more proper to speak of "Judaisms" or various Jewish communities when also speaking of Jewish interpretative approaches.

For example, Enns could have briefly evaluated David Instone Brewer's work that argues that pre-AD 70 Pharisaic exegesis attempted to find the literal meaning of Old Testament texts, though they did not always succeed at it.[15] In this respect, there may be a distinction in the interpretative approach of pre-AD 70 Judaism and that of later Judaism.[16] In addition, there is a strong strain in early Jewish apocalyptic texts that reveals a contextual awareness of the Old Testament contexts from which they

---

13. Ibid., 653.

14. The same focus is found in Enns, "Biblical Interpretation, Jewish," in *Dictionary of New Testament Background*, ed. C. A. Evans and S. E. Porter (Downers Grove, IL: InterVarsity, 2000), 159–65.

15. D. Instone Brewer, *Techniques and Assumptions in Jewish Exegesis before 70 C. E.*, TSAJ 30 (Tübingen: Mohr [Paul Siebeck], 1992).

16. Brewer's criteria for dating pre-AD 70 materials were not as clearly developed in his *Techniques and Assumptions* (11–13) as in his subsequently published *Prayer and Agriculture: Traditions of the Rabbis from the Era of the New Testament* I (Grand Rapids: Eerdmans, 2004), 38–40; see also the secondary sources cited therein by Brewer for further discussion of dating criteria.

cite.[17] Furthermore, when one thinks of Hillel's seven rules of (Jewish) interpretation, all of them in one way or another do not show a concern to twist the meaning of Old Testament texts but could well be compatible with a contextual interpretation of the Old Testament; e.g., none of the rules include allegory or a necessary atomistic interpretation of the Old Testament.[18]

In this respect, the sage assessment of Samuel Sandmel at least needs to be acknowledged; he concluded after long study of the relationship of Egyptian Judaism to Palestinian Judaism that "independent, parallel developments seem the better explanation than that of major dependency in either direction."[19] The first context for understanding the hermeneutical approach, as well as interpretative presuppositions, of New Testament writers is their own community under the influence of Jesus, then the Old Testament, and then Judaism. Both early Judaism and the New Testament are spurs off the Old Testament, rather than the New Testament's being primarily dependent on one branch of Jewish hermeneutics, though it was certainly aware of and in dialogue with sectors of Judaism.[20] Also, when one looks at early Jewish interpretation through the lens of a biblical-theological approach or a typological approach, the exegesis less often appears so twisted.[21]

17. See, e.g., G. K. Beale, *The Use of Daniel in Jewish Apocalyptic Literature and in the Revelation of St. John* (Lanham, Maryland: University Press of America, 1984), 12–153, and L. Hartman, *Prophecy Interpreted*, ConBNT 1 (Lund: C. W. K. Gleerup, 1966): 11–141; e.g., see his summaries on pp. 126 and 139, the latter of which where he makes a distinction between the contextual use of the Old Testament in apocalyptic Judaism but not in Qumran. Hartman sees the use of Daniel 7–12 in Mark 13 (and parallels) to reflect the pattern of the contextual use of the Old Testament in Jewish apocalyptic texts (ibid., 145–47, 158–59, 174, 207, 235).

18. See E. E. Ellis, *The Old Testament in Early Christianity* (Grand Rapids: Baker, 1991), 87–91, 130–32, for a convenient definition and examples of Hillel's seven rules. Rabbi Hillel died in AD 10.

19. S. Sandmel, *Philo of Alexandria: An Introduction* (Oxford: Oxford University Press, 1979), 133–34.

20. E.g., one New Testament heremeneutical presupposition that has its roots in the Old Testament is the notion of corporate solidarity or "the one and the many"; thus the idea that Jesus the Messiah corporately represents his people as true Israel is an outgrowth of the concept that Israel's kings represented their people (e.g., Israel was punished for David's representative sin of numbering the people [1 Chron. 21:1–17]). Likewise, the New Testament writers' presupposition that they were living in the inaugurated eschatological age comes directly out of the Old Testament prophecy that the messianic age was to be an "eschatological period" (e.g., Gen. 49:1, 8–12; Num. 24:14–18; Dan. 2:28–45; Isa. 2:2–4; 11:1–4; etc.). See further G. K. Beale, "Questions of Authorial Intent, Epistemology, and Presuppositions and Their Bearing on the Study of the Old Testament in the New: a Rejoinder to Steve Moyise," *IBS* 21 (1999): 169 and passim 151–80. On "typology" as a presuppositional hermeneutical approach also rooted in the Old Testament, see Ellis, *Paul's Use of the OT*, 131, as well as Beale, "Questions of Authorial Intent," 169.

21. E.g., Enns concludes that the use of the Old Testament in the Qumran commentary on Habakkuk (1QpHab) is very non-contextual and inconsistent with the original meaning (pp. 128–31), but it may well be that when this use is seen through a "typological" lens, the Qumran author's approach

One may disagree with these perspectives and attempt to argue against them, but why does Enns not even acknowledge them? Enns needed to adduce not only what he thinks are examples of non-contextual Jewish exegeses, but also cases where there are straightforward attempts to understand Old Testament texts, of which there are plenty of examples.

Therefore, exegetical approaches differed in Judaism, and to say there was a generally uniform approach that was non-contextual not only fails to acknowledge some of the key features of Second Temple exegesis, but it also produces an artificial reductionism and an artificial monolithic hermeneutical appearance. We may say that just as there were variegated views in Judaism on many things rather than one systematic theology, e.g., on the notion of the law in relation to faith, works, and final reward, so hermeneutics was variegated. Thus, there is not one dominant pattern in Second Temple Jewish exegesis that predetermines how the New Testament authors must behave hermeneutically.

In contrast to Enns, a good argument can be made that the interpretative method of the New Testament is rooted in the Old Testament's viable interpretative use of earlier Old Testament texts and that various early Jewish communities practiced an interpretative approach shaped by the Old Testament's exegetical method, including the early Jewish-Christian community. True, they share some things with other Jewish communities, but they also differ significantly. C. H. Dodd, no evangelical, contended that the greatest influence on the apostles' method was Jesus, whom Dodd contended had a very contextual approach to understanding how the Old Testament related to him and his redemptive work.[22]

In fact, even granting for the sake of argument that there was a monolithic non-contextual Jewish hermeneutic, could not Jesus, who in other ways came to break a lot of the traditional taboos of Jewish tradition, have also come with an approach to biblical interpretation formed more by the Old Testament's use of the Old Testament than by that of contemporary Judaism?[23]

This is not to have a fundamentalist approach to the Old in the New, or one that is too conservative. In fact, among others, some of the leading contemporary German scholars who work in this area affirm the same

---

to the Old Testament may be like that in a number of New Testament texts that understand the Old Testament typologically.

22. C. H. Dodd, *According to the Scriptures* (Welwyn, Herts: James Nisbet, 1952).

23. Enns would likely respond here that later Old Testament authors did not contextually interpret earlier Old Testament writings, but, again, he produces little evidence to substantiate this claim, focusing only on the interpretation of Jeremiah's "seventy years" by Daniel 9 (pp. 117–20), one of the thorniest passages in all of the Old Testament to interpret!

methodological approach to the relation of Jewish exegetical procedures and that of Paul. For example, note the comments of Hans Hübner:

> In fact, it has turned out by the preliminary work to this biblical study of the New Testament, that, for example, Paul through his exegetical procedure modified quite strangely what we know as Jewish methods of interpretation. Actually, concerning Paul as an exegete, and to be precise to understand him as a Christian exegete, who understood himself as the reader inspired by the Spirit and interpreter of the scripture, the characteristic of his exegesis must be brought out. And this characteristic is not deduced just when one takes Jewish methodology as the key of understanding. Its modification by Paul is crucial for his theological acquaintance with the scriptures!

> This fact is clearly recognized also in that work, which, today, is the standard work on Paul and the Old Testament, and which, therefore, has replaced Otto Michel's book in this function, namely the Mainzer *Habilitationsschrift* by Dietrich Alex Koch, *Die Schrift als Zeuge des Evangeliums, Untersuchungen zur Verwendung und zum Verständnis der Schrift bei Paulus.* [Eng. trans., *The Scripture as a Witness to the Gospel: Investigations into the Use and into the Understanding of the Scriptures by Paul.*] Koch identifies divergences between the Jewish-Hellenistic and Rabbinic interpretation of scripture, on the one hand, and that of Paul, on the other hand. Therefore, he arrives at a correct methodological principle: "One is dependent, therefore, regarding the methods of interpretation of scripture which must be assumed for Paul, on conclusions from his own letters." So also, the acquaintance of the New Testament authors with the scripture should be analyzed in the Mesolegomena [the following volume of Hübner's work] first of all, independently from the Jewish methods of interpretation, and there, where it is meaningful, where it is necessary because of the understanding of the procedure of a New Testament author, the Jewish methodology will also be discussed.[24]

4) A Hermeneutical Grid

Enns says conservative evangelicals have a hermeneutical grid that they "impose" on the text through which to read the Old Testament in the New (p. 156), but Enns also has his own version of a christoltelic systematic grid. The question is which grid best explains the evidence. Both Enns and his purported opponents—"conversation partners"—use so-called modern reason to investigate the Bible. The key is which

---

24. H. Hübner, *Biblische Theologie des Neuen Testaments*, Band 1: *Prolegomena* (Goettingen: Vandenhoeck and Ruprecht, 1990), 258–59.

hermeneutical grid best makes reasonable sense of the majority of the biblical data.

5) Basis for Jewish Traditions in the New Testament

Enns comments on Jewish traditions that are reflected in the New Testament (pp. 143–51), which, for the most part, he implies have a precarious historical basis. He gives the impression that the New Testament is permeated with such traditions, but he provides only six examples. With so few examples, readers will not be persuaded that such Jewish traditions are part of the warp and woof of the New Testament. He could, at least, have listed more examples, even if he did not choose to discuss them.

Most of the examples Enns cites are not problematic with respect to questions of historical reliability. Many of the traditions may be understood by recollecting that there was oral tradition that arose together with written Old Testament Scripture, and some of what Judaism and the New Testament reflect may well be this, or at least prior traditions, some of which may well not be of fictitious origin but have historical roots, or they may be understood as mere interpretative expansions of the Old Testament, perhaps based on Jewish exegetical tradition.[25] Though Enns leaves the impression that these examples are historically problematic, the ultimate sources of these Jewish traditions are so speculative that it is not wise to make decisions definitively one way or another about them; e.g., to say they are definitely legend, fiction, or non-historical would be a speculative conclusion.

It is too speculative for Enns to say, as in the case of Paul's reference to the "rock that followed" in 1 Corinthians 10:4, that "the brevity of the allusion [by Paul to the Jewish tradition about the following rock] bespeaks the fact that it must have been in wide circulation already in Paul's day."[26] Although it is possible, it is not as probable as Enns maintains. The brief allusion could just as well be to Paul's biblical-theological understanding of Yahweh's identification with the "rock" that "walked after" Israel. No argument should be based primarily on the brevity of the allusion.

Enns concludes that Paul's allusion to the "rock which followed" in 1 Corinthians 10:4 is dependent on a Jewish tradition about a well

---

25. Cf. R. Bauckham, "The Liber Antiquitatum Biblicarum of Pseudo-Philo and the Gospels as 'Midrash,'" in R. T. France and D. Wenham, eds., *Gospel Perspectives* 3 (Sheffield: JSOT Press, 1983), 33–76.

26. Enns, "The 'Moveable Well' in 1 Cor. 10:4: An Extrabiblical Tradition in an Apostolic Text," *BBR* 6 (1996): 32.

that followed Israel around in the wilderness.[27] There is, however, only one Jewish reference to this tradition that plausibly is dated around the first century AD, but even part of this reference is clouded by textual uncertainty.[28] Thus, it is difficult to be sure what form of the legend existed in Paul's time.[29]

27. This section of Enns's book is based on his above article in *BBR*, 23–38.

28. The lone Jewish source is Pseudo-Philo, which is dated by the majority of scholars as early as the first century AD, though there is some debate even about that (see Bauckham, "Liber Antiquitatum Biblicarum of Pseudo-Philo and the Gospels as 'Midrash,'" 33, and, more recently, B. N. Fisk, *Do You Not Remember? Scripture, Story and Exegesis in the Rewritten Bible of Pseudo-Philo*, JSPSup 37 [Sheffield: Sheffield Academic Press, 2001], 34–40). Enns adduced three texts in Pseudo-Philo that he believes together support the idea that a well-shaped rock followed Israel in the wilderness (Pseudo-Philo 10:7; 11:15; 20:8); however, since 20:8 does not explicitly refer to a well or water that "follows," only 10:7 (God "brought forth a well of water to follow them") and 11:15 could clearly support the idea, the latter reading: "*and the water* of Marah became sweet. And it [the well or the water] followed them in the wilderness forty years and went up to the mountain with them and went down into the plains." However, while some very good manuscripts (the Δ-group of mss. [A, K, P]) have "it followed," the majority of manuscripts (the π-group of mss. [H, R, W, X, Y, Z, S, Ad, D, E, V, M, B, C, O, G]), which are also manuscripts of very good, indeed almost equal, authority with the Δ-group of manuscripts, have "the Lord [*Dominus*] followed," on which see the critical edition of the Latin text of Pseudo-Philo, D. J. Harrington and J. Cazeaux, eds., *Pseudo–Philon: Les Antiquités Bibliques*, vol. 1, Sources Chrétiennes series 229 (Paris: Éditions du Cerf, 1976), 124; see pp. 53–57 for the relative values of both ms. groups. Though Harrington does not prefer "Lord" in his English translation ("Pseudo-Philo," in *The Old Testament Pseudepigrapha* 2, ed. J. H. Charlesworth [Garden City: Doubleday, 1985], 319), in fact, the quality of the external evidence for both readings is almost equal. It is difficult to determine the original reading. Whichever is original, the variant could have been caused possibly by an unintentional error or, more probably, an intentional one. The more difficult reading, and thus more likely original, in the light of the clear reference to the "following well" in 10:7, would appear to be "Lord" (a scribe with 10:7 clearly in mind would tend to want to harmonize 11:15 with 10:7, thus deleting "Lord," so that the well or the water from the well is viewed as the subject of the "following"). This could be debated, but our intention here is merely to point out the textual uncertainty. If "Lord" is the correct reading, then the identification of the "following well" in 10:7 (as well as, presumably, in 20:8) would apparently be the Lord himself in 11:15 (who, accordingly, would also be identified with "the water" in the preceding clause of 11:15), which may have been inspired by the close identification of the rock from which water came in Ex. 17:6 with the phrase "is the Lord among us?" in 17:7 (on which see further the next note below [n. 29] for the rationale). Put another way, if "Lord" is original, then the "following well" in 10:7 and the "water" in the preceding clause of 11:15 could well be viewed as metaphorical for the "Lord" in 11:15, which would take the legendary punch out of the evidence. At the least, even if "Lord" is unoriginal, the variant came to represent part of the exegetical tradition that may well have been existent in Paul's day and would need to be reckoned as part of the possible background for Paul's reference in 1 Cor. 10:4. It is noteworthy to observe that the only early texts (presuming, for the sake of argument, an original "Lord" in Pseudo-Philo 11:15 or that this reading was early) that identify the water from the rock with the divine presence is Pseudo-Philo 10:7 and 11:15 and 1 Cor. 10:4 (remembering Paul's divine identification of Christ in 1 Cor. 8:6), which could point to a link between this Jewish tradition and Paul, but in a different way than Enns contends. Unfortunately, Enns does not mention this significant textual uncertainty in his *BBR* article.

29. The other references to a "following well" are in the later midrashic and targumic literature, though Enns still contends that "some form of the legend apparently did exist" earlier ("Moveable Well," 25), which is expressed with much less conviction than his conclusion about Paul's knowledge of this legendary tradition in the book: "I think it is beyond reasonable doubt" that "Paul's com-

Furthermore, Paul does not refer to a well. He may well be doing a biblical-theological exegesis of Exodus 14 to 17 in the light of Psalm 78:14–20 (e.g., "he split the rocks . . . and gave them abundant drink . . . he struck the rock so that waters gushed out") and 78:35 ("God was their rock"), the latter of which appears to identify God with the "rock" of Psalm 78:15–16, 20.[30]

But what does Enns himself mean when he says that Paul is dependent on this Jewish "tradition"? One must refer to his article "The Moveable Well" to which he himself refers the reader for further discussion. In his *BBR* article, though Enns says that he prefers to use the phrase "exegetical tradition" or merely "tradition" instead of "fable" or "legend,"[31] he is not uncomfortable referring to Paul's conscious dependence on this spurious tradition of the moveable well as "legend." Elsewhere in his article, he uses "legend" in place of his preferred "tradition." For example, he affirms that Paul believed the legend "was really the case" and that he was "relaying information that for him was trustworthy," though, of course, it was, in reality, "legendary."[32] In this respect, he says, "In fact,

---

ment be understood as another example of this tradition" (p. 151). In this light, a more judicious assessment is that it is difficult to be sure what form of the legend existed in Paul's time. Note also some of the differences between Paul's reference and that of later Judaism: (1) he identifies the rock as the Messiah, (2) he does not use the language of a "well," and (3) he refers to the "rock" from which they drank as a *spiritual* rock from which "spiritual drink" was obtained (1 Cor. 10:4), not a literal rock, significant differences with the later Jewish legend, which appears to see a literal traveling well that "followed" Israel. Incidentally, note also that the idea of God in association with a rock that followed Israel in the wilderness is not unique to the later Jewish midrashic literature but occurs also in Ex. 14:19 in relation to Ex. 17:5–7, where the presence of the rock from which drinking water came is also interpreted to be affirming that or is directly linked to the phrase "the Lord is among us" in response to the people's doubt about this. In this respect, note the "following" concept in Ex. 14:19: "The angel of God, who had been going before the camp of Israel, moved and *went behind them*; and the pillar of cloud moved from before them and stood behind them." And the presence of God continues to move between the Egyptians and the Israelites as the latter go through the sea. Note similarly that Isa. 52:12 and 58:8 allude to Ex. 14:19 and prophesy that in the new, second exodus God would also be Israel's "rear guard." Thus, in light of the fact that Ex. 17:6 very closely associates God with the "rock" (as does Psalm 78 [see below]), it does not take much ingenuity to see how Paul could posit that Christ was a "following rock" in his preincarnate divine existence as the "angel of the Lord." Paul may be doing intratextual and intertextual exegesis, which is a form of biblical theology. Thus, Enns's attempt to say that the "following" aspect is unique to the Jewish well legend is not correct, since both linguistically and conceptually the notion occurs in the Old Testament itself.

30. As we have seen, commentators like Ellis, *Paul's Use of the Old Testament*, 66–70, see Paul using a typological hermeneutic in 1 Cor. 10:4 and not being dependent on the Jewish legend.

31. "The 'Moveable Well,'" p. 29, n. 14.

32. Ibid., 37. Also he says, "the following rock, however, 'clearly brings him [Paul] into connection with the Palestinian legend'" (following the position of H. S. J. Thackery [ibid., 25, n. 8]). Likewise, on p. 33 Enns affirms, "I would push this one step further, that for Paul such 'Jewish lore' actually represented his own understanding of the event"; recall here that Enns in the immediate context refers to this as legendary lore that does not correspond to historical reality.

there is no indication in any of the examples listed [including 1 Cor. 10:4] that suggest that the 'legendary' material about to be introduced into these otherwise authoritative works [of the apostolic writers] were of lesser value."[33] That Enns believes that Paul unconsciously absorbed this legend and believed it was true is also clear from a question that he poses and to which he gives a positive answer:

> After all, if at the very climax of redemptive history, the Holy Spirit can do no better than communicate the supreme Good News through *pedestrian and uninspired Jewish legends*, in what sense can we claim that the New Testament revelation is special, distinct, and unique? The question, however, can be put on its head: on what basis ought we to assume that Paul's understanding of the Old Testament was unique? To put it another way, is there anything about the nature of God's revelation itself that necessarily demands its uniqueness over against the environment in which that revelation is given?[34]

Enns answers *no* to each of these questions. The New Testament revelation was not "unique" to its environment, which believed in "legends," though he would certainly say that the New Testament writers believed that Christ and the God of the Old and New Testaments were, respectively, the true Messiah and true God, in contrast to the gods of other religions. He also assumes that divine revelation is communicated through these legends. He provides a fuller answer to the above questions a little later:

> To affirm that Paul's "the rock that followed them" is an unconscious transmission of a popular exegetical tradition ["legend" elsewhere in his article] does not compromise revelation but boldly affirms it at its very heart. Scripture was revealed in time and space, so it bears the marks of that historical quality at various levels [including, Enns means, the level of the presence of legend].[35]

33. Ibid., 37. Why he puts legendary in quotation marks is not clear, but quotation marks are not the ordinary stylistic convention to indicate a caveat; so we take no caveat intended here. See also p. 32, where Enns says that Paul "was simply talking about the biblical story [of the rock in the wilderness] in the only way he knows how, in accordance with the way he (and his audience as well) had received it" (i.e., we understand Enns to mean that they had received it as legend). Likewise, he quotes and disagrees with the following views of some scholars who deny that 1 Cor. 10:4 is based on legend: "Godet makes explicit an apologetic motive by arguing that 'the most spiritual of the apostles' could hardly have 'alluded to so ridiculous a fable.' . . . C. Hodge comments that the presence of this tradition in 1 Cor. 10:4 would make 'the apostle responsible for this Jewish fable, and is inconsistent with his divine authority.'" Enns's point throughout the article is that dependence on legend is not inconsistent with divine authority.

34. Ibid., 35 (my italics).

35. Ibid., 36. See also p. 32, where Enns makes the same point.

For Enns, the New Testament is still authoritative, even in those places where legend is present. Readers will have to decide whether Enns has made a convincing case about the influence of the moveable well legend upon Paul. I, for one, am not persuaded. But this, for Enns, is only one example of the kind of legendary material that exists in the New Testament, and, as we have labored to show elsewhere, also in the Old Testament.

Conservative commentators have not been averse to observing "myth" or "legend" in the Old or New Testaments. But when it has been observed, it has been fairly clear to most conservative scholars that the biblical writers refer to such false traditions in order to conduct a polemic against them and to repudiate false religious tradition (its gods and their titles or attributes; its way of salvation, etc.),[36] as well as to reflect that even pagan peoples have a perception of truth through general revelation or access to very ancient traditions, which have been integrated in flawed ways into their false religion[37] (Rom. 1:19–23 testifies to this). Likewise, biblical writers did not always directly counter ancient Near Eastern concepts but sometimes used them in creative ways, though still revised in significant manner by special revelation, without an unconscious absorption of myth.[38]

But Enns is saying something quite different: that Paul in 1 Corinthians 10:4 did not distinguish his own beliefs from the false beliefs of the Jewish culture around him. I find this unlikely, especially because I am unconvinced that he has made his case that Paul, indeed, is dependent on Jewish legend. In addition, I am not persuaded by Enns's thesis at points throughout his book that God communicates truth through such full-blown myth unconsciously held by Old Testament writers. I have elaborated on this elsewhere.[39]

The Implications of Enns's Book for Providing Guidelines for Biblical Interpretation

What are some of the implications of Enns's views on the use of the Old Testament in the New? In commenting on the ramifications of his

36. For many examples in the New Testament, see G. K. Beale, "Biblical Faith and Other Religions in New Testament Theology," in *Biblical Faith and Other Religions,* ed. D. W. Baker (Grand Rapids: Kregel, 2004), 79–105.

37. See *Inspiration and Incarnation,* 41, where Enns himself acknowledges something close to this possibility.

38. For elaboration and expansion of the ideas in this paragraph, see my review of the other chapters of Enns's book in "Myth, History, and Inspiration: a Review Article of Peter Enns, *Inspiration and Incarnation: Evangelicals and the Problem of the Old Testament,*" *JETS* 49 (2006).

39. On which see my reviews of the other chapters of Enns's book in chaps. 1–2, where I contend that there are hermeneutical, theological, epistemological, and logical problems with such a view.

conclusions, Enns offers the following reflections about preachers, who, he hopes, will hear what he says:

> I see regularly the almost unbearable burden we place on our preachers by expecting them, in a week's time, to read a passage, determine its meaning, and then communicate it effectively. The burden of "getting it right" can sometimes be discouraging and hinder effective ministry. I would rather think of biblical interpretation as a path we walk, a pilgrimage we take, whereby the longer we walk and take in the surrounding scenes, the more people we stop and converse with along the way, and the richer our interpretation will be. (p. 162)

In developing this thought further he says, "There do not seem to be any clear rules or guidelines to prevent us from taking this process [of biblical interpretation] too far. But again, this is why the metaphor of journey or pilgrimage is so appealing" (p. 171).

This conclusion comes on the heels of his conclusion that the interpretative method of the New Testament writers is not sensitive to the contextual ideas of Old Testament authors' original intentions. He thinks we should model our interpretative method on that of the New Testament (p. 170). But, according to his view of apostolic exegesis, this means there are really no rules for good interpretation, and, carried to its logical practical conclusion, it suggests that there is no method of good exegesis that ultimately can be a reasonable guard against preachers not "getting it right." Enns's following comment is also consistent with such a conclusion:

> A christotelic coherence is not achieved by following a few simple rules of exegesis. It is to be sought after over a long period of time, in community with other Christians, with humility and patience. Biblical interpretation is . . . a path we walk rather than a fortress we defend. (p. 170)

Ultimately, the clear implication of Enns's position is that there is no interpretative approach to restrain our eisegetical tendencies. He does acknowledge that "what helps prevent (but does not guarantee against) such flights of [interpretative] fancy is grammatical-historical exegesis" (p. 159). But then he significantly qualifies this:

> However much we might regard certain Second Temple interpretive methods and traditions as unworkable in our modern context, we still cannot simply fill the void by adopting the grammatical-historical methods as the default and exclusively normative hermeneutic for modern Christians. Why? To lift up grammatical-historical exegesis as the ultimate standard

means we must either (1) distance ourselves from the christotelic hermeneutic of the apostles or (2) mount arguments showing that apostolic
hermeneutics is actually grounded in the grammatical-historical meaning of the Old Testament, and that all this talk about the Second Temple
context is just nonsense that can be safely avoided. (p. 159)[40]

Of course, by this point in the book the reader will understand why
Enns says that neither of these is a viable option. At the end of the day,
it appears evident that for Enns the christotelic hermeneutic is accorded
pride of place as the more determinative hermeneutical approach rather
than the grammatical-historical, since the latter approach by itself "is
not a Christian understanding in the apostolic sense" (p. 159). Consequently, "getting it [biblical interpretation] right" (p. 162), i.e., attempting to understand an Old Testament author's authorial intention,
in a particular pericope of Scripture is for Enns not the ultimate proper
focus, even though, as we have seen, he still wants to affirm some kind
of important, though subordinate, and exceptional role for grammatical-historical exegesis.

What then does one make of Paul's admonition to Timothy, "Be diligent
to present yourself approved to God as a workman who does not need to
be ashamed, accurately handling the word of truth" (2 Tim. 2:15; likewise 1 Tim. 4:15–16)? James says that "teachers . . . will incur a stricter
judgment" (3:1). Presumably, Enns would say that the New Testament
writers' standards of "accurately handling the word of truth" are different
from ours. So, there *is* a great responsibility incumbent upon preachers
and teachers of God's Word. Should it be alleviated in the way that Enns
advocates or in relativizing the Pauline admonitions for the modern church
by affirming that they were uniquely applicable to an ancient Christian
mindset? While paying attention to some of Enns's admonitions, should
not pastors be encouraged to rest on God's grace and realize that no one
has an exhaustive grasp on comprehending God's Word? Should not
those with the gift of teaching have the ability and obligation to grasp
sufficiently, more richly, and, therefore, definitely, what God would have
them convey to his people Sunday after Sunday?

In this respect, it is unfortunate that the conclusions of Enns's book
have led him to such a pessimistic pedagogical and homiletical conclusion.

---

40. The same qualification is made on p. 160, where he says that he does "not mean to make sweeping statements against exegetical methods or grammatical-historical exegesis. But . . . we can only
conclude that there must be more to Christian biblical interpretation than uncovering the original
meaning of an Old Testament passage." In context, he emphasizes the latter over the former. Likewise,
on p. 154 he says the "grammatical-historical reading" is "absolutely vital," but again he makes
similar qualifications as above. So similarly, see p. 117.

Enns's book is a good example of the fact that one's exegesis has practical application, an application in this case that is not a felicitous one. To repeat, if Enns had allowed for other interpretative approaches (such as a biblical-theological approach,[41] a typological approach,[42] etc.) beside the polarized grammatical-historical vs. the christotelic, then he might not have been so constrained to make the kind of conclusions he did.

This problem of method is compounded by the fact that Enns's examples of non-contextual exegesis in the New Testament include only his view of each example; he does not cite or interact with other representative views that differ from his own.

The Implications of Enns's Book for Providing Guidelines for Doing Biblical Theology

The significance of this discussion should not be limited to exegetical method, because it also has a bearing on how to do biblical theology, since the use of the Old Testament in the New is commonly considered essential to understanding the theological relation of the testaments, which many scholars have acknowledged.[43] If New Testament writers did not interpret Old Testament passages *in some manner* commensurate to the original meaning, then a hiatus remains between the way they understood the Old Testament and its theology and the way Old Testament authors understood their own writings, both exegetically *and* theologically.

Geerhardus Vos, himself, that great biblical-theological icon of the old Princeton-Westminster tradition, affirmed that at the heart of biblical theology is "the organic progress . . . from seed-form to the attainment of full growth" and that "in the seed form the minimum of indispens-

---

41. There is not space to elaborate on a definition of this here. Suffice it to say that a biblical-theological approach attempts to interpret texts in the light of their broader literary context, their broader redemptive-historical epoch of which they are a part, and to interpret earlier texts from earlier epochs, attempting to explain them in the light of progressive revelation to which earlier scriptural authors would not have had access. So, one aspect of biblical theology is the reading of texts in an intratextual and intertextual manner in a way not ultimately distorting their original meaning, though perhaps creatively developing it. As noted earlier, I believe that an example of such an approach can be found in, among other places, my recent book *The Temple and the Church's Mission* as well as Enns's comments above on how Matthew might have understood Hosea 11:1.

42. For the different definitions of such an approach and literature discussing it, see Beale, *The Right Doctrine from Wrong Texts?* 313–71, 387–404. (My own view is aligned with the articles by G. P. Hugenberger, F. Foulkes, and my own last article in the volume.)

43. E.g., see G. Hasel, *Current Issues in NT Theology : Basic Issues in the Current Debate* (Grand Rapids: Eerdmans, 1978); D. L. Baker, *Two Testaments, One Bible: A Study of Some Modern Solutions to the Theological Problem of the Relationship between the Old and New Testaments* (Downers Grove, IL: InterVarsity, 1977); G. Reventlow, *Problems of Biblical Theology in the Twentieth Century* (London: SCM, 1986). So also R. Longenecker, "'Who Is the Prophet Talking About?' Some Reflections on the New Testament's Use of the Old," *Them* 13 (1987): 1.

able knowledge was already present" for the revelation later in the Old Testament and subsequently in the New.[44] While the later progressive revelatory apple tree might appear different from its earlier biblical seed form, Vos would maintain that they are, nevertheless, organically linked and that, ultimately, the latter develops naturally from the former, just as happens in nature between seeds and their later organic developments.

Enns's perspective cuts the cords of this organic revelation, so that later biblical writers do not develop the original ideas of earlier biblical writers. At best, he can posit that broad Old Testament themes are picked up by New Testament writers. Even in this respect, however, he cannot see such themes to be rooted in a collection of Old Testament texts, since he does not believe that the early Christian writers could perceive the original thematic intention of Old Testament texts, even apparently collections of such texts. Indeed, we may ask, in what sense would a New Testament author perceive an Old Testament theme if it were not originally present and perceivable in several texts throughout the Old Testament? Accordingly, it seems that it would be difficult for Enns to say that broad themes from the Old Testament are relatable to the New.

Consequently, it appears that Enns's approach on the Old in the New will necessitate developing a new approach to biblical theology, which will be quite different methodologically from that of Vos and other similar approaches. Indeed, it would appear that biblical theology as conceived over the past century in conservative scholarly circles is now outmoded, if Enns's perspective is correct.

Conclusion

Enns answers the question "did Jesus and the apostles preach the right doctrine from the wrong texts?" with a resounding "yes," and he says that God's people today should do the same. I have given reasons why I disagree with this assessment.

I have written this chapter in some depth because the issues are significant for Christian faith, and popular readers may not have the requisite tools and background to evaluate the thorny issues that Enns's book addresses.[45] I have also written for a scholarly evangelical audience, since Enns's book appears to be secondarily intended for them[46] and, as we have observed, there have been different evaluations of Enns's book by such an audience.

---

44. G. Vos, *Biblical Theology* (Grand Rapids: Eerdmans, 1948), 7.

45. Note where Enns indicates his purpose in addressing a more popular audience (e.g., pp. 13, 15, 168), though these statements do not exclude a scholarly audience.

46. E.g., recall that the publishers distributed complimentary copies to biblical scholars at the recent November 2005 Institute for Biblical Research Meeting.

Many of Enns's assumptions are wide-ranging and debatable and the primary evidence of Judaism and the New Testament selective, as are the secondary sources he cites,[47] so that it is hard to do justice in evaluating this fourth chapter of his book in a brief manner.

Enns's perspectives on the use of the Old Testament in the New Testament are, no doubt, generally representative of others, including scholars within the evangelical academic guild. So, I am grateful for Enns's further elaboration and development of this approach, even though I have registered disagreement with it. As we all interact with varying perspectives, we are bound to examine our own views in more depth, which is a healthy enterprise, for which I am also thankful to Enns for inspiring me to do. I have been sharpened by reading and interacting with this part of his stimulating book.[48]

Nevertheless, can one hold to Enns's view that Jesus and the apostles taught the right doctrine from the wrong Old Testament texts without diluting the nature of the divine inspiration of the Bible? Is not the purpose of the divine authority of much of the Old Testament nullified if the New Testament writers often could not perceive sufficiently the original inspired meaning? Is it consistent with the divine inspiration of the New Testament to believe that Jesus and the apostles typically used flawed methods of interpretation in interpreting the Old Testament? Can such an interpretative method be neatly distinguished from its resulting interpretations without significantly watering down the notion of inerrancy? Can one hold to a viable view of biblical inspiration while believing that biblical authors like Paul appealed to legends (naïvely believing they were historically true)?

I believe the answer to all those questions is a resounding *no*. It is certainly possible to hold such views and still maintain some kind of nebulous concept of biblical authority, but to do so is to erode the meaning of biblical inerrancy and authority down to doctrinal insignificance. Accordingly, the doctrine of biblical inerrancy and authority dies the death of too many qualifications.

---

47. Enns does cite bibliography for "further reading" at the end of his chapter on the Old Testament in the New Testament (with very brief abstracts), but he does not engage them evaluatively in the body of his chapter; indeed, very few of the nineteen sources listed clearly offer contrasting views of the biblical texts that he discusses. This often leaves readers with the impression that Enns's perspective and evidence for his arguments is the primary or only viable perspective or evidence. The only way readers would learn otherwise is by doing some research and reading in secondary literature.

48. I am grateful to several scholars for reading and commenting on this article. I am especially indebted to Peter Spychalla, my doctoral student, for reading and proofing the article, and particularly for discussing with and obtaining for me the critical edition of the Latin text of Pseudo-Philo referred to in note 28, concerning the textual variant in Pseudo-Philo 11:15.

CHAPTER FOUR

Is a Traditional Evangelical View of Scripture's Authority Compatible with Recent Developments in the Study of the Old Testament in the New? *Part 2*

Dr. Enns responded to my review of his lengthy chapter on the use of the Old Testament in the New with his "Response to Professor Greg Beale" (*Them* 32 [2007], 5–13). I then replied to his response, which comprises most of the present chapter, with minor revisions. My reply appeared originally as "A Surrejoinder to Peter Enns on the Use of the Old Testament in the New" (*Them* 32 [2007], 14–25).

Mitch Kim, my research assistant, offers the following summary of Enns's response to my critique of his use of the Old Testament in the New, which I again requested him to do for the sake of achieving more objectivity.[1]

Peter Enns's Response to Greg Beale's Review in the Preceding Chapter

Peter Enns begins his response to Beale: "It seems clear to me from reading both of Prof. Beale's reviews . . . that his disagreements with me are not merely academic, but touch on issues that are important to him for the very faith we both share."[2] Such deep-seated disagreements

---

1. The reader should feel free to consult Peter Enns's full, original response, which is being summarized here.
2. P. Enns, "Response to Professor Greg Beale," *Them* 32 (2007): 5–13. From here in this chapter, page numbers parenthetically noted in text indicate this article.

are evident from Beale's comments on the "'pessimistic pedagogical conclusions' of [Enns's] approach to apostolic hermeneutics." Enns strives to continue the dialogue about such disagreements with mutual respect, emphasizing "what unites us both is an earnest engagement of Scripture as evangelicals." Consequently, the differences Enns has with Beale are not so much on "basic theological principles, namely the inspiration and authority of Scripture, but in how the rubber of those principles meets the sometimes bumpy road of historical analysis and the realities of our canon" (p. 5). In this light, Enns articulates five basic areas of disagreement and then explores some implications of these disagreements.

1) *Need to Acknowledge Different Points of View.* Enns maintains the importance of the popular focus of his work. Beale charges that Enns's neglect of extensive engagement with differing opinions forces his readers to trust Enns's word for it. However, Enns contends that his annotated bibliographies provide the reader with the means to explore differing perspectives, and his popular focus precludes such involved discussion in knotty issues without compromising his "apologetic purpose and accessible style" (p. 6). Nevertheless, lay readers, while supportive on the whole of his approach, have still provoked dialogue, showing that they "may not be as easily swayed as we academics sometimes think" (p. 6).

2) *Hermeneutical Diversity in Second Temple Judaism.* While Beale correctly asserts that Second Temple Judaism is not a hermeneutical monolith, the midrashic dimension of Second Temple hermeneutics is, according to Enns, "far, far more pervasive than any concern to be 'sensitive' to the Old Testament context." While the rules of Hillel were not the same as, say, Qumran pesher, these rules also were not intended to bring ancient readers closer to a reading that Enns says is "compatible with a contextual interpretation of the OT." Rather, he says, these rules "guided Jews in extracting safe and useful teaching from the Bible for the life of the people gathered around the primacy of divine Torah." Also, the Mishnah and Talmud indicate that these rules could even result in "conflicting and contradictory interpretations." Indeed, the "correct" conclusion was determined by the needs of the interpretive community and not the reading which was more "compatible with contextual interpretation of the Old Testament." Furthermore, Enns says, a "broad but accurate sketch" of Second Temple hermeneutics must span more than rabbinic interpretation but also encompass the pseudepigrapha, Apocrypha, and the Dead Sea Scrolls (pp. 6–7).

"Midrash" seems to describe adequately the general hermeneutical tenor of Second Temple hermeneutics. The diversity of *Jubilees*, the pesher on Habakkuk, the Wisdom of Solomon, and Pseudo-Philo's *Liber antiquita-*

tum biblicarum is nonetheless unified by a hermeneutical posture that Enns says seeks "(1) to mine Scripture for hidden, richer meanings in order to hear God speak once again in a community's present circumstances, and (2) to preserve these interpretive traditions for successive generations." Enns labels this hermeneutical posture "odd" in the sense that it is "not operating from the interpretive standards we take for granted when we open our Bibles and read" (pp. 7–8).

3) *The Question of "Consistency" with the Old Testament.* According to Enns, describing Second Temple hermeneutics with terms such as *twist* or *distort*, as Beale does, "erects at the outset a wall of hostility between the NT and its environment" (p. 8). Such language passes judgment upon the hermeneutical conventions of that era on the basis of the present. Furthermore, Enns argues, Beale recognizes that New Testament exegesis cannot always be explained by grammatical-historical exegesis, yet he defends such exegesis by asserting that (1) such hermeneutics is not as odd as some may think, and (2) that the New Testament is on the whole more contextually bound to original Old Testament meanings than to other Second Temple texts.

Enns has already noted his disagreements on the first point; he goes on to say that the second point further reveals in Beale "a palpable tension between acknowledging the similarities between the New Testament and its environment and wishing to maintain some distance between them." Enns believes that Beale's language seems unnecessarily defensive, even protectionist, as "we read that the NT authors are 'not inconsistent' with the OT context, or their interpretations do 'not contravene' that context, while also being willing to 'creatively develop' that OT passage." Enns affirms that the terminology of consistency, sensitivity, and context must be understood historically within the framework of *ancient* interpreters, and not in the light of our own modern framework.

Enns continues, "Beale's terms suggest an uncritical adoption of etic hermeneutical categories, and so we are presented with a picture of apostolic hermeneutics where it is assumed that the NT writers share Prof. Beale's concerns with matters of contextual exegesis" (pp. 8–9). Against Beale, the complexity of apostolic hermeneutics cannot be reduced to an attempt to remain sensitive to the Old Testament context, but rather it must be understood primarily in light of the climactic revelatory event of the person and work of Christ.

4) *Biblical Theology.* Beale asserts that biblical theology, though technically not grammatical-historical exegesis, does not yield odd uses of the Old Testament. Enns agrees that biblical theology cannot be equated with Second Temple practices and that it "takes in wider biblical contexts than merely the one being quoted" (Enns here is using

Beale's words). Yet the problem lies precisely in these "wider biblical contexts," because, Enns says, "the *very act* of taking in wider contexts is precisely the problem to be discussed, and it demands of us that we assess *how* those wider contexts are 'taken in' to the apostles' exegetical program" (p. 10).

Enns asks, how are these wider contexts taken into account? In Matthew 2:15, for example, Matthew takes the retrospective observation of Hosea 11:1 as a prophetic utterance. And in Galatians 3:16, 29, Paul reinterprets a promise in Genesis of countless offspring to refer to one person, Christ, on the basis of a subtle grammatical point (pp. 9–10).

Beale takes this use of Hosea 11:1 in Matthew 2:15 as a clear counter example to non-contextual exegesis because it is biblical-theological, but this is not persuasive to Enns. Enns counters that these examples "are truly 'odd' uses of the OT (in keeping with Second Temple interpretive practices), and they are *also* powerful examples of biblical theology (Christ embodies Israel's story; God's promises are fulfilled in Christ)" (p. 10). Indeed, these biblical theological messages are born on the wings of Second Temple interpretive practices, not a "sensitivity" to concerns about being consistent with the Old Testament context.

Matthew's use of Hosea shows that Hosea's ultimate meaning is not constrained by his original context but, Enns says, "*transforms* Hosea's words in light of the grand, ultimate context of the eschaton inaugurated at Christ's resurrection." Christ's death and resurrection provide the eschatological lens through which broader biblical themes are understood, not fully constrained by the original Old Testament context. Yet, according to Enns, such biblical theology fails to "serve as a buffer between the NT and the interpretive practices of the world in which the NT writers lived" (pp. 10–11).

5) *The Moveable Well of 1 Corinthians 10:4.* Here, Beale seems concerned primarily with an apologetic issue regarding the precarious historical nature of a tradition within an inspired biblical text. Yet Enns wonders if apologetics drives Beale's historical analysis and whether Beale fails to address fully the issues raised in his 1996 *Bulletin of Biblical Research* article.[3]

Enns notes that the evidence for the significant textual variant in Pseudo-Philo's *Liber antiquitatum biblicarum* 10:7 is not as damaging as it may seem. While the D manuscript indeed has "it [the rock] followed" and the P group has "the Lord followed," it is not true that the latter group is of almost equal authority to the former. Ambiguity inevitably surrounds such technical textual discussions, yet H. Jacobson's

---

3. P. Enns, "The 'Moveable Well' in 1 Cor. 10:4: an Extrabiblical Tradition in an Apostolic Text," *BBR* 6 (1996).

commentary argues that the latter manuscript group routinely deviates from the Latin archetype, with often intentional changes of the meaning of the text.[4]

Should the latter family (P family) then be always rejected? Not necessarily, for each individual instance must be explored on a case-by-case basis. Since the *Liber antiquitatum biblicarum* only exists in Latin, Christians likely ensured its existence by copying it into Latin.[5] Two possible scenarios for the variant in 10:7 are possible: (1) "Lord" was the original Hebrew reading, with "it" introduced later, grounded in an early Jewish interpretive tradition; (2) "it," referring to a miraculous and mobile source of water, is original, and "Lord" is introduced by later Christian copyists. Space precludes further exploration of this difficult issue, but Beale's simple assertion that "Lord" is the more difficult reading, and possibly original, is not persuasive. Further, Enns says, Beale's explanation for why Paul says "the rock that followed" seems "no less midrashic than the Second Temple texts from which he wishes to distance Paul" (pp. 11–12).

Implications

Enns agrees with Beale that historical conclusions affect contemporary method, yet Enns says the difference remains in "how we explain apostolic hermeneutics in its historical setting and the degree to which this should stand as a model for contemporary exposition." Enns affirms that while "all things necessary for [God's] own glory, man's salvation, faith and life"[6] are plain in Scripture, the Bible nonetheless has gaps or irritants, in the words of James Kugel, which defy smoothing out in biblical interpretation. Even with exegetical care and contextual sensitivity, interpretative breadth is unavoidable.

Thus, Enns says, the use of the Old Testament in the New suggests a "metaphor of 'path' rather than 'fortress' for contemporary biblical exposition" (p. 13), though Beale worries (according to Enns) that such a metaphor jeopardizes the possibility of deriving true meaning from a text. Enns concludes that though proper method may not inevitably bring exegetical clarity at every point, this does not necessarily drive us to the "pessimistic pedagogical and homiletical conclusion" about which Beale warns. The reality of interpretive diversity and breadth within Scripture must be addressed, Enns says, with grave implications for failing to do so (p. 13).

---

4. H. Jacobson, *A Commentary on Pseudo-Philo's* Liber Antiquitatum Biblicarum, *with Latin Text and English Translation* (Leiden: Brill, 1996), 1.257–73, esp. 260–64.
5. Jacobson, *Commentary*, 1.276–77. Although note Jacobson's caution against M. R. James's overstatement of the role of the church in perpetuating the book (1.210).
6. *Westminster Confession of Faith*, 1.4.

Greg Beale's Counter-Reply

My first response to Enns's critique is to encourage readers to go back and read my review again (chap. 2). I do not think that he has advanced the argument much beyond what I have said.[7] For example, he offers no substantive response, in my view, to the evidence that he holds various significant narratives in Genesis and in the New Testament (e.g., 1 Cor. 10:4) to be myth or legend according to its classic definition, and that he acknowledges that the biblical writers mistakenly thought such myths corresponded to real past reality.

Nevertheless, I elaborate here upon some of what Enns considers to be major critiques in my review of his book.

The Question of the Genre of Enns's Book

Enns contends in both his *Themelios* and *JETS* responses that I misread the genre of his book and that I evaluated it as a scholarly work instead of a popular book. He says that my critique is unfair in saying that he should have given both sides of various issues with some representative footnoting. Enns acknowledges that his book was written for a scholarly audience only secondarily, so this in itself allows for the critique that I gave. But, in fact, Enns claims that graduate and college-level students are included in his popular audience. Certainly such students should be given both sides of this kind of explosive debate, including, of course, the dispute over the use of the Old Testament in the New Testament. But, in addition, I clearly acknowledged that the primary audience was popular and the secondary audience scholarly, and I wrote with this fully in mind.[8] Even if his conception of a popular audience did not include students, should not we as scholars do the best we can to present both sides of debated issues such as Enns discusses? This was not a felicitous move by Enns, since the book appears as a one-sided attempt to convince readers without presenting all the evidence.

Second Temple Judaism in Relation to the New Testament

I argued that there was more diversity in Second Temple Judaism on the issue of non-contextual hermeneutical approaches to the Old Testament. In contrast, Enns contended that there was a dominant uncontrolled, so-called midrashic approach. In his response to my review, he agrees that Second Temple Judaism was not a hermeneutical monolith. But then he immediately says that "whatever diversity is there cannot be used to

---

7. Readers should feel free to consult Enns's full article in *Them*, "Response to Professor Greg Beale."

8. See, again, Beale, "Myth, History, and Inspiration: A Review Article of *Inspiration and Incarnation* by Peter Enns," *JETS* 49 (2006): 312.

minimize the midrashic . . . dimension of Second Temple Judaism that is far, far more pervasive than any concern to be 'sensitive' to the OT context."[9] Thus, while he is willing to admit that there was hermeneutical diversity in Judaism on this issue, it is a token acknowledgment. My review of Enns in the last chapter set forth some significant exceptions to the idea that Judaism, especially early Judaism, operated by an uncontrolled hermeneutic. In contrast, Enns apparently does not consider this evidence to be significant.

The verdict is out about the degree of diversity in early Judaism on this issue, but circumspect conclusions are more profitable than sweeping statements one way or another. There needs to be much more investigation on a case-by-case basis in the works of early Judaism before broad conclusions can be reached.

Part of the problem in assessing this is that particular kinds of interpretative approaches are seen by some to have no concern with an Old Testament author's original intention while others see the same approaches to have an understandable rationale that is consistent with such authorial intention. Typology is a case in point. Enns responds to my mention of Hillel's rules, contending that such rules were not to be understood as being consistent with a contextual approach to the Old Testament. As a basis for his conclusion, he cites some hermeneutical presuppositions that are unclearly grounded in *early* (pre-AD 70) Judaism and do not support his thesis.

In this respect, it is unfortunate that Enns does not mention David Instone Brewer's work[10]—a work I mentioned in the preceding chapter—which, as far as I know, is the only one that has attempted on a broad scale to evaluate pre-AD 70 rabbinic exegesis, and who comes to conclusions different from Enns's. One may disagree with Instone Brewer, but, at least, his is a work that should be acknowledged. Enns's comments about the Mishnah and Talmud are not as relevant, since they represent later Judaism, which is further removed from the period of early Judaism and the New Testament.

Enns contends that what unites some early Jewish texts—*Jubilees,* the Qumran Habakkuk pesher, the Wisdom of Solomon, and Pseudo-Philo—is the pursuit of "mining Scripture for hidden, richer meanings in order to hear God speak once again in a community's present circumstances" (p. 7). This is likely the case at many points, but to say with confidence that this is the major trend of how the Old Testament

9. Enns, "Response to Prof. Greg Beale," *Them*: 6.
10. D. Instone Brewer, *Techniques and Assumptions in Jewish Exegesis before 70 C.E.*, TSAJ 30 (Tübingen: Mohr [Paul Siebeck]), 1992.

is used in these texts could only be concluded after doing more work on each Old Testament reference in these texts. Furthermore, such a revelatory stance is not necessarily irreconcilable with an attempt to interpret the Old Testament in ways that still have links to the original meaning. I remain unconvinced that even if this revelatory stance were true of other early Jewish texts (e.g., 4 *Ezra*, 2 *Baruch*, the *Testaments of the Twelve Patriarchs*, 1 *Enoch*, and the Qumran *War Scroll*), it does not necessitate an uncontrolled hermeneutic, as the evidence of chapter 3 attempted to show.

Enns also claims I said that "although it has its moments, Second Temple hermeneutics is overall not nearly as 'odd' as some people think." This is not precisely what I said, since the way Enns has phrased it makes it sound as though I think the overall thrust of Judaism is to interpret the Old Testament in line with the original authorial intent. More precisely, my point was merely to assert that there is more significant diversity on this issue in early Jewish (pre-AD 70) interpretative approaches than Enns and others allow.

Contextual Interpretation of the Old Testament?
Enns disagrees with my contention that New Testament writers are characterized by using the Old Testament with the context in mind. He suggests that my approach is "an *uncritical* adoption of etic hermeneutical categories" and that I "assume . . . the New Testament writers share [my] concerns with matters of contextual exegesis" (p. 9; italics mine). In other words, he argues that I make use of predetermined modern categories of exegesis for organizing and interpreting the New Testament rather than familiarizing myself with the hermeneutical categories that are well recognized within the ancient Jewish culture.

In a similar manner, Enns says that for me to "use words like 'twist' or 'distort' to describe non-contextual exegesis of the Second Temple period erects at the outset a hermeneutical wall of hostility between the NT and its environment." His point in the context of the dialogue is that such exegesis may have been legitimate for ancient Judaism and Christianity, since it was the accepted socially constructed approach of the day. Just because we have a different accepted approach today does not make that ancient non-contextual approach wrong nor should we evaluate Jewish exegesis through what we modern exegetes consider to be a correct contextual method of interpretation. The problem with this is its failure to recognize that in the contemporary period there is not necessarily an accepted approach. Enns says the accepted method today is the contextual approach that tries to obtain an author's original meaning. There is, however, a significant movement among some scholars today that affirms we cannot obtain such an original meaning, since it is impossible to interpret objectively. Consequently, they conclude that interpreters are left to reading into the texts the reflection of their own socially constructed thoughts. Could Enns himself be reading the Jewish material through such a contemporary lens?

I agree with Enns's basic assumption that all interpreters, including Enns and me, have presuppositions that influence their interpretative approach. So, the issue is which lens makes best sense of the New Testament data—Enns's lens or mine. This is where we disagree. Let us hope that neither of us is being uncritical as we examine the material through our respective lenses. In order to support Enns's contention that I am uncritical he would need to show evidence of having evaluated my writings over the past twenty-plus years, most of which have been studies of the Old Testament in the New Testament and, often, about how Jewish exegetical perspectives relate to this. He does not adduce such evidence.

I doubt that it is helpful to evaluate one another as "uncritical" scholars, since that lowers the level of the dialogue to ad hominem argumentation. In fact, Enns says, "Some of our differences can be attributed to my Reformed, specifically presuppositional, theological and epistemological starting point."[11] As alluded to earlier, I doubt that this is helpful either, since I cut my teeth early in my graduate studies on the presuppositional viewpoints of such Reformed theologians as John Calvin, Abraham Kuyper, and Cornelius Van Til and on the biblical-theological approach of Geehardus Vos, perspectives which I still hold.

Enns lists only eight "odd" uses of the Old Testament in the New Testament in his book, and apparently on the basis that these texts are representative of many more, he deduces that New Testament hermeneutics is reflective of Jewish hermeneutics. In his reply, he does not attempt to list any other examples of texts of which he considers the eight to be representative. If he had other examples in mind as representative of the New Testament approach, he could have listed them in his reply. Consequently, he has left himself open to being considered unduly prejudicial toward only his view.

Also, in similar manner, he does not address my critique that we do not define New Testament hermeneutics by first going to Judaism, studying their approach, and then coming to the New Testament and beginning with the assumption that the Jewish approach is most likely the New Testament approach. In this respect, he has not heeded S. Sandmel's

---

11. Enns, "Response to G. K. Beale's Review Article of *Inspiration and Incarnation*," 315, n. 6.

warnings against "parallelomania."[12] As historians we study, for example, Paul, and then (ideally at the same time) we study other sectors of Judaism, each in their own right. Then we make comparisons and, finally, conclusions. In this respect, I made the point in chapter 3 that even contemporary, critical non-evangelical German scholars working in this area take the methodological approach just mentioned (e.g., H. Hübner and D. A. Koch).

It seems that Enns so opposes a contextual approach by New Testament writers because he sees a different approach in Judaism, but he might see the New Testament data in a different light if he let them speak for themselves first rather than seeing them through the lens of Judaism. It is for these reasons that my language about New Testament authors using the Old Testament in a way that is not inconsistent with the Old Testament or is sensitive to the Old Testament or does not contravene the Old Testament or reveals a contextual awareness or creatively develops the Old Testament is not unnecessarily defensive, even protectionist, as Enns concludes. Rather, such language is an attempt to describe the phenomena of the New Testament in its first-century context. I am not a voice crying in the wilderness on this issue, since others both outside and within an evangelical perspective also have noticed the New Testament writers' awareness of broader Old Testament contexts of specific passages that they quote.[13] Of course, this issue is greatly debated in New Testament scholarship in general.

Enns also believes that the New Testament writers' belief in Christ, especially in his death and resurrection, gave them christotelic lenses that changed their interpretation of the Old Testament, so much so that only Christian believers with the same lenses could read the Old Testament in the same way. Others, such as the unbelieving Jews, who did not have such lenses, could not understand the Old Testament in this manner. While it is true that belief in Christ caused them to perceive their former moral blindness and be better able to interpret the Old Testament Christianly in the light of progressive revelation; it is also true that they would insist that the Old Testament can be understood even by unbelieving Jews to anticipate a Priest-King, a suffering Servant-King, a new High Priest, etc.

---

12. S. Sandmel, "Parallelomania," *JBL* 81 (1962): 1–13.

13. In this respect, the following are a representative sampling of works: C. H. Dodd, *According to the Scriptures* (London: Nisbet, 1952); more recently, e.g., see R. B. Hays, *The Conversion of the Imagination* (Grand Rapids: Eerdmans, 2005) on which see my review in *JETS* 50 (2007): 190–94, and F. Watson, *Paul and the Hermeneutics of Faith* (T & T Clark, 2004); see also G. K. Beale and D. A. Carson, eds., *Commentary on the New Testament Use of the Old Testament* (Grand Rapids: Baker, 2007).

For example, while Luke 24:45 says that the resurrected Christ "opened their minds [his followers'] to understand the Scriptures," he also says a little earlier (vv. 25–27), "O foolish men and slow of heart to believe in all that the prophets have spoken! Was it not necessary for the Christ to suffer these things and to enter into His glory? Then beginning with Moses and all the prophets, He explained to them the things concerning Himself in all the Scriptures." Thus, Jesus holds his followers accountable *even before the time of the resurrection* for not understanding that the Old Testament foresaw this event.[14]

D. A. Carson says, in response to Enns, that because the interpretations by Christ and the apostles "truly are there in the text, readers can be berated for not having seen them, i.e., the assumption is that if it were not for their moral turpitude and their ignorance of God, they would have seen how the texts are put together, would have grasped more clearly what this God is truly like, and would have understood their Bibles properly."[15] By "properly," I assume that Carson means "sufficiently" but, of course, not with the full richness of meaning that fulfillment brings on the other side of the resurrection. Consequently, the apologetic of the New Testament writers is not only "believe in Christ and you will understand the Bible better," but it also demonstrates to their unbelieving audience that, even as non-Christians, they can perceive from the Scriptures that the Messiah was to die and rise again.[16]

This is why Luke says in Acts 17:11 that the Bereans to whom Paul and Silas were witnessing were "examining the Scriptures daily to see whether these things were so." And Luke can also say that Apollos, who "was mighty in the Scriptures," though "acquainted only with the baptism of John," was "teaching accurately the things concerning Jesus," apparently concerning Old Testament fulfillment in Jesus. Then, when he was taught about the rest of Jesus' ministry "more accurately," he was able to refute Jewish opponents by "demonstrating by the Scriptures that Jesus was the Christ" (Acts 18:24–28). Note that he had an accurate understanding of the Old Testament in relation to John's baptizing activity, which likely includes Jesus' baptism, but after receiving the full revelation about prophetic messianic fulfillment in Jesus, he was able to have a more accurate understanding. This shows that there can be an accurate understanding of the Old Testament even before

---

14. I am thankful to D. A. Carson, "Three More Books on the Bible: A Critical Review,"*TJ* 27NS (2006): 43–44, who has reminded me of these most basic points; see his entire review of Enns's whole book, where many good insights can be found.

15. Ibid., 44.

16. Ibid.

understanding its fulfillment in Jesus, and then a greater understanding in the light of progressive revelation about Jesus. There is no reason to understand this word *accurate* any differently than we generally would today, i.e., having an understanding that significantly corresponds to a realistic perception of the object of understanding in view, with which the other uses of *accurate* (*akribōs*) in the New Testament are consistent (cf. BAGD, 39).

Other New Testament passages likewise support the notion that Jesus and the apostles believed that the Old Testament foretold the revelatory events connected with Jesus to such a degree that people could be held accountable for their understanding of and response to such Old Testament prophecies and their fulfillment in Jesus (Matt. 13:17ff.; John 5:45–47; 1 Pet. 1:10–12 in relation to 1 Pet. 1:13–21).[17]

1 Corinthians 10:4

While Enns replies to my critique of his analysis of 1 Corinthians 10:4 concerning Christ as the "rock which followed," he does not address my major point. Enns had concluded that Paul is referring to a Jewish legend about a well that followed Israel in the wilderness; he says that though Paul believed the legend was true, in reality, we now know that it was legend. I wish that Enns had responded to this very important issue.

It is relevant that Paul himself says in 1 Timothy 1:4 "not to pay attention to myths and endless genealogies, which give rise to mere speculation." Ironically, the kinds of myths that Paul is combating appear to be those fanciful speculations based on the Old Testament, which do not correspond to actual past events, especially perhaps genealogies in Genesis, as for example, those found in *Jubilees* and Pseudo-Philo.[18] Likewise, 2 Peter 1:16 affirms, "For we did not follow cleverly devised tales when we made known to you the power and coming of our Lord Jesus Christ, but we were eyewitnesses of His majesty." The word used for *tales* (*mythos*) here refers to that which historically did not happen in contrast to that which did occur, indeed was "witnessed" (see in the commentaries on 2 Pet. in loc, e.g., by Bauckham, Kelly, and Neyrey).

So, if Enns is correct about the legendary nature of 1 Corinthians 10:4, then not only was Paul unaware that what he was recording was legend, as Enns actually says, but, if he had known, he would have repudiated it, as he does in 1 Timothy. Is this really a likely scenario? Enns would have us believe that the New Testament writers

---

17. I am grateful to Richard Gaffin for pointing out the significance of these passages in an unpublished paper titled "Observations on a Controversy," which is his response to Peter Enns's views.
18. On which see in the commentaries on 1 Timothy in loc, e.g., among others, by Stott and Collins; similarly Fee, Lea and Griffin, and Marshall.

imbibed the myths that were held in the surrounding Jewish culture, but 1 Timothy, Titus, and 2 Peter indicate that they were much more discerning than this and believed that God had broken into history through Christ and had revealed salvific truth in doing so—a *histori-cal truth* that was different from the surrounding religious myths of pagan and Jewish culture.

Enns responds to me concerning the textual problem in Pseudo-Philo (LAB) 10:7 (*sic*; actually the reference is 11:15), and produces an argument that counters my proposal that the original reading in 11:15 was "Lord" instead of "it [the water, or by metonymy the rock-shaped well]" that "followed" Israel in the wilderness. Readers will have to decide how persuasive they think this is. But my major point in discussing the textual problem was not the probability of my textual analysis, which I would still be happy to debate, but that Enns never mentions the existence of the textual problem in his discussion of the Jewish background of 1 Corinthians 10:4, even in his article dedicated to 1 Corinthians 10:7.

In fact, in my review of Enns's use of the Old Testament in the new (chapter 3 of this volume), I said that my evaluation of the textual prob-lem "could be debated, but our intention here is merely to point out the textual uncertainty" of the reference in Pseudo-Philo 11:15. The point is that this is not a minor textual problem, despite one's final conclusions about it, and to base a major conclusion in 1 Corinthians 10:4 on this Pseudo-Philo text is precarious. Enns says, "The presence of a 'moveable well' in Pseudo-Philo demonstrates that such a tradition was roughly contemporaneous with Paul."[19] But, in fact, the textual tenuousness of Pseudo-Philo 11:15 removes this text from being a sure first-century wit-ness to this tradition, which leaves only Tosephta Sukka 3.11 (c. AD 300) and Targum Onquelos Numbers 21:16–20 (c. AD 250–300). These are the only really solid textual witnesses to the kind of Jewish legend that Enns says Paul was dependent on; however, because of their late date, it is difficult to say that the legendary tradition was even extant in the first century.[20] If one consults the discussion by A. C. Thiselton on 1 Co-

---

19. Enns, "The 'Moveable Well,'" 27.

20. In this connection I must comment on a misrepresentation, unintentional no doubt, by Enns concerning the textual evidence for the problem in Pseudo-Philo. He says, "H. Jacobson, in his massive commentary, argues at length that the latter manuscript group [the π family, which supports the "Lord" reading in 11:15] routinely deviates from the Latin archetype, and that the changes made are at times stylistic but other times quite intentional so as to change the meaning of the text." This citation from Jacobson is made by Enns to indicate that the "Lord" reading is more likely a scribal corruption and not representative of the original wording. But this is only what Jacobson says at the beginning of his discussion; he goes on to say that "we can find an additional—and more rational—explanation of our textual variants beyond a perhaps somewhat irresponsible and

rinthians 10:4, then it will be readily seen how incomplete, imbalanced, and misrepresentative Enns's analysis of this passage is.[21]

Concerns with Jesus' Use of the Old Testament

Let us remember that Enns does not exempt Jesus from being just as culturally determined as are the apostles in their use of the Old Testament. This means for Enns that Jesus was not concerned with the original meaning of Old Testament authors and that he read in meanings that had nothing to do with the original meaning.[22] It would be helpful to hear Enns explain how this view fits into his understanding of the incarnation. For example, it is obvious that the supernatural could break through in Jesus when he did miracles; why could not the same kind of breakthrough occur in his hermeneutics? Would not even those evangelicals who stress kenosis much more than others, at least, allow for this?

Interpretive Approaches

One of my replies to Enns's contention that New Testament writers do not employ a grammatical-historical approach to interpreting the Old Testament is that there are other approaches that can still develop in consistent though creative manner the original authorial intentions of the Old Testament. I referred earlier to a typological approach and a biblical-theological approach. The latter uncovers how the New Testament writers explore and tease out intertextual and intratextual relationships within the Old Testament itself. I argued that the use

---

egoistic scribe." More likely, he says, the scribe for the above manuscript group (π) was a "translator-reviser" who was copying from the Latin archetype but also was making changes to that archetype based on a "Greek version that served as a model for his [Latin] exemplar," and he made changes on the basis of the Hebrew original or of "a second—and different—Greek translation" of that Hebrew original (Jacobson, *A Commentary on Pseudo-Philo's Liber antiquitatum biblicarum*, 261). Thus, the π scribe was not making changes based purely on his own interpretative interests but also on earlier Greek or Hebrew manuscripts that served as the original from which the Latin archetype was copied. Thus the π scribe had access to earlier Greek and/or Hebrew manuscripts of Pseudo-Philo than did the Δ scribe, who had access only to the Latin. After considering all the evidence, Jacobson finally concludes that "each family [of mss. π and Δ] has a fairly equal claim on our attention. Every textual problem must be resolved on its own, with internal criteria of evidence" (ibid., 264). This is a fuller picture of Jacobson's evaluation of the manuscript families, which presents a quite different, much more positive picture of the p family than Enns's incomplete comments convey. Could a Christian scribe later have added "Lord," a possibility Enns suggests? It is possible, but up to this point no one has adduced sufficient evidence to make this a probable scenario. Indeed, a text-critical proverb in some circles is "all things are possible, but not all things are probable." Why would not such a purported Christian scribe substitute "Messiah" or "Christ" or "Jesus" instead of the more ambiguous "Lord," the latter of which a Jewish scribe could have felt comfortable with?

21. A. C. Thiselton, *The First Epistle to the Corinthians*, NIGTC (Grand Rapids: Eerdmans, 2000), 727–30.

22. *Inspiraton and Incarnation*, 114–15, 132.

of Hosea 11:1 is a good example of a New Testament writer doing a biblical theology of Hosea by exploring intratextual relationships between Hosea 11:1 and other texts within Hosea. Enns responds that I am acknowledging that apostolic exegesis does some things that "might be left open to a . . . charge of twisting and distorting." No, I would not concede this, though I would concede that there might be some difficult uses of the Old Testament in the New Testament that are hard to understand.

My view of the way typology and biblical theology work are not at odds with what could be referred to as an organic approach to Old Testament meanings. In chapter 3 I explain how such uses make sense of the Old Testament passages cited in line with the Old Testament original meaning. Indeed, once one considers these other methods of organic development of the Old Testament, Enns's list of odd uses by New Testament writers is reduced potentially to almost nil.

Conclusion

According to Enns, biblical writers were consciously intending to be understood as writing a historical genre, *but, in fact, we now know such events are legend.* Enns says that although such accounts do not convey historical truth, they still have important theological truth to tell us—we are to worship the God of the Bible and not pagan gods. Enns differs here even from Robert Gundry, who contended that some narratives by gospel writers, which traditionally had been taken to be history, in fact are not, since they were intentionally and consciously employing a midrashic method that added significant non-historical but interpretative features.

But Enns is saying much more than this. He is saying that the biblical writers like Paul thought they were recording history but they were wrong, since we now know they were unaware that they were recording myth.

Enns's attempt to argue that the New Testament writers "preached the right doctrine but from the wrong texts" I still find unpersuasive. Is it really inappropriately modernist to believe that Jesus and the apostles could have had understandings of the Old Testament that had significant links to the Old Testament's original meaning? If this conclusion can be reached concerning some significant aspects of early Jewish interpreters, why not also arrive at the same conclusion concerning the New Testament?

And should not the element of divine inspiration also affect the answer to this question to some degree? Could not divine revelation break through to cause New Testament writers to perceive the original intention of Old Testament texts? I am also troubled by the implications of Enns's conclusions, which leaves us with a Bible written by *inspired authors*, who at significant points thought they were writing historical accounts but that, indeed, unbeknownst to them, were really mythical.

CHAPTER FIVE

A Specific Problem Confronting the Authority of the Bible: Should the New Testament's Claim That the Prophet Isaiah Wrote the Whole Book of Isaiah Be Taken at Face Value?

We began this book by thrusting the reader into the midst of a hypothetical dialogue between two biblical scholars about the inspiration of the Bible. That dialogue represents just one of a variety of issues related to the inerrancy of the Scriptures that are being debated by evangelicals today. There are a number of contemporary evangelical scholars who do not take at face value the repeated affirmations by Jesus and the New Testament writers that the prophet Isaiah wrote the entire Old Testament book known as Isaiah. This particular debate has significant bearing on the overall debate about the Bible's authority; if Isaiah did not write the book attributed to him, the New Testament's assertion that he did write the book is wrong. But, of perhaps even greater significance, if the prophet Isaiah was not responsible for the contents of the whole book, then we are left with a christological problem, since Jesus understood that the prophet Isaiah wrote the entire book.

The dialogue in the introduction reveals the typical give-and-take in this debate. It is important to recognize that some, especially evangelicals, who contend that Isaiah was not the author of the book by that name do not believe such a position is inconsistent with the inspiration of Scripture. As the dialogue reveals, some believe that the New Testament refers only to a collection of writings known as "Isaiah," and therefore such allusions do not have to be understood as referring to a personal prophet whose handprint is over the whole work. Others believe that Jesus' intention was not conveying that the historical prophet Isaiah was the author but on communicating only the meaning of the prophecy.

Nevertheless, the dialogue also reveals the problem with these particular views, which is my perspective, so that the difficulty of how the Bible can be authoritative and espouse the view of multi-authorship of Isaiah remains.

The Shift of Opinion among North American Evangelicals Concerning Authorship Claims by the New Testament about Old Testament Books

Up until the late 1970s, the consensus among evangelical scholars was to accept the Bible's claims about the human authorship of some of its books, whether that be Isaiah's authorship of the entire prophecy,[1] the Mosaic authorship of the Pentateuch, or the attribution of the psalms to David. This was the position taken by the drafters of the Chicago Statement on Biblical Inerrancy. It is noteworthy that in almost as brief a period as thirty years, there has arisen in American evangelical scholarship a willingness to accept formerly liberal, higher critical views of the Bible's claims about authorship of particular biblical books such as Isaiah,[2] though some contemporary Old Testament evangelical scholars still hold to the traditional view about this book.[3]

The main conservative arguments for the single authorship of Isaiah were summarized in the mid-twentieth century by Oswald Allis:

1) All fifteen of the latter Old Testament prophets begin with a heading of the prophet's name, but Isaiah 40 to 66 does not, so it appears likely that the author of Isaiah 1 to 39 is the same as that of chapters 40 to 66.

---

1. E.g., see E. J. Young, *The Book of Isaiah*, 3 vols., NICOT (Grand Rapids: Eerdmans, 1972), 538–49; R. K. Harrison, *Introduction to the Old Testament* (Grand Rapids: Eerdmans, 1969), 765–95.

2. See, e.g., R. B. Dillard and T. Longman III, *An Introduction to the Old Testament* (Grand Rapids: Zondervan, 1994), 268–74, commonly used at many evangelical institutions and published by a traditionally conservative evangelical publisher.

3. J. N. Oswalt, *The Book of Isaiah*, NICOT (Grand Rapids: Eerdmans, 1986), 23–28; J. A. Motyer, *The Prophecy of Isaiah* (Downers Grove, IL: InterVarsity, 1993), 25–30; see N. H. Ridderbos, "Isaiah: Book of," *New Bible Dictionary*, 3rd. ed. (Leicester: Inter-Varsity, 1996), 513–16, who holds a mediating position, i.e., that it is acceptable to affirm that Isaiah 40–66 contains an Isaianic core, which Isaiah's disciples expanded according to the spirit of Isaiah but that it is not possible to determine what belongs to the core and what to the later editors.

2) For twenty-five centuries no one questioned the authorship of Isaiah, except for one insignificant Jewish medieval interpreter.

3) The New Testament writers quote from all parts of the book of Isaiah and attribute those quotes to the prophet Isaiah.

4) The Qumran scroll of Isaiah shows no kind of literary break between chapters 39 and 40, just where the critics locate the most major break in authorship of the book.[4]

Reconsideration of Jesus' and the New Testament's References to Isaiah

It is certainly true that cogent arguments by Old Testament scholars have been made for multiple authorship of Isaiah, which in fact is the ruling model today for understanding the book's authorship.[5] Yet viable arguments for the unity of Isaiah's authorship continue to be offered. Interestingly, within the last ten to fifteen years, there has been less study emphasizing evidence for diversity of authorship. Nevertheless, great strides have been made by those who, while still affirming multiple authorship, perceive an overall unity of subject matter from various angles, which they propose is the result of a final editor's work. The cumulative effect of these arguments has been to highlight the book's unity. The longer these arguments continue to be made, the thinner the line will be between a final redactor who imposed unity on the diverse strands of the book and Isaiah as the original author, who is responsible for its unity from the beginning.[6]

Though there is much to discuss about the authorship of Isaiah from the perspective of the book itself, this discussion will focus primarily on the authorship of Isaiah from the claims of the repeated references to Isaiah found in the New Testament. Most Old Testament scholars holding to multiple authorship consider their arguments so overwhelmingly convincing that the New Testament evidence must be explained in such a way as to be consistent with their conclusion. Some have concluded that Jesus and his followers were wrong, like the rest of early Judaism, or that Jesus knowingly accommodated himself to false Jewish tradition, or that the New Testament merely refers to a literary collection known

---

4. O. Allis, *The Unity of Isaiah: A Study in Prophecy* (Phillipsburg, NJ: Presbyterian and Reformed, 1950), 39–43.

5. For the typical critical arguments, see the summary (and responses) in Harrison, *Introduction to the Old Testament*, 765–95.

6. See R. Schultz, "How Many 'Isaiahs' Were There and Does It Matter? Prophetic Inspiration in Recent Evangelical Scholarship," in *Evangelicals and Scripture*, ed. V. Bacote, L. Miguelez, and D. Okholm (Downers Grove, IL: InterVarsity, 2004), *passim*, for a convenient survey of this issue, as well as the current status of evangelical views from an Old Testament perspective on the authorship of Isaiah.

as "Isaiah" not written by the personal prophet himself. This is a view often preferred by more conservative scholars holding to diversity of Isaiah's authorship.

The New Testament evidence is so strongly in favor of the prophet Isaiah's authorship of the complete book that to hold that there were multiple authors must lead those who are consistent to one inevitable conclusion—Jesus and the New Testament writers were wrong in their assessment of the book's authorship. Yet I believe that the New Testament position on this issue vindicates the traditional arguments within Isaiah itself, that Isaiah wrote the whole book. This best explains the various kinds of unity that scholars have more recently recognized while attributing the whole to a later redactor(s). In arguing this, I am merely trying to develop in more detail and to update the traditional argument that the New Testament evidence for Isaianic authorship is significant and cannot be dismissed lightly.

Consideration of Actual Attributions of Quotations to Isaiah the Prophet in Early Judaism, the New Testament, and Early Christianity

Probably the best and most precise manner by which to study how the ancients viewed Old Testament authorship, especially the book of Isaiah, is to survey the actual evidence about Isaiah in early Judaism and Christianity. Without exception, this evidentiary literature understands that the prophet Isaiah was the author of the entire book.

Below are all of the references to Isaiah in the Dead Sea Scrolls, Josephus, Philo, Old Testament Apocrypha and pseudepigrapha, the New Testament, New Testament Apocrypha, and the apostolic Fathers. This list shows that throughout all of the early Jewish and Christian literature there are references to quotations from all parts of the book of Isaiah, so-called First, Second, and Third Isaiah, which are attributed to the person of Isaiah.

New Testament References

For this is the one referred to by Isaiah the prophet *when he said*,
   "The voice of one crying in the wilderness,
   'Make ready the way of the Lord,
   make His paths straight!'" (Matt. 3:3, quoting Isa. 40:3)

This was to fulfill what *was spoken through Isaiah the prophet*. (Matt. 4:14, introducing a quotation of Isa. 9:1–2)

This was to fulfill what *was spoken through Isaiah the prophet*: "He Himself took our infirmities and carried away our diseases." (Matt. 8:17, quoting Isa. 53:4)

This was to fulfill what *was spoken through Isaiah the prophet*. (Matt. 12:17, introducing a quotation of Isa. 42:1–4)

"In their case the *prophecy of Isaiah is being fulfilled*, which says,
    'You will keep on hearing, but will not understand;
    you will keep on seeing, but will not perceive. (Matt. 13:14, quoting Isa. 6:9)

"You hypocrites, *rightly did Isaiah prophesy of you . . .*" (Matt. 15:7, introducing a quotation of Isa. 29:13)

As it is written in *Isaiah the prophet*:
    "Behold, I send my messenger ahead of You,
    who will prepare Your way." (Mark 1:2, introducing a quotation from Isa. 40:3)

And He said to them, "*Rightly did Isaiah prophesy of you* hypocrites, as it is written:
    'This people honors Me with their lips,
    but their heart is far away from Me.'" (Mark 7:6, quoting Isa. 29:13)

As it is written in *the book of the words of Isaiah the prophet*,
    "The voice of one crying in the wilderness,
    'Make ready the way of the Lord,
    make His paths straight.'" (Luke 3:4, quoting Isa. 40:3)

And the *book of the prophet Isaiah* was handed to Him. And *He opened the book and found the place where it was written.* (Luke 4:17, introducing a quotation of Isa. 61:1–2)

He said, "I am a voice of one crying in the wilderness, 'Make straight the way of the Lord,' *as Isaiah the prophet said.*" (John 1:23, quoting Isa. 40:3)

This was to fulfill *the word of Isaiah the prophet which he spoke*: "Lord, who has believed our report? And to whom has the arm of the Lord been revealed?" (John 12:38, quoting Isa. 53:1)

For this reason they could not believe, for *Isaiah said* again . . . (John 12:39, introducing a quotation of Isa. 6:10)

And he was returning and sitting in his chariot, and was reading *the prophet Isaiah.* . . . Philip ran up and heard him reading *Isaiah the prophet,* and said, "Do you understand what you are reading?" And he said, "Well, how could I, unless someone guides me?" And he invited Philip to come up and sit with him. Now *the passage of Scripture which he was reading* was this:

"He was led as a sheep to slaughter;
and as a lamb before its shearer is silent,
so He does not open His mouth.

"In humiliation His judgment was taken away;
who will relate His generation?
For His life is removed from the earth."

The eunuch answered Philip and said, "Please tell me, *of whom does the prophet say this? Of himself or of someone else?*" Then Philip opened his mouth, and *beginning from this Scripture he preached Jesus to him.* (Acts 8:28–35, quoting Isa. 53:7–8)

And when they did not agree with one another, they *began* leaving after Paul had spoken one *parting* word, "*The Holy Spirit rightly spoke through Isaiah the prophet to your fathers.*" (Acts 28:25, introducing a quotation of Isa. 6:9–10)

Isaiah cries out concerning Israel, "Though the number of the sons of Israel be like the sand of the sea, it is the remnant that will be saved. (Rom. 9:27, quoting Isa. 10:22)

And *just as Isaiah foretold,*
"Unless the Lord of Sabaoth had left to us a posterity,
we would have become like Sodom, and would have resembled Gomorrah." (Rom. 9:29, quoting Isa. 1:9)

However, they did not all heed the good news; for *Isaiah says,* "Lord, who has believed our report?" (Rom. 10:16, quoting Isa. 53:1)

And *Isaiah is very bold and says,*
"I was found by those who did not seek Me,
I became manifest to those who did not ask for Me." (Rom. 10:20, quoting Isa. 65:1)

Again Isaiah says,
"There shall come the root of Jesse,
and he who arises to rule over the Gentiles,
in Him shall the Gentiles hope." (Rom. 15:12, quoting Isa. 11:10)

Philo

But it is not allowed to every wicked man to rejoice, as it is *said in the predictions of the prophet*, "There is no rejoicing for the wicked, says God" (Isa. 48:22). (*Names* 169)

They then very fairly compare this vine of which we were only able to take a part, to happiness. *And one of the ancient prophets bears his testimony in favour of my view of the matter, who speaking under divine inspiration has said,* "The vineyard of the Lord Almighty is the house of Israel" (Isa. 5:7). (*Dreams*, 2, 172)

Then, like an affectionate mother, it shall pity the sons and the daughters whom it has lost, who now that they are dead are, and still more were, when alive, a grief and sorrow to their parents; and becoming young a second time, it will again be fertile as before, and will produce an irre-proachable offspring, an improvement on its former progeny; for she that was desolate, *as the prophet says*, (Isa. 54:1) is now become happy in her children and the mother of a large family. Which prophetic saying has also an allegorical meaning, having reference to the soul. (*Rewards* 158)

Josephus

But king Hezekiah was not concerned at his threatenings, but depended on his piety towards God, and upon *Isaiah the prophet, by whom he inquired, and accurately knew all future events:*—and thus much shall suffice for the present concerning this king Hezekiah. (*Antiq.* 9:276 [9.13.3.276])

Now *as to this prophet* [clearly Isaiah in context], he was by the confes-sion of all, *a divine and wonderful man in speaking truth; and out of the assurance that he had never written what was false, he wrote down all his prophecies, and left them behind him in books, that their accomplishment might be judged of from the events by posterity. Nor did this prophet do so alone; but the others, which were twelve in number, did the same.* And whatsoever is done among us, whether it be good, or whether it be bad, comes to pass according to their prophecies; but of every one of these we shall speak hereafter. (*Antiq.* 10:35 [10.2.2.35])

This was known to Cyrus *by his reading the book which Isaiah left behind him of his prophecies; for this prophet said that God had spoken thus to him in a secret vision:*—"My will is, that Cyrus, whom I have appointed to be king over many and great nations, send back my people to their own land, and build my temple." (*Antiq.* 11:5 [11.1.2.5])

The chief reason why he was desirous so to do, was, that *he relied upon the prophet Isaiah, who lived about six hundred years before, and fore-*

told that there certainly was to be a temple built to Almighty God in Egypt by a man that was a Jew. Onias was elevated with this prediction, and wrote the following epistle to Ptolemy and Cleopatra. (*Antiq.* 13:64 [13.3.1.64])

For the prophet Isaiah foretold, that "there should be an altar in Egypt to the Lord God: *and many other such things did he prophesy relating to that place.*" (*Antiq.* 13:68 [13.3.1.68])

But since *thou sayest that Isaiah the prophet foretold this long ago,* we give thee leave to do it, if it may be done according to your law, and so that we may not appear to have at all offended God herein. (*Antiq.* 13:71 [13.3.2.71])

Accordingly, he [Onias] thought that by building this temple he should draw away a great number from them to himself. There had been also a certain *ancient prediction made by a [prophet] whose name was Isaiah, about six hundred years before,* that this temple should be built by a man that was a Jew in Egypt. And this is the history of the building of that temple. (*War* 7:431–32 [7.10.3.431–32])

The above references to a temple in Egypt are likely to be Isaiah 19:18–25, which pertains to the final eschatological restoration of Egyptians and Assyrians at the same times as Israel's end-time restoration.

Qumran[7]

Belial is unrestrained in Israel, *just as God said by Isaiah the prophet, the son of Amoz* . . . saying, Fear and pit and snare are upon thee, dweller in the land (Isaiah 24:17[8]). The true meaning of this verse. (CD 4:13–14)

When the oracle of the prophet Isaiah son of Amoz came true [in context the reference is to Isa. 7:17] . . . (CD 7:10)

As it is written in the book of Isaiah the prophet in reference to the Last Days, "And it came to pass, while His hand was strong upon me, [that He warned me not to walk in the way of] . . . this people (Isaiah 8:11). These are they about whom it is written in the book of Ezekiel the prophet." (4Q174 3:15–16)

---

7. The following quotations from Qumran are from M. O. Wise, M. G. Abegg, and E. M. Cook, eds., *The Dead Sea Scrolls: a New English Translation* (New York: HarperCollins, 1996). Brackets indicate lacunae filled in by the editors.
8. This is a text typically viewed as non-Isaianic by many scholars.

[*As it is written in the book of Isaiah the prophet,*] "This year eat what grows [by itself, and next year the aftergrowth" (Isaiah 37:30). The meaning of] "what grows by itself" is [. . . *that is written*] *about them in the book of* [*Isaiah the prophet* . . . for] the Law of the [. . .]. (4Q177 1:2, 5)

It calls them, as [*it is written about them in the book of Isaiah the prophe*t, "He] thinks up plots to [destroy the humble with lying words" (Isaiah 32:7) . . .]. (4Q177 1:6)

[. . . just as] *it is written in the b[ook] of Isaiah the prophet* . . . ["Sing, O barren one who did not bear; burst into song and] shout, you who have not been in labor! For the children of the desolate will be more . . . [than the children of her that is married, says the Lord.] Enlarge the site of [your] ten[t and let the curtains . . ." (Isaiah 54:1–2)]. (4Q265 f1:3–5)

In Israel, just *as God said by Isaiah the prophet, the son of Amoz,* (CD 4:14) *saying* . . . [against] them. Al[l of them are kindlers and lighters of brands (Isaiah 50:11); the webs of (CD 5:14) a spider are their webs]. . . . [and the eggs of vip]ers are t[heir] eggs (Isaiah 59:5). [Whoever touches them (CD 5:15) shall not be clean. The more he does so, the more he is guilty,]. (4Q266 f3i:7–f3ii:2)

Old Testament Apocrypha

I will send you help, my servants Isaiah and Jeremiah. According to their counsel I have consecrated and prepared for you twelve trees loaded with various fruits, [this is in a clear context of chapter 2 of God's promise to bring Israel out of captivity into all the blessings of the restoration promises]. (2 Esd. 2:18)

But they called upon the Lord who is merciful, spreading forth their hands toward him; and the Holy One quickly heard them from heaven, and delivered them by the hand of Isaiah. . . . For Hezekiah did what was pleasing to the Lord, and he held strongly to the ways of David his father, which *Isaiah the prophet commanded, who was great and faithful in his vision.* In his days the sun went backward, and he lengthened the life of the king. By the spirit of might *he [Isaiah] saw the last things, and comforted those who mourned in Zion. He revealed what was to occur to the end of time, and the hidden things before they came to pass.* (Sir. 48:20–25; italics mine)

He reminded you of the scripture of Isaiah, which says, "Even though you go through the fire, the flame shall not consume you" [Isaiah 43:2]. (4 Macc. 18:14)

Old Testament Pseudepigrapha

Isaiah and the prophets who (are) with him prophesy against Jerusalem and against the cities of Judah that they will be laid waste, and also (against) Benjamin that it will go into captivity, and also against you, lord king, that you will go (bound) with hooks and chains of iron. (*Mart. Ascen. Isa.* 3:6)

"And the rest of the words of the vision [by Isaiah] are written in the vision of Babylon [Isaiah 13]. And the rest of the vision about the Lord, behold it is written in parables in the words of mine [Isaiah] that are written in the book which I prophesied openly. And the descent of the Beloved into Sheol, behold it is written in the section where the Lord says, 'Behold, my son shall understand'" [Isa. 52:13, LXX]. (*Mart. Ascen. Isa.* 4:8)[9]

New Testament Apocrypha

O Lord Jesus Christ, the resurrection and the life of the dead, permit us to speak mysteries through the death of your cross, because we have been adjured by you. For you ordered your servants to relate to no one the secrets of your divine majesty which you did in Hades. And when we were, along with all our fathers, lying in the deep, in the blackness of darkness, suddenly there appeared a golden heat of the sun, and a purple royal light shining upon us. And immediately the father of all the human race, with all the patriarchs and prophets, exulted, saying: "That light is the source of eternal light, which has promised to transmit to us co-eternal light." *And Isaiah cried out, and said*: "This is the light of the Father, the Son of God, as I predicted when I was alive upon earth: 'The land of Zabulon and the land of Nephthalim across Jordan, Galilee of the nations, the people who sat in darkness, have seen a great light; and light was shining among those who are in the region of the shadow of death.' And now it has come and shone upon us sitting in death." (*Acts Pil.* 18:1 [2.1])

And all the multitude of the saints, hearing this, said to Hades, with the voice of reproach: "Open your gates, that the king of glory may come in." And David cried out, saying: "Did I not, when I was alive upon earth, prophesy to you: 'Let them confess to the Lord His tender mercies and His wonderful works to the children of men: for He has shattered the brazen gates, and burst the iron bars; He has taken them up out of the way of their iniquity'?" And after this, in like manner, *Isaiah said: "Did not I, when I was alive upon earth, prophesy to you: 'The dead shall rise up, and those who are in their tombs shall rise again, and those who are upon earth shall exult; because the dew, which is from the Lord, is their*

---

9. In the Charlesworth edition of the pseudepigrapha, this reference is *Mart. Ascen. Isa.* 4:20–21. *Martyrdom and Ascension of Isaiah* is dated variously either to the first or second century AD.

health'? (Isaiah 26:19) And again I said, 'Where, O Death, is your sting? where, O Hades, is your victory?'"[10] (Acts Pil. 21:2 [5.2])

And when all the saints heard this from Isaiah, they said to Hades: "Open you gates. Since you are now conquered, you will be weak and powerless." (Acts Pil. 21:3 [5.3])

Apostolic Fathers

And in Isaiah he also says, "This people honors me with their lips, but their heart is far from me." [6] (2 Clem. 3:5)

And *again in another prophet [Isaiah] he says:* "All day long I have stretched out my hands to a disobedient people who oppose my righteous way" [Isaiah 65:2]. (Barn. 12:4)

And *again, Isaiah says as follows:* "The Lord said to the Messiah my Lord, whose right hand I held, that the nations would obey him [Isa. 52:15; 60:11–12], and I will shatter the strength of kings" [114]. (Barn. 12:11) [Observe how David calls him "Lord," and does not call him "son."]

Conclusion to the Isaiah Quotations

References to all parts of the book of Isaiah are found attributed to the personal prophet Isaiah. It is true that some of the general references to Isaiah could be taken figuratively to refer merely to a literary collection known as "Isaiah." It is clearer, however, from the majority of the above citations that they should not be understood in that way. That the references are not made merely to a literary collection but to sayings spoken by the actual prophet is apparent from the specific personal language often used: there is allusion not typically to the *prophecy* or *prophecies* of Isaiah but to Isaiah as a *prophet*:

"Isaiah the son of Amoz"; "what was spoken through Isaiah the prophet"; "referred to by Isaiah the prophet"; "the prophecy of Isaiah"; "rightly did Isaiah prophesy"; "as it is written in the book of the words of Isaiah the prophet"; "the book of the prophet Isaiah"; "the word of Isaiah the prophet which he spoke"; "of whom does the prophet say this"; "the Holy Spirit rightly spoke through Isaiah the prophet to your fathers"; "Isaiah cries out"; "Isaiah foretold"; "Isaiah says"; "the predictions of the prophet"; "one of the ancient prophets bears his testimony"; "as the

10. This last clause is actually a quotation from Hos. 13:14, but the author has taken the verse as an interpretation of the resurrection prophecy of Isa. 25:8 (LXX), probably under the influence of 1 Cor. 15:54–55, where the same Hosea text directly follows the same Isa. 25:8 citation as an interpretation of it. This is quite close to the same phenomenon we will observe below in the use of the Old Testament in Mark 1:2–3.

prophet says"; "Isaiah the prophet . . . and [he] accurately knew all future events"; "reading the book which Isaiah left behind him of his prophecies"; "he relied upon the prophet Isaiah, who lived about six hundred years before, and foretold"; "the prophet Isaiah foretold"; "there had been also a certain ancient prediction made by a [prophet] whose name was Isaiah, about six hundred years before"; "as God said by Isaiah the prophet"; "the oracle of the prophet Isaiah."

When these references are read straightforwardly, they refer to the active, personal role of Isaiah writing and prophesying in all parts of the book. The cumulative effect of these references shows no substantial evidence that such references could have been seen as merely part of a literary work known as "the book of Isaiah."

Repeatedly, however, there are a variety of expressions alluding to the personal activity, role, or involvement of a person named Isaiah. Very interestingly, the quotations come from all parts of the book of Isaiah —so-called First, Second, and Third Isaiah[11]—all of which are attributed to the actual prophet. The first-century Christian and Jewish view was that a single prophet, Isaiah, wrote the entire book attributed to him.

In conclusion, a stylistic convention of attributing an Old Testament prophet's name, such as "Isaiah," to a quotation not written by that prophet does not appear to be supported from the evidence surveyed. Therefore, when Isaiah is quoted in Acts and by Jesus and Paul, those writers and speakers have in mind the actual prophet. This is supported by references in early Judaism and other early Christian literature. So Jesus, Acts, and Paul are either wrong in so referring to Isaiah or they are correct. The option that does not seem feasible is that those writers were reflecting a stylistic convention that referred only to a literary work known as "Isaiah." At least, the early evidence about Isaianic authorship points away from this option.

A similar view to the stylistic convention perspective is that Jesus and the New Testament writers did not intend to speak specifically about actual human authorship when referring to Isaiah but were concerned only about the divine meaning of the text being quoted. If they did not intend to communicate the identity of the human author, they cannot be charged with inaccuracy, even if a real person known as Isaiah did not actually write the entire book.

As mentioned toward the end of this book's opening dialogue, when someone says, "I went to work when the sun rose this morning," the

---

11. The typical critical view divides the book into three parts, written by three different authors at different times: First Isaiah (chaps. 1–39), Second Isaiah (chaps. 40–55), and Third Isaiah (chaps. 56–66).

intent is not to make a scientific statement about the movement of the sun but merely to communicate at what time the person went to work. Accordingly, references to Isaiah are like window dressing through which the divine message is conveyed. But, again, the problem with this is that our survey of references to Isaiah—not only in Judaism but especially in the New Testament—reveal repeated references to the active, personal role of Isaiah in writing and prophesying in all parts of the book. Consequently, such references are not merely the pipe through which the water of the real message flows but are part of the message.

But how is it part of the message? These references convey the notion of the authority of one who was appointed by God, so his message is to be seen as having divine authority: "*Rightly* did Isaiah prophesy of you [hypocrites]" (Matt. 15:7; Mark 7:6); ". . . *to fulfill* what was spoken through Isaiah the prophet" and similar such phrases (six times); and "the Holy Spirit *rightly* spoke through Isaiah the prophet to your fathers" (Acts 28:25). The word translated "rightly" is *kalōs*, which can also be rendered "correctly" or "accurately" (as elsewhere in the NT).[12] The authority of the prophet Isaiah is integral to the message communicated, as is also apparent from recalling Jesus' comparable appeal to Moses (Luke 20:37; 24:27, 44; John 1:17, 45) and David. This underscores the authority of the message and its speaker, demonstrating that the authority of these personages is inextricably bound up with their message. Note Jesus' appeal to David in Mark 12:35–37, where he is quoting Psalm 110:1:

> And Jesus began to say, as He taught in the temple, "How is it that
> the scribes say that the Christ is the son of David? David himself
> said in the Holy Spirit,
> 'The Lord said to my Lord,
> "Sit at my right hand,
> until I put your enemies beneath your feet."'
> David himself calls Him 'Lord'; so in what sense is He his son?"
> And the large crowd enjoyed listening to Him.

Also significant in this regard is that Jesus understands that parts of his ministry are modeled after the prophetic vocation of the actual prophet Isaiah himself. For example, he views his parabolic ministry as

---

12. See *A Greek-English Lexicon of the New Testament and Other Early Christian Literature*, rev. and ed. F. W. Danker (Chicago: University Press, 2000), 505–6, who surveys various ranges of meaning and correctly places the uses in Matt. 15:7, Mark 7:6, and Acts 28:25 in the category of "being in accord with a standard, rightly, correctly."

a recapitulation of the ministry of Isaiah, which the prophet explains in Isaiah 6:9–10. Jesus said:

> "Therefore I speak to them in parables; because while seeing they do not see, and while hearing they do not hear, nor do they understand. In their case the prophecy of Isaiah is being fulfilled, which says,
>   'You will keep on hearing, but will not understand;
>   you will keep on seeing, but will not perceive;
>   for the heart of this people has become dull,
>   with their ears they scarcely hear,
>   and they have closed their eyes,
>   otherwise they would see with their eyes,
>   hear with their ears,
>   and understand with their heart and return,
>   and I would heal them.'"(Matt. 13:13–15)

What applied to the historical Isaiah's ministry is now seen by Christ as applying to his own ministry. In fact, Isaiah 6:9–10 is a commission that the prophet is to fulfill, and Jesus understands that it "is fulfilled again" (*anapleroō*) in him. Isaiah's ministry was a historical foreshadowing of the even greater ministry of Jesus. Thus, the authority of this statement by Christ is, at least in part, derived from its origin with the prophet Isaiah.

All of the above references to Isaiah do not provide sufficient evidence to conclude that they are the insignificant husk that surrounds the real message intended. Rather, they are part of the message.

Was There a Stylistic Convention in Ancient Hellenism or Judaism by Which Specific Passages from Literary Works Could Be Attributed to Authors Who Did Not Actually Write Them?

One of the reasons for some reconsidering what it means in Acts and for Jesus and Paul to refer to all parts of Isaiah—so-called First, Second, and Third Isaiah—is the purported idea that there was a common stylistic convention in the ancient world by which people referred to passages from literary works by authors' names who had, in fact, not authored those works. The evidence, however, for such a way of referring to particular passages from ancient works is nonexistent. More work needs to be done in this area, but we are well served to a significant degree by Christopher D. Stanley's book on Paul's use of the Old Testament.[13]

---

13. Christopher D. Stanley, *Paul and the Language of Scripture*, SNTSMS 69 (Cambridge: University Press, 1992).

Stanley argues primarily that it was common for later authors to quote earlier authors, not verbatim but with small or larger changes. Sometimes the changes have no interpretative significance but there are times that the changes do represent interpretations by the quoter.[14] Stanley surveys early Greco-Roman and Jewish writers contemporary with the New Testament. He argues that Paul appears to follow the same general procedure as the non-biblical writers in his quotation technique.

Stanley does a good job of showing whether an author is dependent on earlier textual traditions or whether the changed wording reflects an independent rendering by the author. This is helpful; it provides a lot of the manual labor, especially in Paul, in supplying textual comparisons. But Stanley does not discuss very much the interpretative significance of these changes when they are attributed to the quoting author or even when they represent a textual tradition that appears already to be interpreting the earlier text (such as the LXX in relation to the MT). Stanley also makes the point that this style of quoting was not unique to the ancient world but is even common to our modern usage.[15] In this respect, it is not a very groundbreaking book.

With specific regard to the issue at hand, however, Stanley presents no evidence that it was an accepted stylistic convention at the time of Jesus and the New Testament period to quote from earlier authors and attribute to them quotations that did not come from those authors. Thus, he adduces no support that would make it understandable and acceptable that Jesus might have attributed to Isaiah the prophet quotations of so-called Second and Third Isaiah—quotations not actually written by Isaiah.

This is our main purpose in summarizing Stanley's book, though he himself does not draw this implication. But even if there were evidence of such a stylistic convention reflected in the Greco-Roman world, one would also have to show it operating in early Judaism.[16]

---

14. Ibid., 242–43.

15. See ibid., 355–56; though on p. 345 and p. 350 Stanley contradicts this assessment.

16. It is possible that the Jewish pseudepigrapha could offer a parallel to taking Isaiah 40–66 as written by a different author than Isaiah but in the name of Isaiah, which would have been assumed from chapters 1–39, but we are here more concerned with Jesus and the apostles quoting particular verses from "Isaiah" and attributing these verses to the prophet Isaiah. The pseudepigraphical group of writings, on the other hand, are not taken into consideration here because this body of works, while attributing an ancient heroic biblical name to a later writing composed by someone else, does not primarily quote from or expand on specific passages from a body of writings that were composed by that ancient biblical figure, as is argued for the authorship of Isaiah 40–66 (though these works do make plenty of allusions to Old Testament passages). Rather, a completely new and later composition is attributed to the earlier biblical character; thus, these pseudepigraphic names are attached to "new" works, not as references to Old Testament works. Furthermore, some of the biblical names attributed

Stanley does make the point that later writers did "correct" an earlier ancient text to "bring it into line with later sensibilities." This may
involve correcting the ancient author's wrong geographical reference or
a statement apparently contrary to the morality of a later age. Sometimes such "corrections" are mere additional statements set alongside
the original without comment.[17] These kinds of quotations, of course,
would not be applicable to New Testament writers quoting Old Testament texts and "correcting" them. Stanley concludes this discussion by
saying, "Modern notions of the inviolability of an author's original text
simply cannot be transferred to the ancient world."[18] Yet at other points
he asserts that such things are not uncommon in modern quotations.[19]
In this respect, he exhibits some inconsistency.

In another instance, Stanley mentions Heraclitus, who "can quote two
or more verses back-to-back with no indication of their diverse origins
[i.e., from different parts of Homer]. In every case the materials thus
combined deal with similar topics, producing a single 'quotation' that
better supports or exemplifies the author's [Heraclitus'] point."[20] After
the preceding reference, however, Stanley gives an example:

> One peculiarity worth noting is a single instance in which an introductory
> formula anticipates a quotation concerning Athena . . . is actually followed
> by a "quotation" that combines one passage on Athena with another that
> originally referred to Artemis. Though a memory lapse is always possible,
> it may be that here again one sees a certain willingness on the part of the
> author to adapt the Homeric text to his own purposes.[21]

to these pseudepigraphical works were people who wrote nothing of which we know (e.g., Enoch,
Abraham, Jacob, etc.). In the case, however, of Isaiah, the contention is that chapters 40–66 were
composed by a school of disciples or editors, who expanded on chapters 1–39, which were written
by the historical Isaiah. Indeed, one reason the large collection of pseudepigraphical works was not
included in the Old Testament canon was likely because the works were known at the time not to
have been written by the purported biblical person whose name was attached to them, and thus
were seen to lack the same biblical authority of Old Testament writers. Most holding a Second and
Third Isaiah view believe that chapters 40–66 were written around the sixth century BC, long before
the time when the literary genre of Jewish pseudepigrapha even arose and flourished (which began
around the beginning of the second century BC). In addition, if Isaiah 40–66 were a pseudepigraph,
would not the fake author go to clear and repeated lengths to insert the name of Isaiah at various
points throughout those chapters, as happens typically in the pseudepigraphical books? The survey
of early Jewish and Christian views (including that of Jesus) of Isaianic authorship will clearly reveal
that they did not view the book to be a pseudepigraph. In this connection, neither Jesus nor the
apostles ever *formally* quote from a pseudepigraphical book, presumably because they were held
not to have divine canonical authority.
17. Stanley, *Paul and the Language of Scripture*, 274.
18. Ibid.
19. Ibid., 356.
20. Ibid., 283–84.
21. Ibid., 284.

If this is not a memory lapse, then it is an interpretative attempt to describe Athena with the attributes of Artemis, a similar procedure that John uses in Revelation: "The one who was and is and is coming" is a name for Zeus, taken and applied to the God of the Bible, though there is also Old Testament influence.[22] But both quotations are apparently from Homer, not from Homer and a different author.

But none of what Stanley has said so far has any parallels with attributing a specific quotation to an author such as "Isaiah" that is not really from that author. Indeed, in surveying the Greco-Roman authors, he focuses on their quotations of Homer, and, as far as I can tell, not one time is there any question of attributing to Homer statements or segments from another author.[23]

Stanley, however, does introduce something that could appear to fit this kind of thing. He cites *1 Esdras* 1.58 (= 1:55, LXX), which I cite here in its immediate context:

And they were servants to him and to his sons until the Persians began to reign, in fulfilment of the word of the Lord by the mouth of Jeremiah. (*1 Esd.* 1:57 = 1:54, LXX)

"Until the land has enjoyed its sabbaths, it shall keep sabbath all the time of its desolation until the completion of seventy years." (*1 Esd.* 1:58 = 1:55, LXX)

In the first year of Cyrus as king of the Persians, that the word of the Lord by the mouth of Jeremiah might be accomplished. (*1 Esd.* 2:1 = *1 Esd.* 2:1a, LXX)

The Lord stirred up the spirit of Cyrus king of the Persians, and he made a proclamation throughout all his kingdom and also put it in writing. (*1 Esd.* 2:2 = *1 Esd.* 2:16, LXX)

Stanley says that *1 Esdras* 1:58 (=1:55, LXX) is "a verse framed as an indirect statement in 2 Chr 36.21 (a midrashic conflation of Jer 25.12 and Lev 26.34), appears as a direct quotation and is attributed in its entirety to the prophet Jeremiah."[24] On the surface, I suppose, one might be able to say that *1 Esdras* is attributing to Jeremiah words from Moses (Leviticus) and the Chronicler. But there is a very thin line between what Stanley calls "an

---

22. On which see a number of examples like this in Acts and Revelation in G. K. Beale, "Biblical Faith and Other Religions in New Testament Theology," in *Biblical Faith and Other Religions*, ed. D. W. Baker (Grand Rapids, MI: Kregel, 2004).

23. E.g., see Stanley's conclusion in *Paul and the Language of Scripture*, 339.

24. Ibid., 309.

indirect statement in 2 Chr 36:21" and "a direct quotation in *1 Esdras*," since both have virtually the same introductory phrasing "to fulfill the word" [or "for fulfillment of the saying"] of the Lord through the mouth of Jeremiah. Note the textual comparisons of the relevant texts:[25]

Passage	Greek	English Translation	Overlap
1 Esd. 1:57–58 (= 1:54–55, LXX)	εἰς ἀναπλήρωσιν τοῦ ῥήματος τοῦ κυρίου ἐν στόματι Ιερεμιου ἕως τοῦ εὐδοκῆσαι **τὴν γῆν τὰ σάββατα αὐτῆς πάντα** τὸν χρόνον **τῆς ἐρημώσεως αὐτῆς σαββατιεῖ εἰς συμπλήρωσιν ἐτῶν ἑβδομήκοντα.**	In fulfillment of the word of the Lord by the mouth of Jeremiah; until the land has enjoyed its sabbaths, it shall keep sabbath all the time of its desolation until the completion of the seventy years.	The bold font reflects overlap with 2 Chron. 36:21–22.
2 Chron. 36:21–22 (LXX)	**τοῦ πληρωθῆναι λόγον κυρίου διὰ στόματος Ιερεμιου ἕως τοῦ** προσδέξασθαι **τὴν γῆν τὰ σάββατα αὐτῆς** σαββατίσαι **πάσας τὰς** ἡμέρας **τῆς ἐρημώσεως αὐτῆς** ἐσαββάτισεν **εἰς συμπλήρωσιν ἐτῶν ἑβδομήκοντα** . . . μετὰ τὸ **πληρωθῆναι ῥῆμα κυρίου** διὰ στόματος Ιερεμιου.	. . . that the word of the Lord by the mouth of Jeremiah might be fulfilled until the land should enjoy its Sabbaths in resting [and] sabbath-keeping all the days of its desolation until the fulfillment of seventy years . . . after the fulfillment of the word of the Lord by the mouth of Jeremiah.	The bold font reflects overlap with 1 Esd. 1:57–58.
Lev. 26:34 (LXX)	τότε εὐδοκήσει ἡ γῆ **τὰ σάββατα αὐτῆς** καὶ **πάσας τὰς ἡμέρας τῆς ἐρημώσεως αὐτῆς** καὶ ὑμεῖς ἔσεσθε ἐν τῇ γῇ τῶν ἐχθρῶν ὑμῶν τότε σαββατιεῖ ἡ γῆ καὶ εὐδοκήσει **τὰ σάββατα αὐτῆς.**	Then the land shall enjoy its Sabbaths all the days of its desolation, and you shall be in the land of your enemies; then the land shall also keep its Sabbaths.	The bold font reflects overlap with 2 Chron. 36:21–22.
Jer. 25:12 (LXX)	καὶ ἐν τῷ **πληρωθῆναι τὰ ἑβδομήκοντα ἔτη** ἐκδικήσω τὸ ἔθνος ἐκεῖνο φησὶν **κύριος** καὶ θήσομαι αὐτοὺς εἰς ἀφανισμὸν αἰώνιον.	And when the seventy years are fulfilled, I will take vengeance on that nation, and will make them a perpetual desolation.	The bold font reflects overlap with 2 Chron. 36:21–22.

Clearly, *1 Esdras* 1:57–58 (=1:54–55, LXX) is essentially a quotation from 2 Chronicles 36:21, as the above chart makes clear. In fact, *1 Esrdas* 1:1–2:5 is essentially a verbatim copying of 2 Chronicles 35:1–36:23.

25. Greek script is used here instead of English transliteration in order that the textual comparisons may be observed more readily.

Thus, like 2 Chronicles 36:21, so *1 Esdras* 1:54b–55 attributes the saying to Jeremiah. Therefore, Stanley is likely correct that 2 Chronicles itself combines Leviticus 26:34 and Jeremiah 25:12. So the problem is not how *1 Esdras* can attribute a saying to Jeremiah that includes what Moses said, but how the Chronicler can do it.[26]

The answer seems to be along the following lines: Jeremiah could be developing Leviticus, though more conceptually than verbally, or the Chronicler could be interpreting that Jeremiah is developing Leviticus, and so he combines the two. The reason the Chronicler attributes the entire saying to Jeremiah is likely that it is the part of the prophecy that he mainly had in mind. Leviticus has become subsumed interpretatively in Jeremiah. This is classic midrash, in which one key biblical text is combined with another to be interpreted by it. The Chronicler is not citing an entire segment of chapters and attributing them to an author who really did not write them. The Chronicler is interpreting one verse (in Jeremiah) by another verse (in Leviticus), and the author he mentions, Jeremiah, is the one that he mainly has in mind to interpret, which is interpretatively supplemented by the secondary author, Moses, in Leviticus.[27]

This then is not an issue of authorship but one of midrashic interpretation. The same phenomenon occurs with the attribution of Isaiah to Malachi in Mark 1:2–3. Rikk Watts has demonstrated quite plausibly the reason for this: Mark is dominated by Isaiah throughout the book—being concerned with narrating Jesus as inaugurating the end-time second exodus predicted by Isaiah and other Old Testament references adduced throughout Mark supplement interpretatively the Isaianic picture.[28] What better way to start off that project than to adduce Malachi to interpret Isaiah 40:3, so that Malachi becomes subsumed interpretatively into Isaiah.[29] This is not, as far as I can tell, about a forgetful memory nor a stylistic convention whereby an author is adduced who could be seen to have written a passage that that author, indeed, did not write.[30]

---

26. Of course, *1 Esdras* also appears to supplement two further possible words from Leviticus, under the influence of the precedent-setting 2 Chronicles, which had already combined other parts of Leviticus with Jeremiah: *eudokēsa* and *sabbatiei* (though the latter is a mere minor change in verbal form).

27. Note that Stanley concludes his discussion by noting that there is some textual lack of clarity in the *1 Esdras* quotation: "The origins of this conflation and adaptation remain obscure [in *1 Esdras* 1:55]" (ibid., 309). So one should be careful of basing too much on this particular example.

28. On which see R. Watts, *Isaiah's New Exodus in Mark* (Grand Rapids: Baker, 1997), 53–90.

29. Indeed, Mal. 3:1 alludes to the leading angel of Ex. 23:20, guiding Israel in the first exodus, which fits admirably with the Isa. 40:3 reference to the messenger preparing for the second exodus.

30. The same thing is going on in Matt. 27:9–10 where Jeremiah and Zechariah are combined, but the entirety is attributed to Jeremiah. See D. A. Carson's explanation in *Matthew, Chapters*

It may be in some cases that only the main text to be interpreted is mentioned, since not only one but more secondary texts brought in to interpret the focus text are present, and it would be too cumbersome to mention all three of the texts or authors.[31] Similarly, would we demand that Paul, when intentionally referring to a phrase from an earlier letter, explicitly say something like, "As I said in Galatians . . ." in order to preserve his historical authorship of that earlier saying? In so doing, does he deny that earlier authorship of the statement? I don't think so.

Of course, Isaiah 40–66 may be one big midrashic interpretation of the preceding part of Isaiah. If so, Jesus attributes parts of this latter section to Isaiah, since the anonymous author of Isaiah 40–66 is interpretatively expanding the focus text of the first part of the book, which was penned by the prophet Isaiah. But such an interpretation would be very close to the Jewish pseudepigraphical genre, which we have already noted as an unlikely category in which to place Isaiah 40–66. Such a large-scale midrashic view of Isaiah 40–66 would be quite different from citing specific quotations or combining parts of verses for interpretative purposes, which is the topic of concern here. Indeed, we are talking about intertextuality, whereby the main text to be interpreted is mentioned but not the interpreting text.

Why have we included a summary of Stanley's work here? This survey of his work does not support the notion that there was an ancient stylistic convention among Greco-Roman or Jewish writers contemporary with the New Testament period of attributing a specific quotation to someone other than the original author. Therefore, when some scholars assert that there was such a stylistic habit and that this habit explains the New Testament references to particular verses from Isaiah, such an assertion is not supported by evidence. Until there is further evidence forthcoming to the contrary, scholars should be hesitant to appeal to this kind of argument.[32]

13–28, EBC (Grand Rapids: Zondervan, 1995), 562–67, which is very much along the lines that Watts follows.

31. In fact, this could be the case in Mark 1:2–3, where Mal. 3:1 and Ex. 23:20 may both be adduced as secondary enhancing texts of the main focus text of Isaiah. Again, see Watts, *Isaiah's New Exodus in Mark*, 53–90, who discusses the influence of Ex. 23:20 in Mal. 3:1, but concludes that only Malachi is present in Mark 1; but both the Exodus and Malachi texts may well be in mind, as the margin of NA[27] contends (though on p. 89 Watts refers to the Exodus/Malachi conflation in Mark 1).

32. Though I suspect it is unlikely that Stanley would draw the conclusion that Isaiah the prophet was the author of Isaiah 40–66, it would probably be for other reasons than his disagreement with the evidence adduced in this section. Of course, one could hold that Jesus and the apostles thought Isaiah was the original author of sayings from this section, so that from this vantage point their citations still fit with Stanley's study. However, such a conclusion poses other problems dealt with

Was Jesus' Reference to Isaiah an Accommodation to an Incorrect Jewish Tradition?

Many of those who may not be persuaded that the references to Isaiah were part of an understandable stylistic convention would contend that the belief of early Judaism and Christianity in the authorship of Isaiah was not historically correct but had somehow become part of their socially constructed tradition. Consequently, they say, it is only natural that Jesus himself expressed this belief, since not only did he have a divine nature, but also he *was* human—speaking Aramaic, accepting the various customs of his Jewish culture, presumably including traditions that were unbiblical or not true to past historical reality. This is sometimes understood as part of a kenosis theory of Christ's incarnation, whereby "he emptied himself" or "gave up the use" of his divine attributes. Accordingly, he was, in part, a typical person of his time and culture, naturally and unconsciously accepting some of the untrue traditions of that culture. This may be referred to as an "unconscious accommodation" of Jesus to his culture.

To further support this view, it is sometimes said that Christ himself admitted he was ignorant of some things and, therefore, fallible in his knowledge, though the main thrust of his message was reliable. Matthew 24:36 is a text sometimes adduced to this end, where Christ says that the "day and hour" of the end of history "no one knows, not even the angels of heaven, nor the Son, but the Father alone." But ignorance of the future is not the same thing as making an erroneous statement; if Christ had predicted something that did not take place, it would be an error. In support of this, ironically, is the directly preceding verse: "Heaven and earth will pass away, but My words will not pass away" (v. 35). In other words, any assertions about past, present, or future reality that Christ makes have a truthful force that cannot be blunted.[33]

---

in the remainder of this study, among which are theological problems (e.g., Christology). One could object to my application of Stanley's work to Jesus' quotations, since Jesus never wrote anything; his references to Isaiah were oral. But the same thing could be technically said of Paul's letter to the Romans and Peter's first epistle (on which see below). Anyway, what Stanley has adduced with respect to authors would appear to be just as applicable to speakers.

33. I am grateful to J. I. Packer, *"Fundamentalism" and the Word of God* (Grand Rapids: Eerdmans, 1957), 60–61, for this point about the link between Matt. 24:35 and 24:36. In this connection, note also B. B. Warfield's comment on Christology: "In the case of our Lord's person, the human nature remains truly human while yet it can never fall into sin or error because it can never act out of relation with the Divine nature into conjunction with which it has been brought." *The Inspiration and Authority of the Bible* (Phillipsburg, NJ: Presbyterian and Reformed, 1970), 162f (cited by Packer, ibid., 83, but I have been unable to find this precise quotation in Warfield's book, though he says as much on pp. 158–76).

In this respect, some evangelical postmodernists might even conclude that some of the erroneous tradition was not wrong for first-century Jews to hold, even though, according to our modern historical standards, we would judge it to be erroneous. But, so goes the argument, we should not impose our standards of historical correctness on ancient literature. Thus, God communicated fully inspired truths to first-century Jews in their own linguistic and cultural language.

But, again, Matthew 24:35 says that no matter how many cultures come and go, Christ's truthful word remains the same. Cultures, with their idiosyncratic beliefs, will rise and fall until Christ comes a final time; ultimately this "heaven and earth will pass away, but Christ's words shall not pass away." The truth of Christ's words and teachings are not culturally bound but transcend all cultures and remain unaltered by cultural beliefs and traditions that contain untrue elements. This is said in another way in Isaiah 40:7–8, quoted partly in James 1:10–11 and more fully 1 Peter 1:24–25: "The grass withers, the flower fades, but the word of our God stands forever" (see also Isa. 55:11; Matt. 5:17–18).

As argued earlier, ancient cultures had logical categories for observing and assessing the world and distinguishing the true from the false, which were in significant ways commensurate to our modern categories.[34] In line with this, Jesus' propositional statements about such things as sin, his deity, his saving death, his resurrection, the final resurrection of humanity, and the end of world history are truths that transcend all cultures.

Others take a different tack and contend that Jesus, as the God-man, may well have known that Isaiah was not the author of the work that went by his name; rather, he consciously "accommodated" himself to the false Jewish view in order to facilitate his communication of the message from the book. Accordingly, to have exposed the error of the false Jewish tradition about Isaiah would have altered the center of attention from the main point of Isaiah's message to a pedantic point about technical historical authorship. Therefore, Jesus adjusted his message to permit this belief to remain unchallenged.

There is a common problem with both the preceding perspectives about Christ's "accommodation." It is clear that part of Jesus' mission was to confront and expose the false traditions of Judaism that had gradually grown and come to be held by the time of the first century.[35]

---

34. On which see chap. 1, "The Issue of Socially Constructed Cultures, Presuppositions, and Biblical Interpretation."

35. On which see further, e.g., N. B. Stonehouse, *The Witness of Matthew and Mark to Christ* (Philadelphia: Presbyterian Guardian, 1944; repr. Grand Rapids: Eerdmans, 1958), 195–211; and

J. I. Packer aptly put his finger on this point as far back as the late 1950s, when he concluded that Jesus "did not hesitate to challenge and condemn, on His authority, many accepted Jewish ideas which seemed to him false."[36] He adds:

> Scripture, indeed, contains emphatic warnings against uncritical deference to traditions and speculations in theology. Christ deals with the question of the authority of tradition in Mk. vii.6-13. The Pharisees claimed their oral law was derived from Moses and should therefore be treated as an authoritative supplement to and exposition of the written law. Christ rejects this idea, contrasting the written word with the oral law as "the command-ment *of God*" and "the commandments *of men*" respectively. . . . The fact that they are bowing to man-made tradition rather than God-given Scripture, He says, shows that their hearts are far from God. To Christ, ecclesiastical tradition was no part of the word of God; it must be tested by Scripture and, if found wanting, dropped.[37]

Significantly, the Jews here believed that since a well-known Old Testament figure, Moses, was the author of their oral law,[38] their oral laws had equal authority with the written Scripture that had also come from Moses. Jesus says no and that such traditions did not have the authority of Mosaic Scripture. In fact, in Mark 7:1–13, Jesus contrasts Isaiah's prophesying (v. 6, citing Isa. 29:13) and Moses' written word (v. 10), which had divine authority, with "the tradition of the elders," which has no divine authority. Therefore, while Jesus opposed the pseudo-authority of untrue Jewish traditions, he always affirmed the definitive authority of the Old Testament (e.g., John 10:35, "the Scripture cannot be broken"), and he "never qualified the Jewish belief in its absolute authority in the slightest degree."[39] This appears to be a case where Jesus disagrees with a pseudo-oral source, the false attribution of Jewish oral tradition to Moses.

In the light of this, is it possible that Jesus would have gone along with a false Jewish view about the authorship of Isaiah? It is unlikely, especially since the Old Testament was foundational for Jesus' teaching and thought about his vocation and his identity; he made appeal

---

R. V. G. Tasker, *The Old Testament in the New Testament* (Grand Rapids: Eerdmans, 1954), 32. I am thankful to Packer, *"Fundamentalism,"* p. 56, n. 2, for alerting me to these two sources.

36. Packer, *"Fundamentalism,"* 55.

37. Ibid., 70–71.

38. On which see, e.g., J. Neusner, "Rabbinic Literature: Mishnah and Tosefta," in *Dictionary of New Testament Background*, ed. C. A. Evans and S. E. Porter (Downers Grove, IL: InterVarsity, 2000), 895.

39. Ibid., 55.

to the Old Testament repeatedly as the primary warrant for the things he did and said. Is it likely, in this light, that he would knowingly or unknowingly be wrong about who was the authoritative author of what some scholars refer to as the "gospel of Isaiah"? If he were wrong here, why should we have confidence that he was not also wrong in other of his important appeals to the Old Testament?[40] As R. V. G. Tasker has concluded, "If [Christ] could be mistaken on matters which He regarded as of the strictest relevance to His own person and ministry, it is difficult to see exactly how or why He can or should be trusted anywhere else."[41]

Reconsideration of the Material in the Book of Isaiah Itself

Superscriptions referring to the prophet Isaiah in the book of Isaiah itself are found at 1:1, 2:1, 13:1, and 20:2:

> The *vision of Isaiah* the son of Amoz concerning Judah and Jerusalem, which he saw during the reigns of Uzziah, Jotham, Ahaz *and* Hezekiah, kings of Judah. (Isa. 1:1)

> The *word which Isaiah the son of Amoz saw* concerning Judah and Jerusalem. (Isa. 2:1)

> The *oracle concerning Babylon which Isaiah the son of Amoz saw.* (Isa. 13:1)

> The LORD *spoke through Isaiah the son of Amoz, saying*, "Go and loosen." (Isa. 20:2)

See also 2 Chronicles 26:22: "Now the rest of the acts of Uzziah, first to last, *the prophet Isaiah, the son of Amoz, has written.*"

In this respect, Richard Schultz's recent conclusion about the superscriptions is one with which I am still in agreement:

> Given 1) the clear assertion in Isa 1:1 that what follows is "the vision of Isaiah son of Amoz, which he saw concerning Judah and Jerusalem in the days of Uzziah, Jotham, Ahaz, and Hezekiah, kings of Judah" and 2) the absence of any additional ascriptions of authorship within the book, the "one Isaiah" position may be the only one that takes the book's own claims seriously.[42]

---

40. Packer, *Fundamentalism*, 60, though Packer is speaking generally about Christ's view of the authority of the Old Testament and not focusing merely on Jesus' appeals to Isaiah.
41. Tasker, *The Old Testament in the New Testament*, 37.
42. Schultz, "How Many 'Isaiahs'?" 153.

I still find the traditional view of Isaianic authorship for the whole book preferable, though in the academic guild I am not considered to be an Old Testament practitioner but a New Testament one. The most recent work of which I am aware that argues for this position is Richard Schultz's article on the authorship of Isaiah.[43] The article presents a brief but viable conservative view of the significance of the superscriptions in Isaiah as well as of the unity of the book.

As evident from reading in the field of Isaiah scholarship, one of the main reasons for reconsidering the authorship of Isaiah 40–66 is that it is so specifically aware of circumstances in Babylon, and it addresses those who were in exile there rather than Isaiah's earlier audience in the land of Israel. In fact, a date for Isaiah 40–66 around the time of Israel's exile or soon after fits in with a presupposition of the majority of Old Testament scholars, who are convinced by higher-critical views of dating. Such views claim that prophecy contained material that was mainly relevant for a prophet's contemporary audience and did not contain predicted events that had no relation to the present. Thus, most predictions are viewed as *vaticinium ex eventu*, which means "prophecy after the event."

In other words, recent events in the lives of a prophet's audience were written down as if they had been prophesied many years, or even centuries, earlier. I am not convinced of this presupposition about Old Testament books but am persuaded generally by the evidence of Schultz's article. Most who hold to a different authorship of Isaiah believe that the author was someone living directly after the prophecies were fulfilled and writing historical accounts as if they were prophecy. A minority of scholars holding to non-Isaianic authorship still affirm, however, that the anonymous author of Isaiah 40–66 was living in the midst of the Babylonian exile and was genuinely prophesying about events that would happen in about thirty or forty years.

But Isaiah 13 is just as specific in a more extreme manner in discussing the decisive judgment of Babylon at the hand of the Persians. This thirteenth chapter is introduced by the phrase, "The oracle concerning Babylon which Isaiah the son of Amoz saw." Does this not indicate a positive answer to the question posed skeptically by some that the only way Isaiah 40–66 could have been written by Isaiah the prophet was

---

43. See also his forthcoming commentary on Isaiah for Baker; note, in addition, Schultz's monograph (based on his Yale PhD dissertation), *The Search for Quotation*, JSOTSup 180 (Sheffield: Sheffield Academic Press, 1999), which focuses not on authorship issues but on intertextuality in the Old Testament, especially with a focus on Isaiah.

if he had seen a vision of the future or had been transported by vision into the future?

Isaiah 13:1 makes this scenario quite viable. The oracle likely continues into Isaiah 14:1–23, where Israel is said repeatedly to have been in bondage to Babylon and that Babylon will be judged and Israel will be restored from Babylon. Isaiah 21:1–2 likewise refers to Isaiah's oracle and vision, which are about the judgment of Babylon ("fallen, fallen is Babylon," [21:9]). Of course, I am aware that commentators place Isaiah 13–14 and parts of 21:1–10 late as well.[44] And, of course, commentators place Isaiah 24–27 at a late date because of its eschatology (resurrection, Israel's restoration, etc.). I am not persuaded by these arguments. Wherever Isaiah appears to make specific prophecies, the critics too often assume that such prophecies are *vaticinium ex eventu*. Thus, I think presuppositions drive these various late datings of parts of Isaiah.

Interestingly, "I" in 24:16 and 25:1 refers likely to "Isaiah" in continuation of the fifteen times it has already occurred in Isaiah 6–21 in that manner. In addition, "But I say, 'Woe to me! Woe to me! Alas for me!'" (Isa. 24:16) appears uniquely similar to Isaiah 6:5, "Then I said, 'Woe is me, for I am ruined!'" In this respect, "oracle" (in Isa. 21:1) is used about ten times in Isaiah (chaps. 13–30) and "vision" (Isa. 21:2) about seven times in the same segment. Also, the name "Isaiah" occurs about sixteen times in Isaiah 1–39. In particular, the intensive use in Isaiah 37–39 (ten times) may be significant, since there Isaiah is reported to have prophesied the exile to Babylon:

> Then Isaiah the prophet came to King Hezekiah and said to him, "What did these men say, and from where have they come to you?" And Hezekiah said, "They have come to me from a far country, from Babylon." (Isa. 39:3)

> "Behold, the days are coming when all that is in your house and all that your fathers have laid up in store to this day will be carried to Babylon; nothing will be left," says the LORD. (Isa. 39:6)

> "And some of your sons who will issue from you, whom you will beget, will be taken away, and they will become officials in the palace of the king of Babylon." (Isa. 39:7)

Considering this together with the prophecies of Israel's bondage to Babylon in chapters 13–14 and of her restoration in chapters 24–27,

---

44. E.g., with respect to Isaiah 13–14, see S. Erlandsson, *The Burden of Babylon: A Study of Isaiah 13:2–14:23*, ConBT 4 (Lund: Gleerup, 1970).

are the prophecies of the very same things in Isaiah 40–66 so alarming and different? The main difference is the extended nature of this latter section, but the actual nature of the material does not appear to be that much different, except for the specific reference to the idols of Babylon. Intriguingly, "Babylon" appears nine times in Isaiah 13–39 and only four times in chapters 40–66. But even this theme of idolatry in chapters 40–66 has its clear roots in Isaiah 1–39.[45] Note in this respect Isaiah 21:1–10:

> The oracle concerning the wilderness of the sea.
> As windstorms in the Negev sweep on,
>> It comes from the wilderness, from a terrifying land.
> A harsh vision has been shown to me;
>> The treacherous one still deals treacherously, and the destroyer
>> still destroys.
>> Go up, Elam, lay siege, Media;
>> I have made an end of all the groaning she has caused.
> For this reason my loins are full of anguish;
>> Pains have seized me like the pains of a woman in labor.
>> I am so bewildered I cannot hear, so terrified I cannot see.
> My mind reels, horror overwhelms me;
>> The twilight I longed for has been turned for me into trembling.
>> They set the table, they spread out the cloth, they eat, they drink;
>> "Rise up, captains, oil the shields."
>
> For thus the Lord says to me,
>> "Go, station the lookout, let him report what he sees.
> When he sees riders, horsemen in pairs,
>> A train of donkeys, a train of camels,
>> Let him pay close attention, very close attention."
>
> Then the lookout called,
>> "O Lord, I stand continually by day on the watchtower,
>> And I am stationed every night at my guard post.
> Now behold, here comes a troop of riders, horsemen in pairs."
>> And one said, "Fallen, fallen is Babylon;
>> And all the images of her gods are shattered on the ground."
> O my threshed people, and my afflicted of the threshing floor!
>> What I have heard from the LORD of hosts,
>> The God of Israel, I make known to you.

---

45. On which see G. K. Beale, "Isaiah 6:9–13: A Retributive Taunt against Idolatry," *VT* 41 (1991): 257–78, on which see also expanded comments in my *You Become Like What You Worship: A Biblical Theology of Idolatry* (Downers Grove: InterVarsity, 2008).

Isaiah[46] here sees a vision of the future fall of Babylon and hears the message from God about this fall several generations after his own, including the judgment of Babylon's idols, a theme expanded in Isaiah 40–48. Isaiah 21:2 not only prophesies about the fall of Babylon but explicitly names the nation, "Media," that will defeat Babylon (as also in Isa. 13:17), which is very similar to though not as specific as Isaiah 44:28 and 45:1–3, 12–13. Is this not virtually equivalent to Isaiah's being transported to the future or seeing a vision of the future or hearing about it in an oracular manner and then prophesying about it?[47]

Likewise, Isaiah 2:1–4, introduced as "the vision which Isaiah the son of Amoz saw," and its prophecy of the eschatological temple and the incoming Gentiles to Jerusalem is a very specific restoration prophecy of very distant eschatological events. If all of Isaiah 1 to 39 is from Isaiah's hand, it would seem that the nature of especially chapters 13–14, 21, 24–27, and 39 would assuage one's unease at the same—though more extended—material in Isaiah 40–66. Of course, again, if these earlier six chapters are not from Isaiah, then that would change the nature of this conclusion.[48]

Additionally, in Isaiah's own day, the northern kingdom was already in Assyrian exile, and "Sennacherib claimed to have conquered forty-six walled cities in Judah and deported more than two hundred thousand of its citizens."[49] In view of this, together with the fact that Babylon was already on the ascendancy (see Isaiah 39), does it not make sense that Isaiah would have seen the captives belonging eventually to Babylon (which he actually says in chapter 39) and the future distant restoration necessarily being from Babylon?

In this respect, the appeal to Isaiah as the author of Isaiah 40–66 by early Judaism and the New Testament is to underscore, at least in part, that God can predict the end from the beginning—God can make long-range prophecy. The best explanation for their appeal is that they were

---

46. That Isaiah the prophet is in mind is apparent from the repeated first-person pronouns (vv. 2–4, 6, 8, 10) in continuation of the repeated first-person pronouns referring to "Isaiah" in the preceding chapters.

47. For support of the ideas offered in this paragraph, see Young, *The Book of Isaiah* 2, 59–75.

48. Of course, the most specific and alarming prophecy is the prediction about "Cyrus" (Isaiah 44–45), but this is not as much of a problem for an exilic prophet as for a preexilic prophet (i.e., Cyrus may not have been reigning at the time of the purported exilic prophet's writing). You may recall that Harrison, *Introduction to the Old Testament*, 794, attributes this to a later scribal gloss, which does not *necessarily* compromise a "unity of Isaiah" view, but if genuine prophecy is allowed for, then why cannot such a prophecy be made, especially since (1) the Messiah is specifically prophesied, (2) the "Medes" have already been prophesied about in chapters 13 and 21, and (3) predictive prophecy is often referred to throughout all parts of Isaiah as evidence of God's sovereignty?

49. Schultz, "How Many Isaiahs?" 164.

following the original intention of Isaiah 40–66, written by Isaiah long before the exile and restoration. To claim that these were not prophecies at all, but history written to appear as prophecy, does not appear to do justice to the polemic that Isaiah 40–66 is conducting. If those to whom this section of Isaiah was originally addressed knew that it was not prophecy, then the polemic against the idols' inability to predict becomes vapid and impotent.

Even to say that an anonymous prophet living during the exile issued actual short-term prophecies while still technically affirming real predictions comes too close to affirming that such predictions were virtually like weather or political prognostications. The author was living so close to the events that he prophesied that he was able, from the human perspective, to predict what was going to happen; the fact that these events did occur demonstrates the divine inspiration of the prophecies, at least, according to an unusual conservative view of such an anonymous *exilic* prophet.

To say that the prophecies came from an exilic anonymous prophet even though they were in the mind of God a few hundred years earlier appears to be special pleading. Such short-range prophecy also dilutes the polemic against the idols, that they cannot make long-range prophecies. While short-range prophecy can occur in the Old and New Testaments, the point of the Isaianic statements supports a long-range perspective, as the following texts show. These prophecies below are specifically of restoration from Babylonian exile and are to be understood as long-range prophecies that were issued before even the Assyrian exile, most likely by Isaiah the prophet:

> Do you not know? Have you not heard?
> Has it not been declared to you from the beginning?
> Have you not understood from the foundations of the earth? (Isa.
>   40:21)

> "Who has performed and accomplished it,
> Calling forth the generations from the beginning?
> 'I, the LORD, am the first, and with the last. I am He.'" (Isa. 41:4)

> Who has declared *this* from the beginning, that we might know?
> Or from former times, that we may say, "*He is* right!"?
> Surely there was no one who declared,
> Surely there was no one who proclaimed,
> Surely there was no one who heard your words. (Isa. 41:26)

"Thus says the LORD, the King of Israel and his Redeemer, the LORD
   of hosts:
   'I am the first and I am the last,
   And there is no God besides Me.
'Who is like Me? Let him proclaim and declare it;
      Yes, let him recount it to Me in order,
      From the time that I established the ancient nation.
      And let them declare to them the things that are coming
      And the events that are going to take place.
'Do not tremble and do not be afraid;
      Have I not long since announced it to you and declared it?
      And you are My witnesses.
      Is there any God besides Me,
      Or is there any other Rock?
      I know of none.'" (Isa. 44:6–8)

"Declaring the end from the beginning,
      And from ancient times things which have not been done,
      Saying, 'My purpose will be established,
      And I will accomplish all My good pleasure.'
Calling a bird of prey from the east,
      The man of My purpose from a far country.
      Truly I have spoken; truly I will bring it to pass.
      I have planned it, surely I will do it." (Isa. 46:10–11)

"I declared the former things long ago
And they went forth from My mouth, and I proclaimed them.
Suddenly I acted, and they came to pass." (Isa. 48:3)

"Therefore I declared *them* to you long ago,
      Before they took place I proclaimed them to you,
      So that you would not say, 'My idol has done them,
      And my graven image and my molten image have commanded
      them.'
"You have heard; look at all this.
And you, will you not declare it?
I proclaim to you new things from this time,
Even hidden things which you have not known." (Isa. 48:5–6;
   cf. also Isa. 43:9–19).[50]

---

50. Though cf. the following text that uses the same language as the above Isaiah texts and affirms
that the king of Assyria's recent past victories over other nations was planned long ago by God:
   "Have you not heard?
   Long ago I did it,
   From ancient times I planned it.
   Now I have brought it to pass,
   That you should turn fortified cities into ruinous heaps" (Isa. 37:26).

The New Testament perspective is that Old Testament prophets made long-range predictions. First Peter 1:10–12 affirms:

> As to this salvation, the prophets who prophesied of the grace that *would come* to you made careful searches and inquiries, seeking to know what person or time the Spirit of Christ within them was indicating as He predicted the sufferings of Christ and the glories to follow. It was revealed to them that they were not serving themselves, but you, in these things which now have been announced to you through those who preached the gospel to you by the Holy Spirit sent from heaven—things into which angels long to look.

Not only does this underscore long-range prophecy by prophets from the Old Testament but also that the prophets consciously knew that they were predicting things that would occur well after their own generation. This is just the opposite of the presupposition noted above by so many in the contemporary Old Testament guild, that prophecy included primarily material that was relevant for the contemporary audience of the prophet. Other New Testament passages make the same point (e.g., Matt. 13:16–17; John 8:56; Heb. 11:13).

Also interesting about the 1 Peter text is that among the Old Testament prophets within Peter's purview is the prophet who predicted the restoration prophecies of Isaiah 40:6–8 (1 Pet. 1:24–25) and Isaiah 53 (1 Pet. 2:22–25, where repeated references are made to Isaiah 53[51]). These Isaiah texts are found in the portion of the prophecy typically attributed to "second Isaiah," not to the prophet Isaiah himself, due to the guild's presupposition about the relevance and fulfillment of prophecy in the prophet's contemporary audience. Yet these very texts are connected not to short-range prophecy but to the programmatic statement about *long-range* prophecy in 1 Peter 1:10–12! And, indeed, the New Testament writers understand that Isaiah 53 was fulfilled in Christ, which means that Isaiah 53 predicted the Messiah's coming seven centuries earlier. Even according to the late dating of Isaiah 53, the prediction would have been around five centuries earlier. If this is so, why is it so hard to believe that Isaiah could have predicted two centuries earlier Israel's return from Babylonian captivity, including the

---

51. On which see most recently, D. A. Carson, "The Old Testament in the General Epistles," in *Commentary on the New Testament Use of the Old Testament*, ed. G. K. Beale and D. A. Carson (Grand Rapids: Baker, 2007).

specific prophecy about Cyrus being instrumental in that restoration (Isa. 45:1–13)?[52]

The typical response is that the New Testament did not have the same perspective as the Old Testament, and therefore this issue about Isaiah must be settled only by studying the book of Isaiah itself. This response is fueled typically by two notions: (1) the accepted idea that because Old Testament studies is a separate discipline that the New Testament's perspective on and interpretation of the Old Testament is not only secondary but often enough does not reflect the true state of things in the Old Testament. Rather, the New Testament reflects only the evolved beliefs and traditions of first-century Judaism. (2) The Bible is not fully inspired, so there is no ultimate divine author of the whole. This means that the New Testament's commentary on the Old (e.g., the authorship of Isaiah) is not reliable. The plea of this chapter, however, is that there are also reasonable and cogent arguments within Isaiah itself that have viability for the unity of Isaiah. Furthermore, the New Testament should also be considered as part of the evidence of the authorship issue.

The degree of "intratextuality"—some would say "intertextuality"—between Isaiah 1–39 and 40–66 has become so recognized that there is an apparent trend among Isaiah scholars who hold to diversity of authorship to recognize a "final literary unity."[53] The line between "unity of authorship" and "final literary unity" is becoming thinner and thinner.

I also find Schultz's conclusion pointing in the right direction:

> Rather, the issue is whether we legitimately can posit a series of inspired authors or editors when the involvement of multiple "prophets" is *not* acknowledged in the text and when one of the reasons for positing such a complex compositional process is the claim that the Spirit of God *could not* (or at least probably *did* not) reveal the diversity of contents identified in the book of Isaiah to just one individual.[54]

If Isaiah 40–66 was written by an unknown prophet, why include it in the canon together with Isaiah's book (Isaiah 1–39)? Why not make it a separate book following Isaiah's, without any attribution of authorship, which is the case elsewhere in the Old Testament? There is no other

---

52. Following Schultz, "How Many Isaiahs?" 162–63. If Peter was the dominant oral source behind Mark's Gospel, as many think, then he would have seen Isa. 40:6–8 (cited in 1 Peter 1) to have been prophesied by Isaiah, as Mark 1:2 so views Isa. 40:3. For a recent argument for a Petrine oral source behind Mark, see Richard Bauckham, *Jesus and the Eyewitnesses* (Grand Rapids: MI, Eerdmans, 2006), 202–39.

53. E.g., Schultz, "How Many Isaiahs?" 169.

54. Ibid., 161.

precedent in the Old Testament for such an extended segment (24 chapters) being attributed to a pseudonymous author, though I realize that a number of higher critics would take exception to this statement.

Does Minor Updating or Editing of Isaiah Nullify the New Testament's Witness to the Single Authorship of Isaiah?

One of the well-known contenders for the single authorship of Isaiah was Oswald Allis. A recent writer, J. H. Wood, has criticized Allis for allowing that the account of Moses' death at the end of the Pentateuch was not written by Moses but by some subsequent editor. Allis acknowledged that not every word was actually written by Moses; why did Allis not allow for the same thing in Isaiah? Specifically, the argument has been made that "if the NT authors assert that the Pentateuch is from Moses even though he did not write every word, then is it possible that NT ascriptions of Isaianic origin do not necessarily imply that the eighth-century prophet wrote every word?"[55]

Wood's critique of Allis assumes that the New Testament ascriptions of Mosaic and Isaianic authorship are so diluted by allowing for some statements not originating from Moses or Isaiah that the notion of the traditional authorship of these two books must be seriously questioned. But this is a legalistic view of authorship, which Wood also assumes in his critique.[56]

---

55. J. H. Wood, "Oswald T. Allis and the Question of Isaianic Authorship," *JETS* 48 (2005): 256–57.

56. Wood's article contains several such flawed assumptions and illogical leaps. For example, Wood says that Allis was inconsistent since he acknowledged that Moses used and edited earlier sources about prior biblical history up to his own time but would not allow the notion that there were editors who used Isaiah as an earlier source and built on him within the book of Isaiah. This is comparing apples with oranges. First, Moses was writing his own work, not editing an earlier source with an author's name and writing in that earlier author's name, though that he was editing earlier sources, whether they be oral or written, we do not know, and what we certainly do not know is if there were authors' names attached to those sources. Second, there is no problem at all with later biblical writers' using earlier sources when writing their own works. This occurs throughout biblical literature (e.g., note the New Testament's use of the Old Testament, sometimes with interpretative paraphrases). Third, Moses was not primarily taking earlier prophecies and reediting them but prior history and reediting it, whereas in Isaiah the critical view is that later editors built significantly on Isaiah's earlier prophecies, not historical narratives, and even created many prophecies that did not emanate from Isaiah. With respect also to Moses' use of sources, Wood says that "Allis allowed for the possibility of a historical discrepancy between the original situation of Moses' source . . . and the situation in which Moses wrote" (ibid., 257). Why Wood believes that Moses' use of prior sources means that there could be a "discrepancy between" Moses' situation and that of Moses' source is a mystery, since he gives no reason for this conclusion. The use of earlier sources does not indicate the probability of discrepancies, unless the one using the source does the distorting, and this Wood does not even attempt to show in the case of Moses. Likewise, Wood confuses the nature of the prophecy in Deuteronomy 18 with that of the Servant in Isaiah 53, but there is not space to elaborate on this hermeneutical fallacy (ibid., 258–59), except to say that partial fulfillments of earlier Old Testament

A viable understanding of single authorship of any writing can be held without assuming that every word is verbatim from that author. Two examples will suffice. It is clear that much of what Moses said in the Pentateuch was written down by scribes, or secretaries in contemporary parlance, and that this scribal record is what became part of the written Pentateuchal record.[57] Such scribes may have used some liberty in their recording, but it is unlikely that Moses and other Israelite officials would have let such scribal records circulate if they did not genuinely reflect what Moses said.

Likewise, Paul himself likely did not write the epistle to the Romans; Tertius was his secretary and wrote down what Paul dictated (Rom. 16:22). Yet the epistle has always been called Paul's epistle to the Romans because it is really from him, not Tertius. There were at least two ways to take dictation in the first century: a whole segment would be read and then the secretary would write it down, or a scribe copied syllable by syllable.[58] We do not know which method Tertius followed. The former mode of dictation may well have allowed for some creative composition on the part of the secretary. Even if Tertius copied in this manner, the letter would have been read back to Paul to make sure that everything there was really what Paul intended. Therefore, it is possible that at various points we do not have the exact words of Paul, but we certainly have his clear conceptual voice. Paul starts the letter saying it is from him to the Romans (Rom. 1:1–7); nowhere does Paul say the letter is from Tertius. The same thing is true of 1 Peter, where Peter says that Sylvanus is his secretary (1 Pet. 5:12).

It is for this reason that Oswald Allis could see that Moses was the ultimate author of the Pentateuch, even if every word was not written by him. Even the record of Moses' death, which may well have been intended to serve as a transition to the book of Joshua, might have been commissioned by Moses for someone else, perhaps one of

---

prophecies do occur within the Old Testament epoch itself, with the climactic fulfillment in the New Testament era, which we believe to be the case of the prophecy of a prophet like Moses in Deuteronomy 18 (see G. P. Hugenberger, "The Servant of the Lord in the 'Servant Songs' of Isaiah," in P. E. Satterthwaite, R. S. Hess, and G. J. Wenham, eds., *The Lord's Anointed: Interpretation of Old Testament Messianic Texts* [Carlisle: Paternoster; Grand Rapids: Baker, 1995], 105–40, who sees the Isaiah 53 Servant as modeled on Moses, which is partly based on the Deuteronomy 18 forecast of a prophet like Moses). Oswald Allis could certainly acknowledge near and distant fulfillments in the Old Testament, but precise exegesis of each prophecy in particular, together with surveying subsequent recorded redemptive history, will show whether a passage prophesies near or distant fulfillment. Allis believed, correctly, that Isaiah 53 prophesied a distant time.

57. On this, e.g., see Daniel I. Block, "Recovering the Voice of Moses: the Genesis of Deuteronomy," *JETS* 44 (2001): 385–408.

58. See Cicero, *Att.* 13.25.3.

his scribes or even Joshua,[59] to record. But the New Testament writers can say that Moses wrote the Pentateuch because it is ultimately from him, even if he did not actually write it all. His handprint is over the book.

It is certainly possible that there were scribes of Isaiah who wrote down some of his discourses, so literary style may vary within the book. Furthermore, later inspired editors could have done some minor editing of Isaiah's prophecies. But the conceptual essence of each prophecy should be seen as stemming from what the historical Isaiah said or wrote in his lifetime; each prophecy is like a footprint left by Isaiah, even if later scribes or editors may have filled in a little tread here and there. This is not very different from the situation in the Gospels, where Gospel writers may have paraphrased Jesus' sayings, giving them various kinds of interpretative nuance, perhaps not explicit when Jesus spoke them. Nevertheless, the later evangelists bring out Jesus' true intention without altering the conceptual essence of what Jesus said. This is also not much different from the kind of creative secretarial activity spoken of above with respect to Paul.

Thus, along the same lines as we have shown with Moses and the Gospel writers as well as Paul and Peter, the New Testament writers can attribute prophetic sayings throughout Isaiah to the prophet Isaiah, even if he did not write down every word of his book. Isaiah's historical conceptual handprint is over the whole book. We noted earlier that there are some who believe that Isaiah 40–66 has an Isaianic core upon which later editors built and expanded, but no one is able to say precisely which belongs to Isaiah and which to his editors.[60] This position is too loose. Rather, it is likely that each prophecy is entirely from what the historical Isaiah said in a conceptual sense even though some of the actual words and phrases may have been later altered for interpretative purposes. Further refinements and elaborations need to be made to the position just laid out, but space does not allow for this.[61]

---

59. Joshua is an excellent candidate in light of the repeated mention that he was commissioned (by Moses or God) to have the authority Moses had possessed in leading Israel (Num. 27:18–23; Deut. 3:27–28; 31:7–23; 34:9; Josh. 1:1). How appropriate would it have been for Joshua, having had Moses' prophetic mantle passed on to him, to have recorded Moses' death to complete the book that Moses wrote.

60. In this respect, see the earlier reference to Ridderbos, "Isaiah: Book of," 513–16. Similarly R. Schultz, "How Many Isaiahs?" 158–59.

61. E.g., further work would need to be done on how the genre of the Pentateuch, the Gospels, and the epistolary literature bears upon the issue of secretarial/scribal/editorial work.

Conclusion

The earlier section of this chapter reflected on views holding that Isaiah was not the author of the entire book by that name: that the attribution of Isaiah as author of the whole book was a mere stylistic convention or that Jesus accommodated himself knowingly or unconsciously to the false Jewish tradition of Isaianic authorship. None of these views is sufficiently compatible with the use of Isaiah in the New Testament except the perspective that understands these instances as references to the actual prophet Isaiah, who wrote the entire book that goes by that name. Neither do these views comport with the traditional evangelical notion of the inspiration of Scripture. In one way or another, these views understand the repeated mention of Isaiah to be the ultimately irrelevant husk that contains the "true" message of the particular Isaiah passages being quoted.

Accordingly, this irrelevant husk is really not a significant part of what Scripture *intends* to say. This amounts to the "insignificant part" of Scripture being uninspired and thus this leads to a limited view of the inspiration of the Bible and of Christ himself, who accordingly could make errors even in his affirmations about holy Scripture itself. Though those with whom I disagree might cry foul and say that I am mischaracterizing their view at this point, it is difficult for me to see that this is not what their view entails.

Packer's conclusion about proposals concerning pseudonymity of New Testament books applies just as much to Old Testament books:

> [The] position, that their canonicity cannot be affirmed if their authenticity is denied, thus seems to be the only one possible; and we may lay it down as a general principle that, when biblical books specify their own authorship, the affirmation of their canonicity involves a denial of their pseudonymity. Pseudonymity and canonicity are mutually exclusive.[62]

In this chapter I've tried to demonstrate that the New Testament's repeated affirmation of Isaiah as the sole author of the book that bears his name is so clear and probable that to maintain multiple authorship of it will, unavoidably, take a person down one path: the New Testament writers and Christ were mistaken in their conviction about the authorship of the book. For some scholars this may not be a problematic conclusion, but for those of a more conservative persuasion, this is a difficult position to hold. Nevertheless, the clear New Testament stance on this

---

62. Packer, *"Fundamentalism" and the Word of God*, 184.

topic confirms the long-established arguments within the book of Isaiah itself—the prophet Isaiah authored the complete book.

The New Testament view of one author also explains quite well the different kinds of unity proposed by a variety of Old Testament scholars over the past two decades, unity they credit to a final redactor(s). Should the authorship of Isaiah be a litmus test for a biblical view of the inspiration of Scripture? No more so than any other aspect of Scripture that is not being affirmed as true. One's position on this issue, especially in recent times, can be an indicator of one's overall view of the authority of Scripture.

Most of the same kinds of arguments offered for Isaiah in this chapter are applicable to the Mosaic authorship of the Pentateuch, though there is more abundant testimony for this in the Old Testament itself, and, to a lesser degree, Davidic authorship of the psalms attributed to David in the superscriptions.

CHAPTER SIX

Can Old Testament Cosmology Be Reconciled with Modern Scientific Cosmology? *Part 1*

The purpose of this chapter and the next is to offer a perspective on the cosmic language of the Old Testament, its parallels with that of the ANE, its uniqueness, and how this may or may not be acceptable to modern scientific and theological sensibilities. An entire book needs to be written on this topic! Nevertheless, though this proposal is of a more tentative nature, we will attempt to provide enough evidence to make it an attractive, viable option for understanding the cosmic descriptions of the Bible.[1]

Introduction

A common objection to the complete, definitive authority of Scripture is the contention that the Old Testament conveys a view of the world and universe that is unscientific and inaccurate and thus impossible for modern people to affirm as scientific truth. Karl Barth affirms, "In the biblical view of the world and man we are constantly coming up against presuppositions that are not ours, and statements and judgments we cannot accept."[2] He specifically applies this to the Old

---

1. I am very grateful to Gordon P. Hugenberger who has read this chapter and the next and has made many helpful suggestions, which I have explicitly noted, though his influence has extended even beyond these.
2. K. Barth, *Church Dogmatics*, I.2 (Edinburgh: T. & T. Clark, 1958), 508-509.

Testament's view of the cosmos,[3] though he contends that there is theological truth, nevertheless, to be gleaned from such accounts. This understanding and impression has been enhanced with the recent escalation and profusion of ancient Near Eastern studies, including publications on the conceptions of the cosmos by the Mesopotamians, Egyptians, and others.

Accordingly, Old Testament writers' minds were shaped by the typical language and conceptions of the world that were a part of the overall way of thinking in their ancient culture. The universe was commonly understood as a composition of three tiers: the heavens, the earth, and the netherworld. The significant features of each of these parts include the following: (1) the earth was composed of only one continent that had mountains at its perimeters to hold up the sky; (2) the sky was a solid mass, a tent or dome, which separated the earthly seas from the heavenly sea that was just above the dome; (3) deities dwelt in the heaven above the earth; (4) the heavens were a composition of three or more levels with pavements of different kinds of stone; and (5) the earth was understood either to float on or be surrounded by cosmic waters or to be supported by pillars.[4]

Many scholars believe that this ancient conception of the world was not merely an attempt to describe things as they appeared to the naked eye, but it was bound up with the various mythologies and scientifically inaccurate views of the different ANE cultures, especially with respect to how the gods were related to the cosmos. The Mesopotamians, for example, believed that the gods maintained cables that linked heaven and earth and caused the sun to remain stable in the sky. Generally, divine powers were at work behind the visible physical phenomena, and even this very observable, material reality was an expression of the gods or their attributes, which amounts to a pantheistic notion.

Increasingly some conservative biblical and theological scholars are acknowledging the existence of such a cosmology and see it as so overlapping with Israel's cosmology that the latter is thought incompatible with the modern scientific view of the universe. There are at least four forms in which this position has been held.

3. E.g., see Barth, *Church Dogmatics*, III.1, 139: with respect to the "expanse" of Gen. 1:6–8, he says, "It is self-evident that the author was not thinking of 'allegorical or metaphysical water,' but of real water, as in the myth and indeed the natural science of his day, which in this respect was that of the 17th century as well" (likewise see III.1, 147, 160).

4. This summary of ANE portrayals of the cosmos is dependent on John Walton's recent summary of these parallels, who cites the main primary and especially secondary sources discussing the parallels in *Ancient Near Eastern Thought and the Old Testament* (Grand Rapids: Baker, 2006), 165–78.

1) In order to maintain a high view of Scripture, some have adapted a postmodern sociology of knowledge perspective. This becomes a rationale by which their conception of Scripture's authority can be maintained. Accordingly, Old Testament writers are seen to have not only written in the typical language of their time but to have conceived of the cosmos through the same socially constructed thought of their ancient culture, as we summarized above. Since such expressions were not a part of the theological point that they were making, these references do not negatively affect the infallible (though not inerrant) theological message of the Bible.[5]

2) Also in line with a postmodern stance, others acknowledge that although such expressions are judged as errors by modern standards, these represented the truth for the ancient Hebrews. Modern people must not impose their cultural standards of truth on ancient cultural assumptions about truth. Such cosmic perceptions must be viewed as unique to ancient Israel and, while not applicable to contemporary Christians, they were relevant and true for ancient Israelites and should be viewed still as fully inspired by God.[6]

3) Still others, like Karl Barth, would see these references to cosmology as non-scientific and erroneous, even though God's Word can speak even through the fallible expressions of the human biblical writers.

4) Finally, some contend that these expressions are either purely phenomenal expressions that overlap with similar expressions today, e.g., "the sun rises and sets," or that the biblical writers expressed their theological—not scientific—conception of the universe and understood it to be a huge temple for God. Accordingly, the architectural depictions of a massive temple-house are to be taken figuratively. This is a conception that should have the same significance for us today!

This chapter and the next will argue that only the fourth position is consistent with a high view of Scripture.

---

5. So, for example, P. H. Seely, "The Firmament and the Water Above, Part 1: the Meaning of *rāqîaʿ* in Gen 1:6–8," *WTJ* 53 (1991): 240. He asserts that "it is not the purpose of Gen. 1:7 to teach us the physical nature of the sky," so that "the reference to the solid firmament" as a solid dome over the earth "'lies outside the scope of the writer's teachings' and the verse is still infallibly true." While I agree with the first statement, that the purpose of Gen. 1:7 is not to teach modern science, the following deduction does not follow, both because the verse probably is not teaching about a "solid dome" and because the reference to the "expanse" or "firmament" is very important to the teaching of Gen. 1:7. This theological topic will be discussed in the next chapter, where further interaction with Seely's view can also be found.

6. Peter Enns (*Inspiration and Incarnation*, 54–55) would be an example of a scholar who combines both of these first two perspectives.

Israel's Temple as a Small Model of the Whole Cosmos, Which Was a Huge Temple

This issue of the use of cosmological language and how it relates to an ancient author's socially constructed reality and to our modern notions of the cosmos is certainly a complex one. The following is one thumbnail sketch of the view that biblical writers used certain expressions to convey their theological conception of the universe as a big temple. This sketch is a summary of a section of my book *The Temple and the Church's Mission.*[7]

Israel's small temple was understood to be a microcosm of the entire heaven and earth, which was one massive cosmic temple in which God dwelt. This view needs to be laid out in some depth before we turn to the questions about how Old Testament writers used cosmological language and how it relates to an ancient author's socially constructed reality, to our modern scientific notions of the universe, and to our view of Scripture's authority.

One of the most explicit texts affirming the design of Israel's temple as a small model of the cosmos is Psalm 78:69: "He built His sanctuary like the heights, like the earth which He founded *forever* [or from eternity]." The psalmist is saying that, in some way, God designed Israel's earthly temple to be comparable to the heavens and to the earth. Similarly, several passages affirm that the earlier "pattern of the tabernacle and the pattern of all its furniture" was made "after the [heavenly] pattern . . . which was shown . . . on the mountain" (Ex. 25:9, 40; cf. Ex. 26:30; 27:8; Num. 8:4; Heb. 8:5; 9:23–24).

The symbolism of the tabernacle is essentially the same as that of Israel's subsequent temple. This equivalence is implied by their many overt similarities and clearly seen when comparing Exodus 25:9, 40 with 1 Chronicles 28:19, which say that both the plan of the tabernacle and of the temple came from God.[8] Since Israel's temple was viewed as a small model of the cosmos, then the cosmos itself was likely seen as a massive temple.

The temple was composed of three main parts, each of which symbolized a major part of the cosmos. The first part was the outer court,

---

7. Leicester: Inter-Varsity, 2004, especially pp. 1–165, where also there is reference to and interaction with Old Testament and ANE scholars who have made these observations. Those desiring to see the full argument about this cosmic thesis concerning the temple should consult this section of the book, where much more elaboration and documentation is provided.

8. The equivalence was also made by early Judaism (so Wisdom 9:8: the temple was "an imitation of the holy tabernacle which you prepared from the beginning"). For the close link between the tabernacle and the temple, see 1 Kings 8:1–6 (= 2 Chron. 5:2–5), which may imply that the tabernacle was even incorporated into the temple.

which represented the habitable world where humanity dwelt. The second part was the Holy Place, which was emblematic of the visible heavens and its light sources. The third part was the Holy of Holies, which symbolized the invisible dimension of the cosmos, where God and his heavenly hosts dwelt.

The identification of the outer court as the visible earth and sea is suggested further by the Old Testament description where the large molten washbasin and altar in the temple courtyard are called, respectively, the "sea" (1 Kings 7:23–26) and the "bosom of the earth" (Ezek. 43:14). The altar also likely was identified with the "mountain of God" in Ezekiel 43:16.[9] The altar was also to be an "altar of earth," in the early stages of Israel's history, or an "altar of [uncut] stone" (Ex. 20:24–25), thus identifying it even more with the natural earth.[10] Thus both the sea and the altar appear to be cosmic symbols that may have been associated in the mind of the Israelite with the seas and the earth.[11]

Enhancing the water imagery were the ten smaller washbasins, five on each side of the Holy Place enclosure (1 Kings 7:38–39). The arrangement of the twelve bulls "entirely encircling the sea" and the "lily blossom" decorating the brim would also seem to present a partial miniature model of land and life surrounding the seas of the earth (2 Chron. 4:2–5). The twelve bulls also supported the washbasin and were divided into groups of three, facing to the four points of the compass, which could well reflect the four quadrants of the earth. Twelve oxen were pictured holding up the sea, and designs of lions and oxen were on the washbasin stands, both of which point further to an earthly identification of the outer courtyard (though cherubim were also depicted on the basin stands). That the outer court was associated with the visible earth is also intimated by the fact that all Israelites, representing humanity at large, could enter there and worship.

9. Translations of Ezek. 43:14 typically have "from the base on the ground" but literally it is "from the bosom of the earth [or ground]." See also G. A. Barrois, *Jesus Christ and the Temple* (Crestwood, NY: St. Vladimir's Seminary Press, 1980), 65–66, who renders the respective phrases in Ezek. 43:14, 16, as "bosom of the earth" and "the mountain of God," which he sees to be symbolic cosmic names.
10. The altar's association with the earth may be enhanced by noticing that it is repeatedly described as having a "foundation" (*yᵉsôḏ*: Ex. 29:12; Lev. 4:7, 18, 25, 30, 34), imagery typical elsewhere of structures rooted to the earth (e.g., Ezek. 30:4; Micah 1:6; Ps. 137:7; Job 4:19; Lam. 4:11) and sometimes used of mountains (Deut. 32:22; Ps. 87:1); that the altar was "bronze" may point further to a mountain association, since this metal was mined from mountains, and Zech. 6:1 enhances this association ("mountains of bronze"); the Hebrew word for the "horns" of the altar can refer elsewhere to a mountain peak or hill (see Isa. 5:1). I am indebted to G. P. Hugenberger for pointing me to these observations.
11. That Solomon's "bronze sea" was symbolic is evident from recalling that it was over 7 feet high and 15 feet in diameter, holding about 10,000 gallons of water and weighing between 25 and 30 tons when empty. Priests would have had to climb a ladder to wash in it.

There is also reason to view the second section of the temple, the Holy Place, as a symbol of the visible sky. The seven lamps on the lampstand might have been associated with the seven light sources visible to the naked eye in the sky—five planets, the sun, and the moon. This identification is pointed to by Genesis 1, which uses the unusual word *lights* (m^{e}ōrōt) five times rather than *sun* and *moon*. The word *lights* is used throughout the remainder of the Pentateuch—ten times—for only the lights on the tabernacle lampstand.

A contemporary commentator on Genesis has made virtually the same observation on the same basis and has proposed that this is the first hint that the cosmos itself was conceived of as a huge temple.[12] In addition, John's apocalypse also closely identifies the seven lamps on the lampstand with stars by the observation that each of the seven churches symbolized by a "lampstand" is represented in heaven by an angel who is symbolized by a star (Rev. 1:20).[13]

Vern Poythress, also, contends along similar lines that the lamps signify the seven main lights of the heaven:

> The lampstand is placed on the south side of the Holy Place. Perhaps this placement is intended to correspond to the fact that from Israel's point of view, north of the equator, the circuit of the heavenly lights would be primarily to the south. That there are seven of the lamps correlates not only with the seven major lights of heaven . . . but with the general symbolism for time within Israel. The heavenly bodies were made in order to "serve as signs to mark seasons and days and years" (Gen. 1:14). The whole cycle of time marked by the sun and moon and stars is divided up into sevens: the seventh day in the week is the Sabbath day; the seventh month is the month of atonement (Leviticus 16:29); the seventh year is the year of release from debts and slavery (Deuteronomy 15); the seventh of the seven-year cycles is the year of jubilee (Leviticus 25). Fittingly, the lampstand contains the same sevenfold division, symbolizing the cycle of time provided by the heavenly lights.[14]

12. So J. H. Walton, *Genesis*, NIVAC (Grand Rapids: Zondervan, 2001), 148. Among the three other uses elsewhere in the Old Testament, two also refer to the "lights" of the heaven. The only other use is Ps. 90:8 ("the light of your presence"), which may suggest that the lampstand "lights" also symbolized the light of God's glorious presence, just as the stars were held to reflect God's glory (Pss. 19:1; 148:3–4; cf. Pss. 8:1; 50:6; 57:5). Such an identification may be represented in the Qumran Hymn Scroll (IQH VII, 24): "I [the Teacher of Righteousness] will shine with a *seven-fold li[ght]* in the E[den which] Thou has [m]ade for Thy glory."

13. G. K. Beale, *The Book of Revelation*, NIGTC (Grand Rapids: Eerdmans), 211–19.

14. V. Poythress, *The Shadow of Christ in the Law of Moses* (Brentwood: Wolgemuth and Hyatt, 1991), 18–19. See also Poythress, *Redeeming Science* (Wheaton, IL: Crossway, 2006), 322–23, for the mathematical proportions of the tabernacle as a reflection of God's creation of mathematical proportionality in the cosmos.

The third, innermost section of the temple symbolized the invisible dimension where God dwelt. The sculpted cherubim around the ark of the covenant in the Holy of Holies (1 Kings 6:23–28) reflect the real cherubim in heaven who presently and in the future will stand guard around God's throne in the heavenly temple (cf. Rev. 4:7–9; 2 Sam. 6:2; 2 Kings 19:15; 1 Chron. 13:6; Pss. 80:1; 99:1). The preceding Old Testament references may have double reference to the earthly and heavenly cherubim.

Furthermore, no human could enter the inner sanctum and look upon the luminous divine glory. Even the high priest, who could enter only once a year, offered incense that formed a cloud so thick that he could not see God's glorious appearance (Lev. 16:13). The cloud itself could easily have been associated with the visible heaven that pointed beyond to the unseen heaven, where God dwelt. Finally, the ark itself was understood to be the footstool of God's heavenly throne (1 Chron. 28:2; Pss. 99:5; 132:7–8; Isa. 66:1; Lam. 2:1). First Chronicles 28:2 asserts, "King David rose to his feet and said, 'Listen to me, my brethren and my people; I had intended to build a permanent home for the ark of the covenant of the LORD and for the footstool of our God. So I had made preparations to build it.'"

Hence, the ark is part of God's heavenly throne room, and, appropriately, the space directly above the ark is empty. God cannot be seen, and no images of him are to be placed there because he has no human form and his special glorious dwelling is primarily in heaven and not on earth.[15] Thus, the Holy of Holies was a representation of God's unseen heavenly dwelling in his temple amidst ministering angels and spirits (Isa. 6:1–7; Ezekiel 1; Rev. 4:1–11).[16]

Thus, Israel's temple appears to be a small model of the massive temple of the universe. The innermost sanctum represented the invisible dimension of heaven; the Holy Place symbolized the starry visible heavens, and the courtyard signified the earth and sea.

The Focus upon the Heavenly Symbolism of the Temple

The Old Testament highlights particularly the heavenly symbolism of the temple with respect to both the visible and invisible heavens. One of the best examples of this is the account of the dedication of Solomon's temple. The cloud that filled Israel's temple when it was completed and dedicated by Solomon may, in part, have an association with the clouds

---

15. Poythress, *The Shadow of Christ in the Law of Moses*, 15.
16. So also Poythress, *The Shadow of Christ in the Law of Moses*, 31, who cites also in this respect 1 Kings 8:30; Job 1:6; Ps. 89:7.

in the visible heavens that pointed beyond themselves to God's unseen
heavenly dwelling place:[17]

> It happened that when the priests came from the holy place, the cloud
> filled the house of the LORD, so that the priests could not stand to minister
> because of the cloud, for the glory of the LORD filled the house of the LORD.
> Then Solomon said, "The LORD has said that He would dwell in the thick
> cloud. I have surely built You a lofty house, a place for Your dwelling
> forever" (1 Kings 8:10–13; cf. almost identically 2 Chron. 5:13b–6:2).

Two different Hebrew words for *cloud* are used in this passage, but they
are generally synonymous. The repeated mention of the cloud and the
temple's being "a lofty place" point more clearly to a link between the
temple and the heavens.

Cloud obviously refers elsewhere to a constituent part of the visible heavens or sky. Job 26:8–9 says, "He wraps up the waters in His
clouds; and the cloud does not burst under them. He obscures the
face of the full moon and spreads His cloud over it" (cf. also Gen.
9:13–14, 16; Job 7:9). And just as *lightning* is part of literal clouds
(Job 37:11, 15), so Ezekiel portrays God's theophanic glory as "a
great cloud with fire flashing forth" and "as the appearance of a
rainbow in the clouds on a rainy day" (Ezek. 1:4, 28). That Ezekiel
views such heavenly descriptions of God's presence as occurring in a
temple is also clear from the cloud that hides the divine presence in
the temple (cf. 10:3–4).

The visible cloud that filled the temple was certainly identified with
the visible heaven but likely also pointed to the invisible heaven. The
preceding references to the cloud in Ezekiel's vision confirm this, since
there the word refers to both a visible meteorological phenomenon and
the invisible presence of God in the unseen heaven. Furthermore, it is
well known that the same Hebrew word for "heaven" in the Old Testament is used for both the seen and unseen dimensions.[18] The upper part
of the visible cosmos came to represent God's dwelling place, pointing
beyond the physical to the divine transcendence and an "invisible spiritual created order" (cf. 2 Kings 6:17; Ps. 2:4; Job 1:1, 16; Zech. 3:1).[19]

---

17. That the visible heavens pointed beyond themselves to the unseen heavens is apparent from
Dan. 7:13, where the "Son of Man" approaches God's unseen heavenly presence "coming with the
clouds of heaven"; likewise 2 Sam. 22:10: God "bowed the heavens . . . , and came down with a
cloud under his feet."

18. Poythress, *The Shadow of Christ in the Law of Moses*, 17–18, who cites Ps. 19:1–6 as an example
where the inaccessibility and majesty of the visible sky points to God's glory.

19. A. T. Lincoln, *Paradise Now and Not Yet*, SNTSSup. (Cambridge: Cambridge University, 1981),
140–141.

Thus, again the temple is associated with the physically created observable heavens and the invisible heavenly dwelling of God to which the seen sky pointed.

The same luminescent cloud that filled Solomon's temple had also hovered over and covered Sinai and the tabernacle during Israel's wilderness wanderings, suggesting that the earlier forms of the temple were also reflective of or associated with the heavens.[20] Hence, the visible bright clouds of the heavens came to be appropriate vehicles to express the invisible heavenly, radiant presence of God in the tabernacle and subsequent temple (Ex. 16:10; 40:35; Num. 16:42; Isa. 4:5; Ezek. 1:28; 10:3–4).

Solomon's reference to his building of "a lofty house" in 1 Kings 8:13 refers to an elevated dwelling. The word *lofty* ($z^e \underline{b}ul$) occurs only three times elsewhere in the Old Testament, but when it does it always refers to the "elevated places" in the visible heavens where the "sun and moon stood" (Hab. 3:11) and to the invisible "holy and glorious elevated place" where God "looks down from heaven" (Isa. 63:15).[21] It is this invisible place that Solomon sees being symbolized in 1 Kings 8 by the earthly temple. Accordingly, he describes the temple figuratively as being in the visible heavens, so that the bright clouds appropriately surround it.

The reference to winged figurines around the ark of the covenant in 1 Kings 8:6–7 may add further to an upper atmospheric symbolism. This symbolism appears to have been enhanced in the tabernacle where its numerous curtains, including the veil before the Holy of Holies, were all made of the variegated colors resembling the sky—"blue and purple and scarlet material"—and had woven into them figures of flying cherubim, i.e., winged bird-like creatures (Ex. 26:1, 31; 36:8, 35). Apparently the scarlet color was intended to resemble the fiery color of lightning and, perhaps, of the sun, with the blue and purple resembling sky blue and the dark blue of dark clouds.[22]

So also the screen for the gate of the court and doorway of the tent was to be made of "blue and purple and scarlet material" (Ex. 26:36;

20. For Sinai, cf. Ex. 19:16; 24:15–16; for the tabernacle, cf., e.g., Ex. 13:21–22; 14:19; note the "cloud" descending and covering the tabernacle in Ex. 33:9; 40:35; Num. 9:15–16; 16:42; for the luminosity of the cloud at Sinai and the tabernacle, cf. respectively Ex. 19:16 and 14:20, 24; 40:38; Num. 9:15.

21. The only other usage is in Ps. 49:14, which refers to earth as an "elevated place" above Sheol; in Qumran the word occurs four times, all pertaining to God's heavenly dwelling.

22. More overtly, Josephus (*Ant.* 3.183) says the "blue" of the "tapestries" symbolized "the air" (so also *War* 5.212), and Philo (*Mos.* 2.88) interprets the "dark blue [*huakinthos*]" to be "like the air, which is naturally black."

27:16; 36:37; 38:18). Even the loops on the edge of some of the curtains were to be of blue (Ex. 36:11). Likewise, the priests were to cover all the furniture of the tabernacle with blue material when dismantling the tabernacle for transport (Num. 4:5–13). All the colors of these inner tabernacle furnishings were likely reproduced in Solomon's temple; it was the permanent establishment of the mobile tabernacle, and the first-century historian Josephus testifies that the later Herodian temple of Jesus' day, modeled on Solomon's, contained the numerous curtains that the tabernacle also had (see *J. W.* 5.210–14; *Ant.* 3.132, 183).

The above evidence, that Israel's temple was designed to be reflective of the heavenly part of the cosmos, points further to the heavenly sphere of the cosmos itself being understood as a part of a huge temple.

Symbolism of the Priest's Robe in Relation to the Temple

It is apparent that aspects of the priest's robe contained cosmic symbolism. Like the tabernacle curtains, the various parts of the high priest's attire were also woven of blue and purple and scarlet material because it was also meant to reflect the cosmos. The square shape of the breast piece corresponded to the square shape (*tetragōnos*) of the Holy Place and temple, the altar, and the mercy seat (see LXX of Ex. 27:1; 30:2; Ezek. 41:21, 43:16; 43:17; Alexandrinus).

Interestingly, the Greek Old Testament even applies the term *four-square* to the high priest's "breast piece of judgment" (Ex. 28:16; 36:16). If this symbolic identification by the Greek Old Testament of the priest with parts of the temple is correct, then it is natural that the priest's clothing was also of the same color as the various inner furnishings of the temple. There are about twelve instances where parts of his attire are said to be of blue and purple and scarlet and where his robe was all blue—phrases also used to describe the curtains of the tabernacle (cf. also "a blue cord" on the turban: Ex. 28:37; 39:31).

I have argued in an earlier work that the jewels on the priest's breast piece, which was a small replica of the Holy of Holies, symbolized the earthly or heavenly cosmos, and the same jewels are part of the new city-temple in Revelation 21.[23] Accordingly, one needs to picture the precious stones on the priest's breast piece set within the larger background of the long blue robe as an apt model of the stars set within the cosmic tent of the dark-bluish heavens. Correspondingly, the same scene on a larger scale was depicted with the seven luminaries on the lampstand placed within the broader backdrop of the sky-colored curtains covering

---

23. See Beale, *Revelation*, in *loc.*, "The High Priest's Breastpiece," following the discussion of 21:18–20.

the inside of the tent-like tabernacle. The seven lamps on the lampstand especially stood out in the Holy Place, since the four thick curtains so thoroughly covered the tabernacle that no natural light would have come in unless the curtain at the entrance were pulled back.[24]

Both the priest's robe and the tabernacle were designed to represent the creative work of God, "who stretches out the heavens like a curtain and spreads them out like a tent to dwell in" and "who has created . . . [the] host" of stars to hang in (Isa. 40:22, 26). Similarly, Psalm 19:4b–5a says that in the "heavens" God "has placed a tent for the sun, which is as a bridegroom coming out of his chamber" (cf. Amos 9:6a: "the One who builds His upper chambers in the heavens and has founded His vaulted dome over the earth"). These expressions suggest further that God built the cosmos as a sanctuary in which to dwell.

It is, in fact, discernible that there are broadly three sections of the priest's garment that resemble the three sections of the temple. First, the outermost part at the bottom—the outer court—on which were sewn "pomegranates of blue and purple and scarlet" along "with variegated flowers" (so *Let. Aris.* 96),[25] represented the fertile earth. Second, the main body of the bluish robe—the Holy Place—within which and on the upper part of which are set the jewels, symbolized the stars that are set in the sky. Third, the square ephod resembles the square Holy of Holies, within which were placed the Urim and Thumim, stones representing God's revelatory presence. The priest's crown, inscribed with "holy to the Lord," may represent the divine presence in heaven or above the ark in the temple's sanctuary that the ephod symbolized. Given all this symbolism, one can well understand the assertion in the *Letter of Aristeas* that anyone who saw the fully attired high priest "would think he had come out of this world into another one" (99).

If the precious stones on the priest's breast correspond partly to the lamps on the lampstand, then this identifies them further with the heavenly luminaries, since we have seen that the lampstand lights are likewise identified with the heavenly stars. This link of the precious stones with the starry heavens may provide an important clue to the significance of the precious stones and metals that compose the temple itself. Why is the temple so heavily adorned with these extremely valuable and shiny materials? Before answering this question, it is important to highlight just how much the temple was adorned with these expensive items.

The foundation of the temple building, which contained the Holy Place and Holy of Holies, was laid with gold, silver, and precious stones:

24. T. Longman, *Immanuel in Our Place* (Phillipsburg, NJ: P&R, 2001), 55.
25. The Letter of Aristeas 96 adds the phrase "with variegated flowers" to the biblical description.

"They quarried great stones, costly stones, to lay the foundation of the house" (1 Kings 5:17). Additionally, "the inner sanctuary . . . he overlaid . . . with pure gold. . . . So Solomon overlaid the inside of the house with pure gold" (1 Kings 6:20–21). He also covered with gold the altar (1 Kings 6:20), the cherubim around the ark (1 Kings 6:28), the floor of the temple (1 Kings 6:30), and the engraved work on the temple doors (1 Kings 6:35; see similarly 2 Chronicles 3–4). Indeed, "100,000 talents of gold and 1,000,000 talents of silver" were prepared for the construction of the temple house (1 Chron. 22:14; likewise 1 Chron. 22:16; 29:2–7). First Chronicles 29:1–7 refers to "gold . . . silver . . . onyx stones and inlaid stones, stones of antimony, and stones of various colors, and all kinds of precious stones" to be used for all the various parts, pieces of furniture, and utensils of the temple.[26]

Thus, the same precious stones and metals used in the construction of the temple were also used in the fashioning of the priest's clothing, enhancing some connection between the two even more.[27] Furthermore, the same precious stones are used to describe the heavenly dwelling of God, further associating the same stones of the temple and of the priestly raiment with the heavenly sphere.[28]

How does the connection we have observed between the precious stones and the starry heavens provide an important clue to the significance of the precious stones and metals that were used to adorn the Holy Place and Holy of Holies? It may not be too risky to guess that part of the reason for so many precious stones and metals in one place, with their glistening nature, is that they were intended to remind one of the luminous splendor of the starry sky, which, we have seen, itself pointed to God's transcendent, glorious dwelling place, which was concealed from human sight. Indeed, even today, one of the main uses of our En-

26. See 2 Chron. 3:6 also for "precious stones and the gold."

27. 1 Chronicles 29 mentions only gold, antimony, and onyx specifically, whereas Exodus 28 mentions explicitly by name each of the various metals and gems. Nevertheless, Chronicles does mention "inlaid stones . . . and stones of various colors, and all kinds of precious stones," which probably included all the specific stones noted in Exodus 28.

28. Cf. "sapphire" as a part of the heavenly temple (Ex. 24:10; Ezek. 1:26; 10:1; Rev. 21:19), likely included in the earthly temple (1 Chron. 29:2), and a facet of the priest's clothing (Ex. 28:18; 39:11); cf. onyx as a part of the priestly clothing (Ex. 25:7; 28:9, 20; 35:9, 27; 39:6, 13) and of the temple (1 Chron. 29:2), though not mentioned explicitly in the heavenly visions; cf. "jasper" as a part of the priest's attire (Ex. 28:20; 39:13) and of the appearance of the heavenly temple (Rev. 4:3; 21:11, 18–19), the latter of which also suggests that "jasper" (or a stone essentially identical to it) was included among the precious stones of Solomon's temple; cf. "beryl" as part of the priestly apparel (Ex. 28:20; 39:13) and of the structure of the heavenly temple (Ezek. 1:16; Rev. 21:20; cf. Dan. 10:6), which shows again that it was presumably included among the "precious stones" of Solomon's temple.

glish word *metallic* is to indicate that which is "shiny, glossy, gleaming, or lustrous."[29]

The following considerations further support the conclusion that the metals in the temple were intended to recall the starry heavens and, ultimately, the luminous glory of God in his heavenly temple, to which the stars themselves pointed. First, the precious materials adorn only the temple house proper and not any part of the courtyard. This fact fits with our identification of the Holy Place with the starry sky and inner room as the unseen heavenly domain. However, the only metal used in the courtyard is the less expensive and less radiant bronze (e.g., the altar), which is also the only area of the temple complex that common Israelite worshipers could enter.[30]

Second, Scripture itself, in Exodus, Ezekiel, and Revelation, describes part of God's glory in his heavenly palace-temple through portrayals of precious stones. The first such depiction occurs at the Sinai theophany; when Moses and the elders of Israel saw God in the cloud at the top of Mount Sinai, "under His feet there appeared to be a pavement of sapphire, *as clear as the sky itself*"[31] (Ex. 24:10; cf. 19:16–20). Here we find a conglomeration of precious stones describing the divine environment of God's heavenly temple, which had temporarily descended to the top of Sinai. In fact, Sinai itself was thought to be a temple, with God's transcendent heavenly sanctuary breaking through from the invisible into the visible realm at the mountain's peak.[32] Furthermore, this gem-like pavement is said to be "as clear [or pure blue] as the sky itself." Thus, the blue color of the stone is comparable to the majestic appearance of the heavens.[33]

Likewise, Ezekiel's description of the heavenly dimension that corresponds to the earthly temple includes virtually the same reference as that found in the Exodus 24 passage: "Now above the expanse that was over the heads" of the living cherubim "there was something resembling a throne, like lapis lazuli in appearance," which itself was under a human-like depiction of God (Ezek. 1:26). Ezekiel 10:1 has an almost identical description, though there "something like a sapphire stone . . .

---

29. E.g., see J. I. Rodale, *The Synonym Finder* (Emmaus, PA: Rodale Press, 1978), 726.

30. Poythress, *The Shadow of Christ in the Law of Moses,* 16.

31. My translation of the Hebrew. LXX reads, "Under his feet there was the likeness of a sapphire slab, and it was just as the appearance of the firmament of heaven in purity."

32. For a more detailed analysis of Mount Sinai as a temporary mountain temple, after which the tabernacle was modeled, see "Excursus 1: Sinai as a Temple" at the end of Beale, "The Descent of the Eschatological Temple in the Form of the Spirit at Pentecost: Part 1," *TynBul* 55 (2005).

33. See also U. Cassuto, *A Commentary on the Book of Exodus* (Jerusalem: Magnes Press, 1967), 314.

resembling a throne" was not above but "*in* the expanse that was over the heads of the cherubim." Ezekiel describes the divine figure:

> . . . like glowing metal that looked like fire . . . and there was a radiance around Him. As the appearance of the rainbow in the clouds on a rainy day, so was the appearance of the surrounding radiance. Such was the appearance of the likeness of the glory of the LORD. (Ezek. 1:27–28)

It is clear that the sapphire is not only directly compared to the appearance of the heavens but is also associated with another startling feature of the sky: the brilliant colors of a rainbow reflective of the sun. Furthermore, the sapphire is part of the immediate heavenly surroundings that, like the glowing metal, reflected the radiance of the divine glory.[34] The precious stones in Revelation also describe the radiant glory of God's dwelling in the heavenly temple (Rev. 4:3; 21:11, 18–20).

Therefore, though every part of our analysis of the astronomical significance of the precious metals and stones will not necessarily be equally persuasive, it is plausible to understand that the gleaming stones and metals composing Israel's temple and the priest's garments functioned to remind one of the sparkling stars in the heavens, which themselves pointed to God's glorious presence in his invisible heavenly temple-court. Our evidence lends additional enhancement to the earlier conclusion that parts of the temple symbolized the heavens, suggesting further that the heavenly sphere was part of God's big cosmic tabernacle.

Jewish interpreters of the Old Testament reflect on the temple and understand it and develop it in ways that are similar to and consistent with our analysis. What was more implicit in the Old Testament portrayal of the temple becomes explicitly drawn out by commentators in Judaism.

Israel's Temple in the Light of the Ancient Near Eastern View of the Earthly Temple as a Reflection of the Heavenly or Cosmic Temple

Some scholars, such as de Vaux,[35] allege that early Judaism's explicit cosmic understanding of the temple was a late allegorical development. A good response may be found not only in the above-cited evidence from the Old

---

34. Ezek. 1:16 also refers to the "workmanship" of the "wheels" that accompanied the cherubim to be "like sparkling beryl." The words "workmanship" and "sapphire" also describe the heavenly environment of the theophanic presence in Ex. 24:10, which links the Ezekiel portrayal even more closely to the earlier Exodus appearance.

35. R. de Vaux, *Ancient Israel* (New York: McGraw-Hill, 1965), 328–29.

Testament but also from the observation that ancient Near Eastern archaeology and texts portray ancient temples as microcosms of huge heavenly temples in a manner similar to that of the Old Testament. In more recent times, it has become widely known that archaeological ruins and texts from the ancient Near East portray ancient temples as small models of heavenly temples or of the universe conceived of as a temple.

As noted, we should not think that Israel's temple was like those of her pagan neighbors because she merely copied the religious traditions around her. Rather, the likeness of the Israelite temple to pagan temples should be viewed, at least, from two perspectives. First, the similarity is intended at times to be a protest statement that, while the pagan nations think that they have cornered the market on divine revelation from their gods who dwell in their temples, their gods are, in fact, false and their temples purely idolatrous institutions—the den of demons (Deut. 32:17; Ps. 106:37; 1 Cor. 10:19–20).

From another angle, it is appropriate to ask whether anything in ancient pagan religion and its institutions resembled the truth about the true God and his designs for humanity. Certainly, pagan nations had not received any special revelation to draw them into saving relation to the true God. Nevertheless, just as the image of God is not erased but distorted in unbelieving humanity, it is plausible to suggest that some of the affinities in ancient pagan beliefs and religious institutions to that of Israel's may be due to the fact that they are garbled, shadowy representations about the being of the biblical God and of his design for his dwelling place.

Keeping in mind these perspectives, we will now investigate the ancient Near Eastern beliefs about the temples that housed their gods. At the end of this segment on the ANE, we will see further how these ancient pagan parallels contribute to an understanding of Israel's temple as a little cosmos and of the cosmos itself as a temple.

General Symbolism of Ancient Near Eastern Temples

One of the best examples of cosmic symbolism of temples is the notion in the *Enuma Elish* VI, 113, where it is said concerning the building of Marduk's temple, "He shall make on earth the counterpart of what he brought to pass in heaven."[36] Likewise, the Egyptian pharaoh Thutmose III restored a temple for the god Amon and made it "like the heavens."[37]

---

36. Following the translation of B. R. Foster, "Epic of Creation (1.111)," in *The Context of Scripture* 1, ed. W. W. Hallo (Leiden: E. J. Brill, 1997), 402.

37. J. H. Breasted, *Ancient Records of Egypt*, vol. 2 (New York: Russell & Russell, 1906), 239 (§601); see also 240 (§604).

And Ramses III (1195–1164 BC) affirmed about his god: "I made for thee an august house in Nubia . . . the likeness of the heavens."[38] The same Pharaoh said of an Amon temple, "I made for thee an august palace . . . like the great house of [the god] Atum which is in heaven."[39] It was not unusual for Egyptian temples to be called "heaven" on earth.[40]

One of the earliest Mesopotamian accounts of a temple being compared with the heavens is that found in the commemoration of King Gudea's building and dedication of a temple in Lagash for the god Ningirsu (c. 2112–2004 BC). "The building of the temple" was done "according to its holy star(s),"[41] and the builders "were making the temple grow (high) like a mountain range; making it float in mid-heaven like a cloud."[42] The new temple was like "brilliant moonlight . . . shining. It illuminated the land, (and) . . . rivaled the newborn Suen (the moon god)."[43] Depicting temples with heavenly descriptions is a phenomenon that spans the centuries in the ancient world. Almost two millennia later, in a hymn to Mar, the god of the kingdom of Rashu and Arashu near Babylonia and Elam (third century BC), there is the exhortation, "Oh, let them build, in heaven, your house, concealed, with stars."[44] Here the god's house is clearly said to be "in heaven."

As noted earlier, the most explicit Old Testament parallel to these references is Psalm 78:69: "And He built His sanctuary like the heights, like the earth which He has founded *forever* [or from eternity]." Similarly, Solomon's description of the temple is quite similar to that of King Gudea's temple. The latter was clearly compared to the heavens and its light sources: "the LORD has said that He would dwell in the thick cloud. I have surely built You a lofty house" (1 Kings 8:12–13). Recall the comparable portrayal of the builders of Gudea's temple, who "were making the temple grow (high) . . . making it float in mid-heaven like a cloud." Like Israel's temple, in some way the temples of Marduk, Amon, and other gods were designed to symbolize not merely heaven but the entire cosmos.

---

38. Breasted, *Ancient Records*, vol. 4, 123 (§218); see also vol. 2, 240 (§604).

39. Ibid., vol. 4, 115 (§ 192); see directly below for similar phraseology concerning Egyptian temples being made in "the likeness of the heaven" (with respect to the temples built by Thutmose III, Ramses I, and Seti I).

40. See O. Keel, *The Symbolism of the Biblical World* (New York: Crossroad, 1985), 172, for several examples.

41. R. E. Averbeck, "The Cylinders of Gudea (2.155)," 421, in *The Context of Scripture* 2, ed. W. W. Hallo and K. Lawson Younger (Leiden, Boston, Köln: Brill, 2000), 421.

42. Ibid., 428.

43. Ibid., 430.

44. R. C. Steiner, "The Aramaic Text in Demotic Script (1.99)," in *The Context of Scripture* 1, 315.

Symbolism of Particular Parts of Ancient Near Eastern Temples

Not only were temples as a whole designed to portray the cosmos, but various parts of earthly temples were made to resemble aspects of the entire earth, envisioned as a huge cosmic temple. The arboreal lampstand of Israel's temple was analogous to the portraits of and actual presence of trees in ancient temples that were viewed as "cosmic trees," symbolizing the life essence of the entire world. In particular, taken together with other cultic appurtenances of cosmic symbolism, the tree image pointed to the temple as "the cosmic center of the universe, at the place where heaven and earth converge and thus from where God's control over the universe is effected."[45] The metaphorical picture is that of a huge tree atop a cosmic mountain whose height reaches heaven, whose branches encompass the earth, and whose roots sink down to the lowest parts of the earth.[46] This tree was the central life-giving force for the entire creation. There is portrayal of such trees in Daniel 4 and Ezekiel 17, 19, and 31.

Similarly, the bronze sea basin in the courtyard of Israel's temple, which represented the cosmic seas, finds striking correspondence to ancient temples of the Levant, which also have artificial replicas of seas, symbolizing either the chaotic forces stilled by the god or the waters of life at the cosmic center.[47] In still other respects ancient temples reflected cosmic symbolism. Temples were symbolically the "embodiment of the cosmic mountain," representing the original hillock first emerging from the primordial waters at the beginning of creation; these waters themselves were symbolized in temples, together with fertile trees receiving life from such waters.[48]

The names of various Mesopotamian temples also express specific notions about their "cosmological place and function" and hence sym-

---

45. C. Meyers, "Temple, Jerusalem," *Anchor Bible Dictionary*, 6:359–60; C. L. Meyers, *The Tabernacle Menorah: a Synthetic Study of a Symbol from the Biblical Cult*, ASOR Dissertation Series 2 (Missoula, MT: Scholars Press, 1976), e.g., 169–72, 177, 180; see also Beale, *The Temple and the Church's Mission*, 53, 333–34.

46. For actual representations of cosmic trees on mountains from oriental seals, see H. Henning von der Osten, *Ancient Oriental Seals in the Collection of Mr. E. T. Newell*, University of Chicago Oriental Institute Publications, vol. 22 (Chicago: University of Chicago, 1934), 106–9.

47. C. Meyers, "Sea, Molten," *Anchor Bible Dictionary*, 5:1060–61. Gudea, king of Lagash, furnished the temple of Eninnum with a limestone basin, decorated with designs of heavenly vases pouring water down to the earth (H. Frankfort, *The Art and Architecture of the Ancient Orient* [Hammondsworth, Middlesex: Penguin, 1954], 490). Quite interestingly, Marduk's temple, Esagil, is said in *Enuma Elish* VI, 62 to be "the counterpart of Apsu" (the cosmic subterranean waters); so see W. Horowitz, *Mesopotamian Cosmic Geography* (Winona Lake, IN: Eisenbrauns, 1998), 122–23, for this translation and discussion.

48. So J. M. Lundquist, "The Common Temple Ideology of the Ancient Near East," in *The Temple in Antiquity*, ed. T. G. Madsen, Religious Studies Monograph Series 9 (Salt Lake City, UT: Brigham Young University, 1984), 53–76, on which see other relevant secondary sources cited.

bolic significance.[49] There are many examples of temples repeatedly called names such as "House like Heaven"; "House of Heaven and Underworld"; "House, Bond of the Land"; "Apsu ["fresh water or sea"]-House"; "House of the Mountains"; and "House of the Pure New Moon."[50] That Apsu was "appointed . . . for shrines" (*Enuma Elish* I.76) suggests that cultic places typically were intended to derive their sacred water from rivers, but it is likely also that temples were to be closely associated and symbolically identified with cosmic water.

One of the famous Mesopotamian inscriptions, portraying the Babylonian king Nabuapaliddin entering a temple, combines some of the prominent symbolic elements noted so far in identifying the temple with the cosmos: the seven main light sources seen by the naked eye—sun, moon, Venus, and four other planets—a palm pillar, and an ocean.[51] Similarly, a wall painting from Mari pictures a temple containing trees, four cherubim, two mountains at its base, four streams, and plants growing out of the streams.[52] There is thus abundant evidence from the ancient world that temples symbolized the cosmos in various ways, suggesting once again that the cosmos itself was seen as a big temple.

Temples in the ancient Near East also generally exhibited the same three-part structure as found in Israel's temple,[53] often with similar symbolic significance. The outer court was equivalent to the visible sea and earth where humans live; an inner court inside a building paralleled the visible heavens and also garden terrain; and a holy of holies symbolized the dwelling of the god. For example, Egyptian cult complexes from the New Kingdom period (1570 BC) onwards exhibited an increasing gradation in sacredness beginning with the outer court and proceeding to a zone of greater holiness and then climaxing in an inner womb-like sanctuary. For the Egyptians "the temple was . . . the cosmos in microcosm."[54] The outer court had its outer wall constructed of mud bricks from the Nile that were patterned to look like waves of sea or lake water. There was also a pond or small lake for ceremonial washing that

49. A. R. George, *House Most High* (Winona Lake, IN: Eisenbrauns, 1993), 59.

50. Ibid., 63–161, where a profusion of examples are listed; see also Horowitz, *Mesopotamian Cosmic Geography*, 122–23, for a similar reference in the *Enuma Elish* VI, 55–68.

51. Keel, *Symbolism of the Biblical World*, 172–74.

52. Ibid., 142–43.

53. See A. Mazar, "Temples of the Middle and Late Bronze Ages and the Iron Age," in *The Architecture of Ancient Israel*, ed. A. Kempinski and R. Reich, Israel Exploration Society (Jerusalem: Ahva Press, 1992), 161–87, for examples of tripartite temple structures.

54. B. E. Shafer, "Temples, Priests, and Rituals: An Overview," in *Temples of Ancient Egypt*, ed. B. E. Shafer (Ithaca, NY: Cornell University Press, 1997), 5, on which see also R. B. Finnestad, "Temples of the Ptolemaic and Roman Periods: Ancient Traditions in New Contexts," in *Temples of Ancient Egypt*, 203, 212, 215.

represented primeval waters.[55] There were scenes on the gateways of the Pharaoh's victories over enemies and of his skill in hunting—typical scenes of the world and the king's rule over it. All Egyptians, regardless of societal rank, could come into this outer section, as was also the case in Israel's temple courtyard.

The second zone of sacredness in Egyptian temples was ornamented with solar images. The two trapezoidal pylon towers forming the gateway leading into it symbolized the peaks of mountains that were on the eastern horizon where the sun rose daily. Could this be the symbolism of the two mammoth pillars leading into the Israelite temple's Holy Place? (See 1 Kings 7:15–22.) Battle and hunting scenes were on the inside of the outer courtyard wall and on the external side of the gate leading into the second court. All of these images were transitional indicators between the earthly symbolism of the outer region to that of the next inner sphere, which apparently symbolized the visible heavens. Stars, moon, and sun were also inscribed on ceilings, though whether this included the most holy sanctum is not clear.[56] Likewise, the east-west orientation of the axial path, which led to the innermost sanctum, signified the daily circuit of the sun and had solar images along its route. The entire temple complex also symbolized the horizon, where the sun rose and set.

It is intriguing that, like the Holy Place in Solomon's temple, the second section of Egyptian temples contained garden imagery: bases of walls symbolized the swamp, columns represented plants, ceilings signified the sky, and the floors symbolized the earth. The temple façade had designs of lily and papyrus plants, and its columns were adorned with images of palms, papyri, lotuses, and reeds. If the two big columns at the outer porch of the Holy Place did not symbolize mountains at the horizon, then, in the light of the Mesopotamian and Assyrian as well as Egyptian, Persian, and Syro-Phoenician evidence, perhaps they represented giant trees, since they were ornamented with vegetation—clusters of pomegranates and lilies—at the top.[57]

55. R. H. Wilkinson, *The Complete Temples of Ancient Egypt* (New York: Thames and Hudson, 2000), 72.

56. Finnestad, "Temples of the Ptolemaic and Roman Periods," 204. See R. H. Wilkinson, *The Complete Temples of Ancient Egypt*, 76, who notes that ceilings were "decorated with stars and flying birds" in order to symbolize the heavens.

57. In a personal communication, G. Hugenberger has expressed the view that the two pillars of the temple are symbolic of God's theophanic presence in a pillar of cloud and a pillar of fire (cf. Ex. 14:19; Num. 14:14), which is said to stand at the entrance to the tabernacle (Ex. 33:9–10; Num. 12:5; Deut. 31:15, though only the pillar of cloud is explicitly mentioned), recalling that the tabernacle had no structural pillars like the later temple (though we cannot discuss all the reasons for this identification).

Depictions of garden imagery in the second part of the temple might seem to contradict the prior conclusion that the second sacred space in both Israel's and pagan temples primarily symbolized the visible heaven. As we will see, especially with respect to Israel's temple, this is not necessarily inconsistent with the star imagery of the Holy Place, since it was also intended to mimic the garden of Eden. This we will argue was the Holy Place in the first primeval temple. The lampstand with seven lamps representing luminaries also alluded to the Tree of Life in Eden. Nevertheless, there probably was some overlap of symbolism in the various sections of these temples, so that while it is difficult to draw hard and fast distinctions between them, the broad symbolic divisions observed above probably remain valid.

Again, the evidence of this section showing that sanctuaries represented the cosmos in different ways, adds to the corollary implication so far argued that the universe was an enormous temple itself.

Symbolism of Precious Metals in Ancient Near Eastern Temples

The precious metals used in the construction of Israel's temple had a sheen that reflected light, apparently designed in part to remind one of the reflection of the sun, moon, and stars in the heavens (see the discussion above and 1 Chron. 29:2–8; 2 Chron. 3:3–9; 4:20–22 for all the precious metals used; likewise for the inner furnishings of the tabernacle, see Ex. 26:32; 31:4; 35:32; 36:36).

Descriptions of other temples in the ancient Orient suggest further that the precious metals in Israel's temple possessed cosmic significance. Royal inscriptions of Assyria regularly compare the inside of renovated or newly built temples to the heavenly abode of the deities.[58] Assyrian kings used precious metals to decorate the interiors of temples in order to produce a shining glimmer like the heavens above.[59]

The Assyrian king Tiglath-pileser I (1115–1077 BC) declared that "the great gods . . . commanded me to rebuild their shrine. . . . Its interior I decorated like the interior of heaven. I decorated its walls as splendidly as the brilliance of rising stars."[60] A later Assyrian king, Ashurbanipal

---

58. J. J. Niehaus, *God at Sinai* (Grand Rapids: Zondervan, 1995), 118, citing in support, among others, A. K. Grayson, *Assyrian Rulers of the Third and Second Millennia B.C.*, The Royal Inscriptions of Mesopotamia, Assyrian Periods (Toronto: University of Toronto Press, 1987), 1:254–55, 11:15–57.

59. J. J. Niehaus, *Ancient Near Eastern Themes in Biblical Theology* (Grand Rapids: Kregel, 2008).

60. A. K. Grayson, *Assyrian Royal Inscriptions*, vol. 2 (Wiesbaden: Otto Harrassowitz, 1976), 18 (vii.71–114); I am indebted to Niehaus, *Ancient Near Eastern Themes* for alerting me to this reference and the following ones in this section.

(668–627 BC), said, "The sanctuaries of the great gods, my lords, I restored with gold (and) [silver] . . . I decked . . . Esarra . . . I made shine like the writing of heaven. Every kind of gold (and) silver adornment of a temple I [ma]de."[61]

Nearly identical descriptions are found of the interior of Egyptian temples. Thutmose III (1490–1436 BC) built an inner sanctuary for the god Amon and called it "His-Great-Seat-is-Like-the-Horizon-of-Heaven." Likewise "its interior was wrought with electrum" in order to serve as an imitation of the light reflected from the heaven itself.[62] Even the liturgical furniture of this sanctuary was composed of precious metals for the same purpose:

A great vase of electrum . . . silver, gold, bronze, and copper . . . the Two Lands were flooded with their brightness, like the stars in the body of Nut [i.e., the sky goddess], while my statue followed. Offering-tables of electrum . . . I made . . . for him.[63]

Similarly the Pharaoh Pi-ankhi I (720 BC) created court furnishings of a temple composed "of gold like the horizon of heaven."[64] Recall that the inside furniture of Israel's temple was covered with precious metal (1 Kings 6:20–28; 7:48–49).

Queen Hatshepsut (1486–1468 BC) constructed a temple for Amon with a floor of silver and gold, and said, "Its beauty was like the horizon of heaven."[65] Along virtually identical lines Amen-hotep III (1398–1361 BC) built a temple in Karnak for the deity Amon and constructed it "of gold . . . unlimited in malachite and lazuli; a place of rest for the lord of gods, made like his throne that is in heaven."[66] And about the temple of the same god in Thebes, the same Pharaoh said, "It resembles the horizon in heaven when Re rises therein."[67] The temple "ceiling is painted blue for the sky and is studded with a multitude of golden stars."[68]

So also Ramses I (1303–1302 BC) constructed "a temple like the horizon of heaven, wherein Re [rises]."[69] The pharaoh Seti I (1302–1290

61. A. C. Peipkorn, *Historical Prism Inscriptions of Ashurbanipal* I (Chicago: University of Chicago Press, 1933), 28–29 (i. 16–23).
62. Breasted, *Ancient Records*, vol. 2, 64 (§ 153).
63. Ibid., vol. 2, 68 (§ 164).
64. Ibid., vol. 4, 495 (§ 970).
65. Ibid., vol. 2, 156 (§375); recollect here that Solomon "overlaid the floor of the house [temple] with gold, inner and outer sanctuaries" (1 Kgs. 6:30).
66. Ibid., vol. 2, 355 (§ 881).
67. Ibid., vol. 2, 356 (§ 883).
68. H. H. Nelson, "The Egyptian Temple," *The Biblical Archaeologist* 7 (1944): 47; see also 48.
69. Breasted, *Ancient Records*, vol. 3, 36 (§ 79).

BC) built for the underworld god Osiris "a temple like heaven; its divine ennead are like the stars in it; its radiance is in the faces (of men) like the horizon of Re rising therein at early morning."[70] This temple was also referred to as "a house like the heavens, its beauty illuminating the Two Lands."[71] Ramses II, a successor to Seti, observed about the temple at Karnak that "its august columns are of electrum, made like every place that is in heaven. (It is) mistress of silver, queen of gold, it contains every splendid costly stone."[72]

This evidence from Mesopotamia and Egypt suggests to some degree that just as ancient Near Eastern temples used precious metals to adorn their temples, the precious metals of Israel's temple also had heavenly symbolism. Interestingly, even the clothing of Egyptian priests was like that of Israel's priests, representing both the inner sanctuary and the heavens.[73]

Conclusion about the Symbolism of Israel's Temple in the Light of Ancient Near Eastern Temples

Evidence from the ancient cultures surrounding Israel points further in the direction that Israel's tabernacle and temple reflect the cosmos, which strongly points to the notion that the cosmos itself appears to be a massive temple or will become such in the future. Occasionally, the ancient pagan descriptions even explicitly assert that there was a temple or a throne in the heaven itself. The ancient Near Eastern temples are also compatible with the three sections of Israel's temple representing the three parts of the cosmos. The outer court symbolized the visible earth—land and sea, the place of human habitation; the Holy Place primarily represented the visible heavens, though garden imagery was included to recall Eden, which, we will see, was the primeval equivalent of the later Holy Place and the Holy of Holies stood for the invisible heavenly dimension of the cosmos where God dwelt.

These ancient pagan commonalities with Israel's temple reflected partial yet true revelation, though insufficient revelation for a personal knowledge of God. Yet Israel's temples are not like her neighbors, merely because they reflected some degree of perception about the true reality of God's dwelling; rather, Israel's temple was intended to be viewed as the

---

70. Ibid., vol. 3, 96–97 (§ 232); likewise ibid., 97 (§ 236–37).
71. Ibid., vol. 3, 98 (§ 240.12).
72. Ibid., vol. 3, 218 (§ 512); similarly, ibid., 217 (§ 510). See Finnestad, "Temples of the Ptolemaic and Roman Periods," 213, for gold covering in temples being metaphorical for sunlight.
73. Betsy M. Bryan, "47 Pectoral of Psusennes I," in Erik Hornung and Betsy M. Bryan, eds., *The Quest for Immortality. Treasures of Ancient Egypt* (Washington: National Gallery of Art and United Exhibits Group, 2002), 130, on which see further Appendix 1.

true temple to which all other imperfect temples aspired. Israel's temple was likely a protest statement against all other pretenders, of whom she was quite aware. In order to make an effective polemical statement, there had to be similarities with the temples of her neighbors, but there also had to be differences.

One of the major differences is whereas in the inner sanctuary of the pagan temple there was an idol, there was no such thing in the Holy of Holies, since God's being cannot be seen, much less an image of it reproduced by human craft. In addition, while there were a variety of temples for various gods in each pagan nation, in Israel there was only one temple, since there was only one true God. Furthermore, in contrast to priests of other religions who practiced magic rituals (incantations, divinization, etc.) to manipulate the gods, Israel's priests, indeed all Israelites, were forbidden to participate in such practices, since God could not be manipulated.

The pagan priests' main function revolved around caring for and feeding their god in the temple, but Israel's God had no needs, so that priests served God only through various rituals designed for worship of the sovereign, self-existing deity that he was.[74] These priests were living images of God. Their attire was designed to reflect the Holy of Holies, where the presence of God himself resided. As such, they were the only images that were suitable for placement in the true temple.

Similarly, the gods of the nations needed housing for rest, but God himself says that no human-made structure could be an adequate dwelling for him (cf. 1 Kings 8:27; Isa. 66:1). One reason for this is that, as we have already hinted and will see in the following chapter, Israel's temple pointed to the end-time goal of God's presence residing throughout the entire cosmos, not merely in the back room of one little, isolated structure.[75] The pagan temples had no such eschatological purpose as a part of their symbolism.

Finally, though parts of Israel's temple, like the neighboring pagan temples, symbolized the starry heavens, that symbolism is not highlighted as much. Why? We believe the reason to be that Israel wanted to make it clear that she did not worship the stars as gods. Therefore, while the stellar symbolism is discernible in Israel's temple, it is not as ornate and ostentatious as in temples dedicated to the sun god and other astronomical deities. Nevertheless, the cosmic symbols that are present indicate that Israel's temple was a small model of the heavens and earth, which not only points to the present cosmos as God's big temple but to the

---

74. I am thankful to my colleague John Walton for this observation.
75. For fuller explanation of this, see Beale, *Temple and Church's Mission*, chaps. 2–4.

end-time goal of God's presence tabernacling throughout the creation as it had only in the back room of the temple.

Divine Rest after Creating the Cosmos and after Constructing a Sanctuary

J. D. Levenson summarizes previous research on the Pentateuch and observes that the creation of the cosmos, the making of the tabernacle, and the building of the temple "are all described in similar, and at times identical, language." The reason for the similarity is to indicate "that the temple and the world were considered congeneric,"[76] that is, they were both realties of the same nature or type. Levenson notes that the similarity is a distillation "of a long tradition in the ancient Near East, which binds Temple building and world building."[77] Such a connection is also linked to divine rest, which occurs subsequently to the work of creating.

God's Rest after Creating the World, the Tabernacle, and the Temple, Which Points to Genesis 1 as a Cosmic Temple-building Narrative

John Walton has observed a link between creation and the tabernacle. In this respect, he cites M. Fishbane, following M. Buber, who observes significant parallels between the creation account and that of the construction of the tabernacle[78] (for example, cf. respectively Gen. 1:31; 2:1; 2:2; 2:3 with Ex. 39:43; 39:32; 40:33). Fishbane notes that Moses' work of constructing the tabernacle is patterned after God's creation of the cosmos, using the same language: "Thus, 'Moses saw all the work' which the people 'did' in constructing the tabernacle; 'and Moses completed the work' and 'blessed' the people for all their labors."[79] Fishbane concludes that the tabernacle's construction was intentionally portrayed in the image of the world's creation. W. J. Dumbrell has also observed some influence from other ancient creation narratives that contain an account of (1) a threat to the deity (Gen. 1:2), (2) combat, and (3) vic-

---

76. J. D. Levenson, "The Temple and the World," *JR* 64 (1984): 286.

77. Ibid., 287–88; so also M. Weinfeld, "Sabbath and the Enthronement of the Lord—the Problem of the Sitz im Leben of Genesis 1:1–2:3," in *Melanges bibliques et orientaux en l'honneur de M. Henri Cazelles*, ed. A. Caquot and M. Delcor (Kevelaer: Butzon & Bercker; Neukirchen-Vluyn: Neukirchener Verlag, 1981), 501–12. Cf. also B. Janowski, "Tempel und Schöpfung. Schöpfungstheologische Aspeckte der priesterschriftlichen Heiligtumskonzeption," in *Schöpfung und Neuschöpfung*, Jahrbuch für Biblische Theologie 5 (Neukirchen-Vluyn: Neukirchener, 1990), 37–69, especially with respect to a depiction of the establishment of the tabernacle according to the thematic lines of the creation narrative in Gen. 1:1–2:4.

78. Walton, *Genesis*, 149.

79. Fishbane, *Text and Texture* (New York: Schoken, 1979), 12.

tory and the construction of a palace-temple, with its image of the deity in the temple.[80]

Along similar lines, J. R. Middleton has concluded that "although not immediately obvious . . . from the perspective of the rest of the Old Testament . . . God is building a *temple* in Genesis 1." He also observes that Isaiah 66:1–2 affirms that the cosmos is a giant temple, a passage that is directly related to a new heaven and earth prophecy (on which see Isa. 65:17–25):

> Thus says the LORD,
> "Heaven is My throne and the earth is My footstool.
> Where then is a house you could build for Me?
> And where is a place that I may rest?
> For My hand made all these things,
> Thus all these things came into being," declares the LORD.
> "But to this one I will look,
> To him who is humble and contrite of spirit, and who trembles at
>   My word."

He notes that the verses do not claim that God does not need a temple but that he does not need a humanly constructed temple, since he already has constructed the entire world as a temple, which is a sufficient dwelling for him.[81] The reference to a throne indicates that this is a palace-temple, and the mention of the footstool probably refers to the notion that the earth itself was intended to be the ark of God's covenant, since that is the typical meaning of footstool elsewhere. M. G. Kline has also argued that Genesis 1 refers throughout to the visible earthly realm as modeled after the temple of the invisible heavenly realm.[82]

More specifically, both accounts of the creation and building of the tabernacle are structured around a series of seven acts: cf. "And God said" (Gen. 1:3, 6, 9, 14, 20, 24, 26; cf. vv. 11, 28, 29) and "the Lord said" (Ex. 25:1; 30:11, 17, 22, 34; 31:1, 12).[83] In the light of observing similar

---

80. Dumbrell, "Genesis 2:1–17: A Foreshadowing of the New Creation," in *Biblical Theology: Retrospect and Prospect*, ed. S. J. Hafemann (Downers Grove, IL: InterVarsity; Leicester: Inter-Varsity, 2002), 58, who also notes that the idea of temple construction in Genesis 1 is also pointed to by observing that elsewhere the Old Testament describes the world in architectural terms: gates, bars, foundations, pillars, canopy, windows.

81. J. Richard Middleton, *The Liberating Image* (Grand Rapids: Brazos, 2005), 81–82. I have made the same point in my *Temple and Church's Mission*, 133–38, while emphasizing that the present cosmos has become tainted with sin and must be destroyed, and that Isa. 66:1–2 envisions a whole new cosmos that will be a temple in which God will live eternally with his people.

82. M. G. Kline, "Space and Time in the Genesis Cosmogony," *Perspectives on Science and Christian Faith* 48:1 (March 1996): 2–15.

83. J. Sailhamer, *The Pentateuch as Narrative* (Grand Rapids: Zondervan, 1992), 298–99.

and additional parallels between the "creation of the world" and "the construction of the sanctuary," J. Blenkinsopp concludes, "The place of worship is a scaled-down cosmos."[84] Similarly, P. J. Kearney argues that each of the seven speeches of Exodus 25–31, describing the commands to build the tabernacle, alludes to some significant feature in the corresponding day of creation in Genesis 1:1–2:3.[85]

Levenson also suggests that the same cosmic significance is to be seen from the fact that Solomon took seven years to build the temple (1 Kings 6:38), that he dedicated it on the seventh month, during the Feast of Booths which was a festival of seven days (1 Kings 8), and that his dedicatory speech was structured around seven petitions (1 Kings 8:31–55). Hence, the building of the temple appears to have been modeled on the seven-day creation of the world, which also is in line with the building of temples in seven days elsewhere in the ancient Near East.[86]

Just as God rested on the seventh day from his work of creation, so when the creation of the tabernacle[87] and especially the temple are finished, God takes up a resting place therein.[88] Psalm 132:7–8, 13–14 says:

> Let us go into His dwelling place; let us worship at His footstool. Arise, O Lord, to Your resting place; You and the ark of Your strength. . . . For the Lord has chosen Zion; He has desired it for His habitation. "This is my resting place forever; here I will dwell, for I have desired it."

Therefore, "the temple and the world stand in an intimate and intrinsic connection. The two projects cannot ultimately be distinguished or

84. J. Blenkinsopp, *The Pentateuch* (New York: Doubleday, 1992), 217–18; cf. also 62–63. One later Jewish tradition similarly identifies the creation with the tabernacle by saying, "The Tabernacle is equal to the creation of the world," and then substantiates the claim by comparing the various things created on each day of creation to seven similar items created in the tabernacle (Tanhuma Yelammedenu Exodus 11.2).

85. P. J. Kearney, "Creation and Liturgy: the P Redaction of Ex 25–40," *ZAW* 89 (1977): 375–78, 384–86. I am grateful to Desmond Alexander for directing me to this source as well as to that of Dumbrell and Middleton above.

86. So Levenson, *Creation and the Persistence of Evil*, 78–79. See also J. Richard Middleton, *The Liberating Image* (Grand Rapids: Brazos, 2005), 83, who recognizes the prominence of the number "seven" in Genesis 1 and in descriptions of the building of the temple and feast days linked to the temple.

87. With respect to the tabernacle, Ex. 25:8 of Targum Onqelos quotes God as saying that the Israelites were to "make before Me a sanctuary and I will let My presence rest among them."

88. I am indebted to Walton, *Genesis*, 149–55, for the discussion here and partly below about the link between the temple and divine "rest."

disengaged. Each recounts how God brought about an environment in which he can rest."[89] Both projects are forms of a temple.

Indeed, in addition to the clear affirmation of Psalm 132, other Old Testament passages indicate that part of the purpose of the temple is as a divine resting place. Among other references in this respect are 1 Chronicles 28:2, in which David intended "to build a permanent home for the ark . . . of the LORD"; Isaiah 66:1: "Where then is a house you could build for Me? And where is My resting place?"; 2 Chronicles 6:41: "Arise, O LORD God, to Your resting place, You and the ark of Your might"; cf. also the apocryphal Judith 9:8: "Thy sanctuary . . . the tabernacle where Thy glorious name rests."[90]

God's rest both at the conclusion of creation in Genesis 1–2 and later in Israel's temple indicates not mere inactivity but a demonstration of his sovereignty over the forces of chaos (e.g., the enemies of Israel) and now has assumed a position of kingly rest, further revealing his sovereign power. Similarly, as we will see below in citations of the *Enuma Elish* and other sources, the building of a shrine for divine rest occurs only after the powers of chaos have been defeated.

Accordingly, it is likely not coincidental that David initially conceived of building God a temple only after "the Lord had given him rest on every side from all his enemies" (2 Sam. 7:1–6, following Levenson).[91] David prepared for the building of the temple (1 Chron. 21:18–29:30), but he did not construct it because he had been "a man of war" and had "shed blood" (1 Chron. 22:8; 28:3). Furthermore, he did not build the temple because while there was rest externally, there was still political unrest internally that needed to be quelled before Solomon could assume the throne and then build the temple (1 Kings 1–2).

Consequently, Solomon decides to "build a house for the name of the Lord" when he recognizes that "now the LORD my God has given me rest on every side" (1 Kings 5:4–5; so almost identically 1 Chron. 22:9–10, 18–19; 23:25–26; cf. 1 Kings 8:56). And, in fact, when God promises that Solomon "will build a house for My name," it is directly preceded and followed by the phrase "I will establish . . . his kingdom" (2 Sam. 7:12–13), thus underscoring the close relation of temple building and complete sovereign rest as a result of defeating all enemies.

89. Levenson, "Temple and World," 288.

90. See also Isa. 57:15 (LXX): "The Most High, who dwells on high for ever, Holy in the Holies, is his name, the Most High resting in the holies." This appears to be a reference not only to God's cultic heavenly resting place but may include the temple in Zion which is the extension of or symbol of the heavenly dwelling. Cf. also Num. 10:33–36; 1 Chron. 6:31; Ps. 95:11.

91. Levenson, *Creation and the Persistence of Evil,* 107.

Exodus 15:17–18 confirms this by saying that God would bring Israel to "the place, O LORD, which You have made for Your dwelling, the sanctuary, O LORD, which Your hands have established. The LORD shall reign forever and ever." God's dwelling in Israel's temple was conceived as the rest of a divine king who had no worries about opposition. God's *sitting* in the temple is an expression of his sovereign rest or reign. This is underscored by the repeated phrase "who is enthroned above the cherubim" (2 Sam. 6:2; 2 Kings 19:15; 1 Chron. 13:6; Pss. 80:1; 99:1), which includes reference to God's actual presence in the temple as a reflection of his reign in the heavenly realm.

Psalm 99:1 even more clearly asserts, "The LORD reigns. . . . He is enthroned above the cherubim." Just as God "ascended and sat in the heights of the universe [to reign]," after he completed the creation (so *The Fathers According to Rabbi Nathan* 1[92]), so he would ascend to the temple and reign from there, after he subdued all Israel's enemies.[93] In like manner, the repeated image of God "sitting on a throne" is another picture of the sovereign who is resting. The phrase occurs at least thirty-five times in the Old Testament, usually with respect to Israel's human kings (cf. though, e.g., Ps. 47:8: "God reigns over the nations, God sits on His holy throne").

Thus, the likely implication of the evidence in this section is that the Genesis 1 creation account is also an account of the building of the cosmos as a massive temple for God's dwelling.[94] This may also be indicated by the fact that the Akkadian, Canaanite, and Egyptian cosmogonies all are inextricably linked in various ways with the building of a temple in heaven or on earth.[95]

The Ancient Near Eastern Concept of Gods Resting after Creating the World and the Temple

Walton notes how well God's rest in Israel's temple corresponds to the purpose of temples in the ancient Near East, which enhances the conclu-

---

92. See *The Fathers According to Rabbi Nathan*, trans. J. Goldin (New York: Schocken, 1955), 12.

93. Levenson, *Creation and the Persistence of Evil*, 108.

94. See R. A. Oden, "Cosmogony, Cosmology," *Anchor Bible Dictionary* 1 (Garden City, NY: Doubleday, 1992), ed. D. N. Freedman, 1170, who notes that the anthropological-sociological explanation (especially that of E. Durkheim), which continues to play the largest role for scholars of cosmology, affirms that cosmologies such as Genesis 1 are patterned after the social organization and have a framework that reflects the forms of societal organization. Thus, such conceptions of cosmology are taken from particular social organizations and projected into the particular culture's conception of the world. This notion fits very well with the present proposal that the Hebrews projected the understanding of their temple onto their understanding of the shape and view of the cosmos, though most of our evidence goes the other way, i.e., that the cosmos is projected onto Israel's temple, so that Israel's temple was a micro-cosmos. Probably both perspectives are true.

95. E. C. Lucas, "Cosmology," *Dictionary of the Old Testament: Pentateuch*, ed. T. D. Alexander and D. W. Baker (Downers Grove: InterVarsity; Leicester: Inter-Varsity, 2003), 133–35.

sions of the preceding discussion. In particular, the *Enuma Elish* narrates that the lack of rest among the gods results in a battle. The higher god Apsu complains to Tiamat about the lower gods:

> Their ways have become very grievous to me,
> By day I cannot rest, by night I cannot sleep.
> I shall abolish their ways and disperse them.
> Let peace prevail, so that we can sleep (*Enuma Elish* I, 37–40).[96]

After defeating Tiamat, Marduk reorganizes the cosmos and the lesser gods under his sovereignty, concluding with the building of Babylon conceived as a shrine-like temple in which the gods can find rest:

> We will make a shrine, which is to be called by name
> "Chamber that shall be Our Stopping Place,"
> we shall find rest therein.
> We shall lay out the shrine, let us set up its emplacement, when we
>   come thither . . . we shall find rest therein.
> When Marduk heard this,
> His features glowed brightly, like the day,
> Then make Babylon the task that you requested,
> Let its brickwork be formed, build high the shrine (*Enuma Elish*
>   VI.51–58).[97]

Similarly, in the Sumerian narrative of Gudea's building a temple for the god Ningirsu, the purpose of the temple was to establish a place of rest for the god and his consort.[98] And when the Sumerian god Ningirsu enters the temple built for him, he is portrayed as a warrior and king (Cyl B v. 1–19[99]). His majestic inactivity shows that the powers of chaos have been ruled over, that stability in his kingdom has been achieved, and no further exertion on his part is needed to achieve victory.

---

96. Here Walton follows the translation of Dalley, *Myths from Mesopotamia* (Oxford: Oxford University Press, 1991), 234; see also the translation of A. Heidel, *The Babylonian Genesis* (Chicago; London: University of Chicago Press, 1942), 19.

97. Here Walton follows the translation of B. Foster, *From Distant Days* (Bethesda: CDL Press, 1995), 39–40; see also the translation of A. Heidel, *The Babylonian Genesis*, 48, who translates with "sanctuary" instead of "shrine" in lines 51 and 58. Like Walton, J. Laansma, *"I Will Give You Rest,"* (WUNT 2 Reihe; Tübingen: Mohr Siebeck), 71, cites the same two segments from Tablet 1 and VI of the *Enuma Elish* in order to make the same point.

98. Walton, *Genesis*, 151: see Cyl. B, 14.21–23. For the text, see T. Jacobsen, *The Harps That Once . . . ; Sumerian Poetry in Translation* (New Haven: Yale Univ. Press, 1987), 438, as well as Averbeck, "The Cylinders of Gudea (2.155)," 430: "O Ningirsu, I have built your temple for you . . . O my Baba, I have set up your bed-chamber (?) for you, (so) settle into it comfortably."

99. Averbeck, "The Cylinders of Gudea (2.155)," in *The Context of Scripture* 2, 431.

After the Egyptian pharaoh Ramses had built a temple for the god Ptah, he made an image of the deity, set it in the most inner holy chamber, and exclaimed that now the god was "resting upon its [the temple's] throne."[100] This theme occurs repeatedly in Egypt.[101] Another passage in the *Enuma Elish* (I.73–76) pertaining to divine rest, not apparently noticed by commentators, explains that after the god Ea defeats other divine opponents, he rests in a shrine:

> After Ea had vanquished (and) subdued his enemies,
> Had established his victory over his foes,
> (And) had peacefully rested in his abode,
> He named it *Apsu* and appointed (it) for shrines.[102]

Similarly, another text (VI.8, 35–36) in the same work affirms that "after Ea . . . had created mankind . . . they had imposed the service of the gods upon them" for the purpose that the gods "may be at rest."

Consequently, "in the ancient Near East as in the Bible, temples are for divine 'rest,' and divine rest is found in sanctuaries or sacred space."[103] The pagan religious material suggests further that after God overcame chaos and created the heavens and earth as his dwelling place and after he overcame Israel's enemies and built the temple, he rested as a true sovereign on his throne in contrast to the pretending, false deities whom pagan worshipers believed had done the same.

Israel's Earthly Tabernacle and Temple as Reflections and Recapitulations of the First Temple in the Garden of Eden

In addition to the notion that the earthly temple reflected the heavenly, cosmic temple, there is evidence that the garden of Eden itself was a sanctuary and that it was the first archetypal temple, which Israel's later tabernacle and temples were intended to reflect in various ways. This points further to the conclusion that the creation account in Genesis 1 is associated with temple building, since Genesis 2 is usually thought to be a second creation account, focusing on the creation of humanity. Accordingly, the sanctuary in Eden was an earthly sanctuary reflecting in various ways the larger cosmic sanctuary. The following list reveals

---

100. Breasted, *Ancient Records of Egypt*, III, 181 (§ 412).
101. For temples as the "resting" place of a deity, see ibid., II, 355 (§ 881) and III, 217 (§510), 220 (§ 517), 221 (§521).
102. Following Heidel, *Babylonian Genesis*, 21.
103. Walton, *Genesis*, 151; see further Levenson, *Creation and the Persistence of Evil*, 100–111, for expanded discussion of the "rest" of gods in temples, both in the ANE and the OT.

a number of ways in which Eden and Israel's tabernacle/temples were uniquely similar.[104]

1) The garden and temple as the unique place of God's presence dwelling with his people.
2) The garden and temple as the place where only priests could dwell.
3) The garden and temple as the place of guarding cherubim.
4) The garden and the temple with an arboreal symbol in its midst.
5) The garden of Eden as formative for garden imagery in Israel's temple.
6) The garden and temple as sources of water.
7) The garden and the temple linked closely to precious stones.
8) The garden and the temple located on a mountain.
9) The garden and the temple with an eastern-facing entrance.
10) The garden and temple as tripartite sacred structures.
11) Adam and Eve are placed as divine "images" in the Edenic sanctuary.

Likewise images of pagan gods were placed in temples, but Adam and Eve were living images of the true God.

In the light of these numerous conceptual and linguistic parallels between Eden and Israel's tabernacle and temple, we should expect to find that Ezekiel 28:13–14, 16, 18 refers to "Eden, the garden of God . . . the holy mountain of God," and also alludes to it as containing "sanctuaries," which elsewhere is a plural way of referring to Israel's tabernacle (Lev. 21:23) and temple (Ezek. 7:24; so also Jer. 51:51). Ezekiel 28:18 is probably, therefore, the most explicit place anywhere in canonical literature where the garden of Eden is called a temple.

The cumulative effect of the preceding parallels between the garden of Genesis 2 and Israel's tabernacle and temple indicates that Eden was the first archetypal earthly temple, upon which all of Israel's temples were based. Some of the similarities drawn may not be as strong as others, but when all are viewed together they have a significant collective effect, pointing to Eden as the first earthly temple in garden-like form. We are not left, however, with only a collection of similarities between Eden and a temple.

Indeed, as seen above, Ezekiel 28 explicitly calls Eden the first sanctuary, which substantiates that Eden is described as a temple because

104. See Beale, *Temple and Church's Mission*, 66–80, for an elaboration of each of the following parallels.

it is the first temple, albeit a garden temple. Early Judaism confirms this identification. Indeed, it is probable that even the similar ancient Near Eastern temples can trace their roots back to the original primeval garden.

Conclusion

Our discussion shows that Israel's temple was symbolic of the cosmos and that the cosmos itself was understood as a gigantic temple for God. It is important to establish this concept, since it will serve as the basis for the next chapter. There we return to our main interest—the subject of the Bible's use of cosmological language and how it relates to modern scientific notions of the universe as well as to the ancient idea that the world and universe were one giant temple. Does such language in the Old Testament contradict modern notions of the cosmos, thus posing a problem for the authority and inspiration of Scripture?

CHAPTER SEVEN

Can Old Testament Cosmology Be Reconciled with Modern Scientific Cosmology? *Part 2*

After investigating the cosmos as a temple and the temple as a reflection of the cosmos, we now return to the issue of the authority of Scripture. Specifically, how does cosmological language relate to an ancient author's socially constructed reality and to our modern notions of the cosmos? Many believe that the Old Testament view of the cosmos cannot be accepted by modern people because it is so inextricably bound up with ancient Near Eastern mythological conceptions that clearly contradict contemporary scientific views. Here we build on the evidence of the preceding chapter to answer this apparent conundrum.

This evidence makes it an attractive, viable option for understanding many of the cosmic descriptions of the Bible not as ancient, naïve, and inaccurate scientific descriptions of the universe but as phenomenological descriptions. Furthermore, even more of these cosmic descriptions are theological expressions of the world as a huge creational temple for God's dwelling. And, I would contend, the same theological understanding is just as relevant theologically for us today.

Old Testament and Modern Cosmology: Cosmos as a Temple?
We have already noted that the Old Testament describes the cosmos in various ways and that there are three possible interpretations of these descriptions: (1) they are phenomenological, i.e., what appears to the naked eye; (2) they are mythological, that is, borrowed from ANE mythologies about the cosmos; (3) they are theological in that many of the

descriptions portray the universe as part of a big temple in which God dwells. We argued that the Old Testament is filled with theologically charged descriptions of the world, especially with respect to how Israel's temple relates to conceptions of the cosmos.

We also saw that the same phenomenon occurs in the ancient Near East. Israel's temple was a small model of the different parts of the entire cosmos. The true temple was intended to be the first cosmos, but the earthly part of it was infected with sinful uncleanness. Nevertheless, there was still a sense in which even the fallen cosmos was God's temple, just as fallen humanity was still in the divine image, though it had become distorted.

God had a redemptive-historical reason in designing Israel's tabernacle and temple as a microcosmic model of the macrocosmic temple. This little model not only reflected the present cosmos but looked forward to the new macrocosmic temple, in which God's glorious presence would dwell as originally intended. This is pictured in Revelation 21:1–22:5, which portrays an eschatologically consummated macrocosmic temple in escalated replacement of the fallen one.[1] Revelation 21:1–22:5 is one of the clearest texts in all of biblical literature that portrays the future cosmos as a gigantic temple,[2] a view also found in the Qumran writings.[3]

We have seen that sometimes Old Testament writers describe the cosmos as a big temple, according to their understanding of Israel's little temple (e.g., Genesis 1; Ex. 25:9, 40; Dan. 2:31–45), and, alternatively and often, that Israel's temple and its various components are depicted with parts of the cosmos (e.g., Ex. 26:30; 27:8; Ps. 78:69), since the cosmos, as we have seen, was viewed as a giant temple, after which the small earthly temple was patterned. The New Testament also understands the cosmos as a colossal sanctuary (e.g., Rev. 21:1–22:5; likewise Heb. 8:5). This means that many of the descriptions of the cosmos are charged with a temple theology to one degree or another, so that in these numerous cases, at least, the writers were *not* thinking according to the mythical conventions of their acculturation or even giving mere descriptions of what appeared to their eyes. While other ANE cultures shared some of

---

1. My entire book *The Temple and the Church's Mission* (Leicester: Inter-Varsity, 2004) argues this point. For a summary of the book, especially on this point, see my article "Eden, the Temple, and the Church's Mission in the New Creation," *JETS* 48 (2005): 5–31.

2. Again, see my "Eden, the Temple, and the Church's Mission in the New Creation," which summarizes my book, *The Temple and the Church's Mission*, where also there is analysis of how Rev. 21:1–22:5 pictures the future cosmos as an enormous temple.

3. The idea of a worldwide end-time temple finds striking similarity to the Qumran community, who were to "honour" God "by consecrating yourself to him, in accordance to the fact that he has placed you as a holy of holies [over all] the earth, and over all the angels" (4Q418, fragment 81 [= 4Q423 8 + 24?], line 4).

these ideas about a cosmic temple, God was filling Israel's understanding with special revelatory truth.

Such descriptions are not scientific but theological, understanding the cosmos as a big temple. The point then is to express a theological rather than a scientific perspective that God's presence filled the entire cosmos and would even more so in the end time. While after the fall God's presence filled the cosmos only in a general revelatory manner, his glorious special revelatory presence was sequestered behind the curtain of the visible heaven in the invisible heavenly dimension, symbolized by the curtain separating the Holy of Holies from the rest of Israel's temple. The Holy of Holies was also the heavenly extension of God's special revelatory presence. Such a theological point, if it is really what Scripture is saying (as we have argued), can be accepted by Christians living in the twenty-first century.

There are obvious places where Old Testament writers give phenomenological descriptions of the cosmos, such as "the sun rose and set," or express the perception that from any high vantage point where the horizon can be seen, the earth appears to be circular (Isa. 40:22; Job 26:10; Prov. 8:27). While these kinds of descriptions are not related to the cosmos as a temple, many cosmological descriptions are tied in to one degree or another to the conception that the cosmos is a temple, after which Israel's little temple was patterned. Consequently, many of the portrayals of the cosmos in the Old Testament betray the writers' theological—not scientific—view to varying degrees that the cosmos was God's dwelling place, i.e., his temple.

If this is so, one cannot make a tidy distinction between a biblical writer's conventional language expressing his worldview and Israel's covenant theology based on God's special revelation. Likewise, of course, if these are theological expressions about a massive cosmic temple, there is no tension between them and our modern scientific understanding of the universe, so that the notion of a "scientific error" does not even come into view. Consequently, there should be no temptation to see the Hebrew conception as unique to their culture and, accordingly, true for them but not for us modern, scientific folk.

One may question whether it is theologically correct to view the cosmos as a temple, but such doubt would be about the theology of the Bible itself, not its scientific inconsistency. Such doubt amounts to doubt about the authoritative theological expression of the Old Testament, if our interpretation about its temple theology is correct.

Do certain descriptions of the cosmos reflect only language expressing the ancient mythological worldview, which was built into the substructure of the biblical writers' thinking through acculturation, and not a phenomenological view or temple-theological perspective? Perhaps. I have discussed this with some ANE scholars, and the best assessment they give me is that sometimes the cosmological language is purely phenomenological (a view with which moderns can identify), sometimes it expresses the cosmic temple notion, and sometimes it reflects the socially constructed mythological geographical assumptions and understanding of the parts of the cosmos, apparently unrelated to the cosmic temple perspective.

For myself, I think the descriptions that scholars might place in the last category may well be tangentially related in one way or another to phenomenological observations, or they could be descriptions related more directly to a cosmic temple. The ancient Hebrews would have thought of every part of the cosmos as part of God's creational temple, a fact pointed to in our earlier discussion where we saw that the Genesis 1 narrative itself is to be understood as God's creation of the world in the form of a huge temple in which he would dwell. Such a primal and foundational first chapter of the Hebrew Bible likely left an indelible mark on the Old Testament writers' view of the cosmos, which could be expressed explicitly, subtly, and even unconsciously.

The following representative list by John Walton of cosmic descriptions in the ANE also found in the Old Testament[4] could easily be—indeed likely are—parts of a cosmic temple description.[5] In fact, the following analysis of these Old Testament descriptions, which parallels ancient Near Eastern cosmology, proposes that they are best understood either from a phenomenological vantage point or from a theological perspective of the temple. They are likely not unconsciously absorbed pagan mythological views of various parts of the cosmos.

Cosmic Descriptions in the Old Testament with ANE Parallels That Are to Be Understood from a Phenomenological or Theological (Temple) Perspective

The "Expanse (rāqîaʿ) of Crystal" in Ezekiel 1:22
"Now over the heads of the living beings there was something like an expanse, like the awesome gleam of crystal, spread out over their heads."

---

4. These examples are taken from a summary of parallels by John Walton, *Ancient Near Eastern Thought and the Old Testament* (Grand Rapids: Baker, 2006), 174–75, though his purpose is only to observe the parallels; he makes no attempt at this point to ask how these parallels could relate to a conception of the cosmos as a temple.

5. The majority of the following parallels mentioned by Walton have also been commented on in the preceding chapter, where both the specific ANE sources and Old Testament references may be found.

This is, at the least, an echo of Genesis 1:6: "Then God said, 'Let there be an *expanse* in the midst of the waters, and let it separate the waters from the waters.'" The expanse or firmament is portrayed as part of an explicit heavenly temple scene in Ezekiel 1. Note the guarding cherubim in the context and the continuation of the vision within a clear temple setting in Ezekiel 8–10. (Josephus [*Ant.* 1:30] says the expanse in Gen. 1:6 was composed of "crystal," thus perhaps identifying Gen. 1:26 with the expanse of Ezek. 1:22.)

The heavenly temple scene of Revelation 4–5 also alludes to Ezekiel 1:22. Revelation 4:6 has "and before the throne there was something like a sea of glass, like crystal" (for the same phrase, "sea of glass like crystal," see also Rev. 15:2). The important observation is that the expanse is viewed as part of a heavenly temple scene in Ezekiel and inextricably linked to the crystal sea in Revelation 4,[6] which is also a temple depiction.

As noted, it is interesting that a number of significant scholars have also identified Genesis 1 as a temple building scene, which would include the expanse there as part of the cosmic temple.[7] This crystal firmament or expanse in Ezekiel may represent the floor of the Holy of Holies in God's heavenly temple, which was viewed as being composed of precious stones. This firmament according to the above descriptions is more fluid-like than solid in substance. It would appear that this firmament or expanse in some way is what separates the visible creation of the sky and starry heavens from the invisible dimension of God's heavenly temple dwelling.

Some believe that the *rāqîaʿ* was rock-solid and formed a dome over the earth, reflecting the ANE mythological viewpoint without any qualification or critique, which is unlikely.[8] For example, P. H. Seely argues for such a view in an article published in the *Westminster Theological Journal*. He contends that the *rāqîaʿ* in Genesis 1:6, 14, 17, 20 and in Ezekiel must be considered solid since this was the common ANE view,

6. This conclusion can be made without analyzing the exact relationship of the "firmament" to the "crystal" in Ezekiel and the relationship of the "sea of glass" to the "crystal" in Rev. 4:6, though in both they are likely virtually identical; this conclusion can also be made by analyzing the use of Ezek. 1:22 in Rev. 4:6. At the least, the "firmament" of Ezekiel 1 is very closely linked to the "sea" of Revelation 4.

7. Genesis 1 and Ezekiel 1 also have in common the following: in Ezek. 1:26–28 the throne of God is located above the "expanse," as is the case apparently also in other texts alluding to part of the "heaven" mentioned in Gen. 1:6, above which sits God's throne (1 Kings 22:19; Pss. 2:4; 11:4; 103:19; Isa. 6:1; 14:13; 66:1, of which Ps. 11:4; Isa. 6:1; and 66:1 are explicit heavenly temple texts [on which see P. H. Seely, "The Firmament and the Water Above, Part 1: the Meaning of *rāqîaʿ* in Gen 1:6–8," *WTJ* 53 (1991): 239, who makes the identification between Genesis 1 and Ezekiel 1 but does not observe that both are part of temple depictions]).

8. See Seely, "The Firmament and the Water Above, Part 1," 227–40.

both from the mythological perspective and from the viewpoint of the ancient common person.

There are several points of disagreement that I have with this article, though space does not allow elaboration of all of them. For example, we just do not know that all ancients believed the sky was a solid dome or that there was anything near unanimity on this point. The mythological portrayal in the *Enuma Elish* of the splitting of Tiamat's body does not prove the point from the Babylonian view, despite Seely's protestation to the contrary,[9] since we cannot be sure that the body of the deity would have been thought of as solid. The deity Apsu is composed of liquid; indeed, even Tiamat is the deity of saltwater deep and equated with that reality. Would the Babylonians have thought of saltwater as something solid? Furthermore, the Israelites and other ancient peoples observed that the sun, moon, and planets move across the sky at different rates, which seems to indicate that these were not implanted in a solid-like dome.

Like Seely, Dennis Lamoureux believes that the ANE viewed the heavens as a solid dome-like structure. Lamoureux cites an illustration of the Egyptian view in which the sun god Re travels by boat on the top

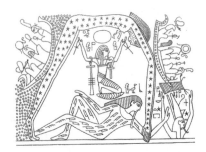

of a dome-shaped sea of the heaven, which is represented by a deity bending over.[10] But there is another Egyptian depiction where the god of the sky, Nut, is held up by Shu, which represents the air itself. Neither the fluid heavenly sea represented by Nut nor the air symbolized by Shu are solid materials![11]

Therefore, rather than considered as a completely solid substance the *rāqîaʿ* is perhaps best thought of as diaphanously spread out and transparent. Thus, "expanse" may be the best translation. The word has this notion in Isaiah 42:5 and 44:24. Even in Exodus 39:3 the verbal form is used for hammering out gold into gold leaf; i.e., the emphasis

9. Ibid., 234.

10. D. Lamoureux, "Lessons from the Heavens: On Scripture, Science and Inerrancy," *Perspectives on Science and Christian Faith," Journal of the American Scientific Affiliation* 60:1 (March 2008): 6.

11. For various ancient Egyptian diagrams of this, see O. Keel, *The Symbolism of the Biblical World* (New York: Seabury Press, 1978), 33–36. The diagram above is taken from Erik Hormung, *Conceptions of God in Ancient Egypt: The One and the Many* (Ithaca, NY: Cornell University Press, 1982), 68. The original is from "Mythological" Mortuary Papers of Tentamun, Paris, Bibliotheque Nationale no. 172 (Twenty-first Dyn).

does not appear to be so much on the substance but on the spreading out of it. Thus, the focus is on the expansive nature in that the *rāqîaʿ*, which Genesis 1:8 defines as "heaven," is spread out from horizon to horizon. If the *rāqîaʿ* is solid, then how does rain get through it, how do the clouds relate to it, how do the sun, moon, and stars move through it, and how do the birds fly in it (on the latter cf. Gen. 1:20)?[12] There is nothing about the word *rāqîaʿ* or about the ancient conception of the cosmos that requires the notion of some kind of solid barrier.

If Seely were correct about the solid nature of the expanse, there would have to be eight solid domes for each light source, evidence of which can be found nowhere in the ancient world. In this respect, biblical writers and ancient astronomers were aware of the five visible light sources—Venus, Mercury, Jupiter, Saturn, Mars—which moved at different rates and sometimes in different directions (retrograde motion) from each other and from all the other stars. This might be feasible if each star were embedded in its own separate dome, but not if each is rooted in the same solid dome that houses the other stars. The ancients also knew about the moon and sun, which travel at different rates from each other and from all the rest. To accommodate all this complexity of motion would, therefore, require eight domes,[13] each with independent rates of rotation, if the ancients thought of these celestial objects as fixed in a solid firmament. Such a view of multiple domes, however, cannot be found to have existed in the ancient world![14]

---

12. See Lamoureux, "Lessons from the Heavens," 14 (n. 23), who prefers that the last clause of Gen. 1:20 should be rendered "[let the birds fly *over* the earth] *across* the face of the *rāqîaʿ* of the heavens," but it is equally plausible to render it something like "in the midst of the expanse" (as in the NASB, ASV, KJV, though other translations do have "across"). Both options are acceptable renderings. The combination of *ʿal-pᵉnê*, which occurs in Gen. 1:20b, refers usually to something being spatially above something else, which is the meaning of the construction in Gen. 1:2, where it is twice used in this way. But it can easily have the meaning of something being "before" or "in front of" something else (e.g., Ex. 34:6; Lev. 16:14; 1 Sam. 24:2 [24:3 = MT]; 2 Sam. 2:24). The preposition *ʿal* indicates that the birds are spatially above the earth in Gen. 1:20a but the preposition *ʿal* plus *pᵉnê* in v. 20b expresses a different notion of the birds flying "in front of the expanse." Though Seely, "The Firmament and the Water Above," 239, says this "is not just phenomenal language" but expresses a belief in a literal solid firmament, many commentators understand the expression in Gen. 1:20b to be only phenomenological, as, e.g., U. Cassuto says, "It seems to reflect the impression that a person receives on looking upward: the creatures that fly about above one's head appear then to be set against the background of the sky—*in front of the firmament of the heavens*" (*A Commentary on the Book of Genesis*, Part 1 [Jerusalem: Magnes Press, 1961], 49; so likewise G. J. Wenham, *Genesis 1–15* [WBC; Waco, TX: Word, 1987], 24). Such a phenomenological view would mean that Gen. 1:20 does not necessarily view the birds actually flying in the expanse. For my understanding of the nature of such phenomenological language, see n. 21 below.

13. That is, one dome each for each of the seven major light sources and an extra dome for all the other stars.

14. I am much indebted to a private communication from G. P. Hugenberger for the thoughts in the last four paragraphs.

Like Seely, Othmar Keel also asserts that the Old Testament and the Egyptians believed that the celestial vault "had a structure similar to a wall or dam," and in partial support he cites Psalm 33:7, rendering the first part of the verse, "[God] holds the waters of the ocean as with a dam."[15] He understands the notion of the dam as similar to a wall or a solid structure. But the word in Psalm 33:7, which he translates "dam" (*nēd*), is not so translated that way in its five other occurrences in the Old Testament. Twice the word refers to the waters of the Red Sea being piled up "like a heap" (Ex. 15:8; Ps. 78:13), and twice it refers to the same phenomenon at the Jordan (Josh. 3:13, 16), where the waters stood up "in one heap." Finally, the word occurs in Isaiah 17:11, where it refers to a "heap" of grain gathered at harvest time. The obviously relevant uses refer to the waters of the Red Sea or Jordan gathering together, so that what Keel considers a solid dam in Psalm 33:7 is really water itself being "heaped up"[16] and perhaps forming a wall-like or roughly-rounded shape.[17] But, again, we find that the material is water, not a solid substance, as we contended above.

Keel, however, expresses more circumspection and caution than Seely in making assessments about this solid vault: "Modern representations of the ancient Near Eastern world view . . . err in portraying the upper regions too concretely, as if they were as well understood by the men of that time as was the earthly environment."[18] Then Keel says more generally but along the same lines:

> Yet another fundamental error of . . . contemporary representations [of the cosmos] lies in their failure to suggest the extent to which the question of the foundations of the universe—of the ultimate basis and security of the sphere of existence—remained a problem. The ancient Near East was not conscious of any answer to this question. Again and again, ciphers and symbols were employed (cf. 28, 33), expressing nothing other than awe in the face of divine, magical power or divine wisdom and grace.[19]

Keel's words here are directly referencing the ancient Egyptian diagrams (his diagrams 28, 33), which we have referenced already, concerning the deities Nut and Shu, where the cosmic sea is represented as being upheld by the air. Keel, again, cautiously concludes his discussion,

15. Keel, *Symbolism of the Biblical World*, 37, 40.
16. The ASV, KJV, NASB, and ESV have "heap" in Ps. 33:7.
17. Accordingly, the LXX renders the Hebrew here as "wineskin," and the NIV has "jars"; similarly the RSV and NRSV have "bottle."
18. Keel, *Symbolism of the Biblical World*, 37.
19. Ibid., 56.

saying, "A wide variety of diverse uncoordinated notions regarding the cosmic structure were advanced from various points of departure."[20] Though I ultimately disagree with Keel's view of a solid vault over the earth, his caution about having too much confidence in assessing ancient conceptions of the cosmos in too precise a manner is a timely word, as is his emphasis on the fact that the ancients used symbols to depict their understanding of the cosmos.

Ironically, Seely commits a categorical fallacy by deducing ancient conceptions of the cosmos from myths and then translating such conceptions into what he thinks are the modern physical equivalents. It is partly this that Keel has warned against. It is interesting that the present editor of the *Westminster Theological Journal*, Vern S. Poythress, disagrees with Seely's position about Genesis 1:6ff. and understands the kind of language that occurs there to be ancient commonsense, phenomenological perspectives about the cosmos that are just as valid as modern commonsense vantage points. For example, it is just as valid today, as it was for the ancients, to think of the sun as a disk that transverses the sky.[21]

20. Ibid., 57.

21. See V. Poythress, *Redeeming Science* (Wheaton: Crossway, 2006), 92–98, upon which this paragraph is based and in which he specifically disagrees with Seely's views. See Lamoureux, "Lessons from the Heavens," 9, who tries to mitigate the force of this shared phenomenological experience by ancients and moderns by saying that the ancient "peoples believed what their eyes saw—the sun literally moved across the sky," though when modern people say the same thing they understand this non-literally (see also ibid., 6). But, in fact, it is speculation to try to know what was in the mind of the ancient biblical writer when making these phenomenological observations in the text, which is an example of a common hermeneutical fallacy sometimes committed by contemporary interpreters. This is known as the "intentional fallacy," trying to discover a writer's fuller intention from material external to the actual text itself, i.e., especially an author's feelings, what motivated him to write, his wider belief system, etc. Most ancient people were not ANE cosmologists; some may have thought more literally about what they saw (as Lamoureux thinks), but others may not have reflected deeply on the heavenly phenomena that they observed in their daily life, and precisely how "the common person on the ancient street" would have theorized about these things is not clear; and Lamoureux gives no primary source data supporting what the common person would have believed. And, as I have said, even what the ANE scholarly cosmological guild held is not perspicuous, as we have seen that Keel has observed. Also, distinction should be made between the recorded observation in Scripture and the broader cosmological worldview behind it (if there was a clear one), since what is inspired is the written expression and not the writer's full thoughts on the general topic of which the expression is a part. Biblical writers are inspired in what they write, but they may certainly be wrong about many of their beliefs that are not recorded in Scripture, even beliefs connected with what they write. This is to say that biblical writers were inspired only in their prophetic capacity of writing Scripture but not in everything they said or believed outside of that task. Thus, a writer could record the observation that the sun traversed the horizon, but his belief about why he thought that happened is external to the text and anyway is speculation. An analogy with the NT may be appropriate: NT writers express the belief that the coming of the Lord could be at any time; I think it is also probable that they thought that that coming would be within their lifetime, but I believe they left that open because of what Christ says in Matt. 24:36 and Acts 1:7. So they likely would have distinguished what they wrote from their own personal expectations of what they wrote, which they held with less certainty. I believe this is analogous to the phenomenological statements of OT writers.

Sapphire Pavement in the Sky at the Top of a Mountain Where God Dwelt in Exodus 24:10

The image of a pavement of stone in heaven may well be thought of as a neutral reflection of the very similar ANE mythological image that we encountered at the beginning of chapter 6. But when one recalls that Mount Sinai was understood to be a temple, the sapphire pavement fits in as the pavement of precious stone that formed the floor of the heavenly Holy of Holies. In this respect, the bottom part of Sinai represented the courtyard where all Israelites could gather; the middle section was more sacred, equivalent to the Holy Place of the later tabernacle where only a priestly caste could come. In Exodus 24 this group was composed of the seventy elders together with Moses and Aaron. The top of Sinai in the midst of the cloud was equivalent to the Holy of Holies, where God dwelt, the tablets of the Law and the ark were created, and only Moses, the temporary high priest, could enter.[22]

Ezekiel's description of the heavenly dimension, which corresponded to the earthly sanctuary, includes almost the same depiction as that found in the Exodus 24 passage: "Now above the expanse that was over the heads" of the living cherubim "there was something resembling a throne, like lapis lazuli in appearance," which itself was under a human-like depiction of God (Ezek. 1:26; see similarly Ezek. 1:22–23, 25). Ezekiel 10:1 has virtually the same portrayal, though there "something like a sapphire stone . . . resembling a throne" was not above but "*in* the vault of heaven that was over [the] heads of the cherubim." It is probably best to view the vault or expanse (*rāqîaʿ*) in both Ezekiel passages as a platform that rests on the four living creatures, which is actually part of the foundation for the throne itself.[23] Though the consistency or nature of this platform cannot be determined precisely, we have already concluded that it is not a solid substance.

In line with this, the jewels in Revelation also describe the shining glory of God's tabernacling in the heavenly sanctuary (Rev. 4:3; 21:11, 18–20). This points further to Exodus 24:10 as being a vision of God's inbreaking heavenly tabernacle, since the Ezekiel vision is clearly of a heavenly temple scene, as Genesis 1:6 is likely part of a temple building narrative, including the whole earth and heaven.

This evidence further supports the concept that the firmament or expanse (*rāqîaʿ*) is not what separates the visible heaven from literal

---

22. For a more detailed analysis of Mount Sinai as a temporary mountain temple, after which the tabernacle was modeled, see "Excursus 1: Sinai as a Temple" at the end of G. K. Beale, "The Descent of the Eschatological Temple in the Form of the Spirit at Pentecost: Part 1," *TynBul* 55 (2005).

23. Cf. Barth, *Church Dogmatics*, 3.1 (Edinburgh: T. & T. Clark, 1958), 136.

waters above it; rather, it appears to be an other-dimensional reality that separates the observable sky from the invisible heavenly temple, so that it may be a reality that overlaps with both the earthly and heavenly dimensions. The bottom part of the expanse is depicted with precious stones that resemble the color of waters underneath and that reach up to the divine throne, though literal waters resembling blue-colored precious stone at the bottom of the heavenly temple may be in view (especially in Genesis 1:6; see Job 37:18 likewise: "Can you, with him, spread out the skies, strong as a molten mirror?"). Psalm150:1 appears to place God's sanctuary and expanse in synonymous parallelism:

> Praise the LORD!
> Praise God in His sanctuary;
> Praise Him in His mighty *expanse*.

These are the only two locations in the psalm where praise is offered. The general identity of the "sanctuary" and "expanse" is pointed to further by the above discussion showing that the "expanse" was the bottom part of the heavenly temple. Thus, the expanse is more precisely not equal to the whole heavenly temple but a part of it. It is likely not coincidental that in the immediate context of Ezekiel 1:26 and Revelation 4:6 the cherubim praise and glorify God in his heavenly sanctuary[24] (see also Isa. 6:1–4), just as praise is to be offered in the sanctuary and expanse in Psalm 150.

Finally, in line with this, Psalm 29:10 asserts, "The LORD sat as King at the flood" (see also Ps. 148:4), which apparently refers to God's dwelling in a heavenly temple above the heavenly sea. Psalm 29:9 confirms that this is a temple scene: "And in His temple everything says, 'Glory!'"

Seely also argues that the notion of literal waters above the firmament in Genesis 1:6 assumes a mythological scientific idea that is inaccurate according to modern standards,[25] but he never entertains the option that Genesis 1 is a cosmic temple building episode shot through with temple theology at every point. It is not an attempt to give an actual depiction of only visible reality but also of the invisible dimension, especially of God's heavenly temple, even if some physical realities were perceived to be in that invisible realm such as waters.

24. See Rev. 4:8–9 and 5:11–14, which allude to the four living creatures of Ezekiel 1. Ezek. 1:24 may imply praise, especially in light of Isa. 6:1–4, and the interpretative paraphrase of the Targ. Ezek. 1:24: "The sound of their words were as though they were thanking and blessing their Master . . . like the sound of the hosts of the angels on high."

25. H. Seely, "The Firmament and the Water Above, Part 2: The Meaning of 'the Water above the Firmament' in Gen 1:6–8," *WTJ* 54 (1992): 31–47.

An analogy of such a mix of physical with heavenly realities is the idea that Christ's physically resurrected body exists in the unseen heavenly dimension now.

It may well be that the literal atmospheric waters above the *rāqîaʿ* in Genesis 1:7 are a part only of the physical cosmos and are a visible counterpart to a heavenly sea that is beyond the seen cosmos, which forms part of the floor to the heavenly temple, or part of the platform for God's throne, as discussed above with Psalm 29:10, Ezekiel 1:22, and Revelation 4:6.[26] Accordingly there would be a dual reference similar to the term *heaven* referring to the physical cosmos or, alternatively, to the invisible heavens, depending on the context. This is a usage commonly acknowledged; i.e., the physical heavens are the furthermost reality from the human perspective and, by analogy, this visible heaven comes to represent the truly most remote reality from human beings, which is the invisible heavenly dimension, where God and his angels dwell.[27]

It must be acknowledged that it is difficult to give a systematically organized depiction of the heavenly temple or cosmos as a temple, since there are only snapshots of such depictions scattered here and there throughout Scripture. A good example is the precise location of the "expanse" in the heavenly temple. Some texts portray the expanse as the floor of the heavenly temple (Ex. 24:10; Ps. 29:9–10?); other passages view it as a platform on which God's throne rests (Ezek. 1:22) or as being in the midst of where the throne is set (Ezek. 10:1). Still others view it as being in front of the throne (Rev. 4:6). Likewise, it is difficult to locate exactly how the expanse of Genesis 1:6–8 fits into a temple depiction. *Our main point, however, is that this expanse in Genesis 1 is associated in some integral manner with the notion of the cosmic temple, including perhaps the heavenly dimension of the temple.*

Seely does not even attempt to discuss the relation of the visible heaven to the invisible heaven found throughout the Old Testament and likely

---

26. I have no problem in viewing the waters "above the expanse" to be literal atmospheric waters from which rain comes. Part of this "expanse" was certainly understood even by the ancients to contain water that was separated from the waters "below" on earth, as, for example, the hydrological cycle described in Job 36:27–39 makes clear (evaporation of water from earth forms clouds from which rains upon the earth come). Thus, many would have viewed the *rāqîaʿ* to have various layers (first air, then multiple levels of clouds filled with water with a further uppermost air space above). This multiple-level view of the "expanse" is still consistent with the notion of Gen. 1:7, that the "expanse" separated earthly waters from heavenly waters, though technically the upper atmospheric waters were really a part of the "expanse" itself.

27. Neh. 9:6 would appear to be a good example of both uses: "You alone are the LORD. You have made the heavens, the heaven of heavens with all their host, the earth and all that is on it, the seas and all that is in them. You give life to all of them and the heavenly host bows down before You." This twofold sense of "heaven" seems to be included in the initial reference to "heavens" in Gen. 1:1.

included, to some degree, in Genesis 1, which is evident from the Old Testament texts cited above in this section with respect to the invisible dimension of God's heavenly dwelling.[28] As we have argued, it is unlikely that there are neutral ancient scientific assumptions in the Old Testament that are not in some way a part of a biblical author's teaching, since everything is charged with theological significance—even cosmic phenomenological language, as we have contended.

Seely argues similarly in his article "The Firmament and the Water Above Part 1: the Meaning of *rāqîaʿ*," where he says that "the reference to the solid firmament "lies outside the scope of the writer's teachings" and the verse is still infallibly true.[29] But note that he does not say "inerrantly true," since he believes he has established a factual scientific error at this very point about the firmament. Again, in this article he makes no reference to Genesis 1 or to the cosmos being part of a temple portrayal. But note Kline,[30] who argues that the firmament in Genesis 1:8 was modeled after the archetype of its corresponding object in the heavenly realm.[31] Seely's two articles need further response, but the limits of this project do not allow further discussion.[32]

The Idea of a Mountain Found at the Center of the World

Such Old Testament texts as Micah 4:1–2, Isaiah 2:2–3, and Daniel 2:31–45 affirm that "in the latter days" a mountain (Zion) will grow and become the central geographical and theological feature of all the earth, and, in the case of Daniel 2, this mountain will "fill the earth" (v. 35). Strikingly, in all three passages this mountain is inextricably linked with a big temple. In Isaiah and Micah, the mountain is possibly equated with "the house of the Lord," and in Daniel a rock becomes a mountain-temple that fills the world.[33]

---

28. On which see further the very important article by M. G. Kline, "Space and Time in the Genesis Cosmogony," *Perspectives on Science and Christian Faith* 48:1 (March 1996): 2–15, with respect to the notion of a heavenly upper invisible register referring to God's temple dwelling and a lower earthly register reflecting the upper heavenly temple in Genesis 1 (e.g., see ibid., 3 and passim).

29. Ibid., 240.

30. Kline, "Space and Time," 6.

31. See also Kearney, "Creation and Liturgy: the P Redaction of Ex 25–40," *ZAW* 89 (1977): 376–77, who argues that the firmament dividing the upper and lower waters has correspondence with divisions linked to the description of the tabernacle.

32. See Lamoureux, "Lessons from the Heavens," 4–15, who argues along the same lines as Seely with respect to Gen. 1:6–8 (though making no significant advancements on Seely's arguments) and comes to the same conclusion about a solid firmament representing ANE views of the cosmos that cannot be accepted as true today but nevertheless is in context part of a teaching that is infallibly true.

33. See Beale, *Temple and the Church's Mission*, 144–53, for the rock-mountain in Daniel being a huge growing temple, on which note also there the close ANE parallel to King Gudea's growing temple.

Daniel 2 is one of the clearest Old Testament texts that portray the whole world becoming a stone temple. Recall again the notion that the sanctuaries of Eden, Sinai, Israel's first and second temples, and the eschatological temple were all understood to be on mountains at the (theological) center of the world, and that the ANE conceived of both earthly and heavenly temples to be built on mountains or to contain the symbolism of mountains. The scriptural portrayals of the mountain temple represent the true depiction of which the pagan parallels were but faint images.

The Idea of a Cosmic Tree in the Center of the World

It was argued earlier that this image apparently had microcosmic symbolism in Israel's lampstand in the middle section of the temple, which several ANE-OT scholars think represents the Edenic tree of life in the middle of Eden. A similar notion of a cosmic Eden and cosmic tree *in connection to a temple* is also found in Qumran (on which, e.g., see 1QH 6.12–19 and other related DSS texts[34]). Recall also that the temple was the center of Jerusalem, which itself was considered the center of the earth.[35] Ezekiel 31 also closely associates such a giant tree with the trees of the garden of Eden,[36] which was considered to be the first primal arboreal temple.[37]

A further observation can be made with particular reference to common tree-like images in both Eden and Israel's temple. In the light of Mesopotamian, Assyrian, Egyptian, Persian, and Syro-Phoenician evidence about columns in ancient buildings and temples having tree-like appearance, the two large columns at the outer porch of the Holy Place perhaps represented giant trees, since, as we saw in the previous chapter, they were ornamented with vegetation—clusters of pomegranates and lilies at the top. Possibly they corresponded to the two well-known trees of life and knowledge in the garden of Eden.[38]

Thus, the description of a cosmic tree in the Old Testament had symbolic significance in connection with the temple and Eden and was not an uncritically regurgitated mythological picture from the ANE.

34. Cited and discussed in Beale, *Temple and Church's Mission*, 155–60.
35. Ibid., 53.
36. On which see ibid., 126–29.
37. On which see the last section of this chapter.
38. As proposed by Bloch-Smith, "'Who is the King of Glory?' Solomon's Temple and Its Symbolism," in *Scripture and other Artifacts: Essays on the Bible and Archeology in Honor of Philip J. King*, ed. M. D. Coogan, J. C. Exum, and L. E. Stager (Louisville: Westminster John Knox, 1994), 27.

The Earth's Foundations, Footings, and Cornerstone (Job 38:4–6)

This passage in Job may merely refer to the phenomenal perception that God made the earth firm and immovable, by human hand anyway. The description, however, resonates with echoes of temple building. The phrase "who *stretched the line on* it?" (Job 38:5) preceded by "who set its *measurements?*" is a combination (composed of the same Hebrew words) occurring only in Job 38 and Zechariah 1:16 and 2:1, the latter of which describes the laying out of plans to build an eschatological temple.[39]

Likewise, the combination of "foundation" with "cornerstone" appears elsewhere only in Isaiah 28:16 and Zechariah 4:7–9 (again with the same Hebrew words), both of which refer to the setting up of a key stone in an end-time temple.[40] Job 38:4–7 together with Job 38:8–11, which refers to God setting boundaries for the seas, is a reflection on God's original creation of the earth in Genesis 1, which we have also seen is a temple-building narrative. In addition, quite intriguing is the observation that the phrase in Job 38:6a, "on what were its bases [or "footings," *ʾeḏen*] sunk?" uses the Hebrew word, which occurs fifty-eight times in the Old Testament, fifty-five of which always refer to "sockets" used in the construction of the tabernacle in Exodus and Numbers (e.g., see Exodus 26–27). Only two times outside of Job 38 does this word refer to something else (a figurative portrayal for Solomon's thighs [Song 5:15] and a person's name [Ezra 2:59]).

In the light of all this, it may be quite understandable that Job 38 employs fairly unique temple-building language in describing God's creation of the world so that it may echo such a concept. Recollect that the reference to the altar's "foundation" (*yᵉsôd*) in the temple courtyard is also used of the foundations of mountains and other structures rooted to the earth.[41] Interestingly, the same word refers to the foundation of the temple itself (2 Chron. 24:27) and, apparently, to one of the foundations of the gates of the temple (2 Chron. 23:5).

The Earth as a Flat Disk (Isa. 11:12)

It is possible that the human eyes would observe the horizon of the earth as a flat disk. The earth (Isa. 40:22) and the heaven (Job 22:14), however, could also be perceived as part of a circle. But some do not

---

39. On which see Beale, *Temple and Church's Mission*, 142–44.
40. Though the Zechariah text has "head" or "top" stone instead precisely of "corner" stone. That Isaiah 28 concerns a temple idea is apparent from its development of Isa. 8:13–15, which refers to "the Lᴏʀᴅ of hosts" as "holy" and the one who "shall become a sanctuary," and refers to people who "stumble," the latter idea also occurring in Isa. 28:13.
41. On which see n. 10 in chap. 6.

think descriptions of a flat earth can be explained only phenomenologically. They view the expression of a four-cornered earth as a reflection
of the naïve ANE view that the earth was flat. Not only could this be a
description of the way things merely "looked" but possibly it could also
contain reverberations of the assumption that the earth was four-cornered
in imitation of the four-cornered tabernacle,[42] the four-cornered outer
court,[43] and four-cornered appurtenances[44] in the tabernacle (e.g., the
altar). Such imitation may be found also in the four corners of Israel's
land (Ezek. 7:2) and perhaps in the four corners of Eden (which some
speculate was the case) to which Israel's temple and land[45] are compared
and actually understood at times to be a recapitulation of.

Recall from the preceding chapter that the square shape of the priest's
breast piece corresponded to the square shape of the Holy of Holies
(1 Kings 6:20), the whole temple complex (Ezek. 45:2–3), and the altar
(Ex. 27:1; 30:2; Ezek. 41:21; 43:16; 43:18). Such uses with respect to
the tabernacle and temple are predominant, but sometimes other more
mundane uses occur. *Four-cornered* can describe an Israelite's field (two
times) or his garment (two times) or even the hair on his head (two times).[46]
Recall that in the end time the temple was to expand to cover Jerusalem,[47]
Israel's land, and then to fill the earth.[48] Such temple associations could
be percolating beneath the expression "four corners of the earth."

*The Earth Founded on the Seas (Ps. 24:2), Divinely Set Boundaries
for the Waters (Ps. 104:9; Prov. 8:29), Doors and Bars of the Sea (Job
38:10), and an Inscribed Horizon (or Circle) on the Seas (Prov. 8:27)*
Again, some of these descriptions may merely express the naked-eye
appearance of the earth's seas (e.g., boundaries of the waters and circle
on the seas). Accordingly, at times the perception of the sea's horizon
may appear as a curved semicircle (so also Prov. 8:27; Job 26:10).

In contrast, some of these descriptions appear to be charged with
theological significance, especially with respect to portraying parts of the

42. As implied in Ex. 26:23–24 and 36:28–29.
43. Ezek. 46:21–22.
44. E.g., Ex. 25:26; 27:2, 4.
45. For the numerous parallels between the garden of Eden and Israel's temple, see the last section
of the preceding chapter, and for the comparison of Israel's land with Eden, see Isa. 51:3; Ezek.
36:35; Joel 2:3; cf. also Gen. 13:10.
46. "Four corners" occurs about 26 times in the OT, 16 of which are descriptions of the tabernacle/
temple or its parts.
47. The new Jerusalem was to be square according to Ezek. 48:13–20, 30–35 and Rev. 21:16, likely
because the square Holy of Holies was to expand out to encompass the city; the idea of the Holy of
Holies expanding to cover Jerusalem is also expressed in Jer. 3:16–17.
48. On which see Beale, *Temple and Church's Mission*, 123–67, 333–34, 365–93.

cosmos as God's temple in which he dwells. The reference to "founding the earth upon the seas" in Psalm 24:2 is perhaps not coincidentally directly related to a temple scene: "Who may ascend into the hill of the LORD? And who may stand in His holy place?" (Ps. 24:3). This is closely followed by an exhortation to "gates" and "doors" to open up so "that the king [the "Lord"] of glory may come in" (24:7–10), presumably into his temple-palace. Just as there was a water source at the back of the Eden sanctuary (Gen. 2:10), and under the Holy of Holies in Israel's first and second temples,[49] as well as in the end-time temple (Ezek. 47:1–12[50]), so waters or seas are portrayed below the earth (Ps. 24:2) and below the structure of God's heavenly temple (Ps. 104:3).[51]

In this connection, Psalm 29:10 asserts, "The LORD sat as King at the flood" (see also Ps. 148:4), which apparently refers to God's dwelling above the heavenly sea, which is separated from the earthly by a firmament (discussed earlier; though here the seas under the heaven could be included). Some may view this as a picture taken from mythological language. More plausibly, however, it probably emerges from Israel's unique covenant theology and not from some mere expression of their acculturated, assumed mythological view of reality.

In fact, it is likely that God's heavenly temple is the assumed context of this statement in Psalm 29, especially in view of the directly preceding verse in Ps. 29:9 (and consistent with Ps. 148:4): "And in His temple everything says, 'Glory!'" In addition Psalm 29:3–9 is commonly understood as a polemic against Baal, since the ascriptions of God are known to have been descriptions of Baal. This then is highly theological and not a mere expression of cosmic acculturation.

Furthermore, in a vision of the heavenly temple that is seeped with references to Old Testament temple-theophany visions, Revelation 4:6 says that John saw "something like a sea of glass, like crystal" before God's throne. This comports with the image in Psalm 29. Thus, this seems to be an example of the heavenly sea above the firmament being part of a cosmic temple conception. This is certainly not a scientific description, since the intention is to describe the cosmos as part of a temple, which I believe, as a modern-day theologian, is still an accurate theological description. As we saw earlier in the heavenly temple scene of Revelation 4–5, Revelation 4:6 alludes to Ezekiel 1:22: "Something like an expanse,

---

49. Ibid., 72–73.
50. So also Joel 3:18; Ps. 46:4; Zech. 13:1, 8. In Ezek. 47:1–12 "water was flowing from under the threshold" of the temple and becoming a river and flowing in the "sea" and "healing" the sea.
51. Note that the preposition *b* can have the meaning "on," so that Ps. 104:3 may be easily rendered "he lays the beams of the upper chambers *on* the waters." But even if the translation were "in," the idea likely would be the same (like a boat "in" or "on" the water).

like the awesome gleam of crystal, spread out over their heads." The important observation is that both the Ezekiel and Revelation 4 texts are viewed as part of a heavenly temple scene.

In the ANE there is found, perhaps not coincidentally, the combined mention of a temple, a cosmic tree, rivers, subterranean waters, jewels linked to sea waters, and divine activity as a description of one cultic place. An apt example comes from a Sumerian-Akkadian text:

> In Eridu the black tragacanth tree grew in a pure place it was created. Its appearance is lapis lazuli stretched out on the Apsu [fresh water or sea] of [the god] Ea—his promenade in Eridu filled with abundance . . . its shrine is the bed of Nammu. In the holy temple in which like a forest it casts its shadow, into which no one has entered, in its midst are [the gods] Shamash and Tammuz, in between the mouths of the two rivers.[52]

This ancient pagan text shows that ancient Near Eastern gods were also thought to dwell in watery abodes or at the source of headwaters. The gods Shamash and Tammuz dwelt in the midst of the holy temple "in between the mouths of the two rivers." The Canaanite god El is also a good example of this.[53] The god's permanent "tent" dwelling was at "the headwaters of the Euphrates River."[54] The dwelling of these gods was apparently in an other-worldly dimension, separate from the observable world. The similar portrayals in the Old Testament of God's dwelling on or over the waters represents the true God's temple in the heavenly dimension in contrast to the false gods who purportedly dwelt in similar cosmic temples.

We noted earlier that Psalm 104:9 was one of the ancient Near Eastern parallels, where divinely set boundaries for the waters is mentioned. That a heavenly temple is also in mind in Psalm 104:3 is indicated by its immediately surrounding context:

> Bless the LORD, O my soul!
> O LORD my God, You are very great;
> You are clothed with splendor and majesty,
> Covering Yourself with light as with a cloak,
> Stretching out heaven like a tent curtain.

52. The text (= CT 16, 46:183-98) is cited by D. Callender, *Adam in Myth and History*, Harvard Semitic Museum Publications (Winona Lake, IN: Eisenbraun, 2000), 50, who is dependent on the translation of R. C. Thompson, *Devils and Evil Spirits of Babylonia* 1 (New York: AMS Press, 1976), 200, lines 183–98, and who also notes other translations.

53. On which see J. Walton, *Genesis*, NIVAC (Grand Rapids: Zondervan, 2001), 167.

54. This is found in a Hittite version of a Canaanite myth, "Elkunirsa and Ashertu," in H. Hoffner, *Hittite Myths*, SBL Writings from the Ancient World (Atlanta: Scholars Press, 1990), 90–91.

> He lays the beams of His upper chambers in the waters;
> He makes the clouds His chariot;
> He walks upon the wings of the wind;
> He makes the winds His messengers, flaming fire His ministers. (Ps.
>   104:1–4)

Verses 1 and 2 allude to God's glorious and majestic appearance, apparently in his heavenly dwelling. God is then said to have "stretched out heaven like a tent *curtain.*" The Hebrew word for "curtain" (*yᵉrîʿâ*) appears about fifty-four times in the entire Old Testament, and the vast majority of the time, mostly in Exodus, it refers to the various curtains in the tabernacle or temple. Only five other times, not including Psalm 104, does the word have a different reference.[55] Even "laying the beams of his upper chambers" is a phrase found elsewhere to refer to the building of the temple (though the Hebrew word for *beams* has a number of other noncultic uses). In fact, that Psalm 104:1–3 concerns a heavenly temple scene is suggested by the very similar portrayal of God in 2 Samuel 22:7–15 (=Ps. 18:6–14):

> "In my distress I called upon the LORD,
>   Yes, I cried to my God;
>   And from His temple He heard my voice,
>   And my cry for help came into His ears.
> Then the earth shook and quaked,
>   The foundations of heaven were trembling
>   And were shaken, because He was angry.
> Smoke went up out of His nostrils,
>   Fire from His mouth devoured;
>   Coals were kindled by it.
> He bowed the heavens also, and came down
>   With thick darkness under His feet.
> And he rode on a cherub and flew;
>   And He appeared on the wings of the wind.
> And He made darkness canopies around Him,
>   A mass of waters, thick clouds of the sky.
> From the brightness before Him
>   Coals of fire were kindled.
> The LORD thundered from heaven,
>   And the Most High uttered His voice.
> And he sent out arrows, and scattered them,
>   Lightning, and routed them." (2 Sam. 22:7–15)

---

55. The Hebrew word "upper chambers" in Ps. 104:3 can refer elsewhere to the "upper chambers" of the temple (2 Chron. 28:11; 2 Chron. 3:9; cf. 2 Chron. 9:4).

Second Samuel 22:9–13 has a very similar description to that in Psalm 104:1–3. In particular, the passage says that the location of God's presence is in the temple (v. 7, *hêkāl*; LXX *naos*) and in his canopies or booths (v. 12, *sukâ*; LXX *skēnē*), the latter a synonym for temple here and elsewhere. The close analogy between these two texts shows how easily such language is closely linked to, indeed part of, heavenly temple language, hinting that the same may be the case in Psalm 104:1–3. The following passages also contain very similar depictions and place them in a heavenly temple setting:

> Can anyone understand the spreading of the clouds,
> The thundering of His *pavilion*?
> Behold, He spreads His lightning about Him,
> And He covers the depths of the sea.
> For by these He judges peoples;
> He gives food in abundance.
> He covers *His* hands with the lightning,
> And commands it to strike the mark. (Job 36:29–32)

> Then the LORD will create over the whole area of Mount Zion and over her assemblies a cloud by day, even smoke, and the brightness of a flaming fire by night; for over all the glory will be a canopy. There will be a shelter to *give* shade from the heat by day, and refuge and protection from the storm and the rain. (Isa. 4:5–6)

Job 36:29 refers to God's "pavilion" (*sukâ*) and Isaiah 4:5–6 to his canopy (*ḥuppâ*) and his shelter or booth (*sukâ*), all of which appear to be references to God's tabernacling dwelling.[56]

John Walton's list of representative parallels between ANE and Old Testament cosmology also includes the following, which can be understood fairly easily by both ancients and moderns, as literal or figurative descriptions of how the world appeared to the naked eye. These are descriptions that even a modern person might give, though even some of them may have intimations of a temple portrayal.

---

56. That Isaiah 4 refers to the entire area of Jerusalem becoming a tabernacle is apparent from recalling that the "fire" and "cloud" were expressions of God's presence both at Sinai (which we have seen was a mountain temple) and in the tabernacle (Num. 9:15–16), and "canopy" is an apt synonym for "tabernacle" (following M. H. Woudstra, "The Tabernacle in Biblical-Theological Perspective," in *New Perspectives on the Old Testament*, ed. J. B. Payne [Waco: Word, 1970], 98–99). Isaiah 4:6 further points to this connection by referring to the "canopy" as a *sukâ* ("booth"), which can be a synonym for "tabernacle" (2 Sam. 11:11; cf. Ps. 31:20; Acts 15:16–18, quoting Amos 9:11–12).

1) The sky or heaven being the abode of light (Job 38:19, phenomenological) and location of storehouses of snow and hail (Job 38:22, figurative).

2) The heavens as the work of God's fingers (Ps. 8:3, figurative for God's power in creating).

3) "Windows of heaven" (Gen. 7:11, 8:2; Isa. 24:18, likely a figurative use).[57]

4) "The deeps were broken up[58] and the skies drip with dew" (Prov. 3:20, virtually literal).

5) "Pillars of the earth" (Job 9:6, figurative, perhaps vaguely reflective of a building structure like a temple[59]).

6) Foundations of the mountains (Deut. 32:22[60] and Ps. 18:7, literal or figurative, again with possible rings of temple associations[61]).

7) The water cycle of evaporation from the earth and the formation of rain clouds followed by rain in Job 36:26–28, which can be fairly literally understood by both very old and contemporary cultures:

> Behold, God is exalted, and we do not know Him;
>   The number of His years is unsearchable.
> For He draws up the drops of water,
>   They distill rain from the mist [or into his mist],
> Which the clouds pour down,
>   They drip upon man abundantly.

Conclusion

Many of the purported socially constructed, mythological expressions of the cosmos reflected in the Old Testament are better understood as descriptions of the way things appeared to the unaided eye or are related

---

57. The phrase is used even more figuratively in Mal. 3:10, while still referencing literal rain; see also 2 Kings 7:2, 19.

58. This expression is difficult with respect to whether it is literal or figurative; sometimes the depiction is figurative (Ps. 77:16) and sometimes it seems literal (Gen. 7:11; Ex. 15:8; Prov. 3:20).

59. Interestingly, the word "pillar" (*'ammûd*) occurs about 112 times in the Old Testament, 80 of which speak of various kinds of "pillars" in the tabernacle or temple. Other uses refer to God's appearance as a pillar of cloud or fire (16x), the supports of other non-temple structures (7x), and "pillars" of heaven is found once (Job 26:11).

60. The Deuteronomy text refers to "Sheol," which throughout the Old Testament refers to the grave, the underworld, and the sphere of the dead. It is not clear how this might be related to a temple notion, if at all.

61. The word for "foundation" (*mûsād*) in Deut. 32:22 and Ps. 18:7 occurs only seven other times in the Old Testament, four times as "foundations of the earth" (Ps. 82:5; Prov. 8:29; Isa. 24:18; Jer. 31:37; Mic. 6:2), twice referring to a foundation in the temple (2 Chron. 8:16; Isa. 28:16, the latter with reference to God as the end-time temple), and once as the foundation of a city (Isa. 58:12).

to a theological understanding of the cosmos (including the unseen heavenly dimension) as a temple. Of course, there will be some portrayals hard to understand and categorize, but most of the portrayals seem to fit rather well into these two categories, the phenomenological and the theological, as well as into other kinds of figurative categories.

How does this conclusion relate to our main theme of biblical authority? Some scholars and students of the Bible have found the Old Testament's conception of the cosmos to reflect an ancient mythological view that clearly contradicts a modern scientific perspective. The purported ANE belief of a solid dome over the sky with water above and below is considered incompatible with how scientists today understand the earth and the sky and the outer space above the earth. The same could be (and has been) said about the description of the heaven having windows or the earth having foundations, pillars, footings, or being a flat disk. Consequently, as we have seen, these biblical expressions have been taken as inaccurate and erroneous.

But we endeavored to show that most of the Old Testament portrayals of the world, sometimes taken to be at odds with the modern scientific view, should not be taken in a woodenly literal manner as anachronistic ancient mythological images or as naïve ancient scientific descriptions. Rather, such portrayals should be understood as theologically charged and ultimately part of Israel's theology.

Cosmic temple language in the Old Testament certainly does not attempt to give a scientific view of the cosmos, but it does convey a theological view of the world and universe being God's massive temple. Thus, the cosmic descriptions of the Old Testament do not pose problems for believing in the absolute authority of Scripture, since they are not contradictions of modern science nor are they mythological beliefs nor naïve scientific portrayals that cannot be held today. I would contend that the view of the cosmos as a temple is one that we as modern-day Christians should also hold.[62] Indeed, if we believe the Bible is authoritative and if our analysis has been correct, we are bound to believe that the cosmos is a temple. Other cosmic descriptions not related to temple portrayals are probably just ways of describing the world as it looked to the eye, much as we do today, neither of which are attempts to give scientific descriptions.

Thus, while it is obvious that God did not reveal to biblical writers a textbook on scientific views of the world and universe, there are some figurative and even literal phenomenological descriptions that are

---

62. This point I develop in my book *The Temple and the Church's Mission*, e.g., see 395–402.

easily understood and even shared by modern readers. Nevertheless, some significant overlaps between Israel's and her neighbors' unique cosmology may seem strange to us today. A significant number of these are expressions about parts of the cosmos being parts of a huge cosmic temple in which Israel's God dwelt.

As we have observed, it is interesting that both in the ANE and Israel there are numerous clear expressions of temples being modeled after the cosmos, implying that the cosmos itself was a temple. While there are some straightforward statements in the ANE that the cosmos was a temple, they are not as numerous. Note the *Enuma Elish* VI, 113 concerning the building of Marduk's temple: "He shall make on earth the counterpart of what he brought to pass in heaven."[63] Such clear statements appear also in the Old Testament, though not as numerously (e.g., Genesis 1; Ex. 25:9, 40; Dan. 2:31–45), as well as in the book of Revelation (Rev. 21:1–22:5).

One reason for fewer portrayals of the cosmos as a temple in the ANE may be that the pagan religions were polytheistic; it might have been awkward to portray the world as multiple temples for multiple deities. But since Israel was monotheistic, such a portrayal was easier, though why there are not more Old Testament descriptions of the cosmos as a temple is not so clear. More to the point, there is evidence in the Bible that God created the world as a big temple to be inhabited by him and his human images, as priests who would worship him in it.[64] In fact, this view is further enhanced by our earlier examination of proposed parallels between ANE and Old Testament cosmology. There we found varying degrees of evidence that the Old Testament description had overtones of temple imagery, which was not typically the case in the ANE parallels. These exegetical explorations are an initial effort; further analysis may yield more connections linking these Old Testament descriptions to God's sacred cosmic dwelling place.

Though Israel and her neighbors shared some commonalities in their view of the geography of heaven and earth, Israel had a different interpretation of these shared features. The religions of the ancient world identified the various parts of the cosmos with divine powers; the heaven, the sun,

---

63. So also, e.g., Pharaoh Ramses III, who said of an Amon temple, "I made for thee an august palace . . . like the great house of [the god] Atum which is in heaven." There is also reference to the whole world being pictured as a garden with a water-ditch around it. See the Epic of Etana, cited in Walton, *Ancient Near Eastern Thought and the Old Testament*, 173; quoting W. Horowitz, *Mesopotamian Cosmic Geography* (Winona Lake, IN: Eisenbrauns, 1998), 60-61, which has affinities to the depiction of the garden of Eden bounded by rivers in Genesis 2, designed to become a worldwide garden sanctuary (on which see Beale, *Temple and Church's Mission*, 66–80).

64. On which see Beale, *Temple and Church's Mission*, esp. 66–121, 313–28, 365–402.

the moon, the earth, and the waters were understood to be actual deities. The Hebrews saw God as separate from the parts of the cosmos and as the sole creator and sustainer of them. "Rather than manifestations of the attributes of deity, they were instruments for his purposes,"[65] and I would add more specifically, for the purpose of creating a massive temple in which he could eternally dwell with his worshiping image bearers.

There are, at least, five different ways that the conceptions and literature of the ancient cultures around Israel relate to the Old Testament writers, including the ancient pagan conceptions of temples that do, in fact, exhibit parallels with descriptions of Israel's temple.[66] (1) The presence of similarities to ANE myth are sometimes due to *polemical intentions*[67] or to direct repudiation of pagan religious beliefs and practices. (2) Others are due to a *reflection of general revelation* by both pagan and biblical writers, and only rightly interpreted by the latter;[68] the recognition of a cultural bridge does not rule out the providential activity of God within those cultures.[69]

3) In addition, still others have attributed purported ANE mythical parallels in the Old Testament to a *common reflection of ancient tradition*, the sources of which precede both the pagan and biblical writers, and the historicity of which has no independent human verification, like creation in Genesis 1. Ultimately the parallels spring from an earlier, ancient, divinely pristine revelation that became garbled in the pagan context but was reliably witnessed to by the scriptural writer.[70]

4) Another view is that revelation did not always counter ancient Near Eastern concepts but often used them in productive ways, though still revised in a significant manner by special revelation. Ancient Near Eastern concepts may have contributed to the theology of sacred space in the building of Israel's tabernacle and temple. Examples include the

65. Walton, *Ancient Near Eastern Thought and the Old Testament*, 175.
66. The remainder of this paragraph and the following two paragraphs are a repetition of a segment from chap. 1, which bear reiterating here (including the footnotes), since it is so important for understanding the present discussion.
67. E.g., see in this respect the article by G. Hasel, "The Polemic Nature of the Genesis Cosmology," *EvQ* 46 (1974): 81–102. Cf. Heidel, *The Babylonian Genesis* (Chicago: Chicago University Press, 1954), 82–140, who does not believe there is enough evidence to be certain that the OT creation narrative was dependent on the Babylonian one, and concludes that some of the significant differences in the former are unparalleled in either the Babylonian or the Assyrian cosmogonies.
68. Peter Enns's discussions of wisdom literature and law in chap. 3 of his book, *Inspiration and Incarnation: Evangelicals and the Problem of the Old Testment* (Grand Rapids: Baker, 2005), would appear to be consistent with this viewpoint.
69. Walton, "Ancient Near Eastern Background Studies," 41–42.
70. E.g., see D. I. Block, "Other Religions in Old Testament Theology," 43–78, who, in essence, affirms these first three views, though the majority of the article elaborates on the first perspective. See also Heidel, *Babylonian Genesis*, 139, who cites a scholar representing the third view.

eastward orientation, the placement of important cultic objects, the designation of areas of increasing holiness, and the rules for access to the Holy Place and Holy of Holies.[71] Accordingly, God often used existing institutions and transformed them to his theological purposes, for example, circumcision and sacrificial offerings, though these examples could also be given for categories 2 and 3 above.[72]

In all four categories, it is common to find similarities at the surface but differences at the conceptual level, and vice versa, especially as divine revelation comes into play in producing different understandings of these surface-level differences.

Of course, another option, in contrast to the preceding four views, is that the biblical writers unconsciously absorbed mythical worldviews about the cosmos, reproduced them in their writings, and believed them to be reliable descriptions of the real world and events occurring in the past real world—creation account, flood narrative, etc.—because they were part of their socially constructed mythological reality.[73] Divine inspiration did not limit such cultural, mythical influence. If this is the case, which is unlikely, it would be impossible not to see ANE myths about the cosmos as inextricably intertwined with Israel's theology, which would be a very difficult predicament for those who believe in the inspiration of Scripture.

Also, I think it is improbable to think, as some do, that biblical writers sometimes thought only from the vantage point of their mythological acculturation and at other times expressed only the distinctive theology based on special revelation. More likely, if they unconsciously imbibed the pagan mythological assumptions about the cosmos, then their unique theology would have been mixed with mythological notions. It is likely a modern conception to suppose that the ancient Old Testament writers could think in such a compartmentalized manner. Would they not have thought that everything they were observing and writing about the natural world was God's creation and, to some degree, a part of their covenantal faith? This distinction seems an artificial imposition onto

---

71. E.g., see Walton, "Ancient Near Eastern Background Studies," 42; see the entire article (pp. 40–45), which is helpful and in which Walton registers agreement also with the preceding three perspectives on ANE parallels, though aligning himself most with this fourth view. See also Block, "Other Religions in Old Testament Theology," 47–48, who also appears partly to align himself with this fourth view.

72. Walton, "Ancient Near Eastern Background Studies," 42.

73. See Walton, "Ancient Near Eastern Background Studies," 43, who repudiates such unconscious absorption and use of myth in the Old Testament, while still affirming that "God's communication used the established literary genres of the ancient world and often conformed to the rules that existed within those genres" (p. 41).

the biblical writers. Did these writers not have a theistic world and life view that encompassed every nook and cranny of creation?

In sum, in this chapter and the preceding one I have labored to demonstrate that the Old Testament's view of the cosmos does not pose problems for the modern-day Christian's trust in the divine authority of the Old Testament. Its cosmic portrayals are not reflections of a naïve, ancient worldview. Many of these depictions are phenomenological and figurative in various ways, as we have discussed. Many also are theological perceptions of the cosmos as a massive temple or parts of such a temple. Such descriptions enhance our theological perception of how God understands the cosmos—it is his temple in which he dwells. If our analysis about the cosmos being a temple is correct for the most part, then we today should have the same theological perspective.

Conclusion

This book has discussed recent challenges to the inerrant authority of the Bible that have arisen within evangelicalism. Chapters 1 to 4 are minor revisions of debates between one particular scholar, Peter Enns, and me over the nature of the inspiration and authority of the Bible. These chapters addressed questions as to whether the Bible can contain myth yet still be considered authoritative, whether the doctrine of inspiration can be retained if the Bible contains distortions of history, and whether Jesus and the apostles misinterpreted the Old Testament, so that their interpretations can still be trusted as authoritative for the church. I concluded with a negative response to each of these questions.

Chapter 5 explored whether Isaiah 40–66 could have been written by someone other than Isaiah, even though Jesus and the other New Testament writers repeatedly attribute the entire book to the prophet Isaiah. Again, I concluded that such a view could not be held while still holding to the absolute authority of Scripture and to the impeccable authority of Jesus himself.

Chapters 6 and 7 posed the question, "Can Old Testament cosmology be reconciled with modern scientific views of the world and the universe?" This issue was addressed because some evangelicals believe that the Old Testament borrows mythological beliefs about the cosmos that are clearly incompatible with modern scientific knowledge. I concluded that these cosmic portrayals that some believe to represent ancient mythology and ancient naïve scientific views are, in reality, better understood as symbolic depictions of the cosmos as a massive temple where God dwells.

Such a perspective does not intend to convey ancient or modern scientific views or mythological views of the world but rather a theological conception about the heavens and earth as God's dwelling place. Israel's small temple was symbolically a little model of the cosmos where God dwelt and would dwell in an even greater way in the new cosmos. I also endeavored to show that other cosmic descriptions not related to temple portrayals are ways of describing the world as it looked to the eye, much as we do today. Since such descriptions were not attempts to give scientific descriptions, they do not contradict the inerrancy of the Bible.

The above issues have been voiced by liberal theologians in the past. What is new about the topics dealt with in this book is that almost the same objections to the Bible's authority are being voiced again but this time from within sectors of evangelicalism. Furthermore, what is especially new is that those who have voiced these viewpoints do not see these former "objections" to pose a problem for the inspiration, even the inerrancy, of the Bible.

The objective of this book has been to address these objections and demonstrate that they are antithetical to the authority and inspiration of Scripture. Therefore, I have sought to show the incompatibility of the postmodern attempt to hold to the high authority of Scripture and the acknowledgment, at the same time, of erroneous views in the Bible. But I have also labored to show that the various supposed contradictions and mistakes in the Bible, set forth by some of the authors discussed in this book, are not contradictions or false views at all.[1]

The new challenges to the absolute authority of Scripture that we have examined in this book ultimately are a new version of an older view known as the infallibility of the Bible. Here *infallibility* becomes a preferred word to *inerrancy*, since the former conveys a notion of Scripture as incapable of misleading in areas of theological doctrines, whereas *inerrancy* affirms that whatever the Bible addresses is without error.[2] Those who held to infallibility did so, since it allowed them to maintain Scripture's authority without holding to inerrancy. Those holding only to infallibility today do so for the same reason. The mere infallibility view inevitably means that the interpreter is the one who decides which parts of the Bible are mistaken and which are correct, which are not theological and which are. This is a precarious position, since ultimately each interpreter or interpretative community decides what constitutes *infallible* Scripture. Packer repeatedly noted the problem of the infallibility view back in the 1950s. He said it was a subjectivist view; that is, the extent of the truth of the Bible is dependent on the interpreter.[3]

---

1. Of course, recall that some of the authors evaluated in this book would not want to refer to "contradictions" or "mistakes," since for them that would be imposing a modern standard of truth on the ancient Scripture.

2. I believe that both the infallibility and inerrancy of Scripture should be held.

3. J. I. Packer, *"Fundamentalism" and the Word of God* (Grand Rapids: Eerdmans, 1958), 50, 72, 140, 158–60.

Some of the more recent challenges noted in this book are issued by those who would object to this analysis and say that all of Scripture is inspired, not just the doctrines, since what we would call "errors" in the Bible, by our modern definition of *error*, would not have been viewed as errors by the ancient biblical writers and readers. Consequently, what is not true for us was true for them. This, however, is a postmodern view of truth and falsehood, which I have argued against. This view really understands that to a significant extent truth is relative. Thus, it is a veiled form of the *infallible* perspective.

Recall, for example, Peter Enns's view that the history of some of the narratives in Genesis are shot through with myth. The important point, Enns contends, was the theological message about the God of the patriarchs being the true God over and against the false gods of the pagan nations. Recall the similar point Enns made about 1 Corinthians 10:4: Paul was dependent on a Jewish legend through which important theological truth was communicated. His stance is virtually identical to the infallibility view of Scripture and to the subjectivist view mentioned by Packer above.[4]

The discussions in this book are representative and reveal the fragmentation of evangelicalism, since its very heart, the absolute authority of Scripture, is under serious debate. There is an erosion of the traditional evangelical notion of what it means for the Bible to be true, as formulated, for example, in the Chicago Statement on Biblical Inerrancy. This slow process of weakening the traditional, biblical view of the Bible's truth is nothing less than the erosion of the very identity of evangelicalism.

My own conclusion is that "the Scripture cannot be broken" (John 10:35). The point of this verse in John is that whatever Scripture addresses has a truthful force that cannot be blunted. I understand this in terms of the *inerrancy* of Scripture, especially as that is formulated in the Chicago Statement on Biblical Inerrancy (see Appendix 2).

4. Ibid., especially see pp. 158–60, where Packer's description of the Biblical Theology movement as subjectivist is uncannily similar to my objection to Enns's view, e.g., "The meaning of factual statements in Scripture may be preserved without any factual [Packer likely means "historical"] reference being ascribed to them. One way is by using the concept of 'myth.' . . . By 'myth' is meant a quasi-factual narrative which, despite its form, is intended only to tell us some truth about our own lives in the present without giving us any information about external events, past or future. 'Myths' tell us nothing of happenings in the physical world. . . . This concept is commonly applied to the stories of the creation."

Appendix 1

Postmodern Questions of Authorial Intent, Epistemology, and Presuppositions and Their Bearing on the Authority of the Old Testament in the New

In chapters 3 and 4 I responded to a postmodern understanding of the use of the Old Testament in the New. This approach, interestingly used by some evangelical interpreters, contends that New Testament writers did not interpret the Old Testament in line with the original intention of the Old Testament authors. This perspective undercuts the authority of Scripture, since there is no consistency between what Old Testament writers meant in addressing their communities with God's authoritative Word and how Jesus and the apostles understood those writers.

Now, one can argue that Jesus and his followers "preached the right doctrine from the wrong texts," so that their interpretative method was flawed; nevertheless, God's Spirit inspired "right doctrinal" conclusions from the writers' fallacious hermeneutical approach, much like ill-prepared preachers who may expound excellent doctrine, but the text from which they are preaching has nothing to do with that doctrine. I have argued against this idiosyncratic view of the New Testament's use of the Old elsewhere.[1]

This appendix explains the theological and hermeneutical foundations for my response to this postmodern approach in chapters 3 and

1. G. K. Beale, "Did Jesus and His Followers Preach the Right Doctrine from the Wrong Texts? An Examination of the Presuppositions of Jesus' and the Apostles' Exegetical Method," *Them* 14 (1989).

4. It is actually based on my past interaction with Steve Moyise, a New Testament scholar, over the same issues of the New Testament's use of the Old.[2] Thus, all of my comments will be aimed at this commentator's views. I have chosen to summarize our previously written dialogue, since he very generally represents the postmodern view covered in the earlier chapters.

In essence, postmodern interpreters contend that we cannot be sufficiently confident about understanding the biblical writers, since our presuppositional lenses shape and, indeed, distort our interpretations of the Bible. Thus, even so-called evangelical postmodernists go so far as to affirm at times that we shape and often distort the meaning of biblical passages according to the image of our socially constructed ideas rather than let the ideas of the biblical writers be the dominant force shaping our views. It is this idea to which I now respond. This appendix will deal with how we can know the meaning of ancient authors' writings and be reasonably confident in our interpretations of them. Hence, I am primarily concerned with explaining a Christian or biblical *epistemology*,[3] and I will argue that we can sufficiently, but not exhaustively, understand the meaning of biblical authors' writings.

The View of a Contemporary Soft Postmodern Interpreter (Steven Moyise[4])

I have argued throughout this book that New Testament writers understood the Old Testament consistent with the Old Testament writers' intention, though with some creativity. Others, however, believe that New Testament writers had no concern for the meaning of the Old Testament passage they were quoting, but gave it a "new" interpretation in the light of the coming of Christ. Steven Moyise, on the other hand, believes that there is a middle road between these two positions, which I refer to as a soft postmodern position.

---

2. G. K. Beale, *John's Use of the Old Testament in Revelation*, JSNTSup 166 (Sheffield: Sheffield Academic Press, 1998), 41–59, and Beale, "Questions of Authorial Intent, Epistemology, and Presuppositions and Their Bearing on the Study of the Old Testament in the New: a Rejoinder to Steve Moyise," *IBS* 21 (1999), 1–26.

3. *Epistemology* may generally be defined as the study of the nature of knowledge and of how one knows what one knows or claims to know. More specifically, for example, *epistemology* may be defined as "the study of the nature of knowledge and justification [for having knowledge]; specifically, the study of (a) the defining features, (b) the substantive conditions, and (c) the limits of knowledge and justification"; see Paul K. Moser, "Epistemology," in *The Cambridge Dictionary of Philosophy*, ed. R. Audi (Cambridge: Cambridge University Press, 1995), 233–38.

4. Though Moyise might not agree to being referenced as a "soft postmodernist," it is my own assessment, according to the definition of postmodernism given above and the following analysis of this excursus, that he is.

In response to the two opposing perspectives, Moyise contends that the real question is not whether the author has or has not respected the Old Testament context; the question is how the Old Testament context interacts with the New Testament context.[5] Is the New Testament use a consistent, organic development, to one degree or another, of the Old Testament passage, or is there such a degree of cognitive dissonance between the two that no harmonious development can be discerned?[6] He answers that John is likely offering new understandings of Old Testament texts, which may have been surprising to an Old Testament readership.

It is important, however, to formulate as precisely as possible what it means to say that John expresses *new understandings* of the Old Testament. Moyise believes that the recently formulated notion of intertextuality can shed light on the issue.[7] Allusion to an earlier text by a later text results in some kind of correspondence between the two. Intertextuality references a reader's attempt to follow the meaning of the later text while being mindful of the prior text, and how the later text redefines and distorts the original by putting it within another cultural and linguistic context.

An intertextual reading must be done with care to analyze the ways in which the two respective contexts interact.[8] "The task of intertextuality is to explore how the source text continues to speak through the new work and how the new work forces new meanings from the source text."[9]

Moyise describes his middle position in terms of the new affecting the old and the old affecting the new.[10] The Old Testament reflects on the New Testament context, even as the New Testament context absorbs and changes the Old Testament allusion.[11] A difficult tension arises between these two interpretative angles. Moyise gives the example of Revelation 5:5–6, where Christ is compared to a lion and a lamb. Even though both are allusions to the Old Testament, they appear to express two very different views of Christ within the space of only two verses.

Some see only the Old Testament-Jewish notion of a conquering messianic figure who defeats and judges enemies in some literal or militaristic

---

5. Steve Moyise, *The Old Testament in the Book of Revelation*, JSNT 115 (Sheffield: Sheffield Academic Press): 19.

6. Moyise contends that this is a different question than whether the New Testament respects the Old Testament context (e.g., ibid., 142), but I cannot detect a material difference between the two.

7. Ibid., 18–19.

8. Ibid.

9. Ibid., 111.

10. Ibid., 19.

11. Ibid., 116.

fashion, since that background utilizes both lion and lamb images in that manner.[12] Others see the New Testament context of the crucified Christ portrayed as a slain lamb swallowing up any original Old Testament notion of a literal conquering messiah, which Gen. 49:9ff., for example, conveys by reference to Judah and to a ruler from Judah being compared to a lion. In this respect, G. B. Caird says that it is as if John wants us to read "Lamb" wherever the Old Testament says "Lion": "Wherever the Old Testament speaks of the victory of the Messiah or the overthrow of the enemies of God, we are to remember that the gospel recognizes no other way of achieving these ends than the way of the Cross."[13]

Caird here seems to support Moyise's view that New Testament writers give Old Testament texts the meaning they think best rather than following the Old Testament notion. I think Caird goes too far in this interpretation, though his idea does apply to Christ's beginning fulfillment of these prophecies; however, the consummation of the prophecies will occur in line with the judgmental tone of the Old Testament. The book of Revelation shows both aspects of interpretation (e.g., see respectively Rev. 5:5–6; 19:13–16).

Moyise also discusses evidence that John does not attempt to resolve the apparent tension and adduces other passages in the book that he believes exhibit an unresolvable tension. For example, he sees passages elsewhere in the Apocalypse (e.g., Rev. 19:11–21) that allude to the Old Testament militaristic notion of a Messiah with no hint at an attempt to tone down or reinterpret the expectation of a military kind of victory.[14] Moyise also contends that John offered no help to readers as to how the sealed 144,000 in 7:1–8 fits with the innumerable multitude that he sees in 7:9ff.

Response to This Postmodern View of the Use of the Old Testament in the New

What Moyise calls "new" interpretations result from the bearing of the new context on the old.[15] Moyise has not gone far enough in explaining how John (or other New Testament writers) has generated his new views of the Old Testament. It is true to say that the Old Testament wording must bear some new meaning by virtue of its placement in the new literary context. This is, however, somewhat general and vague.

---

12. Cf. Ford's view in ibid., 129–30.
13. G. B. Caird, *A Commentary on the Revelation of St. John the Divine* (London: Black, 1966), 75.
14. Ibid., 133.
15. Though Moyise says that John does not create "something completely new" (ibid., 138).

While it is legitimate to recognize new interpretations by New Testament authors, it is important to be as precise as possible in explaining the newness of the meaning that they perceived. Such new meanings emerge because of John's new presuppositional lenses on the Old Testament.

The most significant of these lenses are: (1) Christ corporately represents true Israel of the Old and New Testaments; (2) history is unified by a wise and sovereign plan, so that the earlier parts of canonical history are designed to correspond typologically and to point to latter parts of inscripturated history; (3) the age of end-time fulfillment was inaugurated with Christ's first coming; (4) in light of these latter two, the later parts of biblical history interpret earlier parts—a trend already begun by later Old Testament tradition with respect to earlier Old Testament books—so that Christ, as the goal of history, is the key to interpreting the ultimate interpretative aims of various Old Testament passages and narratives.

Granted the legitimacy of these presuppositions, John's interpretation of the Old Testament shows respect for Old Testament contexts, and his interpretation shows formative influence from the Old Testament itself. If, however, these presuppositions are spurious, then his interpretation must be seen as foreign to the original intention of the Old Testament. Some modern commentators such as Fiorenza view John's own context as injecting new meaning into the Old Testament references that is inconsistent and incompatible with the Old Testament. It is more likely, however, that John would have seen these presuppositions as organically growing out of the Old Testament itself, since the presuppositions are ultimately traceable to Christ's own interpretative approach, which he probably passed on to his disciples. John sees that the events of his time begin to fulfill Old Testament prophecies, and his study of the Old Testament helps him better understand these events, as do the details of the events themselves help him better understand the Old Testament.

There is not space to discuss this at more length; however, I have addressed these questions in more detail elsewhere.[16] If Moyise had been sufficiently cognizant of these presuppositions, he might have been less persuaded to see unresolvable tensions of interpretation within the Apocalypse. For instance, his primary example of the irreconcilable "lion-lamb" notion is solved reasonably well by the "already and not yet" presupposition of John's eschatology. The Old Testament prophecy of the Messiah as a lion who would defeat the enemy has begun in an ironic manner through death and suffering as a "lamb," but the future,

---

16. Beale, "Did Jesus and His Followers Preach the Right Doctrine from the Wrong Texts? An Examination of the Presuppositions of Jesus' and the Apostles' Exegetical Method."

consummate form of the enemy's defeat will be more straightforward. Christ will judge decisively and openly both his earthly and cosmic enemies, including Satan himself.

The judgment commences at the cross in veiled form and is consummated before all eyes in more open and perhaps more literal form at the very end of history, at which time Christ returns finally to deliver his people completely and to judge definitively his foes and consign them to eternal punishment.[17] Thus, Old Testament prophecies about the Messiah's suffering and conquering are fulfilled in two stages: at Christ's first coming and at his final coming. Such a two-stage fulfillment was not seen as clearly in the Old Testament, but New Testament revelation unpacks what lay inherent in the Old. Hence, New Testament writers show creativity (under the influence of the revealing Spirit) in interpreting Old Testament prophecies, yet they continue to see an organic connection between them, so that the conceptual links of the Old Testament are not broken but developed.

John's interpretative resolution between the juxtaposition of Old Testament texts and Christian tradition is to be found either in the broader Old Testament context or in the broader New Testament context, or both. Though there may be times when these contexts yield ambiguous information, it does not mean that John was ambiguous in his own mind. The juxtaposition of texts or ideas that are seemingly incompatible interpretatively is likely best viewed as part of John's overall Semitic style. An expression of Semitic paratactic thinking allowed the setting in close proximity of two different, and sometimes seemingly contradictory, ideas of a word, without the discomfort experienced by some twentieth-century readers. The broader context usually resolved the tension when parataxis

17. I wonder whether Moyise, though he says formally that John offers no resolution to whether the OT interprets the NT or vice versa, could have in mind correctly the reciprocal interpretative interplay of OT influence and the NT presuppositions which read the OT in new but not contradictory or inorganic ways, especially since: (1) he acknowledges formally that "the new affects the old and the old affects the new" (OT in Revelation, 19, 58, 82–83, 102, 110–11, 115, 128), and that "any description of John's use of Scripture must do justice to both the continuities and the discontinuities" (ibid., 22); (2) he acknowledges that significant incidents of John's use of the Old Testament "might come under the category of typology" (ibid., 83) so that many of his interpretative conclusions may fall under Thomas Greene's literary category of those kinds of texts which are "not a pale imitation of the old but its true successor" (ibid., 83); (3) he uncritically acknowledges R. Bauckham's view of the organic relationship of John's use of the OT to OT prophetic tradition (ibid., 98–99), which is similar to my own perspective; he acknowledges that I hold to a similar interplay of OT and NT texts, though not to the degree that he claims he does (ibid., 62, 111); and (4) some of the examples of new interpretation of the OT cited by Moyise, as a result of his purported new hermeneutical perspective, are commonly accepted reinterpretations of the OT which arise from John's obvious Christian presuppositions (ibid., 128–29, 134–35). For similar comments by Moyise, see n. 93 below.

was used in the Old Testament.[18] This appears to account better for the evidence than the formulation of a new hermeneutical theory.

Moyise leaves unclear whether there is ultimate tension between Old Testament references and their uses in the New Testament context, using as his representative example John's use of the Old Testament military imagery of the Messiah as a military kind of conqueror.[19] The upshot of his overall thesis, however, leans toward concluding that the hermeneutical tension often remains. This becomes clearer when he sets out to answer the question, "Irrespective of what John may or may not have intended [as a resolution of the tension between a meaning of an Old Testament passage and its apparently changed meaning in a different New Testament context], does the text offer such a resolution to readers today?"[20]

This question is answered with a resounding no, since Moyise concludes that such an answer is demanded by the observation that major commentators differ profoundly about whether Revelation is essentially Christian or Jewish, which is represented by the different positions of Caird and Ford on the militaristic notion of the Old Testament allusions to the Messiah's victory.[21] This conclusion is bolstered further by the presupposition that "we have no access to the author's mind."[22] Furthermore, even if we were able to discover an author's original intentions, it would not help us toward understanding "how the actual text does work with particular readers."[23]

Moyise tries to qualify this conclusion by acknowledging that John's purposes, in some way, are still of interest to the reader.[24] Yet, as noted above, he is not able to explain exactly how knowing John's intention can help the reader toward better resolving the tension of whether the Old Testament determines meaning in the New Testament or vice versa. This is because Moyise concludes that John himself does not resolve that tension.[25]

Moyise believes that modern readers actually *create meaning* from biblical texts instead of recognizing the meaning already inherent in the text.[26] Two hermeneutical presuppositions form the foundation for this conclusion: (1) "We have no access to the author's 'intention,'" and

18. See G. B. Caird, *The Language and Imagery of the Bible* (Philadelphia: Westminster, 1980), 117–21.
19. E.g., cf. Moyise, *OT in Revelation*, 123–34.
20. Ibid., 131.
21. Ibid., 131–32.
22. Ibid., 132.
23. Ibid.
24. Ibid.
25. Ibid., 133–35.
26. Ibid., 142.

(2) "Meaning is not a 'given' but has to be 'created' by the reader."[27] Modern writers, like Moyise, who operate with these assumptions of reader-response criticism, especially the notion that readers, not original authors, create meaning, usually assume that the readers of their own works are not left to create new meanings but can discover rather easily their own original intention.[28] This is a significant inconsistency.

The notion that readers create meaning is likely due in part to a hermeneutical approach that confuses *original meaning* with *significance*. These two realities are sometimes collapsed into one another rather than differentiated. E. D. Hirsch helpfully distinguishes between meaning and significance, which also has a bearing on the present discussion. The explanation of original, intentional, *verbal meaning* is distinct from the significance of that meaning.[29]

Here we enter into the realm of hermeneutics, with which implicitly we have been involved all along. By way of illustration, we can compare an author's original, unchanging meaning to an apple in its original context of an apple tree. When someone removes the apple and puts it into another setting, say, in a basket of various fruits in a dining room for decorative purposes, the apple does not lose its original identity as an apple—the fruit of a particular kind of tree—but the apple must now be understood not as a unique entity but *in relation to the new context* in which it has been placed. This new contextual relationship is called "significance." The new context does not annihilate the original identity of the apple, but now the apple must be understood in its relation to its new setting. It is the same with meaning and its significance: "'Meaning' refers to the whole verbal meaning of a text, and 'significance' to textual meaning in relation to a larger context" beyond itself, i.e., a context of "another mind, another era, a wider subject matter, an alien system of

---

27. Ibid. The first presupposition was anticipated earlier by Moyise (ibid., 132).
28. Cf. E. D. Hirsch, *The Aims of Interpretation* (Chicago; London: Chicago University Press, 1976), 6, who makes the same criticism: "Whenever I am told by a Heideggerian that I have misunderstood Heidegger, my still unrebutted response is that I will readily (if uneasily) concede that point, since the concession in itself implies a more important point, namely, that Heidegger's text can be interpreted correctly, and has been so interpreted by my accuser. Since the accusation assumes the determinateness and stability of Heidegger's meaning, and the possibility of its being correctly interpreted, I admit the practical error for the sake of the theoretical truth. I was once told by a theorist who denied the possibility of correct interpretation that I had not interpreted his writings correctly." Hirsch contends that Heidegger's disciples, such as Jacques Derrida, had not been able to give a cogent response to this logical criticism at the time he wrote *Aims of Interpretation* in 1976 (ibid., 13). The same kind of criticism against reader-response criticism and deconstructionism is made by D. A. Carson, *The Gagging of God* (Grand Rapids: Zondervan, 1996), 102–5.
29. See below for a further explanation of verbal meaning as a "willed type."

values," etc.[30] What Hirsch calls "significance" some theologians would call "application"—how does the message of a particular ancient biblical text apply to the lives of people living in the twentieth century?

Third, it appears that Moyise sometimes understands the proposal of diverse interpretations of a text (or of an Old Testament allusion),[31] all of which have plausible evidence supporting them, to be evidence of inability to discern an author's original intention. Even if this were true in some cases, which it is, it would not be evidence for a general theory that the original authorial intention behind most or all Old Testament allusions is not discoverable. This would be a logical fallacy in which the evidence of a part is used to represent the remaining uninvestigated whole.

Moyise would have to investigate a much greater range of allusions in Revelation before he could conclude with such a proposal for the whole. In fact, there is not much original exegesis of Old Testament allusions in Moyise's work itself; most of the analysis of actual texts is a survey of what commentators say about texts or a summary of very basic and well-known interpretations of certain texts, whether in Qumran or especially in Revelation.

Furthermore, contrary to Moyise, mutually incompatible interpretations of the same passage do not mean that one interpretation is as good as another.[32] Apparently irreconcilable interpretations may indicate that

---

30. Hirsch, *Aims of Interpretation*, 2–3. The scope of the present work is unable adequately to discuss the hermeneutical debates between the classical and modern positions represented respectively, e.g., by Hirsch and Gadamer; these debates themselves have their roots in two alternative epistemological positions represented by Husserl and Heidegger. For discussion from Hirsch's perspective see ibid., e.g., 4–6; Hirsch, *Validity in Interpretation* (New Haven: Yale University, 1967), 209–74; for an assessment from a similar perspective see Royce G. Gruenler, *Meaning and Understanding* (Grand Rapids: Zondervan, 1991), 74–86; N. T. Wright, *The New Testament and the People of God* (Minneapolis: Fortress, 1992), 18–144 (passim); Carson, *The Gagging of God*, 57–137, 163–74. Both Wright and Carson strike a good balance between the subjective and objective epistemological aspects involved in this debate.

31. Such as in the case of the differing interpretations by Caird and Ford of the messianic images of the lion and lamb in Rev. 5:5–6 discussed earlier.

32. In this respect, Moyise says that readers are addressed by a number of voices within a text, and "how these are 'heard' and what the reader makes of them will differ from person to person," depending on one's prior choice of a hermeneutical key to the overall context of the particular focus text (ibid., 143). Moyise cites Fiorenza in support: "Competing interpretations of Revelation are not simply either right or wrong, but they constitute different ways of reading and constructing socio-historical and theo-ethical meaning" (E. S. Fiorenza, *Revelation: Vision of a Just World*, Proclamation Commentaries [Minneapolis: Fortress, 1991], 3). While Moyise and Fiorenza grant the capability of modern interpreters to recognize the intention of one another's writings and the different presuppositional or hermeneutical perspectives expressed in these writings, they are inconsistent in not being willing to grant the same ability in recognizing the intention and, apparently even, the presuppositions of ancient writers. Though we all have presuppositions that influence the way we read texts, these presuppositions do not blind us from perceiving authorial intentions incompatible

the original author's intention is either unrecoverable in a particular
text or very difficult to assess. Or, such contrary interpretations may
indicate different but ultimately reconcilable or supplementary aspects
of an author's one meaning. Such interpretations should be judged according to degrees of probability and possibility. There is a tradition
of commonsense criteria that has already been established to evaluate
degrees of probability and possibility of interpretative alternatives in
a text.[33]

In this regard, Hirsch's notion of a "willed type" as a further explanation of intentional, verbal meaning may be helpful. A willed type has
two characteristics: (1) an entity with a boundary in which some things
belong within the boundary and others are excluded. It can be represented
by only a single instance among the other things that belong within the
legitimate boundary. (2) The type as an entity can be represented by
more than a single instance, as long as the other representing instances
fall within the boundary.[34]

Suppose I say, "Nothing pleases me so much as the Third Symphony
of Beethoven and other similar kinds of classical music." In response a
friend might ask, "Does it please you more than a walk during a beautiful spring day?" My friend has misunderstood me by taking me too
literally. I was speaking in hyperbole, so that a walk during a beautiful
spring day was not one of the things that fell under what I meant by
"things that please me," for, indeed, such a walk might please me just
as much as Beethoven's Third. I used "nothing" as a hyperbole to stand
for "no other comparable work of musical art." How did I know that
"a walk during a beautiful spring day" was not to be included within
the specific class of "things that please me"? Some overriding principle
in my meaning determined that "a walk during a beautiful spring day"
was excluded from what I meant, and also that Elvis Presley's "You
Ain't Nothing But a Hound Dog" was *not* included as part of a musical
genre that I had in mind, along with a number of other non-classical
music compositions.

I intended to refer to a particular *type* of "thing that pleases me."
I "willed all possible members belonging to that type"[35] and excluded

with our hermeneutical lenses and from discerning the different presuppositions of others, both
modern and ancient writers. Wright, *The New Testament and the People of God*, 18–144 (passim),
refers to such an approach as "critical realism."

33. E.g., see E. D. Hirsch, *Validity in Interpretation*; e.g., note Hirsch's concepts of "intrinsic genre"
and "coherence." Hirsch says that these criteria are part of "the classical, mixed tradition of evaluation" (*Aims of Interpretation*, 12).

34. Hirsch, *Validity in Interpretation*, 49–50.

35. Ibid., 49.

others not falling within the boundary of comparable classical compositions. Certainly, my *conscious* intention did not include all musical works that please me, but only a select few, nor was there before my mind's eye all musical pieces that do not please, but only a few. If my friend were to ask me if I would include Bach's Mass in B Minor in works that especially please me, I would say "yes," even though my conscious intention was to include explicitly only Beethoven's Third and implicitly Handel's *Messiah*, Bach's Brandenburg Concertos, and Vivaldi's *Four Seasons*. My friend could suggest more musical pieces that I would also include and exclude in my willed musical type but which were neither part of my explicit statement nor even part of my implicit conscious intention.[36] Such implicit meanings within my "willed type" can be called "implications" of the explicit verbal meaning.[37] Therefore, in the words of Hirsch: "It is possible to will an et cetera without in the least being aware of all the individual members that belong to it. The acceptability of any given candidate applying for membership in the et cetera depends entirely on the type of whole meaning I willed."[38]

This notion of a "willed type" is instructive for understanding and analyzing John's use of the Old Testament. First, when John alludes to a particular text, it could be asked which feature of the Old Testament context he has in mind, since it is apparent that New Testament writers have varying degrees of contextual awareness when they make reference to an Old Testament passage. In each case, John probably has some specific feature in mind explicitly that, more often than not, is apparent to most readers, and perhaps, implicitly, he has other features consciously in mind that are not apparent in his written expression. If we had opportunity to ask him directly, after he had written, what other implicit features he had in mind, he would probably acknowledge some. Even if we asked him whether some other contextual features could be included in his unconscious intention

---

36. This illustration about classical music has been adapted, with a few changes, from Hirsch, *Validity in Interpretation*, 48–49.

37. Ibid., 61–67.

38. Ibid., 49. Hirsch's view of a determinant meaning is based on Husserl's epistemological presupposition that the mind can perceive an idea of something experienced and that it can "demarcate" that mental act so that it remains the same idea over a period of time (*Aims of Interpretation*, 4–5). An explicitly theistic hermeneutical perspective would add to this the presupposition that the omniscient God's immutable, sovereign transcendence is the enduring foundation for "an absolute transcendent determinant meaning to all texts" (D. McCartney and C. Clayton, *Let the Reader Understand* [Wheaton, IL: Bridgpoint/Victor Books, 1994], 284); the determinant meaning of all texts is known completely by the all-knowing God who is "not mutable or time bound, and so the meaning which He understands of a text is unchanging" (ibid., 284).

or within the parameters of his "willed type," he would probably acknowledge some more.[39]

To go beyond what is his apparently clear, explicit instance of the "willed type" is a matter of guesswork on the part of the interpreter, involving varying degrees of possibility and probability. Indeed, sometimes it is difficult to know whether John even is conscious of some of the very Old Testament references themselves. Such references are apparent to commentators but could be the mere result of a mind so saturated with Old Testament language and ideas that they are unconsciously expressed.[40] Such multiple meanings should not be confused with the kind of contradictory, multiple meanings for which reader-response critics argue.

One of the many examples of this in the Apocalypse is the clear allusion to Isaiah 22:22 in Revelation 3:7. The Old Testament allusion sets up a primary correspondence—and contrast—between Eliakim and Christ. Like Eliakim, Christ was to have absolute power over the Davidic throne as king. Whereas Eliakim's rule over Israel was primarily political and local, Christ's was primarily spiritual and universal. He held authority over those entering the kingdom and over those in the realm of death.

There are, however, other contextual features both within the immediate context of Isaiah 22 and within the broader context of the entire book of Isaiah that could be implicit as a part of John's "willed type." As Eliakim's power was equal to the Israelite king's, so was Christ's to God's; as Eliakim's office likely included priestly connotations, so did Christ's; as Eliakim was appointed to his political office, so Christ was appointed to a greater office. Most of these additional contextual features also find varying degrees of contextual support within both the immediate and broad context of Revelation.[41] How possible or probable they are in relation to John's "willed type" is a matter of possibility and probability judgments. But what we cannot say is that we can make of John's allusion anything we want. There are hermeneutical parameters which exclude many things which we know for certain John did not intend.

39. Perhaps this is what Moyise has in mind when he says, "That is not to say that discussion of the effect of intertextual echo must be limited to John's conscious intention. There is no reason to assume that John thought out all the possibilities of bringing Psalm 89 into a relationship with the living Christ [in Rev. 1:5]," *OT in Revelation*, 118.

40. On which see further Beale, *John's Use of the Old Testament in Revelation*, 163–67.

41. See Beale, *John's Use of the Old Testament in Revelation*, 116–21, for a number of other contextual features in the context of Isaiah which John possibly could also have had in mind.

A Further Response to Steve Moyise

The preceding section is a revised summary of part of a first chapter of my book *John's Use of the Old Testament in Revelation*, in which I reviewed several works on the subject written since the mid-eighties, including Steve Moyise's *The Old Testament in the Book of Revelation*. I thought it important to discuss his book because it was the first to apply systematically recent hermeneutical perspectives to debates surrounding John's use of the Old Testament. Above all, Moyise tried to understand the problems from the related perspectives of "intertextuality" and "reader-oriented criticism." I think the book has some good contributions, though I took issue with him on some points, as summarized above.

He responded to some of my criticisms in an article, "The Old Testament in the New: A Reply to Greg Beale,"[42] and those responses are summarized in what follows. After this, I reply to some of his critiques, with the hope of bringing further clarification to these thorny issues.

The three main issues covered here are, at heart, hermeneutical issues, and they demand book-length treatments. Though I am not a philosopher, I will, nevertheless, try to summarize my views on these issues and refer the reader especially to book-length treatments for elaboration.

The Problem of Equating "New Interpretations" with "New Meanings"

First, Moyise disagrees with my approach to understanding how Old Testament texts could have new meanings in the New Testament.[43] I gave the analogy of picking an apple off a tree and making it part of a decorative table arrangement of fruit. The new context does not obliterate the apple's original identity but it must now be viewed not merely in relation to its original context but also in connection to its new context. Old Testament references gain new significance but not new meaning when placed in a new context. The original meaning does not change but the significance of that meaning changes.

Moyise, however, concludes that "this sounds like a hermeneutical cover-up," since I "speak of New Testament authors offering 'new un-

---

42. *IBS* 21 (1999), 54–58.

43. The conclusions to which Moyise is responding are specifically to my views of John's use of the OT in my *John's Use of the Old Testament in Revelation*. His response goes beyond this to the NT use of the OT in general. Whether the same conclusions can be applied to the rest of the NT was outside the scope of my book to which Moyise is replying. I have briefly addressed this wider issue elsewhere and outlined the approach I would take (esp. see my "Did Jesus and His Followers Preach the Right Doctrine from the Wrong Texts? An Examination of the Presuppositions of Jesus' and the Apostles' Exegetical Method"). My "rejoinder" here is primarily concerned with John's use, since that is what Moyise's response formally addresses and that is the area in which I have done full-scale work, though I believe the study has wider implications for the NT.

derstandings' of Old Testament texts 'which may have been surprising to an Old Testament audience,'" and since I even refer to these "authors offering 'new interpretations.'"[44] He understandably asks, therefore, why such new understandings and interpretations must be called "new significance" and not "new meanings," unless what I mean by the former is ultimately synonymous with the latter. I am happy to try to unravel the distinction between *meaning* and *significance*, since it is important to be precise about terminology in these difficult discussions.

Though I do not have liberty here to expound a full-blown hermeneutical theory, I can attempt to amplify the discussion from my book and to sketch the outlines of a more thorough analysis. It is best, however, to consult E. D. Hirsch, and his most recent developer, K. J. Vanhoozer, for the fuller distinction, since my book relies on Hirsch's work on hermeneutics.[45]

I am a bit perplexed about why Moyise would refer to the distinction between *meaning* and *significance* as a seeming "hermeneutical cover-up," because the distinction is virtually a commonplace in the recent history of hermeneutical discussion. That being said, the distinction may sometimes be termed variously: original intention and contemporary relevance, meaning and application, which might also be understood as the distinction between the author's horizon and the reader's horizon. The following discussion is a summary of Hirsch and Vanhoozer and my own elaboration of their positions, especially with respect to the problem of the "Old in the New."

Interpretation seeks an understanding of an earlier author's original meaning. No interpretation ever reproduces an author's original meaning exhaustively, but it can achieve a truly approximate, partial, and adequate understanding, so that there are some essential points of overlap between the original meaning and the apprehension of that meaning. Therefore *interpretation* or *understanding* is the attempt to reproduce an approximate understanding of the meaning of earlier texts and to explain them. "It is a logical mistake to confuse the impossibility of certainty in understanding with the impossibility of understanding."[46]

If one acknowledges on the epistemological level[47] that an author's original meaning is recoverable from Old Testament texts, not in abso-

---

44. S. Moyise, "The Old Testament in the New: a Reply to Greg Beale," *IBS* 21 (1999), 55.

45. E. D. Hirsch, *Validity in Interpretation*. See for further refinement from an explicitly theistic perspective K. J. Vanhoozer, *Is There a Meaning in This Text?* (Grand Rapids: Zondervan, 1998), to which I am also indebted for making known other sources with which I interact throughout this essay.

46. Hirsch, *Validity in Interpretation*, 17.

47. Recall that *epistemology* is the study of the nature of knowledge and how one can know what one knows or claims to know.

lute completeness but partially, then it is helpful to distinguish between the enduring original meaning and the response to it by later writers, i.e., the significance of that earlier meaning. Hirsch says that *meaning* refers to the "entire verbal meaning of a text" and *significance* refers to "textual meaning in a context beyond itself" in relation to a later time, a later mind, or a wider subject matter.

One must understand a meaning of a prior text before attempting to explain it. Then "the public side of interpretation" includes answering "What does this text mean?" and "What use or value does it have; how is its meaning applied to me, to us, to our particular situation?"[48] Consequently, for Hirsch, there is a sense in which an aspect of later interpretation ("what does this text mean?") but not original authorial meaning overlaps with significance. *That is, for Hirsch, later extended meaning and application make up what he understands as significance.*

If the basic distinction is not maintained, however, between an author's original meaning and what it means for today and for application, then the original meaning and the contemporary relevance of meaning (i.e., later extended meaning + application) are collapsed, and the ultimate meaning of a text becomes merely the reflection of the interpreter's own purely socially constructed thoughts. Thus, "understanding is not the same as authoring."[49] This would mean that "interpreters [would] risk confusing the aim of the text with their own aims,"[50] and that what any interpreter says is the meaning of an ancient text is as valid as what any other interpreter says.

One may disagree with the terms Hirsch uses to distinguish original authorial meaning from significance (i.e., later extended meaning *and* application of that meaning), but whatever terms are used, the distinction needs to be maintained, if one does not hold to the presuppositions of radical reader-response criticism and deconstructionism. In other words, no meaning is recoverable from an original author's intentional acts of writing and, in the case of deconstructionism, the enterprise of interpretation is primarily the exposing of authors' or interpreters' triumphalistic presuppositions. "Hermeneutical realism ultimately rests on this distinction between meaning and significance, on the distinction between an object of knowledge and the context in which it is known."[51]

Hirsch has further defined his view of the dichotomy between meaning and significance by the concept of "transhistorical intentions." While

48. Hirsch, *The Aims of Interpretation*, 19; cf. also pp. 2–3, 156.
49. Vanhoozer, *Is There a Meaning in This Text?* 263.
50. Ibid., 421.
51. Ibid., 260.

maintaining this distinction, he believes that an intended original meaning can go beyond the original content or original context. Authors using some genres will to extend meaning to analogous and even unforeseeable situations so that their meaning is intended to have presently unknowable, future implications.[52] In this respect, one can "speak of open-ended authorial intentions" and "extended meaning" in which an original meaning can tolerate some revision in cognitive content and yet not be essentially altered.[53] It is in this sense that the significance of original meaning may pertain more to the meaning side than the application side. Interpretation should go beyond the author's letter, but it must never exceed the author's spirit.[54]

Therefore, the task of interpretation includes: (1) ascertaining the original meaning; (2) ascertaining the ongoing extended meaning, which may be present in some genres but not others. Ongoing extended meaning is discerned by noticing when authors will to extend implications of their meaning into the indefinite future by espousing principles intended for an indefinite number of applications; (3) recontextualizing meaning by ascertaining creative applications of the meaning to new contexts, which in some genres may not involve extending the original meaning. It bears repeating that parts (2) and (3) make up *significance* for Hirsch.

These three aspects of the overall enterprise of interpretation do not collapse original meaning into the readers' response to that meaning. The two are still kept separate, though there is some overlap between original meaning and significance in the second step. It is helpful to expand a little on Hirsch's middle step, what Vanhoozer calls "extended meaning." Hirsch refers to this as an expansion of the original author's "willed type."

Hirsh gives the illustration of civil codes as good examples of genres in which authors realize that no law can cover all the future instances that will fall under legitimate application of the law originally legislated. The principle of the originally formulated law must be applied to later instances to see whether it is relevant. If the new instance falls within the "willed type" of the original legal author, then the original law applies.

For example, a traffic code may assert that a violation occurs when any wheeled vehicle on a public thoroughfare fails to stop at a red

52. Hirsch, *Validity in Interpretation*, 125, who also elaborates on and gives further refinements of the "meaning/significance" question in "Meaning and Significance Reinterpreted," *Critical Inquiry* 11 (1984): 202–24.

53. Vanhoozer, *Is There a Meaning in This Text?* 261–62, following Hirsch.

54. Hirsch, "Transhistorical Intentions and the Persistence of Allegory," *New Literary History* 25 (1994): 558.

light. Suppose that years later a vehicle was created that had no wheels but moved instead on currents of compressed air. Is such a vehicle still subject to this original law, since the formulation of the law explicitly referred to wheeled vehicles? The original intent of the law would still have in view this new instance, since what was in view from the beginning was a "willed type" of any vehicle. The law might be amended to include "'all vehicles serving the function of wheeled vehicles within the purpose and intent of the law.' The idea of a law contains the idea of *mutatis mutandis*, and this generic convention was part of the meaning that I willed."[55] It should be easy to see that such a genre convention could be included in biblical literature that has legal, ethical, and theological content.

To come back full circle to Moyise's critique and question: "Why is Greg Beale reluctant to say that new understandings and interpretations are not new meanings but new significances?" I am reluctant because I do not want to confuse *original authorial meaning* with the *extension of that meaning* or the *application of that meaning*. Indeed, one cannot judge whether a meaning is being extended or amplified unless there is a clear understanding of a determinate original meaning. And, of course, one cannot apply an original meaning to a new situation without knowing that original meaning. In this light, I am happy to equate *new interpretations* or *understandings* with *interpretative significance* or *meaningful significance* or even with *extended meaning*. I am loath to confuse *original authorial meaning* with anything that is subsequently derivative of it.

Consequently, I can understand that New Testament authors creatively develop new interpretations of Old Testament texts, in the light of Christ's coming, but not absolutely new meanings, since that could be understood to indicate that what they develop is not related in some vital way to the earlier source text written by the original author. I would not be picky about semantics if there were not the potential danger of sliding into saying that *new meanings* indicate something cut off from the conceptual roots of the base text.[56] I am content to see new meanings as creative developments or outgrowths, but not as *absolutely* new meanings. A feature of any good interpretation is some *essential* element of recognizability with the original meaning of the text being interpreted. This does not mean that one can fully understand a text, but it does

---

55. Hirsch, *Validity in Interpretation*, 125, from which this illustration comes.
56. On the other hand, Moyise and others might likely be concerned about the opposite danger that a strict bifurcation of meaning and significance implies a naïve assumption of one's ability to comprehend completely the original meaning and transcend unnaturally one's localized context.

mean that there can be sufficient understanding, which, in the case of inspired biblical literature, one needs in order to experience salvation, sanctification, and glorifying God.

Of course, interpreters can wrongly interpret and have no idea of an original meaning, which is the conclusion many make about New Testament authors' interpretation of the Old Testament, but this is a different matter than saying it is impossible for interpreters to gain some approximate understanding of the original meaning of a text.[57] My apple illustration is an attempt to underscore the indelible line between some unchanging aspect of the original identity of a meaningful act of communication and the effect of that act (i.e., recontextualization through extended implications of "willed types" or applications or both).

Moyise prefers another version of the apple illustration. He thinks the relation of an apple to fruit salad—or one could even compare apple sauce—is an apt comparison, though this might still be compatible with my idea and my analogy of an apple in a decorative basket of fruit: there is still some identifiable aspect of the original apple in fruit salad or applesauce, whether through sight or taste, though I think this illustration could come close to obscuring the original identity of the apple too much. Moyise says that an even better illustration should not be something tangible like apples, since texts do not have firm boundaries that protect them from being altered by changing contexts.

Moyise offers less corporeal analogies of ripples in a pond that combine with other ripples and form new patterns or sound waves that interfere with one another. These analogies, however, seem to me to lose the distinction between some identity between the original ripple and the combination of other ripples or between the original sound wave and the other sound waves that interfere with it.

Upon further reflection, perhaps there is a better analogy than either mine or Moyise's, one that expresses the nature of original meaning as part of a "three-dimensional communicative action."[58] The three dimensions are (1) the literary act of putting words together to make a proposition (locution, e.g., the content of the communicative act);

---

57. See D. Instone Brewer, *Techniques and Assumptions in Jewish Exegesis before 70 CE*, who identifies all the purported examples of pre-70 AD proto-rabbinic exegesis of the OT. His study shows that, while these Jewish exegetes may not have achieved success in each case, they did try to interpret the OT in the light of its context, and never substituted a secondary or allegorical understanding for the primary one. Even if some of his conclusions are judged to be overstated, in my view, the main point of his research still stands. See G. K. Beale, *The Use of Daniel in Jewish Apocalyptic Literature and in the Revelation of St. John* (Lanham, MD: University Press of America, 1984), for the similar observation in some Jewish apocalyptic literature.

58. Vanhoozer, *Is There a Meaning in This Text?* 218.

(2) the particular way in which this literary act is executed (illocution, i.e., what is done with the propositional content, e.g., greeting, promising, commanding, wishing, being ironical, polemical, etc.); and (3) what is effected by or results from the communicative act (perlocution, e.g., obedience, persuasion, surprise, etc.).[59] "If a text is a meaningful action . . . we can . . . have as much confidence in determining what an author is doing in a discourse as we can when we seek to determine what a person is doing in other kinds of action."[60]

The meaning of a communicative act is dependent not on its effect (e.g., how it is responded to by readers, i.e., perlocution or significance) "but on the direction and the purposive structure of the author's action" (illocution).[61] In fact, another way of formulating the distinction between meaning and significance is "a distinction between a completed action and its ongoing intentional or unintentional consequences."

The three aspects of a communicative act are comparable to any physical act that becomes part of history. A professional golfer (1) uses a club to swing and hit the ball, (2) though the kind of swing he uses may put spin on the ball to slice or hook, or he swings to hit straight, or he can swing to make it go high or low—all with the purpose of accomplishing a par on the hole and a low score for the round. (3) The actual effect is how the ball flies and how that particular shot contributed to the overall shots of the round and to the final score. A radio commentator explains the shot to the audience.

The commentator observes the swing (stage 1) and its effect (stage 3), and he also tries to explain the kind of swing and the intent behind it (stage 2). Though he cannot completely understand the precise kind of swing actually used and the exact purpose in the golfer's mind in swinging the way he did, the commentator can still comprehend them adequately so as to make an educated guess (i.e., interpretation) for the listening audience. Too, illocutionary physical and literary actions may be complex, so that there may be multiple ways of describing the action, not all of which will exactly portray the intent of the action.[62]

A golf historian who writes years later about this particular round will rely on the commentator's account and on newspaper and magazine accounts, and perhaps he will add his own understanding to the commentary. Perhaps he has access to something the radio commentator did not; the commentator may have inside information from the golfer's

59. Ibid., 209.
60. Ibid., 216–17.
61. Ibid., 255.
62. Ibid., 327–33.

caddie or his family that the golfer was ill for three weeks prior to the
tournament, which explains why some of his shots were hit poorly and
why he did not win the tournament.

Likewise, a written communicative act is just as historical as any
other act in history, and its meaning is just as accessible. Of course, as
in hermeneutics so in the philosophy of history there is debate about
whether historians can objectively report history. Both the positivistic
objectivist and the postmodern subjectivist skeptic are too extreme.
The truth lies somewhere in between: historians do not record events
fully as they actually happened nor are they unable to record anything
that happened. They are able to recognize, though not exhaustively,
something of what took place. Tom Wright calls this "critical realism,"
which applies both to the historian's as well as the interpreter's craft.[63]
In fact, ultimately, these are not two different disciplines.

Though Moyise does not want to class himself with more radical
"reader-oriented"[64] critics who deny any connection between original
meaning of a text and a later reader's understanding of it, his responses
still appear to place him closely with that position. He says approvingly
in his monograph, "Emphasis on the author's intention has been largely
abandoned in New Testament study and replaced by a focus either on
the text itself or on the role of the reader."[65] Even so, he cites no careful
study that polls what general percentage of scholarship really reflects
this view, a view that is certainly in the minority in the actual exegetical
practice of such leading journals as *New Testament Studies*, *Novum
Testamentum*, and *Biblica*.

In addition, he says, "We have no access to the author's 'intention,'"
and "meaning is not a 'given' but has to be 'created' by the reader,"[66] so
that authorial intention is a social "construct."[67] He adopts the words
of Elisabeth Schüssler Fiorenza to explain his position: "Competing
interpretations of Revelation are not simply either right or wrong, but
they constitute different ways of reading and constructing socio-historical and theo-ethical meaning."[68]

In the light of these clear statements employing the buzz words of more
radical reader-response language, how can Moyise say that his "point

63. N. T. Wright, *The New Testament and the People of God* (Minneapolis: Fortress, 1992),
31–144.
64. Moyise, "Old Testament in the New: Reply to Beale," 57.
65. Moyise, *The Old Testament in the Book of Revelation*, 142.
66. Ibid.
67. Moyise, "Old Testament in the New: Reply to Beale," 58.
68. Moyise, *The Old Testament in the Book of Revelation*, 143.

is *not* that readers make texts mean whatever they like"?[69] Though he does not want to say so that baldly, I cannot see how he can logically resist the conclusion, especially since he does say that "meaning is not a 'given' but has to be 'created by the reader.'" Perhaps, he would want to say that interpretative communities with their own socially constructed view of reality determine how individual readers in the community interpret, so that in a strict sense readers cannot make texts mean whatever they want. But this only moves to the corporate level: communities can make texts mean whatever they want, i.e., communal consensus is the only criterion for a valid interpretation, and interpretative communities who disagree with one another must be content to agree to disagree. That this is Moyise's view is pointed to by his statement, "It is one of the enduring insights of liberation and feminist writings that 'what one knows and sees depends upon where one stands or sits.'"[70]

As far as I can tell, meaning, for him, is not based on the notion that there is a given meaning, a literary communicative act, that resides in a text which can be accessed, not exhaustively, but in some determinant, partial, and adequate manner. While it is certainly true that the situatedness of our perspective on the Bible influences our interpretations, sometimes negatively, sometimes positively, this does not entail that we have absolutely no view of the original meaning of a text.

Moyise tries to explain that meaning is essentially the creation of the reader by arguing that "readers have to make choices" in order to formulate "coherent interpretations." He uses the quotation of Psalm 118:22–23 in Mark 12 as a brief example. The reader is not addressed by only one authorial voice but by a number of voices. Should readers focus their interpretative concerns (1) on the original author of the psalm, or (2) on its meaning in relation to the Psalter, or (3) on how the psalm was interpreted in early Judaism, or (4) on what Jesus had in mind, or (5) on what the evangelist had in mind? Which we should focus on is "simply not 'given' to us by the text."[71]

The decisions readers make about what voice to focus on will shape their interpretation and make it different from other interpretations that have a different focus. Moyise believes that the reason there are differences of interpretation in such cases is that there is no methodological consensus about how to approach an analysis of the plural voices—which voices should be focused on, how to relate them, etc. Several textual voices drift into a reader's mind, and each reader will

69. Moyise, "Old Testament in the New: Reply to Beale," 57.
70. Ibid., 58.
71. Ibid., 57.

organize these voices in a different way so that they become like echoes reverberating with one another in different ways and sounding different. In other words, the voices mean different things to different people. Just as people will connect dots on a paper in different ways to form different shapes, so likewise interpreters connect different voices in different ways to formulate different interpretations.

Vanhoozer's summary of the significance of this kind of intertextuality gets to the heart of Moyise's program:

> Intertextuality is the free association of diverse voices, the centrifugal force that explodes the centripetal constraint of [determinant meaning]. . . . Meaning is not something located in texts so much as something that happens between them. It is precisely because this "between" cannot be stabilized that intertextuality undermines determinancy of meaning.

> "The codependence of texts precludes both the mastery of one text by another and the subservience of one text to another [citing M. Taylor]."[72]

There is, however a method of validating which of the voices should be focused on and which of a text's (or texts') interpretations is more probable than the others. To focus on only one of the contexts of the use of the psalm Mark 12 would be an example of "thin description." One would want to focus on all of them, especially keeping in mind Hirsch's concept of "willed type," in which subsequent new interpretations and applications of a text's primary meaning can be seen as legitimately falling within the willed type of the original meaning and is therefore a legitimate extension of it.

This could be referred to as "thick description," which includes an account of an author's threefold communicative act.[73] The "common-sense" approach, then, would be to study closely all five of the contextual uses of Psalm 118 mentioned above by Moyise. Jesus and the evangelist may have had aspects of all in mind, so that each subsequent use of the psalm develops the richness of the original meaning. Alternatively, they may have had only one or two such contexts in mind, and the evangelist may have had more or less in mind than Jesus.[74] If one presupposes the existence of God and includes God as author of particular biblical texts

---

72. Vanhoozer, *Is There a Meaning in This Text?* 135; for his expanded discussion, see 131–35.
73. Ibid., e.g., 282–85, 291–92, 331–32.
74. In this respect, Vanhoozer, *Is There a Meaning in This Text?* 313–14, following M. Bakhtin, says texts of some genres have a real latent potential meaning which is intentionally open-ended, though it might be better to call such open-endedness a determinate but complex communicative act. In Christian tradition this has sometimes been referred to as *sensus plenior*, which has been defined in various ways.

and of the whole canon, then specific expansions of earlier texts in later ones is part of one complex authorial act of communication. This best represents a summary of a viable view of *sensus plenior*.[75]

Is it mere subjective choice that guides readers to know which of the contexts are in mind or uppermost in mind or whether all could be included, as Moyise seems to think? I do not think so. Those contextual uses that have ideas that correspond in some approximate way with the original meaning are live candidates, together with the original, for texts which the last author or reader may have focused upon—in this case the evangelist.

The more organic correspondences one can muster between the Old Testament text and each of its subsequent uses and the main text being interpreted (in this case Mark 12) will build up a "probability case" that one or more of these contexts is actually in mind in the text under consideration.[76] To put it another way, "The success of any interpretation depends on its explanatory power, on its ability to make more complex, coherent, and natural sense of textual data than other interpretations do."[77]

Hirsch has three chapters in his *Validity in Interpretation* (chaps. 3–5) that discuss a method of how to validate interpretations inductively—not in a purely subjective manner or solely objectively, but according to a "critical realist" perspective. Competing interpretations have degrees of possibility and probability, depending on the number of fundamental correspondences that can be drawn between an interpretation and its source text. Of course, the last author's or reader's own contextual use must be considered in the ongoing trajectory of meaning. In my commentary *The Book of Revelation*, I often show that a number of subsequent exegetical reflections on an Old Testament text (by later Old Testament authors, Jewish writers, and other New Testament writers) together with that text had influence on John and that he himself, in good prophetic fashion, further expanded on the Old Testament text's meaning.

This is not to say that interpretation is not creative. Creativity and, indeed, subjectivity are an inevitable aspect of interpretation. Yet it is not a creativity *ex nihilo* nor does the creative role of interpreters make an author's meaning inaccessible. Good interpretation has an identifiable vital link with the base text being interpreted. Moyise's account

---

75. On which see, again, Vanhoozer, *Is There a Meaning in This Text?* 312–52 (passim).
76. For examples of my own attempted applications of Hirsch's criteria for validation, see Beale, *The Use of Daniel in Jewish Apocalyptic Literature and in the Revelation of St. John*; idem., *The Book of Revelation*, NIGTC (Grand Rapids: Eerdmans, 1998); idem., *John's Use of the Old Testament in Revelation*.
77. R. H. Gundry, *Mark* (Grand Rapids: Eerdmans, 1993), 4.

of interpretation too often obscures this vital link between the text and
its interpretation.

The New Testament Writers' Presuppositions and Their Vital Link to the Old Testament Context of Passages That They Quote

In the first part of this appendix, I contended that John sometimes gives
new interpretations of Old Testament texts that appear different from
their original intended meaning. I argued that such apparently different uses were due to John's new presuppositional perspectives, which
caused him to see Old Testament texts in such seemingly different ways.
I then concluded that if his presuppositions were legitimate, then his
interpretation of Old Testament texts could be seen as showing respect
for the Old Testament contexts from which they come.

Moyise makes a good criticism of my argument: "If 'respect for context' means 'understandable given the author's presuppositions,' then it
surely becomes a truism. Even the most bizarre allegorical use of Scripture could be said to 'respect the context' if we accept the legitimacy
of the author's presuppositions."[78] The reason for his disagreement
is not only that my argument is a truism, but that respect for context
does not fit well with the New Testament authors' habit of giving new
interpretations because of their new presuppositional lenses. Without
further elaboration, Moyise's last point offers no further evidence for
disagreement but only a mere declaration that my conclusion is wrong
because it just seems that way to him.

My responses to this criticism are sixfold—four methodological, one
epistemological, and the last logical.

First, many of John's uses of the Old Testament do not need to be
explained only by referring to his unique Christian presuppositions
(e.g., John's thematic and analogical uses[79]), so that this is not as great
a problem as Moyise implies. A direct messianic prophecy could be seen
as directly fulfilled in Jesus Christ (e.g., Ps. 89:27–37 in Rev. 1:5; Dan.
7:13 in Rev. 1:13). Someone could argue that John was wrong about
applying such passages to Jesus and identifying Jesus as the long-awaited
Messiah. Nevertheless, his actual understanding of the prophecy in its
original context could still well be good. The only problem then would
be *application* of the prophecy, not understanding of the prophecy.

The same is the case with Qumran. Some of the community's understanding of Old Testament prophecies concerning Israel are plausible,
but most commentators would likely disagree with the viability of the

---

78. Moyise, "Old Testament in the New: Reply to Beale," 56–57.
79. Beale, *John's Use of the Old Testament in Revelation*, 93–100.

application of the prophecy to their own community and the identification of themselves as true, eschatological Israel (e.g., cf. the restoration prophecy of Isa. 40:3 in 1QS IX,19–21).

Second, my reference to "respect for context" needs clarification. Moyise prefers "awareness of context" because "'respect for context' . . . suggests some sort of conformity." Does he believe then that there is *no* (or that there could not be) conformity of thought between the meaning of an Old Testament text and a New Testament author's understanding of that text? I do not believe that a New Testament author exhaustively understands the meaning of a prior text but that it is possible to have some understanding. Indeed, "conformity" does not have to entail the notion of an exact replica but carries connotations of "likeness" (cf. the *Oxford English Dictionary*).

I argue, in fact, that John has "varying degrees of awareness of . . . context" and that some uses may be categorized as "semi-contextual," since they have a lower "degree of correspondence with the Old Testament literary context" than do other uses.[80] I also argue it is certainly possible in principle that some uses pay no attention at all to Old Testament context, e.g., rhetorical uses for polemical purposes. My own research on the Apocalypse and other parts of the New Testament over the past twenty-five years, however, has concluded that John uses the Old Testament with significant recognition of Old Testament context.

Third, it is true that presuppositions must be brought into play to explain some uses, e.g., "typological uses" and uses involving some different applications in fulfillment. When a prophecy is said to be fulfilled in a person instead of the nation Israel or in the church, such fulfillments are understandable in that they arise from the Old Testament presupposition of corporate solidarity and the notion of the one and the many, an idea developed even in Judaism.[81] Even the specific idea that Jesus the Messiah corporately represents his people as true Israel is an outgrowth of the notion that Israel's kings represented their people. Israel, for example, was punished for David's representative sin of numbering the people (1 Chron. 21:1–17). Moyise thinks that appealing to New Testament authors' presuppositions to understand and even justify various uses of the Old Testament means that any presuppositions willy-nilly, allegorical or otherwise, could be adduced to justify any bizarre interpretation.

Many of the presuppositions that I mention, however, are not bizarre or new in the sense that they are rooted in the Old Testament itself. In

---

80. Beale, *Use of the Old Testament in Revelation*, 74.
81. Cf. S. Kim, *The Origin of Paul's Gospel* (Grand Rapids: Eerdmans, 1982), 187–92.

addition to the assumption of corporate solidarity, note also the following presuppositions:

1) The New Testament authors assumed they were living in the age of the eschaton, partly because the Old Testament prophesied that the messianic age was to be an eschatological period.

2) History is unified by a divine plan, so that earlier biblical history was designed to correspond and point to later parts of biblical history, a phenomenon often termed *typology*.[82] That allegory is not a method found in the New Testament is, I think, a reflection that its hermeneutical methods are not haphazard.[83] One might want to see the similar presuppositions of the Old Testament as flawed like those purportedly of the New, but at least a common interpretative and presuppositional approach can be seen between the two testaments. This observation makes it more difficult to say that the New Testament's interpretative presuppositions distort the meaning of Old Testament texts. In this respect, the authors of both testaments are part of a broadly related interpretative community that shared the same general worldview and continued to develop earlier meanings with comparable hermeneutical perspectives as time went on.[84]

82. For discussion of the presence of typology as an interpretative method and hermeneutical presupposition in the Old Testament, see F. Foulkes, *The Acts of God: A Study of the Basis of Typology in the Old Testament*, Tyndale Monographs (London: Tyndale, 1958); G. von Rad, *Old Testament Theology* 2 (New York: Harper and Row, 1965), 365–74 (cf. p. 36: "Typological thinking [is] . . . one of the essential presuppositions of the origin of prophetic prediction"); L. Goppelt, *Typos* (Grand Rapids: Eerdmans, 1982), 38–41; M. Fishbane, *Biblical Interpretation in Ancient Israel* (Oxford: Clarendon, 1985), esp. 350–79; D. C. Allison, *The New Moses: A Matthean Typology* (Minneapolis: Fortress, 1993), 11–95, who includes typological uses in Judaism, as does Kim, *The Origin of Paul's Gospel*, 187; G. P. Hugenberger, "The Servant of the Lord in the 'Servant Songs' of Isaiah," in *The Lord's Anointed*, ed. P. E. Satterthwaite, R. S. Hess, and G. J. Wenham (Carlisle: Paternoster; Grand Rapids: Baker, 1995), 105–39; D. Garrett, "The Ways of God: Reenactment and Reversal in Hosea," a paper presented as the author's inaugural lecture as professor of Old Testament at Gordon-Conwell Theological Seminary in fall 1998; Garrett develops the typological use of Genesis by Hosea (in process of submission for publication).

83. As generally acknowledged by both Old and New Testament scholars (respectively see von Rad, *Old Testament Theology* 2, 366, and Goppelt, *Typos*, 32–58, though some disagree). In further support, however, see further C. H. Dodd, *According to the Scriptures* (London: Nisbet, 1952), passim; E. E. Ellis, *Paul's Use of the Old Testament* (Grand Rapids: Eerdmans, 1957), passim; and G. K. Beale, ed., *The Right Doctrine from the Wrong Texts? Essays on the Use of the Old Testament in the New* (Grand Rapids: Baker, 1994), passim (including relevant bibliographical references therein). See, Instone Brewer, *Techniques and Assumptions in Jewish Exegesis before 70 CE*, who sees one dominant strand of early Jewish exegesis also as not employing allegory but "contextual" exegesis of the Old Testament.

84. See N. T. Wright, *The New Testament and the People of God*, as well as *Jesus and the Victory of God* (Minneapolis: Fortress, 1996), for an explanation of this shared worldview common to the

There is yet a fourth response to Moyise's criticism of my view of the bearing of presuppositions on New Testament authors' respect for context. In the light of the earlier discussion of an author's "willed type," can we say with confidence that John's interpretations do not fall in line with legitimate extensions and applications of the meaning of Old Testament texts, since he was so absorbed with the Old Testament? Likewise, to focus on another New Testament author, if someone as steeped in the Old Testament as Matthew could utilize the New Testament community's presuppositions, surely it is possible that someone like Isaiah, if he were living in the first century, might well think the extended application of his prophecies to Jesus would fall within the parameters of his understanding of what he wrote.

In addition, such a possibility is fueled by the fact that the New Testament community's presuppositions are rooted in the Old Testament. It is striking, for example, that the well-known suffering servant prophecy of Isaiah 53 is itself a typological expectation of an anticipated second Moses, who was to do everything and more than the first Moses.[85] Therefore, Matthew's understanding of Jesus as a typological fulfillment of the first Moses is in keeping with anticipations already embedded within the prophetic expectations of the Old Testament itself and in Judaism.[86] Even the notion that Jesus corporately represents true Israel is likely due, in part, to the notion that Israel's past kings represented and summed up the nation in themselves in various ways. The same was true of Moses and was likewise expected to be true of the Servant whom Moses typologically anticipated.[87]

Fifth, should we dare ask the epistemological question "Are John's presuppositions true, and if so, should the answer not have a bearing on his interpretative approach either negatively or positively?" This is not a question often asked in scholarly monographs and journal articles, because the scholarly discipline has been so dominantly descriptive. Tom Wright has broached such questions, though he would not state it in quite the way I have.[88]

There is a "commonsense tradition" by which presuppositions can be challenged, critiqued, and evaluated (cf. the validating criteria of correspondence, coherence, the law of non-contradiction, etc., below). I have argued that the early Christian community's assumptions are

---

Old Testament, early Judaism, Jesus, and the early Christian community.

85. So Hugenberger, "The Servant of the Lord in the 'Servant Songs' of Isaiah."

86. So D. C. Allison, *The New Moses: A Matthean Typology*; cf. Kim, *The Origin of Paul's Gospel*, 187–92.

87. So Hugenberger, "The Servant of the Lord in Isaiah," 111, 121, 131.

88. Wright, *The New Testament and the People of God*, 139–44.

grounded in the Old Testament, so that questions of validity must also be extended to the interpretative assumptions of the Old Testament itself. Furthermore, it is likely that Jesus himself was the originator of the main interpretative approaches and presuppositions employed by his followers, especially the christocentric focus on the Old Testament.[89] While being creative, he was making developments squarely on the basis of the Old Testament and early Judaism.

Can we be bold enough in a scholarly forum to ask the question of whether Jesus' interpretative perspective was wrong? One's view of who Jesus was should determine decisively the answer to this question. Of course, it is a hermeneutical fad today to say that all human thought is a mere expression of each reader's "socially constructed world" *apart from God's in-breaking revelation*, so that ultimately all thought, including that of Jesus, is relative, and no one's thought is any more correct or incorrect than anyone else's.

Of course, much of our understanding as readers is an expression of our socially constructed world. There are perspectives from our cultural world that can give us insights into the true meaning of Scripture, and there are other perspectives that can distort the meaning of Scripture. And, of course, our own fallen natures tend to distort the meaning of God's Word. But if we say that the total influence upon our thought is only from socially constructed influences, then we go too far, since this does not leave necessary room for God's special in-breaking revelation through his Word to mold and reform our perspectives. If our thought is entirely the product of social constructions, then this would result in a closed hermeneutical framework, which allows no outside interference from God's in-breaking truth, leaving only relative truths. Such a limited perspective makes moot asking about the rightness or wrongness of hermeneutical methods and presuppositions and the resulting conclusions derived from them.

There are some evangelical theologians, like Peter Enns and Steve Moyise,[90] who appear to make claims that come close to this position. In the case of Moyise, he is reticent to qualify his statements about our socially constructed knowledge, even in his subsequent responses to the present critique in this appendix. In fact, he gives illustrations that convey a notion that interpretation is relative dependent on the

---

89. See C. H. Dodd, *According to the Scriptures*, who made this point persuasively. In this respect, see my own summary of Dodd's view in Beale, "Did Jesus and His Followers Preach the Right Doctrine from the Wrong Texts? An Examination of the Presuppositions of Jesus' and the Apostles' Exegetical Method."

90. Though Moyise would not want to call himself evangelical, he is somewhat conservative theologically in comparison to the full range of positions held in the scholarly guild today.

interpreter's life situation. Recall, for example, Moyise's water ripple effect in which water ripples become indistinguishable from one another as an illustration of the original meanings of texts combining with one another.[91]

A last response to Moyise's objection to my view of how New Testament writers' presuppositions help shape their contextual use of the Old Testament is in order. This last point entails a logical objection to Moyise. If meaning were a function only of how John as a reader responded to Old Testament texts through his own culturally relative and "socially constructed" presuppositions, and the same is true of all interpreters whether ancient or modern, as Moyise appears most of the time to maintain, then these texts could never be misunderstood, and there would never be such a thing as false interpretation.[92] In fact, the question of whether John respected or was even significantly aware of Old Testament texts is not relevant. He is only able to see mirror reflections of his own mind when looking at and interpreting Old Testament texts.

This last point also touches upon Moyise's final critique of my position, which I will now address.

Modern Interpreters' Presuppositions and the Question of Real Knowledge

Moyise takes me to task because I affirm that though all modern interpreters have presuppositions that influence how texts are interpreted, such presuppositions do not completely blind readers from comprehending an author's meaning that is incompatible with their own hermeneutical lenses and from discerning the different assumptions of others. He disagrees because "since scholars do arrive at positions that differ with Beale, it would appear that what he really means is that *his* presuppositions have not prevented *him* from correctly discerning authorial intention."[93] Following Bruggemann, Moyise agrees with the "insights of liberation and feminist writings that 'what one knows and sees depends upon where one stands or sits. . . . The knower helps constitute what

91. This paragraph is about Christian epistemology. I have argued earlier that all people, including non-Christians, can understand sufficiently oral and written communication because of God's common revelatory grace. God's special revelation does enable believers to understand Scripture better than unbelievers, but this primarily concerns the Spirit's role in giving epistemological assurance about Scripture's authority, in conveying God's presence through his Word, and in applying God's Word to the Christian's life (the area of perlocution, discussed above). There is here, however, not space to elaborate further on these distinctions here.
92. Vanhoozer, *Is There a Meaning in This Text?* 218.
93. Moyise, "Old Testament in the New: Reply to Beale," 58.

is known.'"[94] This is explained by saying that authorial intention "is a 'construct' rather than a 'given.'"[95]

Now, it is plausible to say that authorial intention is a construct in the sense that readers must construct—that is, interpret—what the author is intending to communicate, and that this construct is not a given that we can immediately understand. But it is going too far to say that to construct meaning from an author necessitates that the constructed meaning is a pure, new creation of the reader and has no substantial link to the original meaning intended by the author. This is what Moyise appears to be saying at certain points, since he never qualifies his statements about socially constructed interpretation. For example, he could say at some point that John's interpretation of the Old Testament in Revelation contains some identifiable link with an Old Testament author's intentional speech act, but he rarely makes any statement that approaches this in his discussions.[96]

It is just possible that Moyise and I have neither an exegetical nor even ultimately a hermeneutical disagreement but an epistemological dispute about the nature of knowledge—how we can be confident of what we know or claim to know. He lines up with the more radical side of postmodern reader-response critics. He adamantly protests my placing him with "those reader-response critics who . . . believe that a text can mean whatever they like," since he is "unaware of any reader-response critics who go that far."[97] I did not actually say that Moyise or reader-

---

94. Ibid.

95. Ibid.

96. He does say, however, in his last response to me that "I agree with Beale that there is enough continuity between Revelation and the OT to deny the accusation of misappropriation" (Moyise, "Does the Author of Revelation Misappropriate the Scriptures?" *AUSS* 40 (2002): 17; so see likewise ibid., 20–21, though here he also says that John's focus is not on "the original authorial meaning of the OT authors" but on "seeking to discern the trajectory of interpretation that makes most sense of his present." In this light, there is now a foundation upon which Moyise and I might come to greater agreement in the future.

97. Moyise, "Old Testament in the New: Reply to Beale," 57. Though Moyise may be unaware, there are numerous examples of reader-oriented interpretations of biblical texts whereby authorial intent is not considered as the primary aim or recoverable: cf. OT examples in Vanhoozer, *Is There a Meaning in This Text?* 175–82, and in Wright, *The New Testament and the People of God*, 59–61, where also a "deconstructionist" sample is found and where Wright's assessment of the epistemology of "reader-response" criticism is like mine (in so doing Wright is following others like B. F. Meyer). Likewise, see S. E. Porter, "Literary Approaches to the New Testament: From Formalism to Deconstruction and Back," in *Approaches to New Testament Study*, ed. S. E. Porter and D. Tombs (Sheffield: Sheffield Academic Press, 1995), 90–128, who summarizes and evaluates the milder and more radical forms of "reader-oriented" criticism, and the closely related "deconstructionism," giving examples of how each has been applied to biblical studies. Similarly see D. McCartney and C. Clayton, *Let the Reader Understand*, 280–84; cf. also 51–52. Strikingly, R. Morgan and J. Barton, *Biblical Interpretation* (Oxford: Oxford University Press, 1988), 7, make the programmatic statement, "Texts, like dead men and women, have no rights, no aims, no interests. They can be used in whatever way readers

oriented interpreters affirm "that a text can mean whatever they like," but I do think it accurately represents my view of more radically minded, subjectivist interpreters, among which Moyise sometimes dallies.

In essence, the approach with which he aligns himself generally contends that readers or interpretative communities are the ultimate determiners of a text's meaning rather than the original author's intended speech act in a text. If Moyise only intends that interpretative communities determine a text's significance (in terms of the "application" aspect of "significance" discussed earlier), then I would not be as troubled,[98] but a claim that communities determine *meaning, including extended meaning*, is inherently problematic. In particular, Moyise seems to hold a view that incompatible interpretations of the same texts mean that one interpretation is just as valid, in terms of its "correctness," as another. If this is not Moyise's position, then I will be happy to be corrected, but this appears to be his view, as far as I can tell from his monograph, and his response to me continues to point in this direction.[99]

In contrast to Moyise's subjectivist interpretative perspective, I want to elaborate briefly on Tom Wright's attempt to maintain a balance between the objective and the subjective in the writing of history and of interpretation.[100] The positivistic (observers are neutral and purely objective) and the phenomenalistic (observers only see reflections of their own minds) are two extremes to be avoided. The truth lies somewhere in between, a view Wright styles "critical realism." Ultimately, he sees that all observers have presuppositions, "worldviews," that are private to each individual but that can also be discussed "publicly." The public element includes the ability of people to perceive other presuppositions that differ from and even oppose their own.

Further, the inductive data of reality are also a sharable public commodity. People with differing presuppositional perspectives can discuss with one another how that data fit into their perspectives. The perspective that is the simplest and that makes for the best logical fit of the most data is the most probable perspective. The mindset that is unable to make sense of as much data as another is less plausible. Hence, the

---

or interpreters choose." On the same page the authors say, "But the present point is that in all cases it is the interests or aims of the interpreters that are decisive, not the claims of the text as such. Any suggestion that a text has rights is a deception concealing someone else's interests."

98. Though, if we are speaking of Christian communities, then we would want to posit that the Spirit guides our various applications of the meaning of biblical texts.

99. In this respect, see my analysis of Moyise's discussions of John's use of the OT which seems to fit into a milder "reader-response" outlook, and then compare my analysis of his discussions of the stance of *modern readers* towards John's writing, which are rooted in the more radical form of "reader-response" approaches (*John's Use of the Old Testament in Revelation*, 43–51).

100. Wright, *The New Testament and the People of God*, 31–120.

tests of "logical coherence" and "correspondence" are crucial tests that can be conducted in a public manner.

Wright gives the example of a paleontologist who has the task of fitting together a dinosaur skeleton from some scattered bones.[101] If he creates a simple structure of a known dinosaur that omits the evidence of some significantly large bones that do not fit in, then others may accuse him of satisfying the criterion of simplicity at the expense of the data. The paleontologist might respond by saying that the extra bones belong to another animal that was eaten by, or ate, the one now being constructed. If a second paleontologist produces another skeleton from the same bones and is able to use all the bones, but there are seven toes on one foot and eighteen on the other, then the opposite problem is posed: simplicity has been abandoned for the sake of including all the data, and the first paleontologist will not be persuaded by an unconventional evolutionary explanation. Which of the competing theories will be accepted? The first is more plausible, since it is easier to think that some scattered bones from one animal intruded into the pile of the other than it is to believe that the strange, mutated creature in the second scenario ever existed.

Presuppositional perspectives are comparable to the dinosaur hypotheses, which illustrate that usually no two hypotheses are without problems, yet the one with the least problems is the more likely. Ultimately, in judging history and historical interpretations, Wright is probably correct in placing more weight on the criteria of "inclusion of data" than on the "simplicity of perspective."[102] The same epistemological criteria applied by Wright to verifying historical acts are just as applicable to the verification of authorial literary speech acts of history. In fact, Wright includes hermeneutics within the purview of his discussion.

Wright is apparently unaware that he has espoused an epistemology of presuppositional verification quite close to the Dutch Reformed theological tradition developed earlier this century (e.g., Abraham Kuyper,[103] Cornelius Van Til,[104] and Gordon H. Clark,[105] the latter being Reformed

---

101. Ibid., 104–5.

102. Ibid.

103. Abraham Kuyper, *Principles of Sacred Theology* (Grand Rapids: Eerdmans, 1954).

104. For a summary of C. Van Til's works and thought, see T. Notaro, *Van Til and the Use of Evidence* (Phillipsburg, NJ: P&R, 1980), especially with respect to the relation of presuppositions and inductive data. In the Kuyperian and Van Tilian tradition, see recently J. M. Frame, *The Doctrine of the Knowledge of God* (Phillipsburg, NJ: P&R, 1987).

105. E.g., *Language and Theology* (Phillipsburg, NJ: P&R, 1980); for a summary of his epistemology, see R. H. Nash, "Gordon Clark's Theory of Knowledge," in *The Philosophy of Gordon H. Clark: A Festschrift*, ed. R. H. Nash (Philadelphia: Presbyterian and Reformed, 1968), 125–75, esp. 155–60.

but not standing as squarely in the Dutch tradition). Similarly, Wright's theory of perspectival validation is virtually identical to the classical "commonsense" tradition of hermeneutical validation developed in further detail by E. D. Hirsch, to whom Wright also makes no reference.

The differing presuppositions of people can be discussed and evaluated in the public forum. Such public discussion can reveal how a perspective impinges on or distorts an observation or interpretation by being too narrow or too selective in what is looked at. An apt analogy might be a telescope. Parents may take their three-year-old child to a ridge that overlooks half of a town. They place a telescope there, and have their child look through it. The lens has a red tint, and it has a distorting feature that makes people look as wide as they are tall. The young, inexperienced child concludes that the town is only half as big as it really is, the people are red, and they are as wide as they are tall. This would certainly be a distorted view, but the fact remains that the child still is looking at real objects outside of himself in the real world and has some actual knowledge of that real world.

Working off a similar example, Wright concludes that historians also may have presuppositional lenses that distort in various ways—whether those lenses be white European, feminist, capitalist, Marxist, Latin American liberationist—and "we may well need other lenses and viewpoints to correct such errors; but we are looking at [real] events none the less."[106] Some knowledge can be ascertained, even if it is not exhaustively or perfectly understood. It should be added that some presuppositions are good because they guide us into a right understanding of reality, e.g., presuppositions of the law of non-contradiction, of the existence of the self, and of justice. If the first two are not consistently assumed, then a person cannot operate in society and is categorized as insane. If justice is not consistently assumed, then society itself cannot function but is thrown into civil chaos.

I suspect that Moyise, if he granted the appropriateness of the telescope illustration, might say that the lens is so clouded that the child would be unable to make out a town with people. Such is the nature of his illustration of an initial ripple losing its clear identity when combining with other ripples, or that of an initial sound wave losing its distinguishable identity when combining with other sound waves. It is intriguing that one of the prominent criteria of validating interpretations among the more radical reader-response critics is whether it enables readers to see texts in ways that are new to them.[107]

106. Wright, *The New Testament and the People of God*, 90.
107. Porter, "Literary Approaches to the New Testament," 115.

To deny any real knowledge in historical or hermeneutical investigation is to be skeptical about reality itself, comparable to the solipsistic philosophers who question whether they are presently dreaming or living in a real world. "The philosophical tricks by which authorial intention has been dismissed from the reckoning are, in the last analysis, no more impressive than the well-known trick which keeps the hare in permanent pursuit,"[108] and contending that the hare keeps halving the distance between it and the tortoise into always smaller portions.

Vanhoozer mentions Umberto Eco's similar critique of the postmodern notion of textuality—sentences and texts are all connected to other sentences and texts in a never-ending chain of interconnectedness, so that there is never a determinate but only an open-ended meaning in any particular text. Even such scientific realities as atomic energy, radioactivity, and electricity are considered mere metaphors and cannot be known. Eco has the main character in one of his novels question the common understanding of the shop signs and clouds and other everyday sights and begs them to reveal their hidden meanings. Even a subtext must be sought for a sign that says "No littering."[109]

Finally, Wright argues for another public aspect of hermeneutics: "a hermeneutic of love." Accordingly, "the lover affirms the reality of and the otherness of the beloved. Love does not seek to collapse the beloved in terms of itself."[110] ("Love seeks not its own," 1 Cor. 13:5.) Practically and epistemologically, this means that readers will attempt to be unselfish and not twist the authorial intentions of others to their own selfish ends. Rather, they will deny themselves and seek with all their might the real meaning outside of themselves, which an author has communicated. Of course, for example, this must happen in marriage, else there will be a communication breakdown and the relationship will become chaotic.

Wright is contending that such love must be extended to our neighbor in public, to everyone who crosses our path, including authors whom we read. I hope that I have "loved" Moyise in this manner because he is a real person and author, and I have no right to twist his authorial intentions carelessly in ways that might make criticism of him easier or the fictionalizing of his views. I may have failed in this, but I have tried truly to understand his view.

Likewise, we should "love" ancient authors by denying any modern lenses that distort and by striving to understand what they originally meant and how that meaning might be extended to the present. I agree

108. Wright, The New Testament and the People of God, 58.
109. Vanhoozer, Is There a Meaning in This Text? 122–23.
110. Wright, The New Testament and the People of God, 64.

with Wright and his working assumption that such an ethic is based on a Christian, theistic biblical worldview. Indeed, I believe this worldview makes more sense of particular values such as love than do non-theistic worldviews.

Such a theistic, Christian worldview bases its knowledge on the revelation of God.[111] There is a crucial connection between such a worldview and epistemology. The mind can demarcate the meaning of a communicative act so that the meaning remains constant over time. (Here I am only partially following Hirsch and Husserl,[112] since they propose no formal theistic underpinning for this view.) The enduring foundation for such "an absolute transcendent determinant meaning to all texts" is the presupposition of an omniscient, sovereign, and transcendent God, who knows the exhaustive yet determinant and true meaning of all texts because he stands above the world he has constructed and above all the social constructs his creatures have constructed, yet he has created them to share partly in his attributes and to have some determinant meaning of the communicative acts of others.[113]

Likewise, with particular reference to the biblical text, God not only knows its meaning exhaustively and has created humans in his image to understand it sufficiently, but he has also inspired biblical authors to write his authoritative word in contrast to all other writings of the human race, which are fallible.

Some evangelicals, however, contend that no reader of the Bible has been able entirely to *start* with the Bible alone in order to understand it. Accordingly, it is thought impossible for people, in any ultimate way, to start reading the Bible on their own and to be informed by Scripture alone, as if their mind were a blank slate, not influenced in their initial understanding of Scripture by forces outside the Bible. Such elements as various Christian traditions, past personal experience, family upbringing, cultural location, and social situatedness inevitably color and affect the way an individual approaches and understands Scripture. And, of course, we must not forget that all people are sinners, so that their sin in some way distorts how the Bible is understood.

Thus, it is thought that any idea anyone has about Scripture is shaped by the world in which the reader lives and by the reader's own sinfulness, so that there is no pristine knowledge of God's Word. Ultimately,

---

111. For an in-depth explanation of such a worldview as the basis for the kind of epistemology argued for in this essay, see Vanhoozer, *Is There a Meaning in This Text? passim.*

112. I also allude to this briefly in my monograph *John's Use of the Old Testament*, 55, n. 136.

113. Following generally McCartney and Clayton, *Let the Reader Understand*, 284; likewise G. H. Clark; cf. Nash, "Gordon Clark's Theory of Knowledge," 143–1620.

we have access not to God's Word as it was originally given but only to God's word as it has been understood by others. That is, we have access only to human tradition about the Bible. According to this view, the Holy Spirit does impart knowledge to us, but knowledge is conveyed only through the filter of the particular situations and communities in which we live. The varying interpretative stances about the Bible held among different Christian traditions or communities, even when these interpretations are contradictory to one another, should be mutually respected, since they are all led by the same Spirit.

While it is certainly true that such things do inevitably influence all interpretation of Scripture, whether one is reading the Bible as an unbeliever or a believer, this position as stated above is too extreme and exhibits too much imbibing of postmodern tendencies. But, if it is true that all of our interpretations of the Bible are colored by our socially constructed history and situation, then why is this view too extreme? It is too extreme because it does not allow for God's sovereign revelatory power to break through all of these internal and external elements that color the understanding of Scripture.[114]

While it is true that we do not attain knowledge from the standpoint of neutrality with the Bible, it is true that we can perceive God's in-breaking revelatory presence and communication as that which enables us to see through our aberrant presuppositional lenses and to apprehend God's unerring truth from his perspective or lens. If professing Christians are left with only a closed circle in which our biases influence our interpretation of the Bible, and our resulting jaundiced view of Scripture's interpretation further forms our theological biases, though purportedly led by the Spirit, then all we can do is attempt to evaluate which socially constructed theological tradition best represents Scripture. Furthermore, to attribute the leading of the Spirit to that which guides Christian communities and traditions to different, even mutually exclusive, views of biblical truth is an attempt to baptize a postmodern approach with Christian terminology.

Therefore, while it is, indeed, not possible for people, in any ultimate way, to start reading the Bible independently and to be informed by Scripture alone, as if their mind were a blank slate, they can start having *true* knowledge by having their minds and hearts penetrated by God's in-breaking revelatory presence and Word, which begins to form

114. John Webster helpfully locates the doctrine of Scripture not as prolegomena to address epistemological concerns but within the doctrine of God, as Scripture is a revealing, sanctifying, and inspiring self-communicative act of the triune God; see *Holy Scripture: A Dogmatic Sketch* (Cambridge: Cambridge University Press, 2003), 8.

or reform in them his lenses on reality (e.g., see 1 Cor. 2:10–16; 1 John 5:20).[115] Thus, it is sinful to try to be objective in the sense of trying to perceive Scripture's meaning only by oneself, since we should want God's subjective though true perspective on truth, which can break through the distorting lenses we wear and lead us into the truth.

God is transcendent and separate from the world he has created and from all the sinfully tainted social constructs that his creatures have built. Nevertheless, he has created them to share partly in his attributes in that he has created them to reflect his image and to have some sufficient meaning of his communicative acts of special revelation, especially those who are Christians and have been created in the image of Christ, and who "have the mind of Christ" (1 Cor. 2:16).

But how does all this hermeneutical theory affect our subject of the authority of Scripture, including the New Testament's authoritative use of the Old Testament? *If we cannot know what God has communicated to us in his inspired Scripture, then his authoritative Word has no binding relation to us. What good is an authoritative word of God, if we cannot know what that word has said? This is the ultimate danger of postmodern perspectives on interpreting the Bible.*

Conclusion

Critical evaluation of Steven Moyise has been difficult because of the complex nature of the hermeneutical issues involved and because I know him personally, and I have high respect for him. There are subtleties in both my position and his that are sometimes hard to express precisely, which makes it difficult to be sure whether I have completely understood his views. Nevertheless, I have tried to represent his views as fairly as I can.[116] Indeed, some of his subsequent responses to me provide a clearer foundation upon which we might be able to build together and to come to more agreement.[117]

115. It may be more precise to say, instead of God giving us lenses on reality, that God refines or regrinds our lenses, so that we see reality more truly from the divine perspective. The reason for this is that God originally created Adam and Eve with lenses to interpret rightly the reality within which they were created and to understand God's word spoken to them; after the fall, those lenses were not destroyed but were distorted (as the image of God was not destroyed but distorted). Thus, with belief in Christ, we begin to have our "sight" made better or "reformed" (though we still only "know in part"), until finally at Christ's final coming, we "shall know fully just as we also have been fully known" (1 Cor. 13:12).

116. See G. R. Osborne, "Recent Trends in the Study of the Apocalypse," in *The Face of New Testament Studies*, ed. S. McKnight and G. R. Osborne (Grand Rapids: Baker, 2004), 493–94, who briefly reviews the debate between Moyise and me and gives a similar assessment as I have.

117. On which see n. 96 above, and his last response of which I am aware: Moyise, "Respect for Context Once More," *IBS* 27 (2006): 24–31, where he also surveys and summarizes our published interactions with one another's views.

This essay is a defense in summary form for the hermeneutical and epistemological hope that is in me. It contains the barest outlines of an approach that could only be written fully within the larger parameters of a book. My own thought in these areas is best represented by Hirsch, Vanhoozer, and Wright, from whom I have learned a great deal. I do not expect others to agree with me or those with whom I am in agreement; nevertheless, I believe the hermeneutical and epistemological positions laid out are plausible, and other contrary positions bear the greater burden of proof, though some might think just the opposite.[118] And, at least, whether or not readers agree with my critiques of Moyise, the ultimate purpose of this appendix has been to lay out my own view of epistemology in relation to the hermeneutical understanding of how the New Testament interprets and understands the Old Testament.

---

118. I am grateful to Professor Moisés Silva for his willingness to read the majority of this chapter and for his helpful comments.

Addendum to Appendix 1: Brief Reflection on the Relationship of Globalism to Postmodernism

There are various definitions of globalism. Generally, *globalism* is typically defined as a conviction that worldwide concerns should be taken into account before considering national or local concerns. Such concerns may be economic, cultural, social, political, ecological, or theological. In theological terms, globalism may still involve, to one degree or another, the other matters just mentioned in combination with certain theological issues. For example, liberation theology in Latin America has applied the theology of Israel's exodus and release from Babylonian captivity to the economic and political oppression of the poor. Accordingly, such biblical precedents are applied in a way that gives biblical encouragement to the poorer classes to take social and political action, sometimes even military action, to be delivered from their economic and political disenfranchisement.[1]

In contemporary evangelicalism, a globalistic perspective has become increasingly the focus of theological discussion. This dialogue sometimes becomes combined with postmodern perspectives whereby, for example, Western or North American Christians are told that their "way of doing theology" and of "interpreting the Bible" is very parochial and that other sectors of the church elsewhere in the world do theology and interpret Scripture in a different way from the Western church. Accordingly, it is sometimes said that the way Westerners approach the Bible and theology is good for them but not for Latin Americans, Africans,

---

1. Probably Gustavo Gutiérrez most prominently expresses the hermeneutics of liberation theology: "The theology of liberation offers us not so much a new theme for reflection as a *new way* to do theology. Theology as critical reflection on historical praxis . . ." This historical praxis focuses, for Latin America, on reading Scripture from the perspective of the poor. See G. Gutiérrez, *A Theology of Liberation*, 2nd ed., trans. C. Inda and J. Eagelson (Maryknoll, NY: Orbis, 1988), 12; cf. also M. H. Ellis and O. Maduro, eds., *The Future of Liberation Theology* (Maryknoll, NY: Orbis, 1989).

Asians, and other people groups around the world. One can occasionally receive the impression from such assertions that there is no right or correct theological or interpretative method. Whatever each church global community considers correct is right for them, but not necessarily for other Christians living in other parts of the world.

I have heard some evangelical theologians at times seem to go so far as to imply that even the theological ideas of various sectors of the global church are not merely different but so different as to be virtually irreconcilable with one another. Nevertheless, what biblical ideas or doctrines are thought to be true in one part of the global church, while not considered true in another, must be respected by all. For example, I have heard more times than I can count that the way we Westerners have done systematic theology and biblical interpretation in the past is not the way that Christians in Africa, Asia, or Latin America do these things. And Western missionaries should not be using such methods when teaching in these parts of the world. In fact, it is sometimes said that to do so is another example of Western imperialism and colonialization. Thus, what is a true method of approaching the Bible in one part of the global church is not true for another.

This is merely another version of what we have already discussed about how some postmodern biblical scholars understand the use of the Old Testament in the New. Jesus and the apostles used an interpretative method for interpreting Scripture that we would judge to be wrong according to twenty-first-century standards, but it was right for them, and we should respect the way they so interpreted their Old Testament Bible. Yet, there is certainly a perspective of globalism that is good and healthy, indeed, biblical.

Yet the church in part of the world may focus on methods of theology, or interpretation, or biblical ideas, or doctrines, or applications of these things that are not seen or emphasized in other parts of the worldwide church.

Each sector of the church can learn from the other sectors about those areas in which it is blind or unduly underemphasizing something. It is not that such ideas or methods in parts of the church are inapplicable to others and nonetheless need to be respected. On the contrary, each segment of the global body of Christ learns from all the others true facets of biblical reality. Each supplements the other. What comprises a good method of doing theology or a good interpretative insight in one part of the church should be shared with other parts, since it will prove beneficial to the whole. For example, the poorer parts of the church may have much more insight into the biblical texts that concern poverty and the right response to poverty than those parts of the church that are in prosperous economies. Financially well-off parts of the church, no doubt, have much to learn from the impoverished part. And certainly it is true that some sectors of the church are in situations where certain interpretative and theological methods and doctrines need to be emphasized more than others, just as pastors recognize that not all people who come to them for counseling should be given the same counsel from the same portion of Scripture or on the basis of the same doctrine.[2]

The last 150 years of most of Western theological and biblical scholarship have had a detrimental effect on the worldwide church, since the majority of this scholarship has either denied or underemphasized the inspiration of Scripture, text-based biblical interpretation, and the supernatural element in Scripture.

However, the long, deep tradition of conservative systematic and biblical theology and biblical interpretation in the Western world has much to offer the newer parts of the church that have risen significantly over the last fifty or so years where there was not much Christian presence formerly. The conservative Western sector of scholarship has much to offer other parts of the world, because of its emphasis on the authority of the Bible, text-based interpretation, and affirmation of the supernatural in the Bible.[3] In particular, the more recent emphasis on biblical or narrative theology, in which the redemptive-historical storyline of the Bible has been highlighted, has much with which non-Western churches can resonate positively. Therefore:

> Academic interpretation of the Bible (meaning, among other things, interpretation that is not ruled by current dogmatic convictions . . .) is absolutely necessary for the church to understand, live out, and proclaim to this generation and to future ones. . . . In other words, throughout the world there is an acute need for church leaders with knowledge of original languages and scholarly competencies for verifying the original texts of Scripture, their best translation, and their meaning, and their application. Pastoral leaders need grounding in the history of Israel and OT Scripture and theology, Second Temple Judaism, the first century and its history and

---

2. Craig Blomberg persuasively makes a case that biblical scholars should respond not only to Western questions but also to questions from the majority world church; see his "Where Should Twenty-First-Century Biblical Scholarship Be Heading?" *BBR* 11 (2001): 167; Blomberg, "The Globalization of Biblical Interpretation: A Test Case—John 3–4," *BBR* 5 (1995): 1–3.

3. On which see Robert Yarbrough, "The Last and Next Christendom: Implications for Interpreting the Bible," *Them* 29 (2003): 30–37. For example, Yarbrough argues, "The increase of world Christianity should result in an increase in literacy and learning, precisely because Christians come to faith by hearing, and hearing by the Word of God (cf. Rom 10:17), and that implies reading and analysis and synthesis, all activities calling for intelligence and reason and scholarship" (ibid., 37).

literatures, the NT Scriptures and their theology, the patristic era, and subsequent periods, debates, [and] issues in the history of Christian faith.[4]

The matters crucial to determining what the Bible meant in its context
and what it means for today's church are transcultural concerns applicable to every age. Thus, what Paul says about the body of Christ in
1 Corinthians 12:12–30 is very applicable to this global issue, since we
are discussing the global body of Christ:

> For even as the body is one and yet has many members, and all the members
> of the body, though they are many, are one body, so also is Christ. For by
> one Spirit we were all baptized into one body, whether Jews or Greeks,
> whether slaves or free, and we were all made to drink of one Spirit. For
> the body is not one member, but many. If the foot says, "Because I am
> not a hand, I am not a part of the body," it is not for this reason any the
> less a part of the body. And if the ear says, "Because I am not an eye, I
> am not a part of the body," it is not for this reason any the less a part of
> the body. If the whole body were an eye, where would the hearing be?
> If the whole were hearing, where would the sense of smell be? But now
> God has placed the members, each one of them, in the body, just as He
> desired. If they were all one member, where would the body be? But now
> there are many members, but one body. And the eye cannot say to the
> hand, "I have no need of you"; or again the head to the feet, "I have no
> need of you." On the contrary, it is much truer that the members of the
> body which seem to be weaker are necessary; and those *members* of the
> body which we deem less honorable, on these we bestow more abundant
> honor, and our less presentable members become much more presentable,
> whereas our more presentable members have no need *of it.* But God has *so*
> composed the body, giving more abundant honor to that *member* which
> lacked, so that there may be no division in the body, but *that* the members
> may have the same care for one another. And if one member suffers, all
> the members suffer with it; if *one* member is honored, all the members
> rejoice with it. Now you are Christ's body, and individually members of
> it. And God has appointed in the church, first apostles, second prophets,
> third teachers, then miracles, then gifts of healings, helps, administra-
> tions, *various* kinds of tongues. All are not apostles, are they? All are not
> prophets, are they? All are not teachers, are they? All are not *workers of*
> miracles, are they? All do not have gifts of healings, do they? All do not
> speak with tongues, do they? All do not interpret, do they?

Consequently, theological globalism is nothing more than the different members of the body of Christ needing one another. May God

4. Ibid., 36–37.

give us grace to recognize this. But may he also give us grace to see that the meaning of God's truthful Word in Scripture is the same for all his people, though none of us can know it exhaustively, and though some of us will perceive different insights than others, all such insights are relevant for the upbuilding of the entire church of any age.

Appendix 2

Chicago Statement on Biblical Inerrancy with Exposition

[The following statement and explanation of the Chicago Statement on Biblical Inerrancy is given here, since it well represents my own view.[1]]

Background

The "Chicago Statement on Biblical Inerrancy" was produced at an international summit conference of evangelical leaders, held at the Hyatt Regency O'Hare in Chicago in the fall of 1978. This congress was sponsored by the International Council on Biblical Inerrancy. The Chicago Statement was signed by nearly 300 noted evangelical scholars, including James Boice, Norman L. Geisler, John Gerstner, Carl F. H. Henry,

---

1. Though I do have a few very minor adjustments that I would want to make in some of the language used. For example, in the section of "Exposition" the following is stated: "Differences between literary conventions in Bible times and in ours must also be observed: since, for instance, non-chronological narration and imprecise citation were conventional and acceptable and violated no expectations in those days, we must not regard these things as faults when we find them in Bible writers. When total precision of a particular kind was not expected nor aimed at, it is no error not to have achieved it. Scripture is inerrant, not in the sense of being absolutely precise by modern standards, but in the sense of making good its claims and achieving that measure of focused truth at which its authors aimed." This statement does not take into consideration that even some modern literary genres use non-chronological narration or nonprecise time or geographical measurements or approximations as an acceptable style. Also, I would prefer not to speak of "apparent inconsistencies" in Scripture as "illusions" (also found in the "Exposition" section) but rather as phenomena that will one day be understood at the end of history, when we shall "know fully" (cf. 1 Cor. 14:12). This underscores the partial knowledge that we have in the inaugurated eschatological era in contrast to the "full knowledge" that we will have in the consummated eschatological period (see 1 Cor. 14:9–12).

Kenneth Kantzer, Harold Lindsell, John Warwick Montgomery, Roger Nicole, J. I. Packer, Robert Preus, Earl Radmacher, Francis Schaeffer, R. C. Sproul, and John Wenham.

The ICBI disbanded in 1988 after producing three major statements: one on biblical inerrancy in 1978, one on biblical hermeneutics in 1982, and one on biblical application in 1986. The following text, containing the "Preface" by the ICBI draft committee, plus the "Short Statement," "Articles of Affirmation and Denial," and an accompanying "Exposition," was published in toto by Carl F. H. Henry in *God, Revelation and Authority*, vol. 4 (Waco, TX: Word Books, 1979), on pp. 211–19. The nineteen Articles of Affirmation and Denial, with a brief introduction, also appear in *A General Introduction to the Bible*, by Norman L. Geisler and William E. Nix (Chicago: Moody Press, rev. 1986), at pp. 181–85. An official commentary on these articles was written by R. C. Sproul in *Explaining Inerrancy: A Commentary* (Oakland, CA: ICBI, 1980), and Norman Geisler edited the major addresses from the 1978 conference, in *Inerrancy* (Grand Rapids: Zondervan, 1980).

Clarification of some of the language used in this Statement may be found in the 1982 Chicago Statement on Biblical Hermeneutics.

The Chicago Statement on Biblical Inerrancy

Preface

The authority of Scripture is a key issue for the Christian church in this and every age. Those who profess faith in Jesus Christ as Lord and Savior are called to show the reality of their discipleship by humbly and faithfully obeying God's written Word. To stray from Scripture in faith or conduct is disloyalty to our Master. Recognition of the total truth and trustworthiness of Holy Scripture is essential to a full grasp and adequate confession of its authority.

The following Statement affirms this inerrancy of Scripture afresh, making clear our understanding of it and warning against its denial. We are persuaded that to deny it is to set aside the witness of Jesus Christ and of the Holy Spirit and to refuse that submission to the claims of God's own Word which marks true Christian faith. We see it as our timely duty to make this affirmation in the face of current lapses from the truth of inerrancy among our fellow Christians and misunderstandings of this doctrine in the world at large.

This Statement consists of three parts: a Summary Statement, Articles of Affirmation and Denial, and an accompanying Exposition. It has been prepared in the course of a three-day consultation in Chicago.

Those who have signed the Summary Statement and the Articles wish to affirm their own conviction as to the inerrancy of Scripture and to encourage and challenge one another and all Christians to growing appreciation and understanding of this doctrine. We acknowledge the limitations of a document prepared in a brief, intensive conference and do not propose that this Statement be given creedal weight. Yet we rejoice in the deepening of our own convictions through our discussions together, and we pray that the Statement we have signed may be used to the glory of our God toward a new reformation of the Church in its faith, life, and mission.

We offer this Statement in a spirit, not of contention, but of humility and love, which we purpose by God's grace to maintain in any future dialogue arising out of what we have said. We gladly acknowledge that many who deny the inerrancy of Scripture do not display the consequences of this denial in the rest of their belief and behavior, and we are conscious that we who confess this doctrine often deny it in life by failing to bring our thoughts and deeds, our traditions and habits, into true subjection to the divine Word.

We invite response to this statement from any who see reason to amend its affirmations about Scripture by the light of Scripture itself, under whose infallible authority we stand as we speak. We claim no personal infallibility for the witness we bear, and for any help which enables us to strengthen this testimony to God's Word we shall be grateful.

—The Draft Committee

A Short Statement

1. God, who is Himself Truth and speaks truth only, has inspired Holy Scripture in order thereby to reveal Himself to lost mankind through Jesus Christ as Creator and Lord, Redeemer and Judge. Holy Scripture is God's witness to Himself.

2. Holy Scripture, being God's own Word, written by men prepared and superintended by His Spirit, is of infallible divine authority in all matters upon which it touches: it is to be believed, as God's instruction, in all that it affirms: obeyed, as God's command, in all that it requires; embraced, as God's pledge, in all that it promises.

3. The Holy Spirit, Scripture's divine Author, both authenticates it to us by His inward witness and opens our minds to understand its meaning.

4. Being wholly and verbally God-given, Scripture is without error or fault in all its teaching, no less in what it states about God's acts in creation, about the events of world history, and about its own literary origins under God, than in its witness to God's saving grace in individual lives.

5. The authority of Scripture is inescapably impaired if this total divine inerrancy is in any way limited or disregarded, or made relative to a view of truth contrary to the Bible's own; and such lapses bring serious loss to both the individual and the Church.

Articles of Affirmation and Denial

Article I.
WE AFFIRM that the Holy Scriptures are to be received as the authoritative Word of God.

WE DENY that the Scriptures receive their authority from the Church, tradition, or any other human source.

Article II.
WE AFFIRM that the Scriptures are the supreme written norm by which God binds the conscience, and that the authority of the Church is subordinate to that of Scripture.

WE DENY that Church creeds, councils, or declarations have authority greater than or equal to the authority of the Bible.

Article III.
WE AFFIRM that the written Word in its entirety is revelation given by God.

WE DENY that the Bible is merely a witness to revelation, or only becomes revelation in encounter, or depends on the responses of men for its validity.

Article IV.
WE AFFIRM that God who made mankind in His image has used language as a means of revelation.

WE DENY that human language is so limited by our creatureliness that it is rendered inadequate as a vehicle for divine revelation. We further deny that the corruption of human culture and language through sin has thwarted God's work of inspiration.

Article V.

WE AFFIRM that God's revelation within the Holy Scriptures was progressive.

WE DENY that later revelation, which may fulfill earlier revelation, ever corrects or contradicts it. We further deny that any normative revelation has been given since the completion of the New Testament writings.

Article VI.

WE AFFIRM that the whole of Scripture and all its parts, down to the very words of the original, were given by divine inspiration.

WE DENY that the inspiration of Scripture can rightly be affirmed of the whole without the parts, or of some parts but not the whole.

Article VII.

WE AFFIRM that inspiration was the work in which God by His Spirit, through human writers, gave us His Word. The origin of Scripture is divine. The mode of divine inspiration remains largely a mystery to us.

WE DENY that inspiration can be reduced to human insight, or to heightened states of consciousness of any kind.

Article VIII.

WE AFFIRM that God in His work of inspiration utilized the distinctive personalities and literary styles of the writers whom He had chosen and prepared.

WE DENY that God, in causing these writers to use the very words that He chose, overrode their personalities.

Article IX.

WE AFFIRM that inspiration, though not conferring omniscience, guaranteed true and trustworthy utterance on all matters of which the Biblical authors were moved to speak and write.

WE DENY that the finitude or fallenness of these writers, by necessity or otherwise, introduced distortion or falsehood into God's Word.

Article X.

WE AFFIRM that inspiration, strictly speaking, applies only to the autographic text of Scripture, which in the providence of God can be ascertained from available manuscripts with great accuracy. We further affirm that copies and translations of Scripture are the Word of God to the extent that they faithfully represent the original.

WE DENY that any essential element of the Christian faith is affected by the absence of the autographs. We further deny that this absence renders the assertion of Biblical inerrancy invalid or irrelevant.

Article XI.

WE AFFIRM that Scripture, having been given by divine inspiration, is infallible, so that, far from misleading us, it is true and reliable in all the matters it addresses.

WE DENY that it is possible for the Bible to be at the same time infallible and errant in its assertions. Infallibility and inerrancy may be distinguished, but not separated.

Article XII.

WE AFFIRM that Scripture in its entirety is inerrant, being free from all falsehood, fraud, or deceit.

WE DENY that Biblical infallibility and inerrancy are limited to spiritual, religious, or redemptive themes, exclusive of assertions in the fields of history and science. We further deny that scientific hypotheses about earth history may properly be used to overturn the teaching of Scripture on creation and the flood.

Article XIII.

WE AFFIRM the propriety of using inerrancy as a theological term with reference to the complete truthfulness of Scripture.

WE DENY that it is proper to evaluate Scripture according to standards of truth and error that are alien to its usage or purpose. We further deny that inerrancy is negated by Biblical phenomena such as a lack of modern technical precision, irregularities of grammar or spelling, observational descriptions of nature, the reporting of falsehoods, the use of hyperbole and round numbers, the topical arrangement of material, variant selections of material in parallel accounts, or the use of free citations.

Article XIV.

WE AFFIRM the unity and internal consistency of Scripture.

WE DENY that alleged errors and discrepancies that have not yet been resolved vitiate the truth claims of the Bible.

Article XV.

WE AFFIRM that the doctrine of inerrancy is grounded in the teaching of the Bible about inspiration.

WE DENY that Jesus' teaching about Scripture may be dismissed by appeals to accommodation or to any natural limitation of His humanity.

Article XVI.

WE AFFIRM that the doctrine of inerrancy has been integral to the Church's faith throughout its history.

WE DENY that inerrancy is a doctrine invented by scholastic Protestantism, or is a reactionary position postulated in response to negative higher criticism.

Article XVII.

WE AFFIRM that the Holy Spirit bears witness to the Scriptures, assuring believers of the truthfulness of God's written Word.

WE DENY that this witness of the Holy Spirit operates in isolation from or against Scripture.

Article XVIII.

WE AFFIRM that the text of Scripture is to be interpreted by grammatico-historical exegesis, taking account of its literary forms and devices, and that Scripture is to interpret Scripture.

WE DENY the legitimacy of any treatment of the text or quest for sources lying behind it that leads to relativizing, dehistoricizing, or discounting its teaching, or rejecting its claims to authorship.

Article XIX.

WE AFFIRM that a confession of the full authority, infallibility, and inerrancy of Scripture is vital to a sound understanding of the whole of the Christian faith. We further affirm that such confession should lead to increasing conformity to the image of Christ.

WE DENY that such confession is necessary for salvation. However, we further deny that inerrancy can be rejected without grave consequences, both to the individual and to the Church.

Exposition
Our understanding of the doctrine of inerrancy must be set in the context of the broader teachings of the Scripture concerning itself. This exposition gives an account of the outline of doctrine from which our summary statement and articles are drawn.

Creation, Revelation and Inspiration
The Triune God, who formed all things by his creative utterances and governs all things by His Word of decree, made mankind in His own image for a life of communion with Himself, on the model of the eternal fellowship of loving communication within the Godhead. As God's image-bearer, man was to hear God's Word addressed to him and to respond in the joy of adoring obedience. Over and above God's self-disclosure in the created order and the sequence of events within it, human beings from Adam on have received verbal messages from Him, either directly, as stated in Scripture, or indirectly in the form of part or all of Scripture itself.

When Adam fell, the Creator did not abandon mankind to final judgment but promised salvation and began to reveal Himself as Redeemer in a sequence of historical events centering on Abraham's family and culminating in the life, death, resurrection, present heavenly ministry, and promised return of Jesus Christ. Within this frame God has from time to time spoken specific words of judgment and mercy, promise and command, to sinful human beings so drawing them into a covenant relation of mutual commitment between Him and them in which He blesses them with gifts of grace and they bless Him in responsive adoration. Moses, whom God used as mediator to carry His words to His people at the time of the Exodus, stands at the head of a long line of prophets in whose mouths and writings God put His words for delivery to Israel. God's purpose in this succession of messages was to maintain His covenant by causing His people to know His Name—that is, His nature—and His will both of precept and purpose in the present and for the future. This line of prophetic spokesmen from God came to completion in Jesus Christ, God's incarnate Word, who was Himself a prophet—more than a prophet, but not less—and in the apostles and prophets of the first Christian generation. When God's final and climactic message, His word to the world concerning Jesus Christ, had been spoken and elucidated by those in the apostolic circle, the sequence of revealed messages ceased. Henceforth the Church was to live and know God by what He had already said, and said for all time.

At Sinai God wrote the terms of His covenant on tables of stone, as His enduring witness and for lasting accessibility, and throughout the period of prophetic and apostolic revelation He prompted men to write the messages given to and through them, along with celebratory records of His dealings with His people, plus moral reflections on covenant life and forms of praise and prayer for covenant mercy. The theological reality of inspiration in the producing of Biblical documents corresponds to that of spoken prophecies: although the human writers' personalities were expressed in what they wrote, the words were divinely constituted. Thus, what Scripture says, God says; its authority is His authority, for He is its ultimate Author, having given it through the minds and words of chosen and prepared men who in freedom and faithfulness "spoke from God as they were carried along by the Holy Spirit" (1 Pet. 1:21). Holy Scripture must be acknowledged as the Word of God by virtue of its divine origin.

Authority: Christ and the Bible

Jesus Christ, the Son of God who is the Word made flesh, our Prophet, Priest, and King, is the ultimate Mediator of God's communication to man, as He is of all God's gifts of grace. The revelation He gave was more than verbal; He revealed the Father by His presence and His deeds as well. Yet His words were crucially important; for He was God, He spoke from the Father, and His words will judge all men at the last day.

As the prophesied Messiah, Jesus Christ is the central theme of Scripture. The Old Testament looked ahead to Him; the New Testament looks back to His first coming and on to His second. Canonical Scripture is the divinely inspired and therefore normative witness to Christ. No hermeneutic, therefore, of which the historical Christ is not the focal point is acceptable. Holy Scripture must be treated as what it essentially is—the witness of the Father to the Incarnate Son.

It appears that the Old Testament canon had been fixed by the time of Jesus. The New Testament canon is likewise now closed inasmuch as no new apostolic witness to the historical Christ can now be borne. No new revelation (as distinct from Spirit-given understanding of existing revelation) will be given until Christ comes again. The canon was created in principle by divine inspiration. The Church's part was to discern the canon which God had created, not to devise one of its own.

The word *canon*, signifying a rule or standard, is a pointer to authority, which means the right to rule and control. Authority in Christianity belongs to God in His revelation, which means, on the one hand, Jesus Christ, the living Word, and, on the other hand, Holy Scripture, the written Word. But the authority of Christ and that of Scripture are one. As our Prophet, Christ testified that Scripture cannot be broken. As our Priest and King, He devoted His earthly life to fulfilling the law and the prophets, even dying in obedience to the words of Messianic prophecy. Thus, as He saw Scripture attesting Him and His authority, so by His own submission to Scripture He attested its authority. As He bowed to His Father's instruction given in His Bible (our Old Testament), so He requires His disciples to do—not, however, in isolation but in conjunction with the apostolic witness to Himself which He undertook to inspire by His gift of the Holy Spirit. So Christians show themselves faithful servants of their Lord by bowing to the divine instruction given in the prophetic and apostolic writings which together make up our Bible.

By authenticating each other's authority, Christ and Scripture coalesce into a single fount of authority. The Biblically-interpreted Christ and the Christ-centered, Christ-proclaiming Bible are from this standpoint one. As from the fact of inspiration we infer that what Scripture says, God says, so from the revealed relation between Jesus Christ and Scripture we may equally declare that what Scripture says, Christ says.

Infallibility, Inerrancy, Interpretation

Holy Scripture, as the inspired Word of God witnessing authoritatively to Jesus Christ, may properly be called *infallible* and *inerrant*. These negative terms have a special value, for they explicitly safeguard crucial positive truths.

Infallible signifies the quality of neither misleading nor being misled and so safeguards in categorical terms the truth that Holy Scripture is a sure, safe, and reliable rule and guide in all matters.

Similarly, *inerrant* signifies the quality of being free from all falsehood or mistake and so safeguards the truth that Holy Scripture is entirely true and trustworthy in all its assertions.

We affirm that canonical Scripture should always be interpreted on the basis that it is infallible and inerrant. However, in determining what the God-taught writer is asserting in each passage, we must pay the most careful attention to its claims and character as a human production. In inspiration, God utilized the culture and conventions of His penman's milieu, a milieu that God controls in His sovereign providence; it is misinterpretation to imagine otherwise.

So history must be treated as history, poetry as poetry, hyperbole and metaphor as hyperbole and metaphor, generalization and approximation as what they are, and so forth. Differences between literary conventions in Bible times and in ours must also be observed: since, for instance, non-chronological narration and imprecise citation were conventional and acceptable and violated no expectations in those days, we must not regard these things as faults when we find them in Bible writers. When total precision of a particular kind was not expected nor aimed at, it is no error not to have achieved it. Scripture is inerrant, not in the sense of being absolutely precise by modern standards, but in the sense of making good its claims and achieving that measure of focused truth at which its authors aimed.

The truthfulness of Scripture is not negated by the appearance in it of irregularities of grammar or spelling, phenomenal descriptions of nature, reports of false statements (e.g., the lies of Satan), or seeming discrepancies between one passage and another. It is not right to set the so-called "phenomena" of Scripture against the teaching of Scripture about itself. Apparent inconsistencies should not be ignored. Solution of them, where this can be convincingly achieved, will encourage our faith, and where for the present no convincing solution is at hand we shall significantly honor God by trusting His assurance that His Word is true, despite these appearances, and by maintaining our confidence that one day they will be seen to have been illusions.

Inasmuch as all Scripture is the product of a single divine mind, interpretation must stay within the bounds of the analogy of Scripture and eschew hypotheses that would correct one Biblical passage by another, whether in the name of progressive revelation or of the imperfect enlightenment of the inspired writer's mind.

Although Holy Scripture is nowhere culture-bound in the sense that its teaching lacks universal validity, it is sometimes culturally conditioned by the customs and conventional views of a particular period, so that the application of its principles today calls for a different sort of action.

Skepticism and Criticism

Since the Renaissance, and more particularly since the Enlightenment, world-views have been developed which involve skepticism about basic Christian tenets. Such are the agnosticism which denies that God is knowable, the rationalism which denies that He is incomprehensible, the idealism which denies that He is transcendent, and the existentialism which denies rationality in His relationships with us. When these un- and anti-biblical principles seep into men's theologies at [a] presup-

positional level, as today they frequently do, faithful interpretation of
Holy Scripture becomes impossible.

Transmission and Translation

Since God has nowhere promised an inerrant transmission of Scripture,
it is necessary to affirm that only the autographic text of the original
documents was inspired and to maintain the need of textual criticism as
a means of detecting any slips that may have crept into the text in the
course of its transmission. The verdict of this science, however, is that
the Hebrew and Greek text appear to be amazingly well preserved, so
that we are amply justified in affirming, with the Westminster Confession, a singular providence of God in this matter and in declaring that
the authority of Scripture is in no way jeopardized by the fact that the
copies we possess are not entirely error-free.

Similarly, no translation is or can be perfect, and all translations are
an additional step away from the *autographa*. Yet the verdict of linguistic
science is that English-speaking Christians, at least, are exceedingly well
served in these days with a host of excellent translations and have no
cause for hesitating to conclude that the true Word of God is within their
reach. Indeed, in view of the frequent repetition in Scripture of the main
matters with which it deals and also of the Holy Spirit's constant witness
to and through the Word, no serious translation of Holy Scripture will
so destroy its meaning as to render it unable to make its reader "wise
for salvation through faith in Christ Jesus" (2 Tim. 3:15).

Inerrancy and Authority

In our affirmation of the authority of Scripture as involving its total truth,
we are consciously standing with Christ and His apostles, indeed with
the whole Bible and with the main stream of Church history from the
first days until very recently. We are concerned at the casual, inadvertent,
and seemingly thoughtless way in which a belief of such far-reaching
importance has been given up by so many in our day.

We are conscious too that great and grave confusion results from
ceasing to maintain the total truth of the Bible whose authority one
professes to acknowledge. The result of taking this step is that the Bible
which God gave loses its authority, and what has authority instead is
a Bible reduced in content according to the demands of one's critical
reasonings and in principle reducible still further once one has started.
This means that at bottom independent reason now has authority, as
opposed to Scriptural teaching. If this is not seen and if for the time being
basic evangelical doctrines are still held, persons denying the full truth

of Scripture may claim an evangelical identity while methodologically they have moved away from the evangelical principle of knowledge to an unstable subjectivism, and will find it hard not to move further.

We affirm that what Scripture says, God says. May He be glorified. Amen and Amen.

Appendix 3

Selected Quotations from Karl Barth's
Church Dogmatics on the Fallible and Errant Nature
of Scripture

I am including an appendix on some of Barth's quotations about the fallible nature of the Bible, since some evangelicals appeal to his overall view of the Bible's authority as representing a biblical perspective that should be held.[1] There is not room to present the extensive context of each of these quotations, but I invite the reader to consult his *Church Dogmatics* to check that context themselves.

The point of this appendix is to show that Barth believed that Scripture contained errors but that, nevertheless, God could communicate his message even through such fallible parts of the Bible. Likewise, some of the quotations reveal that Barth did not identify God's Word with the Bible but that the Bible is a witness to the Word.

Book I, 2; p. 65
"It is really not laid upon us to take everything in the Bible as true *in globo*, but it is laid upon us to listen to its testimony when we actually hear it."

Book I, 2; p. 507
"It witnesses to God's revelation, but. . . . The Bible is not a book of oracles; it is not an instrument of direct impartation."

---

1. E.g., see B. McCormack, "The Being of Holy Scripture Is in Becoming: Karl Barth in Conversation with American Evangelical Criticism," in *Evangelicals and Scripture*, ed. V. Bacote, L. C. Miguelez, and D. L. Okholm (Downers Grove, IL: InterVarsity, 2004), 55–75.

Book I, 2; p. 507

"If it [the Bible] tries to be more than witness, to be direct impartation, will it not keep from us the best, the one real thing, which God intends to tell and give us and which we ourselves need?"

Book I, 2; p. 507

"The men whom we hear as witnesses speak as fallible, erring men like ourselves. What they say, and what we read as their word, can of itself lay claim to be the Word of God, but never sustain that claim."

Book I, 2; p. 509

"We have to face up to them and to be clear that in the Bible it may be a matter of simply believing the Word of God, even though it meets us, not in the form of what we call history, but in the form of what we think must be called saga or legend."

Book I, 2; p. 509

"But the vulnerability of the Bible, i.e., its capacity for error, also extends to its religious or theological content."

Book I, 2; p. 509

"There are obvious and overlapping contradictions—e.g., between the Law and the prophets, between John and the Synoptists, between Paul and James."

Book I, 2; p. 510

"For within certain limits and therefore relatively they [biblical writers] are all vulnerable and therefore capable of error even in respect of religion and theology."

Book I, 2; p. 529

"The prophets and apostles as such, even in their office, even in their function as witnesses, even in the act of writing down their witnesses, were real, historical men as we are, and therefore sinful in their action, and capable and actually guilty of error in their spoken and written word."

Book I, 2; p. 529

"That the lame walk, that the blind see, that the dead are raised, that sinful and erring men as such speak the Word of God: that is the miracle of which we speak when we say that the Bible is the Word of God."

Book I, 2; p. 529–30

"To the bold postulate, that if their [biblical writers'] word is to be the Word of God they must be inerrant in every word, we oppose the even bolder assertion, that according to the scriptural witness about man, which applies to them too, they can be at fault in any word, and have been at fault in every word, and yet according to the same scriptural witness, being justified and sanctified by grace alone, they have still spoken the Word of God in their fallible and erring human word."

Book I, 2; p. 530

"If, therefore, we are serious about the fact that this miracle is an event, we cannot regard the presence of God's Word in the Bible as an attribute inhering once for all in this book as such and what we see before us of books and chapters and verses."

Book I, 2; p. 530

"Yet the presence of the Word of God itself, the real and present speaking and hearing of it, is not identical with the existence of the book as such."

Book I, 2; p. 530

"It then comes about that the Bible, the Bible *in concreto*, this or that biblical context, i.e., the Bible as it comes to us in this or that specific measure, is taken and used as an instrument in the hand of God, i.e., it speaks to and is heard by us as the authentic witness to divine revelation and is therefore present as the Word of God."

Book I, 2; p. 531–32

"If God was not ashamed of the fallibility of all the human words of the Bible, of their historical and scientific inaccuracies, their theological contradictions, the uncertainty of their tradition, and, above all, their Judaism, but adopted and made use of these expressions in all their fallibility, we do not need to be ashamed when He wills to renew it to us in all its fallibility as witness, and it is mere self-will and disobedience to try to find some infallible elements in the Bible. But finally we are absolved from having to know and name as such the event or events, in which Scripture proves and confirms itself to us as the Word of God."

Book I, 2; p. 533

"We must dare to face the humanity of the biblical texts and therefore their fallibility without the postulate that they must be infallible, but also without the superstitious belief in any infallible truth alongside or behind the text and revealed by ourselves."

Selected Bibliography

Allis, O. *The Unity of Isaiah: A Study in Prophecy*. Phillipsburg: NJ Presbyterian and Reformed, 1950.

Allison, D. C. *The New Moses: A Matthean Typology*. Minneapolis: Fortress, 1993.

Baker, D. L. *Two Testaments, One Bible: A Study of Some Modern Solutions to the Theological Problem of the Relationship between the Old and New Testaments*. Downers Grove: InterVarsity, 1977.

Bauer, Susan Wise. "Messy Revelation," *Books and Culture*. May/June 2006, 8–9.

Beale, G. K. "Did Jesus and the Apostles Preach the Right Doctrine from the Wrong Texts? Revisiting the Debate Seventeen Years Later in the Light of Peter Enns' Book, *Inspiration and Incarnation*." *Themelios* 32.1 (2006): 18–43.

_____. *John's Use of the Old Testament in Revelation*. Journal for the Study of the New Testament: Supplement Series 166. Sheffield: Sheffield Academic Press, 1998.

_____. "Myth, History, and Inspiration: A Review Article of *Inspiration and Incarnation* by Peter Enns." *Journal of the Evangelical Theological Society* 49 (2006): 287–312.

_____. "Questions of Authorial Intent, Epistemology, and Presuppositions and Their Bearing on the Study of the Old Testament in the New: A Rejoinder to Steve Moyise." *Irish Biblical Studies* 21 (1999): 1–26.

_____. "Review of Richard Hays' *Conversion of the Imagination*." *Journal of the Evangelical Theological Society* 50 (2007): 190–94.

_____. "A Surrejoinder to Peter Enns on the Use of the Old Testament in the New." *Themelios* 32 (2007): 14–25.

_____. "A Surrejoinder to Peter Enns's Response to G. K. Beale's *JETS* Review Article of His Book, *Inspiration and Incarnation*." *The Southern Baptist Journal of Theology* 11 (2007): 16–36.

_____. *The Book of Revelation*. New International Greek New Testament Commentary. Grand Rapids: Eerdmans, 1999.

_____, ed. *The Right Doctrine from Wrong Texts? Essays on the Use of the Old Testament in the New*. Grand Rapids: Baker, 1994.

_____. *The Temple and the Church's Mission.* Leicester: Inter-Varsity, 2004.

_____. *The Use of Daniel in Jewish Apocalyptic Literature and in the Revelation of St. John.* Lanham, MD: University Press of America, 1984.

_____, and D. A. Carson, eds. *A Commentary on the New Testament Use of the Old Testament.* Grand Rapids: Baker, 2007.

Blomberg, C. "The Globalization of Biblical Interpretation: A Test Case—John 3–4." *Bulletin for Biblical Research* 5 (1995): 1–15.

_____. *The Historical Reliability of John's Gospel.* Downers Grove, IL: InterVarsity, 2001.

_____. "Where Should Twenty-First Century Biblical Scholarship Be Heading?" *Bulletin for Biblical Research* 11 (2001): 161–72.

Brewer, D. I. *Prayer and Agriculture: Traditions of the Rabbis from the Era of the New Testament.* Grand Rapids: Eerdmans, 2004.

_____. *Techniques and Assumptions in Jewish Exegesis before 70 C. E.* Texte und Studien zum Antiken Judentum 30. Tübingen: Mohr (Paul Siebeck), 1992.

Carroll, M. Daniel R. "Review of Peter Enns' *Inspiration and Incarnation*," *Denver Journal: An Online Review of Current Biblical and Theological Studies* 8 (2005): n.p.

Carson, D. A. *Becoming Conversant with the Emerging Church.* Grand Rapids: Zondervan, 2005.

_____. *The Gagging of God.* Grand Rapids: Zondervan, 1996.

_____. "The General Epistles." In *Commentary on the New Testament Use of the Old Testament.* Edited by G. K. Beale and D. A. Carson. Grand Rapids: Baker, 2007.

_____. "Three More Books on the Bible: A Critical Review." *Trinity Journal* 27NS (2006): 18–45.

Collins, C. John. "Galatians 3:16: What Kind of Exegete was Paul?" *Tyndale Bulletin* 54 (2003): 75–86.

Currid, J. D. "Review: *Inspiration and Incarnation: Evangelicals and the Problem of the Old Testament*," *Banner of Truth* 521 (2007): 22–27.

Dillard, R. B., and Tremper Longman III. *An Introduction to the Old Testament.* Grand Rapids: Zondervan, 1994.

Dodd, C. H. *According to the Scriptures.* London: Nisbet, 1952.

Ellis, E. E. *The Old Testament in Early Christianity.* Grand Rapids: Baker, 1991.

_____. *Paul's Use of the Old Testament.* Grand Rapids: Baker, 1957; repr. 1981.

Enns, P. "Apostolic Hermeneutics and an Evangelical Doctrine of Scripture: Moving Beyond the Modern Impasse." *Westminster Theological Journal* 65 (2003): 263–87.

_____. "Biblical Interpretation, Jewish." In *Dictionary of New Testament Background*, 159–65. Edited by C. A. Evans and S. E. Porter. Downers Grove, IL: InterVarsity, 2000.

_____. "Exodus and the Problem of Historiography." Paper delivered at the 56th Annual Meeting of the Evangelical Theological Society in San Antonio, Texas, November 2004.

_____. *Inspiration and Incarnation: Evangelicals and the Problem of the Old Testament*. Grand Rapids: Baker, 2005.

_____. "The 'Moveable Well' in 1 Cor. 10:4: An Extrabiblical Tradition in an Apostolic Text." *Bulletin for Biblical Research* 6 (1996): 23–38.

_____. "Pseudepigrapha." In *Dictionary of the Theological Interpretation of the Bible*, 652. Edited by K. Vanhoozer. Grand Rapids: Baker, 2005.

_____. "Response to G. K. Beale's Review Article of *Inspiration and Incarnation*." *Journal of the Evangelical Theological Society* 49 (2006): 313–26.

_____. "Response to Professor Greg Beale." *Themelios* 32 (2007): 5–13.

Eschlebach, M. "Review of Peter Enns' *Inspiration and Incarnation*." *Journal of the Evangelical Theological Society* 48 (2005): 811–12.

Fekkes, J. *Isaiah and Prophetic Traditions in the Book of Revelation: Visionary Antecedents and their Development*. Journal for the Study of the New Testament: Supplement Series 93. Sheffield: JSOT Press, 1994.

Ferry, B. C. "Review of Peter Enns' *Inspiration and Incarnation*." *New Horizons in the Orthodox Presbyterian Church* (October 2005): 23–24.

Fishbane, M. *Biblical Interpretation in Ancient Israel*. Oxford: Clarendon, 1985.

_____. *Text and Texture*. New York: Schoken, 1979.

Foulkes, F. *The Acts of God: A Study of the Basis of Typology in the Old Testament*. Tyndale Monographs. London: Tyndale, 1958.

France, R. T. *Jesus and the Old Testament*. Grand Rapids: Baker, 1984.

Goppelt, L. *Typos*. Grand Rapids: Eerdmans, 1982.

Gruenler, R. G. *Meaning and Understanding*. Grand Rapids: Zondervan, 1991.

Gundry, R. H. *Mark*. Grand Rapids: Eerdmans, 1993.

Hafemann, S. J. "The Glory and Veil of Moses in 2 Cor. 3:7–14." In *The Right Doctrine from the Wrong Texts?* 295–309. Edited by G. K. Beale. Grand Rapids: Baker, 1994.

_____. *Paul, Moses and the History of Israel*. Wissenschaftliche Untersuchungen zum Neuen Testament 81. Tübingen: Mohr (Paul Siebeck), 1995.

Hannah, J. D. "The Doctrine of Scripture in the Early Church." In *Inerrancy and the Church*, 3–35. Edited by J. D. Hannah. Chicago: Moody, 1984.

Hartman, L. *Prophecy Interpreted*. Coniectanea Biblica, NT Series 1, Lund: C. W. K. Gleerup, 1966.

Hasel, G. *Current Issues in NT Theology: Basic Issues in the Current Debate*. Grand Rapids: Eerdmans, 1978.

_____. "The Polemic Nature of the Genesis Cosmology." *Evangelical Quarterly* 46 (1974): 81–102.

Hays, R. B. *The Conversion of the Imagination*. Grand Rapids: Eerdmans, 2005.

Helm, P. "Review of Peter Enns' *Inspiration and Incarnation*." No pages. http://www.reformation21.org/Life/Shelf_Life/Shelf_Life/181?vobId=2938&pm=434.

Hirsch, E. D. *Aims of Interpretation*. Chicago; London: Chicago University Press, 1976.

_____. "Transhistorical Intentions and the Persistence of Allegory," *New Literary History* 25 (1994): 549–67.

_____. *Validity in Interpretation*. New Haven: Yale University, 1967.

Howard, D. M., and M. A. Grisanti, eds. *Giving the Sense*. Grand Rapids: Kregel, 2003.

Hübner, H. *Biblische Theologie des Neuen Testaments*, Band 1: *Prolegomena*. Goettingen: Vandenhoeck and Ruprecht, 1990.

Kline, M. J. "Space and Time in the Genesis Cosmogony." *Perspectives on Science and Christian Faith* 48:1 (March 1996): 2–15.

Long, V. P. *The Art of Biblical History*. Grand Rapids: Zondervan, 1994.

Longenecker, R. "'Who is the Prophet talking About?' Some Reflections on the New Testament's Use of the Old." *Themelios* 13 (1987): 4–8.

Longman, T. "Divine and Human Qualities of the Old Testament." *Modern Reformation* 14 (2005): 33–34.

Lucas, E. C. "Cosmology." In *Dictionary of the Old Testament: Pentateuch*, 130–39. Edited by T. D. Alexander and D. W. Baker. Downers Grove, IL: InterVarsity; Leicester: Inter-Varsity, 2003.

McCartney, D., and C. Clayton, *Let the Reader Understand*. Wheaton, IL: Bridgepoint/Victor Books, 1994.

Morgan, R., and J. Barton, *Biblical Interpretation*. Oxford: Oxford University Press, 1988.

Moser, Paul K. "Epistemology." In *The Cambridge Dictionary of Philosophy*, 233–38. Edited by R. Audi. Cambridge: Cambridge University Press, 1995.

Moyise, Steve. *The Old Testament in the Book of Revelation*. Journal for the Study of the New Testament 115. Sheffield: Sheffield Academic Press, 1995.

Nash, R. H. "Gordon Clark's Theory of Knowledge." In *The Philosophy of Gordon H. Clark: A Festschrift*, 125–75. Edited by R. H. Nash. Philadelphia: Presbyterian and Reformed Publishing Co., 1968.

Neusner, J. "Rabbinic Literature: Mishnah and Tosefta." In *Dictionary of New Testament Background*, 895. Edited by C. A. Evans and S. E. Porter. Downers Grove, IL: InterVarsity, 2000.

Noll, M. A., and D. N. Livingston, eds. *B. B. Warfield, Evolution, Science, and Scripture: Selected Writings*. Grand Rapids: Baker, 2000.

Notaro, T. *Van Til and the Use of Evidence*. Phillipsburg, NJ: P&R, 1980.

Oden, R. A. "Cosmogony, Cosmology." *Anchor Bible Dictionary* 1:1162–71. Edited by D. N. Freedman. Garden City, NY: Doubleday, 1992.

Osborne, G. R. "Historical Narrative and Truth in the Bible." *Journal of the Evangelical Theological Society* 48 (2005): 673–88.

Packer, J. I. *"Fundamentalism" and the Word of God*. Grand Rapids: Eerdmans, 1958.

Porter, S. E. "Literary Approaches to the New Testament: From Formalism to Deconstruction and Back." In *Approaches to New Testament Study*, 90–128. Edited by S. E. Porter and D. Tombs. Sheffield: Sheffield Academic Press, 1995.

Poythress, V. *Redeeming Science*. Wheaton, IL: Crossway, 2006.

_____. *The Shadow of Christ in the Law of Moses*. Brentwood: Wolgemuth and Hyatt, 1991.

Provan, I., V. P. Long, and T. Longman III. *A Biblical History of Israel*. Louisville: Westminster John Knox, 2003.

Reventlow, G. *Problems of Biblical Theology in the Twentieth Century*. London: SCM, 1986.

Sandmel, S. "Parallelomania." *Journal of Biblical Literature* 81 (1962): 1–13.

Schultz, R. "How Many 'Isaiahs' Were There and Does It Matter? Prophetic Inspiration in Recent Evangelical Scholarship." In *Evangelicals and Scripture*, 150–70. Edited by V. Bacote, L. Miguelez, and D. Okholm. Downers Grove, IL: InterVarsity, 2004.

_____. *The Search for Quotation*. Journal for the Study of the Old Testament: Supplement Series 180; Sheffield: Sheffield Academic Press, 1999.

Seely, P. H. "The Firmament and the Water Above, Part 1: The Meaning of *rāqîaʿ* in Gen 1:6–8." *Westminster Theological Journal* 53 (1991): 31–46.

Spear, W. R. "Augustine's Doctrine of Biblical Infallibility." In *Inerrancy and the Church*, 37–65. Edited by J. D. Hannah. Chicago: Moody, 1984.

Stanley, Christopher. *Paul and the Language of Scripture*. Society for New Testament Studies Monograph Series 69. Cambridge: Cambridge University Press, 1992.

Stonehouse, N. B. *The Witness of Matthew and Mark to Christ*. Philadelphia: Presbyterian Guardian, 1944.

Tasker, R. V. G. *The Old Testament in the New*. Grand Rapids: Eerdmans, 1946.

Thiselton, A. C. *The Two Horizons: New Testament Hermeneutics and Philosophical Description*. Grand Rapids: Eerdmans, 1980.

Vanhoozer, K. J. *Is There a Meaning in This Text?* Grand Rapids: Zondervan, 1998.

_____. "Lost in Interpretation? Truth, Scripture, and Hermeneutics." *Journal of the Evangelical Theological Society* 48 (2005): 89–114.

Walton, J. H. "Ancient Near Eastern Background Studies." In *Dictionary for the Theological Interpretation of Scripture*, 40–45. Edited by K. Vanhoozer. Grand Rapids: Baker, 2005.

_____. *Ancient Near Eastern Thought and the Old Testament*. Grand Rapids: Baker, 2006.

Watson, F. *Paul and the Hermeneutics of Faith*. T & T Clark, 2004.

Webster, John. *Holy Scripture: A Dogmatic Sketch*. Cambridge: Cambridge University Press, 2003.

Wood, J. H. "Oswald T. Allis and the Question of Isaianic Authorship." *Journal of the Evangelical Theological Society* 48 (2005): 249–61.

Woodbridge, J. D. *Biblical Authority: A Critique of the Rogers/McKim Proposal*. Grand Rapids: Zondervan, 1982.

Wright, N. T. *The New Testament and the People of God*. Minneapolis: Fortress, 1992.

Yarbrough, R. "The Last and Next Christendom: Implications for Interpreting the Bible." *Themelios* 29 (2003): 30–37.

Author Index

Scripture Index